Cherished Memories

Tales from Perry County Storytellers

Compiled by Debra Kay Noye

Cherished Memories

Copyright © 2021 Debra Kay Noye

All rights reserved. No part of this book may be used or reproduced by any means, graphic, electronic, or mechanical, including photocopying, recording, taping or by any information storage retrieval system without the written permission of the author except in the case of brief quotations embodied in critical articles and reviews.

ISBN 978-1-945169-66-3

Orison Publishers, Inc.
PO Box 188
Grantham, PA 17027
717-731-1405
www.OrisonPublishers.com
Publish your book now, marsha@orisonpublishers.com

Disclaimer: No stories will be printed for other purposes beyond this book. We tried our best to preserve the stories as written, but technology definitely has a mind of its own, and human error may happen.

Special "Thank You"
to
Flo Dunkleberger Loy

There are times in one's life when something good just happens to drop right into your lap --- that was *Flo*!

I had interviewed Flo and her siblings in my home. Once I was finished writing their story, I sent it off to Flo to read, proof, and share with her siblings. Upon receiving the story back, I was very impressed with the additions Flo had made. I realized she was not only able to use a computer but had some serious writing and composition skills. I was wishing she might be willing to help me out.

Mercy Sakes!! She volunteered!

As Larry Reisinger, another book participant and personal friend, likes to say, "It was a God moment". I was blessed, and am extremely appreciative of all the suggestions, proofing, and technical support, provided by Flo.

Another Perry County native, from back over the ridge, outside of Elliottsburg, Flo, like me, also graduated from West Perry High School. Immediately, she entered the work force at Highmark Blue Shield in Camp Hill and remained for forty-three years. She, as the years progressed, became responsible for producing various publications. I could hear the pride in her voice, as she spoke about what she had accomplished.

I'm sure grateful, she stuck with the Perry County 2021 project, because it was not without challenges. We Perry Countians have back bone and don't give up. We're also devoted to preserving and sharing about our special way of life. Flo's expertise was put to good use, to make sure **our** stories become legendary, to be read by future generations.

Flo, "we done good", as our great-granny's would say!

PREFACE
THE WHERE FORES AND WHYS

Antiquing in Bedford, Pennsylvania, almost three years ago, I stumbled across a hardbound book, lying on the floor, of an antique booth. After picking it up, briefly looking through, and putting it safely onto a shelf, I went about exploring. As I and my husband, Fred, were starting for the exit, I was compelled to return to that book. And the rest is history!

"Penny Candy and Grandma's Porch Swing, A Living History of North Central Pennsylvania" was the catalyst, which ultimately brought so many Perry Countians together, to share their stories of growing up, in a very rural area, of Pennsylvania.

I, also, realized that I had become one of the dinosaurs, and with my passing, so to would the idyllic way of life coveted by those of us, who grew up in Perry County. Nobody was documenting how we grew up, unless you include what everybody seems compelled to share to the "cloud", or videography.

Today, there are those, who would distort our past, and re-write our history, in an attempt to demonize our generations, for the ills of society today.

That's another reason, why I decided to publish this book. It is tangible. Something to hang onto and cherish! Leaving a true lasting legacy, for the next generations!

This book is dedicated to you, Perry County!

Debra Kay "Debby" Noye

CONTENTS

Special "Thank You" iii

PREFACE The Where Fores and Whys iv

Perry County Will Always Be Home!
Storyteller Chuck Lamoreaux 1

John & Irene McConnell Family Larry & Jim McConnell
Storytellers Larry & Jim McConnell
Recorded by William & Crista Lyons 3

Perry County Magic!
Storyteller Craig Wallis "Diamond" 12

Just a Kid Free to Roam Millerstown
Storyteller Jim Roush 15

Recollections from Growing Up in a Country Store
Storytellers Cathy Urich Gilbert and Terry Urich 17

Childhood Memories from Along the Juniata River
Storyteller Jeannie Maguire 21

Walking with Grandma Along the Cow Paths
Storyteller Lorie Bolden Goss
Recorded by Debra Kay Noye 25

Memories of Downtown Millerstown
Storyteller Jane Cameron Simonton 30

A Diary of a Perry County Farm Boy Serving in World War 1
Storyteller Jeremiah Ross Lyons
Recorded by William Glenn Lyons 32

Growing up in Perry County
Storyteller Gay Russ Irwin 37

My Fondest Memories of Duncannon
Storyteller Ginny Jones Clark 40

Snippets of Mary F. Lightner's Diary, Living in Landisburg, Perry County
Recorded by Kathy Henry Hughes 41

Childhood Memories
Storyteller Kathy Henry Hughes 49

My Memories of Marysville
Storyteller Barb Stokes 54

From Centerville to Liverpool
Storyteller a Proud Great-Great-Granny Myrtle Hoffman Holman
Recorded by Debra Kay Noye 56

Growing Up at Stoney Point
Storyteller Jane Smith Dobbs 62

Fun Stuff and Memories from Home
Storytellers Deitra Neidigh Hinkle and Christina Cressler Morrow 65

The View from the Back Porch—Submarines and Rafts
Storyteller Larry L Little 66

Amity Hall from a Waitress' Perspective
Storyteller Judith LePere Armstrong 68

Growing Up in Perry County
Storyteller Carol Janet Gabel Ulsh 69

Lyons Family History
Storytellers William & Crista Lyons 72

Early Memories in Perry County
Storyteller Jerry A. Clouse 83

Memories from Ickesburg Elementary
Storyteller Polly McMillen Eby 85

"You don't go out and have fun until the work is done!"
Storyteller Deb Reisinger Nyce
Recorded by Debra Kay Noye 88

Last Class at the Elliottsburg Schoolhouse
Storyteller Dorothy "Dee" Shiffer Wesner 93

Farmer's Daughters
Storyteller Polly McMillen Eby 95

An Eye for the Future
Storyteller Penny Rudy Nicholl 103

Wilt Sisters From Alinda
Storytellers Connie Lupp and SueEllen McElhiney 106
Recorded by Debra Kay Noye

A Perry County Hero
Storyteller Harriet Berrier Magee 112

My Story - Growing up in Loysville
Storyteller Galene Guiles Weller 114

Growing up in the 50's and 60's – My Story
Storyteller Sue Reisinger Binger 117

Perry County Hero's Life During WWII
Storyteller Jeff Dobbs 122

Memories of Growing up in Liverpool in the 1960s
Storyteller Julie Shumaker Harvey 133

Carson Long Military Academy/ New Bloomfield
Storyteller Judith Lepere Armstrong 136

Perry County Farm Girl Gives Up Milking Stool
Storyteller Linda "Rocky" (Dum) Rock 138

Perry County Living in the 1940s and Beyond
Storyteller Frances Ickes Owen... 141
Recorded by Debra Kay Noye

Growing up in Tuscarora Township in the 1950s
Storyteller Patricia Kerr Brodisch 148

Special Memories of Buckwheat Valley
Storyteller Shirley Burd Reisinger
Recorded by Debra Kay Noye.. 150

Just Another Kid from Wila Tech
Storyteller Larry Reisinger
Recorded by Debra Kay Noye.. 153

A Flood of Memories
Storyteller Bradley Halter 158

Growing up in Liverpool, PA
Storyteller Patty Campbell 159

Cherished Memories
Storyteller Steve Hower.. 165

Growing Up in Perry County, PA
Storyteller Vickie Rudy Johnson... 167

Pleasant Valley Memories
Storytellers Patricia Dunkleberger Kretzing, William G. Dunkleberger, Flo Dunkleberger Loy
Recorded by Debra Kay Noye.. 170

My Story - Growing Up on Meadowgrove Road
Storyteller Heather Lynn (Little) Reed.. 176

Growing up in Beautiful Perry County
Storyteller Jane Neely Stambaugh.. 177

Nicknames of Duncannon and Marysville Residents
Recorded by Joe Mutzybaugh, Harriet Magee and Clarence Clouser... 182

Robinson's Store and the Western End of Loysville
Storyteller Dean Robinson 187

Life in New Bloomfield, PA
Storyteller Judy Metzger
Recorded by Steve Metzger... 190

Life & Times in Perry County Growing up in Newport, PA
Storyteller Ray Metzger
Recorded by Steve Metzger 194

Growing up in Oliver Township
Recorded by Steve Metzger 199

Storekeepers Daughter to Accomplished Vocalist
Storytellers Jane Hoffman Roush and Debra Ann Roush
Recorded by Debra Kay Noye 203

My, How Things Have Changed!
Storyteller Gary Eby 209

Perry County Boy–Born and Raised!
Storyteller Jim Kain 216

The View from the Back Porch—A Buzzard in the House
Storyteller Larry L Little 217

No Prissy Miss! Growing up in Andersonburg
Storyteller Mary Jane Nesbit Kint 220

The Night the Barn Burned
Storyteller Linda Martin Gilmore 225

An Entire Life Time in Perdix
Storyteller Franklin Delano Reidlinger
Recorded by Debra Kay Noye 228

Perry County Jargon
Storyteller Steve Hower 240

Little Germany Childhood Memories
Storyteller Donna Rudy Neely 242

Growing Up In Perry County
Storyteller Carl E. Tressler 246

Cloverleaf Connections
Storyteller Lynn McMillen 250

Perry Countians Serving in the Spanish American War
Storyteller James Michael McAteer 253

In Perry County Everybody Knows Your Name
Storyteller Jane Cameron Simonton 257

"Baby Boomer"
Storyteller Fred C. Noye 258

My Thoughts, Observations, and Story!
Storyteller Debra "Debby" Kay Noye 264

Perry County Will Always Be Home!

Storyteller Chuck Lamoreaux

I was raised by my maternal grandparents, Leo and Louise Casner, in the then idyllic village of Wila. They were not only my parents, but they also saved me from a life that would have shaped me into a much different person. These two raised six children on very modest means. Technically, we were poor. We just didn't know it because we were loved unconditionally.

Why do I refer to Wila as idyllic? Back then, it consisted of no more than ninety residents, but I will never call them neighbors. They were family members. Each adult in our village had the right and responsibility to correct any of us who got out of line. These people defined for us the importance of the now popular adage, "it takes a village to raise a child".

As young and healthy guys and girls, we frequently gathered in empty lots for pickup baseball, softball, and tackle football games from morning until night. We had no cell phones and no video games. Instead, we played Strat-o-Matic baseball and had Monopoly games that lasted for weeks.

Unlike today's youth, we umpired and refereed ourselves. Did we argue? Yes. Did we occasionally come to fisticuffs? Once in a while. But, after our contests, we would shake hands and have a Coca Cola at our general local store. We were brothers and sisters to one another, then and now.

We respected our parents, even when we disagreed. I fondly remember us all coming in for the night when we saw our parents flash the porch lights.

Elizabeth Lyons, a widow raising three children alone, was the General Store's proprietor. She was our Walmart, carrying everything from penny candy, to groceries, to hardware, sporting equipment, kerosene and gasoline. In her spare time, she was our village postmaster.

There was no electronic social media. As young people and long into our early adulthood, we sat on her store's porch talking about life, face to face. Inside the store, older gentlemen would perch on the pickle barrels and discuss everything from news to politics to sports. It was our community center.

Just a hundred yards away, the Wila Methodist Church served as our spiritual center, where we each met God for the first time. There, too, we grew closer to the people of our little enclave as family members. Though the church has closed, we who worshiped there remain close.

At age sixteen, my life was forever changed when I was critically injured in an automobile accident. I broke three vertebrae in my neck and began living as a quadriplegic. While this could have been socially isolating, especially in a very small town, the people of our village and surrounding area rallied around my family and me, letting us know we were not in this fight alone.

I first left Perry County at eighteen for college. After earning a few degrees, I moved away for good to begin my career in the federal sector. While I have been blessed to live in Los Angeles, Dallas and now Maryland for the past eighteen years, I took what I learned from that little village – filled with truly loving people and have made a great life for my family and myself. Despite the physical difference, Perry County will always be "home", and its people will forever be my family.

What is the most important thing I have learned in this life? Faith, family, friends … in that order of importance. These elements are the very bedrock of our lives. Neglecting even one of these, our foundations crumble.

Note from Debra Kay Noye, author
Chuck was the very first person to respond to my request for "growing up stories about Perry County". His lifelong friend, Carl Tressler of Wila, sent him my information, which immediately inspired him to begin writing from the heart. Needless to say, his story made my day and confirmed I was on the right path to preserving Perry County's past.

John & Irene McConnell Family
Larry & Jim McConnell

Storytellers Larry & Jim McConnell
Recorded by William & Crista Lyons

John and Irene Keck McConnell were married in 1941. In 1943, they bought the 209-acre farm, four miles southwest of Blain, at the current address of 3100 Fowler Hollow Road, Blain, Pa. The property was up for tax sale when John negotiated a price with the current owner Clark Anderson. Mr. Anderson paid the back taxes due, and the men agreed upon a selling price of $4250.00 with the taxes amounting to $15.00 yearly. John and Irene had $1800.00 to go towards the farm but the banks wouldn't loan them any money. Irene's sister was an old maid that loaned the additional money to them, interest free.

J. Larry was born in 1942 and was 7 months old when his parents bought the farm. Daughter Ida was born in 1943 and died of cancer at the age of 57 in 2001. Son James D. was born in 1950.

When the farm was bought, their income came from 35-40 chickens for eggs. Also, he bought 10 cows from his father, James, to milk by hand. They carried the milk in buckets to the spring house to be dumped into cans to keep cool. The cans were picked up by a truck. John also grew wheat, oats, corn, and hay. There were a few old fruit trees on the farm, but only two or three were any good.

There was no electricity at this time in the early 1940's, but they did have a "Delco light plant" that was powered by a Briggs & Stratton gas engine. The light plant generated 32 volts so you could either run a washing machine or lights, but not both at the same time. Electricity was stored in batteries and the engine would fire up and recharge the batteries as needed. The lights would get bright in a hurry when the motor would first start. The "Delco light plant" went by the wayside in 1945 when Penelec put electric lines in. It was quite a few years later before United Telephone ran their lines through in 1966, even though neighbors half a mile east of the McConnell farm had telephone service in the 1940's.

The McConnells have a good flow of water coming out of their spring house throughout the year. Back in the mid 1950's, the spring drain needed a good cleaning out and it was before the time of anyone having a backhoe. John got the idea to use dynamite since no permits were needed for that back then. He drove to Carlisle to Cochran and Allen hardware store to load up his car trunk with dynamite. To be safe, he made a separate trip to buy the caps and fuses because he took no chances that it would set off the dynamite. They had about 300 feet from the spring house to the road, a culvert under the road, and then a much longer stretch of land to Brown's Creek. It took an 80-pound jar to set off a stick of dynamite along with fuses and wire to tie the sticks together. John had Larry use a crowbar to make a hole in the ground every 18 inches and they would place a dynamite stick in each hole till they did a hundred. They placed the first stick 50 feet from the spring house and John laid under a flatbed wagon to set off the charge. When the first stick went off, it went down the row just like a row of dominos. After the blast, there would be 8 inches of mud on the wagon bed. They repeated the process over several days until they had the whole waterway open and flowing to the creek. The chickens' egg production may have suffered that week as they flew to the back of the barn during the blasting.

Dad sold the cows in 1954 and converted the barn into a three-story egg laying chicken house that held 5,500 chickens. The chickens produced 4,800 to 5,000 eggs a day. That amounted to close 100 cases of eggs a week with each case containing 30 dozen. The eggs were stored in a cool, dry room and were picked up by Emlet Brothers once a week. In 1960, the price of eggs fell from an "at the farm price" of .80/a dozen to .25/a dozen. That was the end of chickens at the McConnell farm.

Larry graduated high school in 1960. At that time, the barn was converted back into a milking barn for 30 cows and 15 dry cows and heifers. He along with his dad, built a milk house that year. It held two can coolers one of which held eight cans and the other four. The cans of milk went to Pensupreme in Lancaster for bottled milk. In 1977, a bulk tank was installed, and the milk went to Sunnydale at Elliottsburg. When the Sunnydale plant closed, the milk went to Eastern Milk Producers.

Around the year 1965; John, Larry and cousin, Paul McConnell, got involved with doing construction. They did all kinds of construction from building barns, laying block, pouring concrete, roofs, and additions to houses. Jim graduated in 1968 and joined in with the farming and construction too. John and his boys continued to milk cows and work at their crops the same as Paul would do with his father, Vern, next door. The cows were sold on October 3, 1983. Somehow, they would get all of that done and continue to work construction until 1986. In 1975, there was a bad storm and from the 4th of April until the 1st of June, the four men put on 30 house and barn roofs, all in the Blain area. There were two days of severe straight-line wind which had to also include a twister that caused all the damage. Ben Bower, the schoolteacher, saw the water stand up out of his pond like a funnel shape. The men would go out and look at jobs, give estimates and come home. Irene, their mom, would tell them you have gotten several more calls to go look at properties.

Two of the Drumgold barn and house roofs were gone. The house roof including the rafters were blown off one. Other properties with damage included Jim Mumper, Jim Koser, Hook Thomas, and Frank Rice. The Rice's back farm lost the barn and house roofs plus the chimneys which the McConnell crew also rebuilt. They would milk and feed the cows, eat breakfast, head off to a roof job, come back to milk and feed the cows, then go back to the roof job and work till dark. Mom always had their lunches packed along with a piece of pie. She was told not to worry about supper till they would get back home. The McConnell men were well known for high quality work because people would call about a project, they wanted them to do; they would be told it will be at least 6 months till we can get to you. The reply would be, we will wait, we don't want anyone else. Early on they bought their building supplies from Forest "Flo" Bolze from Alinda, Landisburg area until he retired. In 1971, they bought from the Allenville Plaining Mill, where they were the third largest buyer of material for one year. It's no wonder these two eligible bachelors, Larry and Jim, never got married, they were always too busy!

There were a number of local barns built by these men. To name a few: in the Blain area - David Trout, Laurence Cauffman, Nevin Rice and Richard Rohm. In Ickesburg area – Dale "Brownie" Fritz and Frank Hoke. Richard Peachy, on Route 35 and Gilbert Adams in New Bloomfield. In Doylesburg, the men built a 440-foot cage layer chicken house and did everything but the electric work. One day starting at 11:00 am, they poured 90 yards of concrete, moving it in place by skid loaders, and finishing it.

Dad started planting fruit trees in 1980 which has been an ongoing thing ever since. There are now twenty different varieties of apples and five different varieties of peaches planted on their farm. Apple trees include Black Twig, Winter Banana, Wolf River, Smokehouse, Sheep Nose, Spizenburg, Northern Spy, Orleans, Grimes Golden, Summer Rambo, Red Delicious, Golden Delicious, and the one they like the best is Stayman Winesap. Their dad always wanted to plant some native Gutshall apple trees that were grown in Perry County. He looked for years but could never find any. The McConnells were told that variety of apple was in its heyday in the 1920's and 1930's. Gutshall apples started getting scarce before 1950. Peach trees include Red Haven, Sunhigh, Loring and Canadian Harmony. Larry and Jim started selling fruit in 1990, along with cider and apple butter. They started out small, but now average selling of 1,500 to 2,000 gallons of cider each fall. The process for making cider includes grind the apples, then squeeze through a cloth, collect cider in a barrel, jug it and refrigerate it in the milk house. On the average, they hand pick 1,100 bushels of apples a year and between 125 to 140 bushels of peaches. Peaches are very time sensitive. Every now and then, a ladder might move on them, and someone may end up on the ground!

To make apple butter is a labor-intensive job. They usually do six kettles of apple butter a fall, that makes 18 gallons of apple butter each. Converted to quarts, that is 72 quarts a kettle times six for a total of 432 quarts. Their process for making apple butter includes peel and core 3 bushels of apples the day before, get up at 3:30 am. the next morning and clean the copper kettle with vinegar and salt, put 30 gallons of apple cider in and make a fire, boiling the whole time, cook the cider down halfway, start putting the three bushels of apples in, but not all at once and stir the whole time. If the kettle gets a frothy head, put a half a stick of butter in (margarine will not work). Forty pounds of sugar goes in next. Once the sugar is in it will cook another hour. From start to finish is about 11 hours till it is put in jars. They usually do a kettle a week. The test to see if the apple butter is done is to pour some on a saucer, take a knife, and separate both ways to see if any liquid runs towards the center. If it does, it's not done yet.

Larry and Jim's Great-Grandma and Grandma on their mother's side always made their own vinegar. Their Great-Grandpa on their dad's side also made vinegar and sold it at the Velma Bistline, Lee "Hacky" Linard and Vern Smith stores, all in New Germantown. Larry and Jim also started to make vinegar to sell when they first started pressing apple cider. They work with four barrels and keep moving the product forward and when it reaches the fourth barrel, it has completely turned to vinegar. In order to make homemade vinegar out of cider, you need to just have "Mother" which is a slimy, whitish, mass. If you don't have "Mother", cider will not turn to vinegar. The best place to get "Mother" is a place that makes vinegar. Sometimes cider will grow its own "Mother", but rarely does that ever happen. Larry and Jim had bought a gallon of vinegar at a store that must not have been pasteurized properly. It had a white, cloudy mass in the jug, in other words, it was starting to grow "Mother". That's where they got their "Mother" and have kept it alive and growing ever since. "Mother" is already in the first barrel along with 30-40 gallons of new cider each fall. Twice a year they move the cider-vinegar from barrel to barrel, take a dipper and dip out some and put it back in to get oxygen in it. When it gets to the fourth barrel, it is vinegar ready to be sold. They always leave 8-10 gallons in the first barrel. Each fall new cider is put in, if you don't, "Mother" will eat up the vinegar and die. If "Mother" dies, it turns black. Larry and Jim sell 50-60 gallons of vinegar a year.

Larry and Jim have been successful at saving some fruit trees in the past years. A bear worked over an apple tree one year that they were able to wire back together, and it is still doing good. Another apple tree had too many apples on it and split the tree apart. The men put a piece of threaded rod through the tree and put washers and nuts on each end and drew the tree back together. The tree grew over the steel rod and is till bearing apples to this day.

The brothers started beehives in 1972 and kept at it until 2000. They at one time had as many as 55 hives and one year 40 hives made 2600 pounds of honey. The main nectar flow usually occurs from Memorial Day through the 4th of July and one time, one hive made 40 pounds of honey from Friday night to Monday. Once in a while you may get stung when checking a hive to see how much honey is in there or if you happen to pinch a bee. They had verona mites get into the hives sometimes and it was expensive to get rid of them, but they continued to keep the hives going for several years. Colony Collapse Disease came along and that caused them to quit the beehives because it was too hard to keep them alive. Larry and Jim used their own honey in their secret deer bologna recipe for many years and after they lost the bees, they bought honey in five-gallon buckets. They bought as many as thirty, five-gallon buckets of honey from a fellow in Berrysburg, Virginia for making deer bologna at a cost of $3100.00.

In 1982, Larry, Jim and their dad started making deer bologna and dried venison for others. This business kept growing and in 1993, it peaked at making 27,000 pounds of bologna. For several years, they usually did 20,000 to 24,000 pounds annually. By 2004, Pennsylvania's deer herd was smaller in size and the amount of bologna tapered off to 12,000 pounds made. As they have gotten older, they decided in 2016 that it would be their last year of making deer bologna although they still process dried venison. They never advertised and their business was always word of mouth. The meat they worked with was mostly local, but over the years they made bologna from Potter, Juniata, Cumberland, Franklin and Dauphin Counties. They once shipped the finished product to a hunter in Raleigh, N.C. by overnight UPS and the hunter volunteered to pay all the shipping costs. Some people have brought meat to be processed from Virginia and the furthest away was from some folks from Connecticut who drove seven hours each way to drop off and pick up for many years. Jim has carried enough meat over the years that he can estimate the weight within a pound or so before weighing.

The process for making deer bologna: Larry and Jim grind, mix and put meat into hand sewn muslin bags from 6:00 am to 1:30 pm., then have 700 pounds ready to go into the smokehouse where it stays for eight hours until it's done. Their recipe is "Top Secret"!

The process for dried venison: sugar cure rear quarters of deer, leave alone for 12 days, then put it in a brown sugar solution (leave sit for a few days), hang the quarters up in the smokehouse for eight hours, then take the quarters out of smokehouse and store in a dry room until it is solid enough to slice, it usually takes four weeks till it is dry enough. When the McConnell's first started processing venison, they had a foot bridge twelve inches wide to cross the run to carry the meat from the butcher shop to the smokehouse. When they wore the foot bridge out, they built a four-foot-wide bridge, fifteen feet long, made out of oak with locust sleepers laid on the ground, on each side of the run. This enabled them to use a wheelbarrow instead of carrying the meat by hand. Low and behold as the years went by, they wore the second bridge out and built a third. Over 550,000 pounds of deer bologna and not counting the number of pounds of dried venison crossed over the bridge to the smokehouse.

They set up a sawmill in 1977 and have sawed logs for many people including themselves for many years. A half-frozen log is hard to saw, but a fully frozen log saws straight and true. The men may very well have sawed over a million board feet over the years. In 1985 the Pennsylvania DCNR based out of New Germantown (Tuscarora State Forest) was contacted by channel ABC27 asking who had an old-time sawmill. The McConnells received a call and a TV crew came out and interviewed their father, John, and took video of the boys sawing logs which was shown on the evening news. A year later, ABC6 out of Philadelphia came out and spent the good part of a day videoing at the sawmill and in their workshop. They have been on TV but remain humble.

The McConnell men always had an interest in guns especially since they hunted. Larry and Jim used Model 94 Winchester lever actions in 32 Winchester Special for many years. They also own family heirlooms in Mod. 64 and also the oldest a Mod. 1894. In 1980, they built a gunshop for Thaddius Book, in Doylesburg, and by doing so, it perked their interest even more. They would go there often, look the guns over and socialize. Their dad bought a .338 Winchester, Larry a .280 Ruger and Jim a .308 lever action Savage. These 2 guns of Larry and Jim's are their go-to hunting rifles. Since the men grow tough in Jackson Township, you'll find that Larry and Jim each have a pistol in their boot; Larry a .22 and Jim a .380, to keep the peace!

After the cows were sold in 1983, they farmed around 80 acres of fields that they grew corn and hay that consisted of timothy and some alfalfa until 1992. They sold some of the hay local including Ray McMillen one spring. Most of it was sold at Lancaster auctions through John Hoover's brother-in-law, Levi Brubaker. The ear corn was sold through Abe Stricker of Lititz for many years until he retired and then my dad, Bill Lyons, bought it the last two years. The farmland was idle for several years after that until Mike Book leased it for his Hyd-A-Del bird hunting operation from 2003 to 2007 when hunters came from all over to enjoy the farm. In recent years, a neighbor, Dennis Hoover, has been renting the acreage for crops.

On May 23, 1993, the brothers decided to make a trip west to the Pacific Ocean and back. Over the three weeks, they went across the northern states and saw the Bad Lands, General Custer's Battlefield, Yellowstone National Park, the Grand Canyon, and on to the state of Washington. In Anacortes, Washington, they took a three-hour ferryboat ride through the Puget Sound to Vancouver Island, British Columbia with stops to other islands along the way. The ferry was five decks above the water and held 120 cars and 21 tractor trailers. From there they headed south down through Oregon and California and then headed east through some southern states to home. It was a great trip and nice to see other parts of the United States. It is always nice to get back home to Perry County. Total cost for the whole trip was around $1400.00 for two people.

In the 1990's they raised long necked pumpkins for pies and also the big round Jack-o'-lanterns for a couple years. They sold the majority of the pumpkins for a $1.50-$2.00 apiece and got as high as $15.00 for a 15–18-pound Jack-o'-lantern. They had no trouble selling them to make some money when not having to spray for blight. As time passed by, blight caused them the need to spray which would have cost more than the pumpkins were worth, so they stopped growing them.

In 1996 and 1997, the McConnell family decided they would really get into planting potatoes. Larry and Jim were at a sale in Snyder County where they bought a single row Farquar potato planter for $15.00 that was probably made around 1918-1920. It had a long tongue that was made for a horse to pull until the brothers modified it to be pulled by a tractor. It has steel wheels, a fertilizer attachment, and a seat that a person would sit on to pull the lever to engage and disengage the planter. It works a lot like a corn planter where it has a shovel plow on the front and two coulters on the back to press the rows shut. The way it works is you put the cut potato pieces in the seed bin and as you go a piece drops out every twelve inches. Planting them was easy since they had a potato planter, so just like that, they had 500 pounds planted on about an acre and a half of land. Each potato was picked up by hand and after a while they would crawl on their hands and knees because it was too hard on their backs. They ended up with wagon loads of potatoes that amounted to a 10-wheeler dump truck load. The potatoes spread over ¾ of the machine shed floor with them being 2 ½ feet deep. A "potatoes for sale" sign was placed at the end of their lane and all the potatoes were sold. There was a lady that had stopped and asked if they were washed, and Larry said no. She said that's what she wanted, potatoes with ground on. They did this for two years and said that this was enough!

The farm's deed was transferred over to Larry and Jim from their parents in 1998.

Larry got in his head one day that they were going to build a cannon to sit in the front yard. Jim and him took two steel mower wheels, made a frame, and then manufactured a barrel made out of wood. When it was all painted up and finished, complete with a ramrod, they placed it in the yard in front of the house. Across the road the men placed a plywood target with big round holes in it. A couple stopped in from the Marysville area looking to have some furniture built. The woman exclaimed that you shouldn't be shooting across the road at your target. She didn't realize that they did not actually shoot off the cannon; they made it look very real!

The brothers have 100 acres of woodland that they had selective cutting of timber in 2016. Ninety percent of the timber cut was oak trees. Some of the trees were very large, so much so, that sometimes one tractor trailer load was made up of a total of three or four trees. Their woods were not cut hard as there are many good-sized trees still growing here. There were over 140 tractor trailer loads of timber cut and some of the nicest went to the Philippines and Sweden.

Woodworking in their shop is something they have always enjoyed doing. They have tackled almost anything over the years. They have made and or repaired all kinds of furniture from tables, chairs, rocking chairs, mirror, corner cupboards, cedar chests, gun cabinets, toy boxes, roll top desks, bedroom suits and turkey box calls. They even repaired Paul Revere's aunt's chair. A man's daughter married into the Revere family. This man from Duncannon had been to McConnell's with deer meat in the past and knew they were skilled woodworkers. The chair, possibly made in England, was a fancy black walnut chair with an upholstered seat. It was broken in shipment from Massachusetts. Jim repaired the chair to the satisfaction of its owner. The men ate at Path Valley Restaurant often and one day in 1994, the owner ask them if they would be interested in making tables, booths, and countertops for him. He had heard from other people that they were very skilled craftsmen. They used oak that grew on their farm, sawed at their sawmill, and was built in their workshop. They installed everything at night when everything was closed for business. To this day everything is looking good. Larry has made over 300 buckets that are put together with no nails or glue. If you don't have one, you should get one because they are so neat. The buckets are one of a kind, numbered and signed.

The brothers have made a lot of homemade ice cream over the years for themselves and others. They have six- and eight-quart freezers, but also bought another freezer that makes twenty quarts. They make for the Three Springs Church of the Brethren socials and the annual church fishing season soup sale, to name a couple. Once they made for the church spring banquet, pulled the beaters out of the twenty-quart freezer and set them in front of Gard Wallace of Blain to clean off. He stalled out, too much ice cream to clean off!

Larry and Jim's Ice Cream Recipe for Eight Quarts

1 big and 1 small box of instant vanilla pudding
4 cups of sugar
4 eggs beaten
2 cups half and half (half milk, half cream)

4 cups heavy cream
2 cans condensed milk
3 tablespoons vanilla
Pinch of salt

Enough milk to make 8 quarts (Put milk in till it touches the bottom of the second fin. If you fill up further with more milk, the ice cream will come up against the lid, which will cause it to overflow or not harden.)

When Larry was looking around in the attic for some old-time things to add to these stories, he found eight gallons of dried apples. That reminded him of his mother and her German/Dutch background. The next evening for supper, Larry put together "Snitz and Nep" for them to eat.

Snitz and Nep Recipe

Take two hand fulls of ¼" thick dried red delicious apples
Add a chunk of butter, ¼ cup sugar and water to apples
Bring to a boil
Add dumplings when the above comes to a boil
Dumplings are made out of Bisquick (recipe on the box)
Cut dumplings in half, spread with apple mixture, can add milk if desired

---

The McConnell's shared some stories about the Newport and Shermans Valley Railroad. The railroad delivered to most all of the local stores which would include sugar, flour, baking powder, crackers and other dry goods in wooden oak barrels for the storekeepers to sell out of. Grandpa, James McConnell, would buy a whole barrel of salted herring. The fish were whole and gutted. They would not spoil for many months since they were salted. There was no refrigeration or freezers in those days! When you wanted to eat fish, you would get some out of the barrel, soak in clear water overnight to remove the salt before preparing to eat. He also had a cream separator to separate the cream and milk. He fed the skim milk to the hogs and would take the cream to the Blain Station to be shipped to Newport. Larry and Jim have a key for the Newport and Shermans Valley Railroad that their mother, Irene's, Uncle Dan Keck, had as the postmaster at the Blain Train Station. Fowler's Hollow is four miles south of New Germantown. The Perry Lumber Company had a sawmill there, where they would cut an area, then move the mill to another area as they worked. The company would lay train tracks to accommodate the sawmill to get their lumber transported to New Germantown by the way of the Perry Lumber Train. There they loaded onto the railroad cars to be taken east to Newport. When the Newport and Shermans Valley Railroad train arrived at New Germantown, it didn't have a turnaround, so it would return to Newport backwards; pull west and push back east.

Larry and Jim's great-grandfather, James, had told their father, John, about the "year of no summer in 1894". In June, it snowed when the wheat was in blossom. The farmers took a hay rope and stretched it out between them, walked through the field, and knocked the snow off the wheat blossoms. When the wheat came to maturity, where the rope took off the snow, there was no wheat, only straw, but where the snow was left on, there was wheat.

Larry and Jim have a few old-time remedies that may never have been heard about anywhere else. Here are a few of them: put elderberry leaves in your pocket and it will keep you from getting prickly heat or gaulded. It will work even when the leaves are dried up. When you start to see barn swallows in the spring, it means warm weather is going to be here to stay. If you have a wart, cut a potato in half, rub it on the wart, then put the two halves together, and bury it under a roof drip of a building. The wart will fall off! You could chew calamus root for high blood pressure. Calamus was growing on the farm in the early 1950's. It grew well near a lot of moisture, especially near the spring house drain. The cows were pastured in that area for a time, so that was the end of the calamus. Larry and Jim's Great-Uncle Ben Leibey always had some in his pocket to chew on.

Larry makes up a monthly weather report that he has been giving to Crista Lyons for at least ten years now.
He uses phrases like "water and the fishes" and "moon turns on edge" which means a possibility of wet weather.
If it rains on St. Swithin's Day (July 15), you will have rain for forty days, chance of rain, shower, or sprinkle.
When the wind blows hard at night, it never stops blowing in the middle of the day or middle of the night. It always stops at sunrise or sunset and most always blows 24, 36 or 48 hours before it stops; it will never stop in between.
If the sun sets behind a cloud on a Sunday night, it will rain before Wednesday and if it sets behind a cloud on a Wednesday night it will rain before Sunday.
If it's cloudy and then clears up at night, it won't last but a half day to a day, then it will rain.
If fog goes up the valley, it's not done raining.
On May 7th, every so many years, a thin moon hangs in the evening sky. After supper look west-northwest to see the moon, off to the right is Mars. It will be a bright object with a reddish tinge.
There are four full moons between spring and summer. This only happens every 2 ½ years.

A lot of times the weather report is very accurate, but Larry does say "subject to change by God"!

Larry and Jim's grandmother, Sarah Hattie Keck had the best black walnut pie recipe. She was born in 1873 and died in 1929 at the age of 56.

Black Walnut Pie

1 cup of molasses or honey (Larry uses honey)
2 cups sugar
1 ½ cups ground black walnuts

4 eggs
5 tablespoons flour
1 ½ cups water

No top crust on the pie, only bottom crust
Bake at 350 degrees for 45 minutes
Makes 2 – 9-inch pies

Larry and Jim are members and attend Three Springs Church of the Brethren. Both men have a strong faith in God and believe in the power of prayer. Larry is a twelve-year cancer survivor and gives credit to God for him and his brother's good health. They have interest in a lot of fun things they like to do beside work. They are excellent deer and turkey hunters and have a lot of proof of that hanging on their shop wall. Another passion is attending gun sales where they are both very knowledgeable on values of guns and accessories. The brothers are master custom builders of furniture and Larry is an excellent cook and baker. Black walnut pie is a specialty and is similar to pecan pie. A piece of advice from Larry is - never say "no" because you wind up doing what you said "no" to. Two examples: He was asked to consider to be placed on the Church ballot for District Delegate, he said no at first, but now has served for several years and really enjoys it. We (Bill & Crista) have been asking Larry and Jim for many years to write down their family history and wealth of knowledge so it wouldn't be lost to future generations. The answer was always no, no, no, but look at what we have on paper now! The further west you go in Jackson Township, the tougher they get! Larry and Jim live in the last house west! Our grandchildren: Adam, Carla and Sam Campbell, Austin and Eli Lyons, refer to Larry as the "weather man" and Jim as the "apple man". These two brothers are both very smart, full of common sense and are a pure pleasure to know. As long as they are both blessed with good health, they will continue to make furniture, pick fruit, process dried venison, apple butter, cider, vinegar and enjoy life to the fullest.

Perry County Magic!

Storyteller Craig Wallis "Diamond"

So how does a Perry County kid growing up on a chicken farm become a world renown, multiple award-winning magician, considered within the magic world to be one of the most traveled entertainers in the industry?

Who knew? Well, if you were around in the 1970's you'll know a bit of this unique story…My grand-father Edwin B. Wallis Sr. started, in the late 1930's, what would become the largest poultry operation in the county, just south of Liverpool. With the addition of peach and cherry orchards, the business would later become Edwin B. Wallis & Sons, to include a farm market, and the Millersburg Ferryboat and campgrounds. My Dad Edwin Jr. "Bud" Wallis, along with working in the family business was also a two term Republican County commissioner in the 1970's; going on to become the Director of Plant Industry for the Department of Agriculture during the Thornburgh administration. So, there's some background for those that don't know, now the magic…

Like all kids in the 1960's, especially boys, I got the magic bug young, after seeing the old Hollywood movie about the magician Houdini. Watching the Saturday morning show the Magic Land of Alakazam, and then the MAGIC KIT! In second grade my teacher Miss Whitekettle had me go class to class showing an amazing trick! (The magical ball and vase, a standard effect in every magic set to this day), well I was hooked. This coincided with the family's addition of the Ferryboat campgrounds. That summer I spent the time going from campsite to campsite doing my little "show". One day a gentleman came up to me at the concession stand and said, "So I hear you like magic?", he then proceeded to remove the top of a ketchup bottle and vanish it in his bare hands! My eyeballs popped! His name was James T. Warmkessel, a retired former vaudevillian magician; one of the first magicians of television featured on the Philadelphia based children's show "The Sally Star Show". He and his wife were seasonal campers, and I was waiting for them the next weekend at their campsite with my bag of tricks. The rest of that summer was sitting around the campfire on Friday and Saturday nights listening to great stories and watching magic. Jim would perform something and then teach it to me. He provided me with my first mail order magic catalog and by the end of that summer I had a full-blown magic show! Now, it gets a little more interesting! The following year, the family that had the campsite next to the Warmkessel's (separated by just feet) would have a regular Sunday visitor friend from Harrisburg. His name was Dr. Don Lederman and at that time he was president of the local magician's organization of the International Brotherhood of Magicians. Seriously what are the odds of all this?? Don was impressed enough with my skills and got me into the local magic club by special vote. You had to be at least 14 years of age and that was four more years away! So, I guess you could call me a child prodigy. I had a terrible absentee rate at school. I would do anything to convince my Mother I couldn't go to school, to stay home to work on my magic. Along with performing at the Ferry Campgrounds I progressed to birthday parties, church events, civic clubs, private parties, carnival's, fairs, political fund raisers, all kinds of special events. Before I turned 16 one of my parents was stuck with the job of driving me to all my shows.

After attending my first national magic convention and competition in Boston, the Society of American Magicians 1974 convention, I saw what I still think as, the greatest array of national and international talent ever. AND it gave me an idea……the following school year I proposed for a class sponsored show. Fund a one-night show that I'll organize and produce, and the class would make more money on that night than selling candles, candy, hoagies, etc. all year. In January of 1975, the very first "The World of Illusion" show appeared at Newport High School to a sold-out crowd. The starring act "The Gustafson's Magic by Candlelight" was a huge act in magic. I first saw them on the Ed Sullivan show, and here along with three other big acts and myself, we're doing a show at Newport! It was a big success and another one was set for the next year with even bigger stars. I do mean stars of magic. This was "pre-David Copperfield days", so many of the names weren't household names but were huge in magic. Del Ray, Tommy Wonder, Lee Allen, Garray & Tomio, I could go on with ten or more names. Magicians from five states would drive to see this one-night show. My last two years of high school I was graciously allowed to use the music office and phone (thank you forever Russ LaForce) to organize the event. Each year it got bigger. I did them in 1975,1976,1977, 1982, 1994, and the last in 2018.

The wonderful county tie in is that another Newport student saw these shows and was bit by the magic bug and would later take magic lessons from me. He would also go on to become a pro and international magic act—that is John Westford of Newport. The two of us starred and produced the 1994 and 2018 version of the show. The stage at the Newport Jr./Sr. High School has quite a magic legacy.

My career took off first with being part of production shows, the Pocono resorts, dinner theaters, etc. Big time management came in 1984. From New York City, the former president of the American Guild of Variety Artists (AGVA) called me on the family farm and wanted to be my manager…. yes please! The next 37 years were a whirl wind of international travel. Literally travelling around the world…. all the time, either by air or sea, 32 to 52 weeks a year. I started headlining with the cruise industry of January 1984. I also was lucky to be an opening act for the likes of Joan Rivers, Phyllis Diller, the Smother's Brothers, Sammy Davis Jr., Bobby Vinton, Tony Bennet, Victor Borge; I could go on and on. They are all pinch me moments to a kid from Perry County. I have travelled to more than 130 countries, performed on every continent, yep even Antarctica! I've performed for Kings and Queens, Prime Ministers, Sheiks, Sultans, and even the White House in 1983 for President Reagan's state dinner for the King and Queen of Nepal. In 1986 I was presented with Master Magician of the Year. Last year I was the cover and feature story for Vanish International, the largest magic magazine in the world. So, there you go, for a kid from Liverpool (south enough that I went to Newport) and for a student of Newport who hardly went…. I did okay. I mention in my show on the cruise ships I'm from a county in Pa. that's very rural and doesn't have a stoplight or parking meter in the entire county (I know about the light now). I can't tell you how many times after the show there is someone or a group waiting for me to inquire Perry County??? Then the stories begin. I changed my surname for stage, "stage name", in 1980 to Craig Diamond. At the time the act was known as Craig Diamond & Crystal. I simply changed because every time a newspaper would write me up my name was misspelled as Wallace. So, after listening to an advisor of Penn & Teller and Copperfield, who explained "they have to spell it right and remember it", Wallis was out and Diamond was in. I met my beautiful wife Dolores on a cruise ship in 1985. She was a professional croupier (blackjack, roulette) working in the casino. Born in Ireland, raised in England. In those days every night in the casino was formal, so it was right out of a James Bond movie. I always say I walked through the casino, saw this beautiful blonde with an English accent and it was love at first sight…. because I know she'll fit in all of my boxes…….and it was, and she did. We married on the island of St. Thomas in 1987. We moved to Florida in 1988, which was the same year my parents retired to there as well. Through the years I brought them out with us on lots of cruises and our years together in Florida were magic too. For Mother and Dad there was always the yearly trip back "home" to the county. Since their passing I try to get back when I can and visit my sister Jill in Bucks Valley. I may be the most travelled person ever from the county, but PECO will always be home. For more interest you can read the article from Vanish magazine and/or visit my website www.craigdiamondentertainment.com https://joom.ag/ZJdC

Just a Kid Free to Roam Millerstown

Storyteller Jim Roush

Until the mid-1960s, US22/322 ran directly through Millerstown. As kids, we spent many Saturday nights sitting on the front porch on Market Street, counting out-of-state license plates on the busy highway.

Cash, along with a note, was placed in our front porch milk box and milk was delivered by Hall's Dairy, three times per week to the box.

Daily Patriot News newspapers, along with the weekly Grit (or Williamsport liar as it was sometimes called), were loaded into bicycle baskets and delivered to homes throughout town early in the morning by paperboys and papergirls.

Western Flyer bikes, with baseball cards clothes pinned to the wheel frames, fluttered in the spokes. A baseball and bat were secured under the seat, a ball glove hung from the handlebar of our bikes just in case we had enough kids to play "scrubby" at a makeshift ball field next to the elementary school, or the Moose parking lot.

If we had enough players for two baseball teams, we chose teams by catching a bat in the air, then alternating hands to the top of the bat, with "no nibs or thumbs up". The player whose hand reached the top of the bat first, picked first. We used sticks, cardboard, or whatever else we could find for bases.

Serving as bat boy for the town team's baseball team was always fun. And if we were lucky enough for them to break a bat, my Uncle Dar would saw the end of it off and we would use it as a "pint sized" bat!

Ladies routinely hung their wash on clotheslines in the backyard. They would meet there and discuss the week's 'goings on'. It was said that gossip would be spread throughout town via the clothesline.

There were three grocery stores (A&P, Bortell's Butcher Shop and Gelnett's) within walking distance, so there was no need to hop in a car to get groceries. On Saturday morning, kids would deliver groceries to homes from Gelnett's store in our wagons.

My Mom often reminds me of the time she sent me to Gelnett's store for a can of red beets. I got to the store and couldn't remember what I was to get, so I picked up a 50 lb. bag of potatoes and struggled my way up the street. I was probably about 8 years old at the time.

Howdy's Hardware Store had everything you ever needed…it just took a while for him to find it!

Homer Kepler and Bob Cameron had barber shops on the square. We would alternate getting crew cuts every other week.

Frosty's ice cream truck made its way through town every Saturday afternoon. We would run for the truck as we heard the bell approaching, to get a large cone of chocolate frozen custard.

We often crossed the river to place pennies on the train tracks. We'd wave to the caboose then collect our flattened copper.

Practically every Saturday morning, my brother and I would wake up early and stare at WGAL TV8's trademark screen, anxiously waiting for Covered Wagon Theater to come on at 8:00 a. m., followed by Percy Platypus and Fury.

The firemen's carnival was held the second week of August each year. Garbrick's rides were the highlight with two big ferris wheels, a paratrooper, merry mixer, and the merry go round playing Sousa marches. When I ran out of ride tickets, I'd take a seat beside my grandmother in the bingo tent…a big double card for 10 cents a game! Don Lorenze's Record Hop and Andy Reynolds and the 101 Ranch Boys were mainstays each year on the stage.

Millerstown seemed to be the mecca of nicknames back in the day—names such as Chuckles, Jiggs, Pickles, Whiskey, Dipper, Nutsy, Sneakers, Frog, Scoopy, etc. One year Ron Drake served as Parade Marshall for a centennial celebration. When he returned to his WHP microphone the following Monday morning, he spouted off all of his new "friends" he met in Millerstown over the weekend.

Each Christmas season, we would go to Joe the Motorist at the 7th Street Plaza in Harrisburg to see the "real" Santa Claus, along with their model train display.

The Mather Family (paternal grandmother) Reunion was held annually on the fourth Sunday in June at Willow Mill Park. Lots of good eats, followed by an afternoon on the amusement rides!

Another family tradition was going to the Red Barn in Lewistown to pick up a large bucket of chicken, then head to the Horseshoe Curve or East Broad Top Railroad for a Sunday afternoon picnic.

Recollections from Growing Up in a Country Store

Storytellers Cathy Urich Gilbert and Terry Urich

Our parents, Stanley Glenn and Catherine Rowe Urich, owned and operated Urich's Grocery from 1948 until our mother's retirement in 1983 (our father passed away in 1980, and our mother continued to operate the business for three additional years, until she sold the business, and our home, in 1983). Our home was connected to the store, so we literally grew up in the store. We knew our neighbors, became friends with all of the salespeople who called on the store, and enjoyed the friendships of everyone who entered our little store. These people were a part of our family, and rejoiced with us during the joyous times, and stood with us during life's difficult changes. We learned how to make change using the old cash register, how to keep books, and in general how to run a small business while always respecting our customers (the customer is always right).

Days were long for our parents as the store opened at 7 in the morning and remained open until 9 at night. Store hours accommodated workers in the morning who stopped for gas or lunch materials and farmers who labored from morning until dark. Our parents successfully raised 4 children in addition to working those long hours. We rarely had anyone else work in the store and during those few, rare times, we relied on trusted neighbors or relatives. It was truly an emergency when one of our parents was not in the store (funerals, hospitalizations, and an occasional wedding).

Country stores were actually general stores and served as the gathering place for everyone; a place to get your groceries (which included fresh meats from local butchers such as Kling's or Trostle's), purchase gas and oil for your car, kerosene to heat your home, clothing, shoes, work boots, hardware and a place to see your neighbors, and ask about those you hadn't seen in a while. Customers stopped in for their daily papers, delivered each day by Mr. Les Wagner of New Bloomfield. We were a full-service business, so we pumped customers' gas, checked their oil, pumped kerosene for their stoves, and loaded their groceries in the car. We delivered groceries to those who weren't able to come to the store, or if the weather was too treacherous for them to drive. We also sold cigarettes (kept behind the counter for security reasons), cigars, chewing tobacco, ammunition, and a little bit of anything needed in the home, farm, or business.

When we were asked to write a few words about our lives growing up in Perry County, and being a part of a "general store" family, we had some similar and some very different recollections. Terry, the oldest of our family, and Cathy, the youngest shared the following:

Mrs. Edith Magee was the local tax collector and used our store to collect taxes at the end of August. Farmers in the area sold their wheat crop and were then able to pay their taxes.

Horseshoe pits were the main attraction during the summer months. Our store had 4 pits outside in the parking lot, made with clay from the Ard Kretzing farm. The boys were tasked to water the pits each day so the horseshoes would stick and prevent them from sliding off the pits. Lights were installed so the pitchers could play after dark.

In the early 1950's, the store had the only telephone in the area. Calls would come and our parents would take messages to the party. Often, the recipients needed to come to the store to return their calls.

Billy Burd would sell watermelons and cantaloupes to the store; 50 watermelons and 5 bushels of cantaloupes were stacked on our open front porch for resale.

The little gray box – Mom and Dad kept a little gray metal box behind the counter to record debts of their customers. During the winter months, when paper-wood loggers had no work, farmers were short on cash, and construction workers and laborers struggled to find employment, our parents kept a running "tab" for those who needed help. Families needed food, gasoline, fuel (kerosene), and boots and shoes. Several of those tabs sometimes grew into thousands of dollars. The bills were always paid as soon as the customers (we never called them debtors!) received money. These transactions occurred with simply a handshake, for all of these folks/friends were true to their word. It was not easy for my folks to carry these debts, but it was necessary for those who needed help.

There was always a large wheel of cheese on the counter and "loose" pretzels in cans that were sold by their weight. Purchases were put into brown paper bags. Bottles of soda (or soft drinks, as they were known at the time) were in a cooler in the back of the store. The sodas were cooled in a case of circulating cold water. Folks would reach into the cooler to make their selection and then dry their hands and the soda bottle on an old dish towel positioned right beside the bottle opener.

There was such a spirit of community at the store. Often, there was a jar on the counter to purchase flowers from "Friends and neighbors of Mannsville" when someone was sick or when a family was mourning the loss of a loved one.

During times of crisis, people would arrive at the store to share the news about a fire in the community or if someone was down on their luck and needed groceries or kerosene to heat their homes. I remember my mother going through the store and getting toothbrushes, toothpaste, and other necessities to give to those who just lost everything.

One Christmas was especially eventful when a neighbor called on Christmas morning to inform my parents that a young boy in the community received no Christmas presents. She asked my folks if they could help the young lad. Mom and dad went into the store and assured the boy would have wrapped presents delivered for Christmas day. A Timex watch, a few small toys that were sold in the store, a new toothbrush, and socks were gift wrapped. In addition, the boys in the family donated a few of their unopened presents; a fact they didn't know until much later.

Snowstorms were a fact of life, and sometimes, we would be "snowed in" for days. In the early 1970's a major storm hit the area, and our Harrisburg Dairies milkman was snowed in with our family for days.

Growing up in the small community of Mannsville was the perfect setting for children. We did not have the privilege of growing up "in town", with access to the library, sidewalks, playgrounds, and public swimming pool, but we had a group of friends that were located close enough to be a community, but far enough away to be in the country. While each family had siblings (our family included Terry, Dutch, Peno, and Cathy), we also had neighbors and friends who were the same age. Lee Campbell, Bill Reisinger, Steve Jury, John and Gary Turnbaugh, Linda and Mike Rudy, Jean and Dave Radle, Joyce Johnson, and Wanda, Sis, and Junior Campbell were all part of the community. We played ball every day with our friends in our backyard, or in the Mannsville Lutheran Church "lot". Balls hit over the chicken house roof were automatic home runs. We went through a lot of baseballs because our neighbor, Minnie Burd, would confiscate them if we didn't jump the fence quickly to retrieve them from her gardens.

Hot, lazy summer days were spent playing ball, riding bikes, and riding our bikes going to Alfred Yohn's stream to fish. Those were Idyllic days without a care in the world. The boys played little league baseball, often with dad coaching, in the evenings while mom and Cathy stayed home to tend the store.

We had a long glass candy case where we sold penny candy. Small, brown paper bags contained these treasures and the children of the community enjoyed shopping with their change. While such decisions were time-consuming, it was important for the little ones to spend their pennies wisely.

There were baskets and crates of apples sitting on the floor of the store. Customers could purchase bushels, half bushels, or pounds of apples. As a teething toddler, it was very tempting to pick up an apple, try a bite, and then replace the apple back into the basket. Our parents would discover this when they were weighing the apples for customers. Our mother said she made a lot of pies and applesauce the year that Cathy learned to walk and commit this misdeed. A picture of Cathy "caught in the act" mysteriously appeared in her high school yearbook with the caption, "one bad apple don't spoil the whole bunch".

Men from the community which included farmers, laborers, construction workers, retired and those in their prime came to the store to "loaf", so we called them the loafers. During the summer months, they congregated on benches on the front porch, greeting everyone who came to the store. During the winter months, they sat in the back of the store, and shared the news of the day. Often, they returned home with their grocery list filled or a half gallon of ice cream for their family. Memorable loafers included, Frankie Barns, George Radle, Leroy Shuman, Bob Sutch, Ard Kretzing, Charlie Brunner, Charlie Burd, Russell Rossback, and Alfred Yohn.

Loafers would gather each night to settle the problems of the world. From those wise discussions, we learned that you could hear the corn growing after a thunderstorm and it was extremely humid. Sitting on the porch of the store, we could hear the corn crackling and creaking in the fields of Ben Beichler, who farmed across the road.

Folks returned their empty soda bottles for the deposit. Many of the returned bottles were found along the road, so it was a dirty task assigned to us children when those bottles needed to be "separated" for return to the distributor.

During deer season, the men would arrive at the store early on the first day and form a "gang" to hunt deer. Bob Sutch, Charlie Brunner, Bud Brunner, Bill Sutch, Don Mitchell, Glenn Mitchell, Guy Kepner, Walker Snyder, Jim Hummel, Ard Kretzing, Ernie Kretzing, Don Sheibley, Red Stoops, Brant Kretzing, Perry Kretzing, Don Stoops, and Dale Haas were familiar names to the "Mannsville Gang".

Fridays were grocery day at the store. We were all up early for the cases and cases of groceries that were delivered from Harrisburg Groceries. We helped unload the boxes from the tractor trailer. Then after everything was accounted for, dad would cut open the boxes while we marked the prices on the top of the cans or bottles, and then stock the shelves. The boxes were kept and used to pack groceries for our customers. At that time, everyone seemed to prefer their groceries packed into boxes instead of paper bags. I'm sure those boxes were used and reused by the customers.

We also sold plants and flowers. Both Frownfelter's Greenhouse and Newport Greenhouse would deliver vegetable plants and flowers to the store for resale. Seed potatoes and onion sets were purchased from Wentzel's Mill and resold. Bulk seeds, such as corn and beans were also sold, and we would weigh the seeds and put them into paper bags for customers.

In summary, we realize how fortunate we were to be with our parents every day, all day. We knew they were there for us all the time. Many of our friends were not that fortunate and only saw one (or both) of their parents at the supper table and the evening hours before bedtime. One of our parents was there for all of the school plays, sporting events, Cub Scouts, Brownies, and after school activities. We worked together, ate all of our meals together (unless we were interrupted when a customer walked in the store), and even had the opportunity to have every Sunday "off" because stores were closed on Sundays when we were growing up. Little did we know at the time that we were indeed blessed to have two hard-working, loving parents who exhibited their kindness to the community in both little and large ways.

Childhood Memories from Along the Juniata River

Storyteller Jeannie Maguire

My first (and only) bicycle was a used, 26" red girl's. I should mention I was only around eight at the time. No training wheels but wooden blocks on the peddle so I could reach them and, of course, no gears. I learned to ride the usual way with one of my parents holding onto the seat. But, only on dirt or grass. We rode that bike in the yard and field, taking turns. Sometimes it was the horse in 'Cowboys and Indians'! Only as a teen did I finally ride on the paved road and only to a nearby neighbor's house, outside of Duncannon.

My grandparents' property was along the Juniata River, in Aqueduct. Almost every evening in the summer, (afternoon on the weekend) swimming trips were taken to the river. The Juniata, unlike the Susquehanna, has few deep holes or swift currents so it was a safe place for kids. Sometimes, when the water was low and the seaweed was "icky" to walk through, and green "slime" lined the bank, we'd take the rowboat out. Especially on weekends, my cousins, aunt, uncles, etc. would join in.

There were trees near the water with heavy vines, that some of the boys would swing out over the water and jump in. On one hot summer day, we had our dog along, in the boat. Everyone was in the water except Tinka. My father (one or both parents were always swimming with us) decided to go to shore for some reason. Next thing we had a diving dog as she jumped from the boat and swam to join him. Happy ending, she was fine but it was the last time we took her out on the boat.

Later when my mom got a car, she'd take us, some neighbor kids, plus a friend and her kids to the public landing for an afternoon swim. Cars were big. No seat belts, so kids sat on each other's laps. It was only a short way!

When we got out of the water, there was always a "leech" check. Don't remember anyone ever finding one, but it was a "left-over" from my parent's childhood! The riverbank was weedy, creating a mad dash to grandpa's, in Aqueduct, to avoid getting "eaten" by the mosquitoes. Oh yes, avoid the "cow itch"!

My father built my brother a motorized go-cart. It was a nice one, but the first time out, the brakes didn't work. As it went down our drive, picking up speed, my brother was laying over, clinging to the seat, and screaming. My mother was chasing after while my dad and I were bent over laughing. As mom always said, it could have been very bad if he'd made it to the road, but somehow it got stopped.

After it was "repaired" it still got my brother in big trouble. One day, he and a friend decided it would go better on a dirt track. They took the garden tractor and made a track in the back yard. My parents were not happy to see the grass that was slowly spreading dug up!

We had lots of snow in the 1950's, so sledding (and shoveling!) was a major activity. The neighbor allowed us to sled in his pasture ... just be careful not to tear up the grass! Our sleds had runners, so trails had to be made. Walking down and back up the hill, packing the snow as you went. Then sledding as far as you could and walking back up the trail, again and again. Eventually you had a fast track to the bottom. You could go down one, two, three or more on the sled... sitting up or laying down. Trains could be made by holding onto the back of the sled in front of you. (Amazingly, we all survived!) When we got cold, a trip to the house - usually ours - since we had a coal furnace with a big register, just right for drying coats, mittens, and boots. After a board game or two, back out for more sledding!

Harrisburg was a distant city to us. My other grandparents lived there and visits were always special. Grandma always had to "feed us" - snacks or sandwiches. Our visits were usually "drop-in". Usually, we walked to the stores on Third Street. Stores like Bill's 5 & 10, The Boston Store (clothing), Joe the Motorist, and Lee's 5 & 10, all seemed grand to us. Lee's 5 & 10 was extra special. We didn't always walk that far, but it had doll house furniture like sewing and washing machines (cost 10 cents so only pick one!). They had other toys not found in our local 5 & 10. We didn't eat at their lunch counter.

When I was a teen, grandma started to have the whole family for Thanksgiving. Two of my cousins lived in the city, so "we kids" were allowed to walk "downtown" to see the Pomeroy's Christmas window displays...they used to put on quite a show.

Part of the fun of growing up in a small town, was that store owners and clerks in the stores knew your family by name. Going into these stores was like visiting friends or family. Joking and laughing was part of the shopping trip.

'Home Delivery' is starting to make a comeback. However, in the1950s, we had a milk man, a bread man and in the summer, an ice cream man. A small, insulated aluminum box sat on the porch for the Juniata or Harrisburg Dairy milk deliveries. In the winter, the milk would freeze and push the cardboard cap up an inch or so. At first milk was only pasteurized, so there was a couple of inches of cream at the top and you had to shake it before pouring!

The Capitol Bread truck carried a little more than bread. It was a treat to get a box of glazed donuts. Sam's Ice Cream truck came, I think, only in the summer. I remember half gallons, but it probably had novelty items, too.

My brother and I were fortunate to have three neighbor kids (from a very large family) near our age. We played together most days and into the summer nights. There were days when we'd fight over something. An hour later, we were begging our mothers to let us play again. Since there were only five of us (sometimes a few of the other kids would join in), we made up rules to suit us. We played most of the games of the 1950s - Kick the Can, Red Light, Green Light, Pops the Ball, I Spy, Hide and Seek, Tag, Fox and Geese, Dress-up, Cowboys and Indians, School and House.

Softball! You had to hit the ball straight, narrow, and not too far, or it became foul or worse, out. This wasn't because there were only five of us. There were gardens, fields, and other obstructions in the areas we were allowed to play!

I feel so lucky to have grown up in the 1950's and to have had parents who liked to play games with the kids. My childhood memories are "spotty" but I do remember hours of 500 Rummy, Tripoli, putting together jigsaw puzzles, playing horseshoes and croquet. Monopoly, though that may have been only one game...it lasts forever! Sledding in winter, swimming, bowling (we had a table version...small wooden pins and large marbles), and other activities, played with my parents and brother.

It was about 1954, when we got a black and white TV with three channels - sometimes! Watching Topper at our grandparents, was a weekly family affair.

Comic Books were plentiful and not just Superhero's, but Donald Duck, Sugar & Spike, Archie, Tom & Jerry, and on and on!

Cut Outs were my Barbies. They came in many different designs. Pink Wedding, anyone? Or a movie star? Or maybe Roy Rodgers? The list went on!

Sometimes when I watch reruns of the TV shows of the 1950s, it is easy to step back in time. Even then the shows did not reflect real life. My mother wore jeans, pants, and shorts frequently. She did have some "house dresses" but I don't think she cleaned in them! After all, clothes were starched and ironed in those days. A lot of work for something you were wearing to scrub floors!

My dad, as were many in this rural area, was a blue-collar worker. He had one suit for "special occasions". He usually wore jeans and tee, flannel, and work shirts. For visits out of the area, slacks and a sport shirt were worn.

The kids on TV were a little more realistic. We had school clothes, which were changed to play clothes, immediately when we got home. Only dresses for girls, and slacks for boys at school, but jeans, twills, and shorts at home, for everybody.

Sad to say the cigarette smoking on the shows really did happen. Ash trays were provided, and it was an accepted practice for adults. Though not everyone liked the "dirty habit" (ashes, odor, stains on hands). Daddy smoked, mom did not but many of our extended family did. Cigarettes were an OK gift if you knew the smoker's brand.

My 1950s childhood was a little different from the ones you read about in the different "memories" posted on Facebook, etc. Unlike the total freedom they describe, we were not given total freedom. When I was very young, we lived within sight of the railroad. Four tracks, at the end of our front yard, so there was definitely no leaving the yard, and most play was at the side or back of the house. Later, we were only allowed in our yard, and when crops were not an issue, in the field between our house and the neighbors. If we wanted to go to their house, permission was needed. Our doors were locked at night.

Walking with Grandma Along the Cow Paths

Storyteller Lorie Bolden Goss
Recorded by Debra Kay Noye

"The cows are laying down, it's going to rain" Lorie's Grandmother Margaret McGuire would say every time she spotted the cows belly down, resting in the fields. So, she didn't find it unusual that her grandmother would carry an onion and long pieces of string along, when they would follow the cow paths through the meadows and woods. She automatically knew there had to be a good reason, and luckily, they were never put to use. Today, Lorie figures it was a remedy for a possible snake bite.

Grandma was learned in the old ways. She was the source of information and inspiration to Lorie, as she stood by her side learning how to identify plants, as well as, appreciate and put God's bounty to best use. On the long walks around the farm, they would suck the "honey" from the flowers on the wild honeysuckle bushes. They discovered "cow-berries", along the stream. They were low lying bushes that had berries resembling, those on a holly tree. The women would eat the lack-luster berries, but not pick them for any other purpose.

Lorie's favorite wild berry was the pink colored, teaberry, hidden under the dark green foliage. She ate them right away, enjoying the unique taste, similar to wintergreen. As they traipsed all around the farm, Lorie's grandma would paint a mental picture of their Irish ancestors, as they worked the land. She would tell how the women would bring lunch and iced tea to the fields, for the men as they prepared for, and tended the crops. She always shared tidbits of family history, with Lorie, on their adventures.

In the early spring, Lorie's grandma was eager to go look for the pink and white flowering arbutus. She always seemed to know exactly where the "May Flower" vines were flourishing, even if the ground was a bit snow covered.

The women searched for wild strawberries in the fields, even-though, Lorie's grandfather had large strawberry patches on the farm. Other close-by relatives also raised strawberries. Lorie picked strawberries for her grandfather, for days-on-end. It was not unusual for her to pick one-hundred-quart boxes of strawberries, per day. Her great-grandmother Pearl Burd, "Mammy Burd", fashioned a basket holder onto an apron, which enabled Lorie to pick berries with both hands. After the berries were picked, her grandfather would sell them at the farm, as well as peddle them all over, even into Duncannon. He sold the berries for one dollar a box. Lorie received ten cents per box picked. She really made "big bucks", for a girl who never received an allowance.

They didn't have to go too far to pick blackberries and black raspberries, because there were large patches, right on the farm. When there was a good yield, they'd freeze them.

Wild fox grapes were plucked from the vines and turned into grape juice; by cooking them with water and straining the liquid. Sugar was added, before it was canned in glass jars, to be enjoyed through the winter months. They'd also make fox grape jelly, which was also sealed in glass jars. What a treat!

Penny royal was picked from the wild vine and dried, to make "penny royal tea". The same applied to sassafras, where the roots were dug up, cleaned, dried, and placed in a glass jar. The dried root was then steeped in boiling water to make a bright tasting tea, to enjoy when the snow was blowing.

Her father, Bob Bolden, would have Lorie take a five-gallon bucket, and fill it with dandelion flowers. She would search the fields, plucking dandelion flower heads, filling her bucket, and proudly take it to her father. He would take his hand, compressing the flowers, and send her back out to fill it to the top once again. It was frustrating, but he wouldn't be content, till she and her cohorts picked enough dandelion, so he could make dandelion wine. Now Lorie swears, she doesn't know how it tasted, but she had a sly grin!

Dandelion greens were another story entirely. The "greens" were picked, washed, and cooked down. Her grandma would make hot bacon dressing, which was added to the greens, cooking it further. The sweet and sour, salty and bitter, mixture was served over "saltwater potatoes", simply salted boiled potatoes.

When they weren't on another summer adventure, there was the huge "truck-patch" put out by the families, to be planted, weeded, and harvested. Lorie's family canned and froze the vegetables, to get them through the winter. Her pappy would plow up the potatoes, while she followed behind, picking them up out of the soil.

Her family would go pick sweet cherries at Evan's cherry orchard in Roseglen, outside of Duncannon. Mr. Virgil Evans was the Susquenita High School art teacher. However, that chore didn't end with the picking. Lorie hand-seeded each cherry before they were canned or frozen. It was a sticky kind of day!

It was the men's job to do the fall butchering of pigs, when Lorie was very young. Uncle Bobby McGuire, owned McGuire's Butcher Shop, outside of Duncannon, where the hams, bacon, and shoulder were smoked.

Her dad hunted, and Lorie actually helped to clean the game.

Her love of cooking came from her grandma, and Great-Aunt Veletta "Let" Smee. Lorie learned the art of making pot pie noodles, plus pies and cakes for special occasions. She wishes she could make her favorite date-nut pin wheels, like her grandma. They were one of many kinds of cookies made for the Christmas season.

Grandma's scrumptious coconut cake was baked each year at Christmas, after Lorie's pappy freshly grated a whole coconut. The six-layer coconut cake is still a family Christmas tradition, as well as a unique sausage fruit cake. The family enjoyed Christmas in their home, with a large dinner. Cousins and their parents would come in the afternoon, to visit and dine on sweets.

Christmas was her father's favorite time of the year, and he made sure it was extra special for everybody. Lorie referred to him as "Mr. Christmas", who would take the family to a local tree farm, to bring back a Christmas tree. However, it would remain bare until Santa decorated it, once the kids went to bed on Christmas Eve. He enjoyed bringing the pine tree to life and placing the tons of gifts underneath. Mr. Christmas' strict rule was that gifts could not be unwrapped, until he came downstairs on Christmas morning. The kids would beg him to hurry, but he would tease saying, he needed to shave or brush his teeth. It was the *one* time of year, that the family splurged!

Lorie would go out into the woods, to look for a patch of "crow's feet", so she could decorate the house for Christmas. Pinecones and boughs were also used. The family decorated a lot, with items gathered from the wild. Afterward, Lorie loved to lay on the couch smelling the pine and seeing all the decorations.

Her father hand-made wooden figurines, like reindeer, that were placed in the yard. The outside decorations wouldn't have been complete without the traditional nativity scene.

Christmas Eve meant traveling along, with Grandpa Ralph McGuire, as he delivered gifts and goodies to family members and friends. Lorie's church, Duncannon Church of God, on Sunshine Hill, would have a Christmas Cantata the Sunday before Christmas, instead of Christmas Eve. The candle-light service, featured the choir, directed by Betty Brinton, singing traditional Christmas songs, along with many depictions of the Christmas story. As the service came to an end, the attendees would circle the interior of the church, and be given a candle. One candle would be lit, and the flame passed to another, till the entire congregation was illuminated, as they sang Silent Night, creating a memorable holy night.

 The children would always sing "Happy Birthday", to baby Jesus. A giant sheet cake was emblazoned with birthday greetings to Jesus, and enjoyed by the church members, after the services. Lorie's church would treat each youngster to an orange and a box of candy.

Easter meant her grandmothers special custard-filled jelly roll, and lemon meringue or coconut custard pies, using Rawleigh pie filling base. The desserts graced the dinner table, after church. Lorie would be dressed in patent leather shoes, white gloves, new clothes, and coat, for the church's Easter service. Her father always asked Weezie Holland, owner of Holland's Flowers, in Duncannon, to create huge daffodil corsages for each of the females in the household. The Easter corsage was something Lorie looked forward to every year. A prankster, like Lorie, her father hid their Easter baskets, anywhere in the house, including the oven.

Some of Lorie's clothes were hand-made by her Aunt Pearl, who often made matching sets for Lorie and her cousin, Judy. If she needed anything else, they would go to Balsbaugh's Store, in Duncannon, where her mother, Lolita McGuire Bolden, worked.

Lorie also enjoyed going to Chapman's Store on Middle Ridge, outside of Newport, or to Harrisburg to shop. Popular catalogs, like Sears, presented other shopping opportunities.

Joining the local 4-H sewing club introduced Lorie to sewing, but she would rather be outside building forts in the hay mow, climbing into the silo filled with fermented corn silage, sliding around in the grain bins, or splashing in the creek, on the look-out for salamanders and crawfish. She even tried riding the cows in the pasture, since to her they were family pets. Each cow had their own name.

When she wasn't riding her bike and outside all day, Lorie loved to read about Nancy Drew's adventures. She, her siblings, and cousins, would pretend to be just like Nancy Drew. They spied under their own kitchen window, and really liked to pester Aunt Let, by doing the same at her home. "We thought, we were very cool! We were spies!" Fortunately, her parents purchased various books for Lorie to read, capturing her imagination.

But that mischievous nature would get Lorie into trouble, especially at Halloween. She and cousins, Judy, and Andy McGuire, decided to soap and toilet paper Great-Uncle Britton and Great-Aunt Letti Smee's home, as a Halloween practical joke. They sneaked out of their homes in the middle of the night and applied harsh bar soap to the Smee's windows. Their trees were adorned with ribbons of toilet paper. The revelers threw the toilet paper rolls high over the trees. Upon being discovered by their uncle, who yelled "Pis' Hunkies", the pranksters high-tailed it across the fields.

Of course, when it became known they surely were the culprits, vinegar and newspapers were used, by the cousins, to remove the soap. They also gathered up all the wasted toilet paper. The following years, their prank was duplicated by town kids.

Who would've thought that Lorie and her friends, would also phone Alfie Miller's Corner Store, on the square of Duncannon, and ask if they had King Albert in a can, which was a popular tobacco product? When Alfie would tell them yes, they would shout out, "let him out"! It was a fad among youth, to play this prank.

Her love of pranking may have come naturally, as she relates the story about some of her relatives, as told to her. Seems some family members decided to disassemble the outdoor privy. Now back in those days, it was the only bathroom, as indoor plumbing just didn't exist! The pranksters must not have had any fear of heights, as they reassembled the outhouse on the barn roof. It turned out to be an unusual cupola!

Her elementary years were spent at Duncannon Elementary School, which remained open, on the snowiest of days. Lorie hated having to travel down Aqueduct Hill because the bus would slide off the road. The driver would ask the older boys to get out and push the bus back onto the slippery highway.

Lorie describes the cafeteria as "a hole in the basement", where she bought and ate her lunch. She got an ice cream novelty if she had any extra money. She also worked at the ice cream stand. When she started sixth grade, it was a big deal to be a trusted hall guard. Lorie enjoyed getting dressed-up for May Day festivities, which included the traditional May pole with streamers.

Lorie recalls the day President Kennedy was assassinated. Teachers and students were crying and the following day, school was closed for a national day of mourning.

When she was in third grade, Lorie wrote a story about a vampire, that she shared with her teacher. Her teacher was so impressed, she gave Lorie a gold star and sent a note of praise, home to her parents.

Once school was out for the summer, Lorie attended Bible School for one week and participated in the presentation to the church, the following Sunday. Aunt Lois McGuire was a constant inspiration to Lorie, as she taught her about Christian faith and to love God.

Lorie would pride herself in achieving perfect attendance at church, for the year. She was so proud when she received a 'perfect attendance pin and Bible'. She dedicated herself to achieving this goal unless she was very sick. To console Lorie when she was ill on a Sunday and had to stay home from church, her father would stop off at Alfie Miller's store, and buy her a comic book and the family a newspaper. This would have been an extravagance, for the family.

Camping at the Duncannon YMCA was the only family vacation. They would pack up necessary belongings, and head out to the campgrounds. Sometimes, staying for weeks, during the summer months. Their father would go off to work during the day and return in the evening, to enjoy family time, swimming in the pool, and cooking over the camp stove or open fire. The open-air cabins, which were merely shelters, was a place to sleep. When raccoon would raid their food supply, her father would travel to Duncannon, to Glass' Bakery. He would bring back empty five-gallon buckets, with lids. The icing buckets were great for storing anything you didn't want destroyed, by pesky critters.

Otherwise, they spent time with family, the grandparents, Isabelle and Ted Bolden, and Margaret and Ralph McGuire, especially on Sundays. They would picnic at various homes and in the Narrows, between current day Wagner's Park on Montebello Road, and Route 849. The church sponsored trips to amusement parks, in the surrounding counties. Occasionally, they went to the Halifax drive-in movie theatre in Upper Dauphin County. Their father, always thinking about the kids, built a special board as an extension of the back seat, so that a sleepy child could stretch out and fall asleep.

***

Lorie's work ethic, love of nature, an appreciation of the olde' days, and strong faith in God were values instilled in her, by her grandparents and parents. Those lessons still ring true today, as their legacy lives on, cherished by Lorie.

Memories of Downtown Millerstown

Storyteller Jane Cameron Simonton

It's surprising how many businesses were in the small town of Millerstown when I was young, during the 1950s - 1960s. There was Moore's Hardware, Botdorf Funeral Home, Botdorf Furniture store, Charles Burn's Appliance store, a dress factory, two restaurants, a doctor's office and a dentist office. The one restaurant on the square was owned by my grandmother's sister-in-law, Edith Chubb. I cannot remember the name of it. The other restaurant was called Mom's Place. A group of us got permission from the school to go down there for lunch once.

There were three groceries stores. Lauver's was the one where my mom bought most of her groceries and it also had a gift shop section. I remember going there to buy presents for my mom. One gift I remember buying were two small flower vases. Bortell's was owned by Blain (Butch) Bortell and Leonard Beasom worked for him. This store is where my mom bought her meat. The A&P was the place my friend and I would go to get the pickles out of the large wooden barrel. We would pick out a pickle to eat on our walk home. Most of the groceries at the A&P were behind the counter and the store clerk, Mr. Harris (his nickname was Bang Bang Harris) had to get what you needed. He would have a long stick to reach some that were way up high. There was also milk delivery from Hall's Dairy and a bread man from Capital Baker's. It was fun when we were allowed to also get doughnuts or some pastry off the truck.

There was a movie theatre in town with a large popcorn machine and Selma Ulsh playing the piano. Three movies I remember seeing at the theatre were *Jailhouse Rock*, *Love Me Tender* and *Three Coins in the Fountain*. I also have memories hearing Christmas music the month of December being played over an outside speaker from the Homer Kepner barber shop and going with my mom to pay the phone bill and seeing all the lady phone operators working on the long switchboards. At that time, the phone we had was the black candlestick style where you spoke into the round mouthpiece and lifted the receiver or earphone to hear. The operator would ask who you wanted to call and would connect you to that person. Years later we had a wall phone with party lines. You weren't able to call whenever you wanted but would wait until the other party's call was completed.

There was also a small store in town that children would go to get candy and ice cream. Clair Coats owned it. She had a big candy counter filled with lots of penny candy and candy bars. We would get our baseball cards, candy cigarettes, mini paraffin drink bottles, candy buttons, sugar daddy pops, Turkish taffy, double bubble gum, and Skybars, just to name a few. At Halloween she would let us pick 5 cents worth of candy.

Summer days were spent going to the town pool, 4-H meetings, and Bible School at the Methodist Church, back then it was for two weeks and during the day. Most evenings were visits to Hall's Dairy for ice cream. If it were a nice evening, we would walk with a group to the dairy or ride our bikes, but mostly we would go in the car. Back then they had the basic flavors – vanilla, chocolate, and fruit flavors. My favorite was their raspberry ice cream or banana splits.

Millerstown had Memorial Day Parades and Halloween Parades. I would march in the Memorial Day parade with my Brownie and Girl Scout troops when I was young, then with Greenwood High School. The Halloween parade was always at night and when I was in elementary school, classes would often go as a group. In first grade we were to dress as scarecrows. My dad made me arms out of cardboard so I wouldn't have to walk with my arms stretched out the whole time. It was a problem though when the teacher said to put your arms down and I couldn't.

There were no clothing stores in town, so it was a treat when the Sears catalog arrived in the mail. My friend and I would sit for hours looking at the catalog and pick out clothes. Mom and dad would also take us to Carlisle to buy clothes at the Lehman Shop (girls) and Israel's (boys) and shoes at Dutrey's. I also remember going to a children's clothing shop on East Main Street in New Bloomfield owned by Virginia Barnes. The owner had grown up in Millerstown and was a friend of my mom.

A Diary of a Perry County Farm Boy Serving in World War 1

Storyteller Jeremiah Ross Lyons
Recorded by William Glenn Lyons

In 1917, several men were drafted into the Army to serve during World War 1. Grandpa, Jere Lyons, 25 years old, and his brother, Ray, were part of the group from Perry County. Grandpa was from Loysville, and Great Uncle Ray came from New Bloomfield. Grandpa rarely talked about his days as an infantryman, but he did keep an accurate journal in a little 2" x 4 ¼" booklet that he had given to me as a boy. My parents, William and Kay Lyons, shared some things that they remembered that he would talk about. He once sat among a group of soldiers that were sitting around eating a meal together, overseas, when one of the men pulled a chicken head out of the gravy. Everything was utilized during wartime! He didn't eat any horse meat, but he saw dead horses that had the meat cut away from underneath their manes. Grandpa Lyons had said that he always had in his mind, while fighting in the trenches, if the German soldiers would have had an opportunity to take him prisoner, he would rather be shot. The American soldiers in his group fought alongside Polish men often. The French people didn't speak English, and we didn't speak French, so if we wanted to buy something like eggs, we would make the sound of a chicken, and point at the eggs, to communicate. Grandpa would take my dad and Uncle Ron hunting sometimes, but he never carried a gun himself, he would always say "I did enough shooting in the war". The group of Perry County veterans always would gather each year on Armistice Day, November 11, at the New Bloomfield or Newport VFW, for a meal. At the same time my Grandma Pearl Lyons, my dad, Aunt Gail, Uncle Ron, and Aunt Miny would travel to my Great Uncle Ray Lyons home. There they met up with my Great Aunt Polly and their cousins Tom, Neil, Ed, Ruby, and Kay. They would feast on fried oysters and all the fixings and eat a bucket of Hattie Harris ice cream made by Harrisburg Dairies for dessert.

Jeremiah Lyons' own words follow:

On April 6, 1917, the war between the United States and Germany was declared.
I was checked out on October 27, 1917 and was sent home through the Y.M.C.A. During Christmas 1917, I was at the base hospital at Camp Meade, in Maryland.
April 4, 1918, we left Camp Meade for Baltimore and had a parade there on the 6th. We camped in David Hill Park overnight and the next day, a Sunday, we hiked 22 miles back to camp.

June 8 & 9, 1918, I was in Washington D.C. Some of the main places that I saw were the White House, Capital, Washington Monument, National Museum, and Glen Echo Park. We were put up at a Red Cross. The Red Cross played an important role during the war with food and a place to sleep, being just part of it. They also provided aid to the victims of natural disasters, of tuberculosis, of Spanish influenza, refugees, and displaced persons.

June 10, 1918, we were taken out to the rifle range and made camp for 10 days.

July 5, 1918 at 7 pm, we left Camp Meade and landed in Jersey City, N.J. the following day at 5 am. At noon, we were fed lunch by the Red Cross. On Sunday, July 7, we loaded luggage all day onto the ship.

On Monday, July 8 at 6 pm, the ship commenced to move and we left Hoboken, N.J. On Sunday, July 14, we had five convoys of submarine chasers with us. The next day at 12:30 pm, we landed at shore somewhere in France. July 16, 135 wounded soldiers were loaded on to our ship. Two days later we were unloaded off the ship, and paraded in the streets of Bretz, in the afternoon, with our full uniforms on.

July 19 it was raining heavy as we broke camp at 2 am. We hiked 4 miles and then were loaded on to boxcars. We were unloaded off the train in Laignes on July 21 at 11 pm and camped there overnight. At 8 am, we were on our way as we hiked 9 miles to a little village named Ampilly. On July 25 at 7 pm, we left the little village on gator trucks, 29 soldiers to a truck, and landed in another village the following day at noon.

On Sunday, September 8 at 12 noon, we left Argilliers for a railroad station. It commenced to rain at 4 pm. We arrived at the train station at 7 pm after hiking 15 miles with full packs on. A full pack included a blanket, shelter half, shelter half pole and pins, entrenching tools, ammo belt, first aid kit, canteen cover, canteen cup, baking tin, condiment can, and boxes of bread rations. A fully loaded pack weighed over 60 pounds not including our weapon. We unloaded off the train the next day at noon and hiked 3 miles to a town named Fains. We left there on the 13th and landed in Ricicourt, a town that had been bombarded. Two days later, we went into dugouts, and in the evening before we left, the town was shelled again.

On September 19, I was repairing a dugout (some dugouts were 30 feet deep) trying to make it shrapnel proof. The next evening, we moved and bivouac overnight. On September 21, we were digging trenches and had to run in to get away from shrapnel. The next 4 days and 4 nights it rained, so we were wet and working in pure mud. Trench warfare was a huge part of World War 1. Both sides would dig in and built networks that stretched hundreds of miles across France. In some places less than 100 yards separated opposing lines. Between these lines of trenches lay no-man's land. "Over the top" a battlefront commander would shout. We, the infantrymen, with fixed bayonets climbed out of the trenches and dashed across no-man's land. We would fling our grenades, struggle through barbed-wire entanglements, and run around gaping shell holes. Machine gun fire took a heavy toll and made successful charges almost impossible. There were second and third lines of trenches parallel to the first line, each line 100 yards apart. Huge underground caverns served as first-aid stations, supply centers, and living quarters for the troops. Life was miserable in the trenches as rain would fill them with water and mud, and rats lived there too.

On September 25 at 7 pm, we were on our way to the front and at 2:30 am, the big guns commenced firing. At 5:55 am, we made the attack in very foggy conditions and ran into machine gun fire. We put up for the night and we then ran into more machine gun fire and fog the next morning. I went into a dugout, and it was raining heavy. In the afternoon, we were chased by artillery fire and we went over the top in the evening. Throughout the next day, more heavy artillery, machine gun fire, and shells dropping all around us. When night came, we dug in until 3:30 am, when we got a cup of coffee. We fought all day and dug in again at night. It continued to rain heavy as shells were flying all around us. On the 29th, we went through more heavy artillery and machine gun fire. At night, we dug in again and it was still raining. At 2:30 am, I went up to a machine gun on the front line. Later, I went out on a detail for eats and could not find any. Dinnertime, we were relieved and started back for rest camp. The whole division bivouac overnight in a field and in the morning, we commenced to hike. We got back to camp by 4 pm on October 1st. We were gone for a week, but only had 2 days of rations with us. Food was scarce. Until food would get to the soldiers it would sometimes be stale. The soldiers would crumble up the stale bread and biscuits, add potatoes, onions, and boil it in a sandbag. It would be eaten as a sandy, stale soup. A staple diet consisted of canned corn beef with bread and biscuits. When flour would be scarce, bread would be made out of dried, ground turnips. Any food was considered a luxury.

On October 2, we moved from a field and into the woods. The next day at 8 pm, we started on a long hike with full packs until we reached our destination at 3 am. We went into the woods that was wet and full of thick underbrush. We put up for the night and were not allowed to make any light. October 4 at 2:30 pm, we left the woods and hiked until 8 pm into an open field for the night. The next day at 8 am, we were on the road again and hiked till 5:30 pm. We were doing good if we got one meal a day. We left the village of Ruht on October 11 at 12:30 am and hiked until 5:30 am where we put up in the woods. "Tell me, there were some boys with the back door trots! I was kept on the go for 2 weeks!" October 12, 5:30 pm, we left the woods and hiked until 8:45 pm and landed in the village of Ambey as it misted rain all evening. This is where we were held in reserve.

October 25 at 6:30 pm, we left the village and hiked until 9 pm to a town called Sammidrui. We bivouac out in the woods overnight and now I'm lying around a bonfire toasting bread and cooking tomatoes for my lunch. On the 28th, we left the woods at 6 pm and hiked until 11 pm. Once there, 5 men were placed in each dugout overnight. Today, on the 29th, we are frying bread and bacon that we found and are using a stove made out of a gasoline can. Later that evening at 6:30 pm, we left the dugout and hiked until 11 pm. We bivouac into the woods and were lucky enough to find a dugout. October 30 at 10:30 am, I am sitting around the fire and the big guns are going off all around us. When they shoot it, it shakes the earth. Last night was pretty noisy. We were supposed to leave last night, but it was called off for some reason.

October 31 at 7 pm, we left the woods and hiked until 1:15 am where we put up in an open field near a canal for the night. The next day at 7 pm, we left for the front and arrived at 11 pm and stayed in a shell hole overnight. In the morning, the Germans sent over a heavy barrage. At 9 am, we hiked back and were shelled heavy the whole time. On November 4, we went back to the front and took our gas masks along. We were chased to dugouts on our way up. Several of our guys got gassed. The poisonous chlorine gas was a greenish-white mist that drifted towards us from the enemy. We set up our guns on November 5. The next evening, we were under heavy gunfire. I and my corporal set up the gun and were almost covered with dust from high up. The rest of the boys ran for a dugout. November 7, the morning started out foggy as we formed a dugout and were cleaning it out. The next evening after dark, we commenced to advance in the rain and slept in an open field in the hills. In the morning as we advanced, we ran into machine gunfire. On November 10, we were still advancing, towards evening we ran into a machine gun nest, and we sent over a barrage. We went over the top and encountered heavy artillery from the enemy all night. I was struck with shrapnel different times while I was lying down. Some shrapnel hit me on my helmet and knocked it off my head. I was not wounded and spent no time in a hospital while in action!! On November 11, we advanced through fog, heavy artillery, along with machine gun fire. Then on the 11th month, 11th day, and the 11th hour, the firing stopped......THE WAR IS OVER!

On November 13 at 12 noon, we left the front and went to the rear. We hiked until 3 pm and ended up at Crefiron. Three days later, we hiked 2 hours and put up in small dugouts, 6 men to a dugout. On November 26, we went out on a practice march for 4 hours carrying a full pack. On November 28, it was Thanksgiving Day somewhere in France. We had for dinner, corned beef, tomatoes, potatoes, bread, and coffee. In the afternoon, I went to a Y.M.C.A. and bought cakes, candy, jam, gum, and peaches for 7 ½ francs. The next day we hiked until 1 pm with packs on our backs, with roads that were certainly muddy. Now we have been hiking 2 days each week while we are here, drill and police the rest of the time. December 10, we left the dugouts near Damullirs at 8:15 am and hiked till 3 pm to Montmedy. We left there on December 12 and hiked 3 miles to do guard duty. There are 14 of us, and don't say we have some homesickness. On December 16, we left and hiked back to Montmedy. Three days later, I was shaved by a French lady.

On December 24, Christmas Eve, I was on guard duty myself and the other 13 guys had a fresh chicken and mashed potatoes cooked by a French lady. On Christmas morning the snowflakes fell thick and fast. For dinner, we had cooked turnips, carrots, gravy, meat, bread, coffee, and 2 pieces of candy. I received for a Christmas gift, 18 pieces of candy, 1 pack of cakes, 2 packs of cigarettes, and 1 cigar. New Year's Day I was on guard.

January 20, 1919, at 1:15 pm, I left Montmedy on an auto truck and arrived at Souilly at 6 pm. I am going away on pass. I left on January 23 at 8 am by rail and landed at Vals les Baines 3 days later at 8:30 am. I stayed in the de Sym Hotel. January 29, I am on a high hill overlooking a farm along with 15 goats as I gathered chestnuts. On February 3, I left Vals les Baines at 5 pm and landed back at Souilly 3 hours later where the ground was covered with snow, and the flakes were falling fast and thick. I left there at 11 pm and arrived at Erize la Brulee at 1:15 am.

On Sunday, March 2 at 11 am, I left Erize la Brulee to go to school and returned back on March 9. On March 15, I was a "mule skinner". In WW1, a mule skinner was a soldier trained to use and care for horses and mules. The animals would be used to take equipment and other essentials places that a truck or jeep couldn't go. March 28, we hiked from 9 am to 12:15 pm in snow squalls and put up for the night. The next day we were on the road again at 8:30 am until 4:40 pm as it snowed and rained the whole time. March 30, we traveled from 8 am until 3:30 pm and again it snowed most of the day. The last day of March we were on the road from 7:30 am until noon with the snow being 8" deep. April 1 we were on the road from 9 am until 11:30 am landing in St. Blin. On April 12, the 79th Division was reviewed by General John J. Pershing as it rained all day. We left St. Blin on April 23 at 1 pm and hiked 5 miles to a train. The train left at 5 pm and we were unloaded off on April 25 at 12:30 pm. We were then loaded on trucks at 1:20 pm and unloaded at 3:15 pm at Beanfreau. We had Division inspection on May 8. On Sunday, May 11, we left at 6:45 am and landed at Cholet at 11:30 am. At 2:15 pm, we loaded on a train that made it to St. Nagarris by 10 pm. We then hiked 3 miles to a camp and ate supper at midnight. In the morning, we had physical examinations and were deloused. On May 14, we had another examination. On May 16 at 6:30 pm, we left camp for the ship. I went up the gang plank at 8:30 pm. The following morning the vessel pulled out at 6 am. Nine days later, on May 26 at noon, we landed on the United States soil and unloaded. The Red Cross gave us lunch and then we were loaded on a boat and taken to Jersey Shore. We left there by rail at 5 pm and landed at Camp Dix at 9 pm and ate. We had a group photograph taken of Headquarter Company 314th Infantry 1919 "Just Back from France", Meuse Argonne -Troyon Sector Valley Of The Neuse.

Grandpa's time fighting in World War 1 all took place in France. The country suffered incalculable property damage since so much of the war took place there. Some areas of France were too badly damaged to ever start rebuilding right away. The economy was ruined after the war, the loss of manpower was way down with so many killed or wounded, agricultural land was wrecked, and a need for so much more to be imported compounded the problems. There was also a huge need for medical care for the millions wounded.

During the war 2,800,000 U.S. men were inducted into military service with 1,400,000 serving in France. The United States had 53,402 soldiers killed in action, 63,114 from disease and other causes, and 205,000 wounded. During World War 1 the number of civilian deaths in areas of actual war totaled about 5,000,000 people with 80% caused by starvation, disease, and exposure. Spanish influenza, which some blamed on the war, caused tens of millions of others to die. The first three years of the war, the fighting nations spent $85,000 every minute and twice that amount in 1918. None of these figures includes additional economic loss involved for servicemen crippled, interest on war debt, or pensions paid to veterans and families.

My family and I are very proud of my grandpa for serving our country in World War I and demonstrating bravery during the time of battle. He never openly talked about the loss of friends, or a special buddy killed, or wounded, during his time serving. I am sure that he had moments when the fighting was fierce, that he was talking to the Lord for strength and protection. He was a very fortunate man not to be wounded or killed as heavy artillery, machine gun fire, and shrapnel was all around him. Travel took a lot of time back in 1917-1919, be it truck, train, ship, and all the hiking that was done. He was drafted, left home, fought the fight, and returned back home with the earned rank of lieutenant, where he married, raised a family, and lived a successful full life. We thank you for all these things, for without you, none of our Jere Lyons family would exist.

Growing up in Perry County

Storyteller Gay Russ Irwin

What could be more fun than growing up in the country where neighbors know you so well that they come to bring their home remedy when they hear you're sick or been stung by a bee? I remember Mrs. Metz coming flying in our door ready to offer her help. Doctors weren't plentiful and emergency rooms were not even a consideration so neighbors became treasured friends. That's what Perry County was to many of its rural residents. We shoveled each other out after a winter snow and did chores when someone was temporarily incapacitated. That care for each other was expressed in so many ways that next door neighbors cannot even imagine today.

As a young child living in the community known as Kistler, near Blain, I remember so many wonderful warm summer days when we played outdoors, and my brother Mike and I made carts to ride down our hills. We created them out of everything from skates to old broken baby buggies. When sleds were no longer useful, we improvised. I'm sure if my kids rode in some of the contraptions that we did, I would have been startled! Mom was so calm (or maybe she just wasn't paying attention). None of our creations lasted long before one final crash did them in but, oh the hours of fun we had. We even got the neighbor boy, Lee Smith, to try out a couple of them.

I started elementary school in Blain which, at that time, held all twelve grades in one building and did not include kindergarten; we started out in first grade. My first-grade teacher, Miss Clark, was my favorite of all. I thought she was really old because she wore funny little wire-rimmed glasses and long dresses with her laced-up "sturdy-but-serviceable" black shoes. Her long hair was pulled back into a braided bun. She often brought in her homemade horehound candy to share with our class. She had a very matter-of-fact style of teaching; I was always a very serious student, so it worked great for me. We started our class with the National Anthem followed by the Pledge of Allegiance. I remember the day when we quit writing 1958 on the top of our papers and we had to start writing 1959. Wow, that was ages ago! I also remember the year we got new flags in all our classrooms because two new states were added to the U. S. - Alaska and Hawaii. Now that piece of information makes me sound ancient! I only went to Blain for a few years before my parents moved to the Carlisle area for a short time.

The elementary school in Carlisle was relatively new and everything was so clean, orderly, and bright! As students, we had to line up and march down the hall to the cafeteria which doubled as an auditorium with a stage at the end. I felt like a soldier taking orders when I first went there. Academically, I had a lot of catching up to do! In math especially, I had to work hard that third grade year. But we moved back to Perry County when I was in fifth grade, and I went to the Landisburg Elementary School which has since been torn down. I had Mr. McAllicher and we had class in a room in the basement that was very dark and dismal. My most horrible experience happened soon after I moved there. I was afraid of the teacher but one day I got so stomach sick in class. He had some of the students at the blackboard doing math problems. I held my hand up for the longest time until I could wait no longer for his attention. I got up, walked up to him at the blackboard and, without warning, began to projectile vomit all over the floor, the trough of the blackboard and Mr. McAllicher's shoes. The whole class watched in horror. I got to meet the kind nurse who took immediate care of my problem and I went home. I'm not sure what happened in the classroom after that. The teacher told our entire class the next day that if we EVER have that kind of emergency, it is okay, even required, that we immediately leave the room! I laugh now but at that time it was NOT FUNNY.

That summer was my first experience going to Girl Scout Camp. It was hard work but lots of fun. We camped in tents, made tripods for our basins which we used for bathing and dug a deep trench to use as our latrine which was sheltered by four walls of canvas to give us some privacy. We cooked all of our meals over the open fire, which had to be started without matches. I quickly learned that "primitive camping" is not my favorite. The rest of the summer was great.

Every year we enjoyed going to two weeks of Bible School. Even the high school kids came. The boys had to hurry home to bale hay, but the girls had plenty of time for other things. Carnivals were a big deal and every community had one. Landisburg's was the second weekend in June and it was the highlight of our summer, a time to get together with all the local kids. There was usually a hayride, a few other carnival rides and games of chance and fireworks on Saturday night. We always hit the paddle wheel to take a chance (or five) to win a homemade pie or cake or a watermelon. Every night there was a variety of homemade ice cream but they often ran out, so you had to get there early. The air was full of the fragrance of homemade soups in the kettles and fresh cut fries fresh from the fryer. Mom never had to cook on Carnival nights, other than what she had made for donations to the event. Friendships were made and families came together to enjoy all the activities and visit with everyone. The fire company always made out well from it because they were the host and major contributor.

Other than that, we kids spent time on bicycle rides back on the dirt roads, swam under the Red Bridge and went to Colonel Denning State Park where there was a little beach, the lake, and a concession stand. Moms liked to take kids there because there were lifeguards on duty and kids were happy to plan on meeting their friends.

In later years, the Lions Club provided a bus that would pick up kids to go to New Bloomfield pool for two weeks of swimming lessons. It was never nice to have the early morning classes and have to jump into that cold water "to get warmed up". I would have rather stayed home but mom and dad insisted we ALL go. I always knew I would see my Girl Scout Leader, June Hench, there. She was so dedicated to the swim program and was there every year.

In the winters when I was older my parents bought a 40-acre farm on the edge of Landisburg. Our backyard and the hills behind became a winter playground, perfect for sledding and tobogganing. Dad even set up a spotlight so we could see to sled at night. Mom always had hot dogs when we came in to get warmed up. A lot of the town kids came and joined the fun. Lyons' pond was next to our property and sometimes we could ice skate there too. Our entertainment was inexpensive but not short on fun or the memories we have for a lifetime.

West Perry School District was created when I was going into 8th grade. I had attended Green Park High School for 7th grade before the consolidation of three school districts and then was transported to New Bloomfield for the rest of Junior High School. For me, the interesting thing was that, in tenth grade, I was back at the Senior High with some of the kids I knew from 1st, 2nd and 3rd grades. They looked a lot different, but I figured most of them out and it was fun to see them again. I graduated with the class of 1969 and was elated to leave those hallowed halls of West Perry High. I shed no tears because I had worked so hard my senior year and it was not fun for me. I was happy to grab my diploma and run. Mr. Liebel had told me that I was not college material (just the affirmation and encouragement every student wanted to hear, right?) so I did not know what I would do next. He would be surprised to know that I actually graduated from Messiah College with a bachelor's degree.

My parents were fantastic people and, as a family, we had an awesome life. Dad worked construction and mom had different jobs over the years. She was a beautician, but also drove a school bus, sold cars, worked for the Office of Aging, was a realtor, always active in the community, and also was a great mom. We did not have all the luxuries that some did but we did lots of things together. Every summer dad took us on a vacation somewhere for a week or two. He loved living in Perry County but he wanted us kids to get to see our country. One year he had planned and saved to take a trip west to California. We had a pop-up camper and for 21 days, we traveled cross-country experiencing the U. S. It was an experience I will never forget or take for granted. This is not one that many folks from Perry County have 'checked off' their bucket list! I must admit though that none of the places we visited gave me the desire to live anyplace other than my home in Perry County. As an adult I have lived in Cumberland County, Juniata County, Wyoming County and Perry. I also lived in Fayetteville, North Carolina for 6 months, but Perry County will always be home!

My Fondest Memories of Duncannon

Storyteller Ginny Jones Clark

My fondest memories of Duncannon are of the dances held at the chapel, on North High Street, which later became the Lion's Club building. Ken Delancey, who owned the jewelry store on the Duncannon square, which is now Rustic Orchid, spun the records. He also sold vinyl records in his store, which made it a popular spot among the teenagers.

We had such great times. Bands would come from Harrisburg and around the area to sing their favorite songs, at the chapel. One band, that comes to mind, were Tom E and the Commands.

My stepdad, Bill Sterner would close the streets from Prospect Avenue to Market Street, so we could sled down the hill, past Forrer's Garage. He even made a swimming pool in our yard, out of concrete cinder blocks. It was probably six feet by five feet and three foot deep. All the kids from the neighborhood, came to swim.

These were the greatest times ever. I will always cherish them in my heart, till the day I leave this earth.

Thanks, Duncannon, for the memories.

SNIPPETS OF MARY F. LIGHTNER'S DIARY

Living in Landisburg, Perry County

MARY LIGHTNER (12/5/1872 - 4/12/1959)
Recorded by Kathy Henry Hughes

Diary/journal from January 1932 to end of 1946. One entry page for 1955--see end. My notes are in italics. Many of the entries are simple weather records--"clear," "snowy," "rain," etc. There are quite a few noting deaths, births, and marriages. I've chosen a selection.

From www.myheritage.com -Mary's parents Samuel Power Lightner 1842-1919, Emma Elizabeth Waggoner Lightner 1848-1929; brother John Clinton Lightner 1870-1895.

Mary and her cousin Ada Keck, Hadessa (Dessie) Keck DeLancey's sister, worked at Charlie DeLancey's store in Landisburg. Hadessa was Charlie's first wife. Mary and Ada both moved into my grandmother Anna's house in Landisburg to board when Charlie died in 1955. There were three bedrooms: My mother and I shared a room; my grandmother had her own room; and Ada and Mary shared a room. I recall my mother telling me that Mary had attended a Normal School. She had great patience and read Little Golden Books to me for hours on end. Ada was a few years younger than Mary, born in 1876. She suffered from dementia and had to be moved to a nursing home around 1957 but lived to 1960.

***

1932

Jan 14. 15. & 16 warm like spring. Had fire in stove until noon then let go out and had door open.

Feb. 29 Chas DeLancey hauled a load of flitting* from Philadelphia for Anna Miller *I had to Google "flitting"--looks like it can refer to moving household goods--to flit from one place to another.*

Rev. Spease fell over dead May 10. Funeral service in the church May 13 with burial at York.

May 27 Went up through Sheaffer's Valley above the C-C Camp, crossed over into Cumb. County, ate supper at Dublin Springs, then came to Plainfield, Carlisle, and home. *Mary consistently refers to Doubling Gap as "Dublin" which started in the 1800s.*

Laid my walk June 20 to 25, cost $111.70. Fixed cellar doors

Had my flue torn down to roof and rebuilt Oct 22 by Lawrence Schey. Cost $3.75.

Truman Clouse sowed my grass Oct. 29 and started to paint

Dec 31 Paid $22.00 for coal.

1933

Feb 8 like spring in the morning, snowing in the afternoon and about zero until evening and snow drifting.

March 4 cold. Franklin Roosevelt inaugurated 32nd President of the United States

Banks closed in United States from Mar 6 to 9th

DeLanceys, Ada and I took trips during July, August, and September through the following: Baltimore, Hagerstown, Williamsport, and Va. Harper's Ferry Honey Locust Inn, Fayetteville at Scott Sundays, State College, Rolling Green Park, Selinsgrove, Port Royal, Hershey, Palmyra, York twice, Dillsburg, Pine Grove Furnace, Caledonia Park.

Re-elected tax collector Nov 7

Mabel Wertz Neely came home from hospital Sat, Dec. 30

1934

Mar 25 DeLanceys, Ada, Mrs. Noll and I were through Harrisburg, Mechanicsburg, Dillsburg on to Gettysburg, were on Little Round Top and part of the battlefield then came home by Biglerville, Carlisle on to Newport and arrived house at 8:30 PM.

Mar 26 Frank Spotts had sale and the sheriff took everything.

Apr 24 planted potatoes and peas and beans

May 20 at Williams Grove, arrived house at 11 P. M.

June 10 DeLanceys, Mrs. Stewart, Ada, and I ate supper. Saw the most beautiful Laurel everywhere on the mountain and the loveliest ferns.

June 17 We took a drive and ate supper in Boiling Springs Park, then went to Williams Grove Park, then home.

June 25 Hard road finished from Landisburg to Dromgolds.

Dr. Hebbinger moved into Mrs. Bowen's house June 22, 1934 to practice medicine.

Chas Boyer shot by Carey Meadow while out hunting Nov 22, buried Nov. 26

1935

Feb 7 coldest morning of the winter

Mr. George A. Waggoner died Feb 11 at 11 o'clock P. M. at Cora Wertz's. He was buried Friday Feb 15 at 11 o'clock A. M., services in St. Peter's Church. He was 94 years old.

Mar 2 Carpenters roofing the Kennedy's store building for C. H. DeLancey

Mar 11 DeLanceys digging foundation for store building

March 17 Sabbath, clear and cold. DeLanceys, Ada and I were to Dillsburg and Carlisle, stopped at Allen DeLanceys. His wife had pneumonia.

several pages of weather reports--no other news for this year

1936

January 23 roads drifted, no mail nor bread trucks

Jan 24 opening roads

Jan 28 continued cold, snow drifting, men shoveling open and cutting ice 12 in. thick.

Jan 29 James Fetter and Sheaffer at restaurant, filling their ice houses

Jan 31 roads drifted and very cold/could not stand the cold to open roads

Feb 17 cloudy, John Garlin shoveled snow off porch roof

Feb 29 clear and warm, I took sick that day

Mar 19 Newport about square-- water to ceilings in stores and water almost up to 4th Street. Terrible floods at Pittsburgh, Johnstown, and all along to Harrisburg, where water was 8 ft deep in buildings. Duncannon was flooded and the New England states had floods.

Mar 29 clear. DeLanceys, Ada and I drove to Lewistown to see the damage done by flood. Saw a bridge that washed down the stream and all broken.

Mar 30 clear. Dessie and Chas took a load of moving for Roy Snyder to near Mechanicsburg

April 19--cold and partly cloudy. Mother dead 7 years.

NO ENTRIES for 1937 and FEW for 1938

1939

Jan 1 Florence Egolf married Lenus Wertz at 8 A. M. by Rev. Menninger assisted by Rev. Jones. We took a drive to Newport, Harrisburg, Carlisle, and Duncannon.

Jan 17 Gov. James inaugurated and Farm Show week

Feb 13 clear--like spring--got my hot-bed ready to sow my lettuce

Feb 14 clear and not cold, Rev Jones and wife celebrating their golden wedding

Apr 6 Clarence Reisinger's baby born

May 6 clear and stormy. Finished planting potatoes, James Armstrong sale

June 11 clear, thunderstorm in afternoon. At Harrisburg to see the rose garden then at William's Grove in P.M. where 500 were in the bands that played.

June 13 clear and cool, planted cucumbers, peas, beets, and lettuce

June 20 clear and warm. Roy Allen, wife, daughter Lois and Mrs. Woods were to see me.

July 29 C.H. DeLancey auction at 7 P.M. Raining at 10 P. M. Heavy rain during night

Aug 30 clear--Harry Roddy called to see me

Raymond Clelan's baby born Sept 14, 1939 (*this is my cousin Vonny, who now lives in Idaho*)

Sept 30 clear--James Fetter has sale and DeLancey has auction

Nov 18 clear and warm Finished DeLancey's chimney at the store

1940

Mar 16 Mrs. Karl Kennedy and baby came home from Hospital

Mar 24 Ice froze in my kitchen in A. M.

Mar 27 Chas DeLancey and Dessie came home from Danville Hospital--were there 8 days

May 24 Leroy Stewart shot himself in the barn, was buried Monday May 27

May 25 rained--A boy drowned at the Orphans' Home

Sept 1 clear. Kennedy's Valley Church reopened

Oct 26 clear--DeLancey had auction

Oct 31 clear--DeLancey traded cars

Nov 5 warm--had no fire in the store--Roosevelt reelected

Nov 9 DeLancey opened a store at East Waterford

Nov 17 clear and not so cold. DeLanceys and I took a drive to East Waterford, Port Royal, McAllisterville, Harrisburg, and Carlisle, arrived home at 7 P. M.

Dec 11 Chester Sherman had his arm torn in corn fodder shredder

1941

Jan 1 clear and mild

Jan 10 Stormy and cloudy

Jan 20 Roosevelt inaugurated for the third term

Jan 24 Winfield Gray, Chas Carl's son-in-law, died of a heart attack buried Monday Jan 27

Feb 9 clear, took a drive around by Harrisburg and Carlisle, arrived home at 7 P. M.

Mar 18 Very cold and stormy, slush ice in my kitchen, the first all winter.

Mar 24 Snow storms, James Morrisons moved

Apr 25 Edgar Dyson married at 3 P. M Duncannon

May 30 rained A. M. then clear

July 14 clear. Dessie went to the Polyclinic Hospital

July 16 clear. Dessie DeLancey was operated on for cataracts in one eye

July 20 clear. Were down to the Hospital to see Dessie

July 27 Chas, Ada and I were to Harrisburg and brought Dessie home from the Hospital

Aug 3 clear, took a drive up Kennedy's Valley

Aug 24 clear and cool, were at Mt Holly and Crestmount road house, bought apples and peaches.

Sept 20 clear and cool, DeLancey had auction at East Waterford

Sept 25 & 26 was sick.

Sept 28 clear and dry, warm like summer. Mabel DeWalt and Helen's family were here.

Oct 5 clear and like summer, took a drive over the new road across Dublin.

Oct 14 clear. Mervin Lightner shot himself in the bank in Duncannon on Tuesday Oct 14, buried Saturday Oct 18 at Landisburg. *Dick Swank, former owner of Swank Publications, the county's newspapers, discovered the body.*

Oct 16 Marshall Adair repaired my porch

Nov 1 Kenneth Rice came home from camp (*Ken "Pickle" Rice was my dad's best friend, ran the Yankee Theater in Landisburg and served in WW II in Germany*)

Nov 12 Dessie DeLancey had insulin shock.

Nov 19 Warmer. Linus Wertz and Specie Bell cleaned my cistern and cemented it.

Dec 3 Clear and warm. Cleaned my windows outside upstairs.

Dec 6 Finished cleaning my side porch.

Dec 11 clear and cold. Japan attacked Hawaiian Islands by surprise

1942

mostly weather reports, then...

Feb 5 Snowing. I took sick at the store. Had a ruptured blood vessel in my right lung. Was in the house until....?

1943

Jan 4 sleeting during night, stormy in morning

Jan 11 mild. Wood from Newt Reisinger cost $7.00

Jan 19 Raining. Martin inaugurated Governor. Very high winds. Roofs torn off, trees blown down and telephone lines broken and snow storms.

Jan 26 Snowing. Harry Carls are moving

Feb 19 Wm Rheams moved beside me.

Apr 3 clear and cold. Luther Keller and E. C. Dile sales

Apr 24 Mrs. Mack Gray was in an automobile accident and had her wrist broken.

Apr 30 Boy rode into Chas DeLancey's truck at Mt. Holly Springs

May 8 clear with shower in afternoon with auction in P. M.

Ernest Schlusser's child died May 11, buried May 12

May 22 clear and cool--commencement

July 22 Rain in morning, DeLancey finished cement building.

July 26 cloudy, Chas and Marshall at Baltimore.

Sept 2 Mrs. John Garlin died, buried Sept 6 at 2 P. M.

Oct 5 clear and frosty. George Murray died and was buried at Landisburg Oct 7 at 1 P. M.

Oct 22 Kennedy Murray & Miss Mitchell married at Mt Holly at 8 P. M.

Dec 15 we all were sick

Dec 16 Had the dr.

Dec 17 Clear. Had the Dr.

Dec 18 clear and cold. Had the Dr.

1944

Jan 3 snowed a little and was slippery

Jan 21 paid $47.00 for 4 tons coal and $1.00 for carrying in.

Jan 31 Mrs. Newt Briner died, buried Feb. 3.

Feb 9 Mr. Chas Carl died, buried Feb 14 aged 85 years

Mar 7 cloudy and slippery. Wm Rheam moved to his new home--the John Stum house.

Mar 8 clear and cold. Geo Womers moved beside me.

Mar 23 clear, Raymond Clelan's baby born (*my cousin Raymond Jr., "Sonny," who now lives in Montana*)

June 4 cloudy and cool. Maria Rumbaugh's surprise birthday party.

June 6 clear and cool, The Allies invaded France.

June 17 clear. DeLancey had a sale.

June 21 Cool and cloudy, planted cucumbers & corn

July 14 cloudy, planted beans & lettuce

Aug 2 clear. Earl Morrows received word Grant was missing in action

Aug 8 clear. Dale Clouse wounded in France.

Aug 22 clear. Margaret Burtnett Emlet's twins born

Sept 2 clear. Had auction.

Sept 10 clear and cool. Wm Lightner's little girl buried

Nov 10 Dessie DeLancey died, buried Nov 14. Services at the house at 11 A.M. Rev Johns preached the sermon. Katherine Nelson & Florence Stusse remained until Nov 24. Ada Metz returned Nov 18

Dec 24 was at DeLanceys

1945

Jan 14 cloudy. Geo Croziers, Lee Shulls and Mary Kellars babies born at the Carlisle Hospital

Jan 16 deep snow and roads drifted

Jan 21 Commodore Morrison died, buried Jan 24

Feb 1 coldest morning and snow drifting

Feb 2 clear and cold, some roads still closed

Feb 5 cold, DeLancey at Harrisburg

Feb 28 a spring morning

Mar 13 clear, ground frozen. David Bolze's son killed overseas Feb 20

April 12 clear. President Roosevelt died, buried Apr 14

Apr 25 Raining and warmer. DeLancey at York

May 30 Were at Carlisle, Shippensburg, Chambersburg, Mt, Union then came home. Unveiled the Honor Roll at 7:30 P. M. - cold & stormy

June 12 clear & warm. Planted 2 rows potatoes

June 13 clear, planted Lima Beans

June 14 Ada Keck fell and broke her arm

June 17 Chas DeLancey took Ada to the Hospital again

Dec 24, 1945 Chas H. DeLancey was married at Enola at 4:30 P.M. (*he was married to my grandmother Anna Fry Maulfair, whose husband Walter had died June 22, 1945*)

Anna Gertrude Kerr died at Deaconess Home at Allentown Dec 31, 1945, buried at St. Peters Thursday June 3, 1946

1946

Feb 13 Chas DeLanceys started their furnace fire

Feb 15 very stormy and cold

Feb 24 changeable--snow & sunshine

Mar 16 & 17 cloudy. 16 at Carlisle

Mar 22 & 23 cool. 22 papered kitchen.

April 4,5,6 clear. 6th planted potatoes

Apr 7 Lee Stewarts went home

Apr 14 clear and warmer. At Breezewood on Super Highway

Apr 21 clear. Easter. Chas DeLancey, wife, Ruth, and I were to Bedford on the Super Highway and took supper at Lewistown (*"Ruth" is my mother, who would have been 19 years old*)

Apr 28 clear. DeLanceys, Ruth, Ada and I were to Lock Haven. Bellefont, and Williamsport.

May 5 were through Williamsport, Gettysburg, Chambersburg, Hagerstown, ate dinner at Charlestown, West Virginia, through Martinsburg at National Cemetery Winchester Va. Ate supper in Maryland, through Harpers Ferry and arrived home 9 P. M.

May 10 clear. Ice in A. M. Were at Rev Johns in evening.

May 16 raining. Neil Lightner made a new top for my cistern

May 23 were over at Johns

May 25 cloudy. Baccalaureate sermon.

May 28 raining. Linus Wertz's baby home

May 29 clear. Went to see the flood at Duncannon, then to Rolling Green Cemetery, Dillsburg where we ate dinner, then to Clelans (*my grandmother Anna's sister Nellie was married to Raymond Clelan, and at this point they and their 7 children had moved from Landisburg to the York Rd in Carlisle*) and to Duncannon again and to Newport

Went west June 18, arrived in Minnesota June 21 at J.E. Metz. Ate supper at Welcome at Stusses, then went to Mrs. Jerome Minich (*I'm guessing Charlie DeLancey was the driver on this trip. Not sure of all the connections here--I know Florence Stuss was Mary's cousin--she and her husband visited us in Landisburg a year or two before Mary died*).

June 23 had a party for us at Roy Minich's. There were 45 of us. Had a fine time.

June 24 Ate dinner at J. E. Metz, ate supper at Mrs. Bev Kecks, spent the night at J. E. Metz in Fairmont the night of the cyclone

June 25 started for Penna, arrived home Sat. June 29 about 10:30 A. M.

June 27 were at the Moody Bible Institute Broadcasting station (*this was in Addison, IL, and Anna's brother Bud was the Chief Engineer there until he retired in the 1960s.*)

July 7 we were at Hershey Park

July 8 planted corn

July 9 we were at Hoyers

July 15, 16, 17 hot and dry

July 17 at Sheaffers at Newville

July 19 hot--at Loysville at carnival

July 26 hot--were at Blain carnival

July 28 Ardus Minich came

July 29 were at Hershey & Gettysburg

July 30 took Ardus Minich to Harrisburg

Aug 4 DeLanceys, Ada and I were at York Springs, got peaches

Aug 5 got my wood

Aug 2 Anna Mary Bolze Henry died and was buried Aug 6, 1946. (*Anna Mary, or Anna Mae, was my father Mark's first wife--they had been married 10 years*).

Aug 5 DeLanceys, Ada, and I were to Bolzes to see Anna Mary Bolze Henry

Aug 8 DeLanceys, Ada, and I were over to Mexico at camp meeting

Aug 10 clear--pulled weeds

Aug 13 clear--cleaning cellar

Aug 17 were to Liverpool to carnival and it rained very heavy

Aug 31 Delanceys, Ada, and I were to Duncannon to a carnival and it was very cool

Sept 1 DeLanceys, Ada, Ruth, and I were across Dublin, Newville, Pine Grove Furnace, Mount Alto, Caledonia Park, Waynesboro, Dillsburg, and back home

Sept 2 Ada and I canned peaches

Sept 3 made grape butter & grape juice

Sept 5 Mary Leonard's sale

Sept 9 heavy thunderstorms. Chas Kennedy's barn burned

Sept 12 were at York Fair. It was fun.

Sept 18 were up through the coal regions to Mt. Carmel and stopped at the Gratz Farm

Sept 19 were to Hagerstown Fair

Sept 25 DeLanceys, Ruth, Ada and I were to Bloomfield Fair

Oct 11 cleaned the side porch

Oct 20 were at North Middleton to hear the Thompson family

Oct 27 clear--took a drive through Cumb. Co. Littlestown, Hanover, York, and home. Had a lovely drive

Nov 5 was in the election house

Nov 28 was at DeLanceys for dinner and supper then we went to Donallys Mills to church

Nov 29 clear, cleaned dining room

Nov 30 Cleaned my kitchen then we went over to Hoyers in evening

Dec 6 cold. The parsonage sold to Roy Neely for $2500.00.

Dec 25 clear, was at DeLanceys for dinner then we went to Hoyers back to DeLanceys for supper then went to Carlisle.

Dec 30 Chas Egolf died Dec 29, 1946, buried Jan 1, 1947 at 2 P. M.

1955

Chas DeLancey died of a heart attack Jan 6, 1955. Had the heart attack Christmas 1954, went to the Hospital on Monday Dec. 26 and lived 8 days. Viewing at Loysville Friday evening Funeral services at Funeral Home Saturday at 2 P. M.

Mr. S. D. Henry *(my grandfather)* died July 1955 of heart attack.

Childhood Memories
Storyteller Kathy Henry Hughes

Born at Harrisburg Hospital, lived in Landisburg until graduating from college--a few months on Water Street next to the building that housed the Odd Fellows Lodge; the remaining years on North Carlisle Street, in my grandmother's house across the alley (High Street) from the election house.

Father Mark Henry, mother Ruth Maulfair Henry. No siblings--my father died when I was 3 months old and my mother never remarried.

Grandparents Sam Henry and Sarah Wilt Henry; Walter Maulfair and Anna Fry Maulfair, later DeLancey (Walter died before I was born).

My father was a mechanic. He maintained trucks for the Coca-Cola plant in Harrisburg. In the 1940s early 1950s he and his two younger brothers, Bob and Roy owned Henry Brothers Garage on Rt 850 between Landisburg and Dromgold's Corner. They repaired vehicles and also sold and repaired large appliances.

My mother worked for Swift and Company, a meat-packing plant, in Harrisburg. She was a receptionist and switchboard operator ("Number puhleeze!"). After I was born, she and her mother Anna ran a shop located in our home. The shop was on the glassed-in sun porch attached to our old brick farmhouse. My grandmother had started the shop in 1955, after her husband Charlie DeLancey died. She named it the Apparel and Gift Shop, and that's how we always answered the phone (a landline, of course, with a party line). There was quite a varied stock: Bolts of fabric, spools of thread and other notions, nylon stockings, blouses and skirts made by my grandmother on her monstrous black Kenmore sewing machine. Men's flannel shirts, pants, wool socks, hunting caps and straw "farmer" hats; candy dishes and other knick- knacky glassware, and jewelry, filled the shelves. There wasn't much merchandise to interest kids, except for a selection of Little Golden and Ding Dong School books which I'd get first crack at when a new batch arrived.

Starting in elementary school, I helped out in the store. I'd check in, sort, and tag new merchandise, greet customers, and help them find what they were looking for in the narrow walkways between floor-to-ceiling shelving and the two large glass display cases in the center of the sun porch. Eventually I was allowed to operate the adding machine and make transactions. I especially liked to wrap gifts for people not adept with tape and scissors.

Who influenced me the most? Had to be my mother and grandmother, as we all lived together. My mother loved Landisburg and liked to reminisce about visiting her cousins there when she was growing up. She and her parents had lived in Enola, where her father was an operator/switchman for the Pennsylvania Railroad.

In Landisburg you could see movies at the Yankee Theater, pick corn right off the stalks and strawberries from the fields, go swimming at Rice's bridge (always known as The Red Bridge), and cruise around country roads in the rumble seats of friends' cars. Enola had cement, pavement, and fresh soot from the rail yards covering the windowsills every morning. My grandmother had grown up on a farm outside of Duncannon and must have been happy to get back to a more bucolic lifestyle when she moved to Landisburg in 1945 or 1946.

On our one-acre lot she had extensive flower gardens, a grape arbor, a little smokehouse for hams, and a large vegetable garden. She canned tomatoes, beans, and peaches, and made her own sweet-smelling soap with lye and animal fat collected from cooking. She had been an independent seamstress in Enola, making all my mother's clothes plus prom and wedding gowns for clients. She made most of my clothing, too, and was very creative--when I was in second grade, I won first prize at the Halloween parade for the snowman costume she'd made from chicken wire covered with cotton batting. She managed to somehow affix real coal chunks for the eyes and mouth.

My mother made sure we went to church every Sunday, to St. Peter's Reformed (later UCC) near Bridgeport. That's where she and my father were married, and all his brothers and sisters attended. When I started junior high school, I began to walk to the sister church, then called Trinity and now New Hope, right in Landisburg, with my best Landisburg friend, Melva. Her dad Melvin was the Sunday School teacher. Melva and I took turns at playing the piano for Sunday School. Favorites were "What a Friend we have in Jesus" and "Rock of Ages"--both easy to play. Neither of us was a virtuoso. We also helped with Vacation Bible School, which consisted (again) of playing the piano, refereeing "Mother, May I?" and "Red Rover" games, and keeping kids from eating paste during art projects. We both were volunteered by our parents or teachers to serve at church breakfasts and suppers. The fishermen's and hunter's breakfasts were the least desirable, as we had to report to the Landisburg Fireman's Hall at 6:00 A M. But looking back, I can feel for those kitchen workers who must have done an all-nighter to prepare pancake batter, bacon, and sausages.

I've been sorry to see St. Peter's church, fall into disrepair. I remember the opening of their annex in the early 1960s, when our Sunday school classes could meet in a spacious new facility, not the cramped, hot balcony of the church that was always plagued with wasps. The churchyard is still well-maintained or was the last time I visited three years ago to have my mother's ashes interred with my father. The Henry plot is at the top of the hill, with a sweeping view of Shermans Creek, cow and sheep fields, and the Blue Mountains beyond--as nice a place as any to spend eternity.

Landisburg Elementary was a two-story rectangular brick building built in 1926. The playground, behind the school, was a sea of asphalt, great for jump rope and hopscotch, but deadly on knees and elbows--or front teeth-- if you happened to fall. The playground equipment was all metal. There were two slides, a hanging bar for "skinning the cat", a couple of seesaws, and flat wooden swings on metal chains that you would "pump" to go as high as you could. Inside at lunchtime 5th and 6th graders would run the candy counter, on the first floor near the playground entrance. From the wooden-framed glass case that looked like any penny candy case in a local grocery store or gas station, you could buy Mallo Cups, Bit-o-Honeys, Squirrel Nut Zippers, Sugar Babies, Bonomo's Turkish taffy, and most any tooth-decaying treat today's school-age kid can only imagine.

The building had originally served as a high school, and the basement contained two fifth grade classrooms in what used to be the "shop"/industrial arts area, the cafeteria, and the furnace room. The first floor had the bathrooms and first through fourth grade plus sixth grade classrooms. Floors, with the exception of tile and cement in the bathrooms and basement, were well-worn wood that was oiled every summer to preserve them from foot traffic, rain, and snow. The sixth-grade classroom doubled as the auditorium, and had a movable wall adjoining the classroom next to it so it could be opened up and seat a big crowd for movies, run on a 2-reel projector.

If you rode the bus, you carried your lunch or picked up a metal tray divided into sections at the cafeteria, to be filled by the lunch ladies, all moms of students, with delicacies such as meat birds (poultry stuffing wrapped with Spam and secured with a toothpick) or porcupine balls (hamburger rolled in rice). You'd then carry your tray to your classroom to eat. Each class had a slop bucket stationed in the corner of the room at lunch, and when you had finished your meal, you'd take your tray and scrape off any remaining food into the bucket. Depending on the lunchtime offerings, the bucket could be nearly empty or full to overflowing. Sixth grade boys were responsible for taking the buckets and empty trays back to the cafeteria.

Since I lived at the bottom of the hill one block from the school, I was a "walker", as opposed to the students who were bused from Sheaffer's Valley, Green Park, Kennedy's Valley, and other areas. Walkers could go home for lunch if they chose, and I often did--although through first and second grade, walkers needed a parent or a Safety Patrol to walk them to and from home. Safety Patrols were carefully screened 5th and 6th graders. They each wore an off-white webbed belt with one shoulder strap, on which was pinned their official silver safety patrol badge. The badge resembled the LAPD badge on Dragnet, and to be named a Safety Patrol was an aspiration for little girls like myself, who had no younger siblings to boss around. We could threaten the underclassmen with the principal's wooden paddle, on display in his office, but to my knowledge never used, if they didn't stay in line.

The school office was just outside the door of the sixth-grade classroom, convenient for Mr. Owen, the sixth-grade teacher and also the principal. The office was a small room with a desk, a couple of chairs, filing cabinets and a telephone. There was no one to answer the phone other than Mr. Owen and a sixth-grade girl, assigned each month. I had a memorable turn on Friday, November 22, 1963. Mr. Owen was off observing another classroom while we had art class, and the office phone rang. I answered--"Landisburg Elementary School!" to hear a woman on the other end say. "Oh! Hello...can you tell me, is it true, that the President has been shot?" I turned around to see Mr. Owen at the door. I handed the phone to him with my hand over the mouthpiece, and laughed, "There's some woman on the phone that says President Kennedy has been shot!" He smirked, most likely thinking it was a prank call, and I returned to class. As usual, everyone wanted to know who had called. I told them, "Some nut who says the President has been shot!"

Everyone laughed and began speculating at what kind of mental case would call an elementary school with such a crazy claim. Mrs. Egolf, the art teacher, finally got us to settle down, and we finished our projects.

When Mr. Owen returned to the room, he announced that since it was such a warm day, we could have an extra recess on the ball field up the hill from the playground, a special treat reserved just for sixth graders. We all ran up through the woods to the diamond, played kickball, and as we were waiting our turns, continued to laugh about the phone call. When we finished and returned to the classroom, we began getting ready to go home for the day. Mr. Owen had us all sit down after we'd collected our bags from the cloakroom. He said, "I have some sad news--President Kennedy was shot and killed today. Your parents will talk with you about it when you get home." There was a chorus of gasps, and many kids began crying.

Since first grade, we had had many Cold War practice drills for when a nuclear bomb dropped, crawling under our desks, or filing to the basement and lining up with our faces to the cement walls. But this was something shocking and tangible. It was an event that we'll always remember, just as I'm sure we can pinpoint where we were and what we were doing when the planes hit the World Trade Center.

From seventh through ninth grade, we were bused to the junior high in New Bloomfield. The bus picked us up at the elementary school, so I had the same walk in the mornings and afternoons, but the nine-mile ride afforded new opportunities for alliances and shared seats with upper-and under-classmates. We were introduced to a whole new group of peers from Ickesburg, New Bloomfield, and Carroll Elementary schools. On the first day there I met Sue Parkinson, who informed me that she and I were born on the same day, December 1, and that our mothers had been in the same maternity ward. Our homeroom and health teacher, Mrs. Long, told me that she had gone to school with my father. My Aunt Ruth was a cafeteria aide.

As with the teachers at Landisburg elementary, I already knew several from their visits to my mother's gift shop. It was a very provincial education compared to todays. Boys had to take Shop/Industrial Arts, while girls took Home Ec. In 9th grade we had the Home Ec teacher, Mrs. Laura Belle Holmes, for homeroom. One wall of her room was all mirrors, perfect for dress-fitting and checking your posture. But in the era of mini-skirts, we used it to make sure our outfits met the standard: If you knelt, your skirt had to brush the floor. We quickly discerned that leaning forward a bit would tip the hem enough to touch.

During junior high my friends and I began having pajama parties. We'd stay up all night, watching Johnny Carson's Tonight Show, playing cards or board games, sharing articles from Sixteen and Tiger Beat magazines, but mostly talking about boys. Some of us were lucky enough to have basement retreats so we could make as much noise as we wanted without disturbing other family members. Years later, as our daughter hosted pj parties and team dinners, I could appreciate how fortunate those families were to escape the ear-piercing shrieks of a group of preteens.

One of my best friends was Vicki, who lived in Green Park and rode the bus with us Landisburg kids. She and I would spend every summer afternoon we could at the New Bloomfield/Carroll Municipal Pool, swimming, playing cards, swapping magazines, listening to top 40 hits on our transistor radios, and basking in the sun on the grass around the pool. Having inherited my father's redheaded complexion, I had some of the worst sunburns of my life, but just peeled off the damaged skin and kept going.

Since my mother had the store open 6 days a week, she could never give me a ride, but Vicki's mother was a great sport, driving the three miles into Landisburg to pick me up, then backtracking through Green Park to New Bloomfield. Vicki had 4 younger siblings, so we would sometimes be charged with babysitting one or two of them at the pool. Her mother figured we'd call her for a ride home if the weather turned cold. She declared the outdoor temperature had to be at least 70 degrees before she'd give us a ride. Vicki and I would call each other a half hour before the pool opened and run back and forth to the thermometers at each of our houses, reporting the mercury levels. Vicki would relay these readings to her mom. If it was 70 in Landisburg but 68 in Green Park, that qualified as a "go".

Senior high school meant a shorter bus ride, to Elliottsburg 4 miles away. There were plenty of opportunities to join a club, a sport, or other activity. I participated in Future Teachers of America, going to the new elementary school up the hill from the senior high to "student teach". Student teaching was a step up from volunteering at Vacation Bible School. We didn't have any paste-eaters to monitor but read stories to first- through third graders and helped with worksheets and art activities. It was a nice way to reconnect with the teachers who had guided us through Landisburg Elementary. The Landisburg school had closed while I was in Junior High, and Green Park Elementary was built to accommodate Landisburg and Ickesburg schools.

We showed our school spirit at football games in the fall and basketball games in winter. I never tried out for teams but had always loved racquet sports. When spring of junior year arrived and I got my driver's license, I'd manage almost every day to convince friends to play tennis. There were 4 courts within 5 miles, two at the high school and two behind the old elementary school in Loysville. The Loysville court had lights, so you could play far into the night--but because it was "in town" and next to the baseball field it was usually busy. There was almost never a wait at the high school, most likely because the asphalt courts weren't in great shape. We quickly learned to aim at the weeds, cracks, and potholes on the opposite side of the court to deaden the ball when we returned a serve.

One of my favorite activities was yearbook. Always interested in photography and writing, I had been looking forward to being on the staff since sophomore year. Although we didn't have the opportunity to take photos ourselves, we helped direct the photographer hired by the publisher where and who to shoot. I enjoyed taking his finished photos and creating page layouts, pairing them with copy we all had written. The whole process was a chance to make new friends and create a keepsake of our years at West Perry.

In the summers throughout my school years, firemen's carnivals were the big draw. Landisburg, New Bloomfield, Ickesburg, Blain, and other towns all relied on them to support fire, ambulance, and other community services for the year. You could find one almost every weekend from June to late August. A country music band played most nights. The fishing booth attracted most elementary school kids. Each player would be given a fishing pole with a line, which had a clothespin attached to the end. A curtain on a shower rod separated the "creek" from the player, who would cast the line over the top of the rod. When the player felt a tug, he or she would reel in his or her line and find a brown paper lunch bag containing a prize clipped to the clothespin. The big attraction for adults was bingo, usually held indoors in the fire hall. There was always great food--homemade ice cream, hand-churned until electric motor churns were perfected; barbeque sandwiches that everywhere outside of Pennsylvania are known as Sloppy Joes; hot dogs; french fries; cotton candy; and barbequed chicken. The carnivals usually ran Thursday to Saturday nights, with fireworks wrapping up the event on Saturdays.

Cherished childhood memories never to be forgotten!

My Memories of Marysville

Storyteller Barb Stokes

My recollections, while memorable to me, are a little sporadic. Marysville has been my hometown and my family's hometown since the early 1800s. Even though we don't live in town anymore, I still regard Marysville as my hometown. My father was in the military, and we traveled around a lot. We always returned to Marysville, it was our home base with family and friends.

I remember when we lived on Kings Highway, we would play ball out in the street. I remember that the street was still dirt. This would have been around 1955 or 1956. We moved to Virginia in 1959 and rented our house in Marysville. From Virginia it was onto Alabama and then to Germany for the second time. We would come home for a visit or I would come home and spend the summer in town with my grandparents, and my aunts and uncles. My favorite thing to do as soon as I got to town was to take a walk from Maple Avenue to Kings Highway or to the Lions Club. I usually stayed with my grandparents on Maple Avenue. I would start from there and go to my Aunt Phyl's, also on Maple Avenue. Then on the other side of the street was my Great Aunt Bertie. Then to the Church of God where I would stop and talk with the Pastor. Next would be my Great Aunt Julia's place. She had a small apartment above Fred White's TV store. At that time that was the yellow building on the corner of Maple Avenue Extended and Valley Street. Next stop was Roth's Cut Rate/Bitting's for some penny candy and purchasing some comic books. Onto Watt's 5 & 10, I could spend hours in that place. The rest of the walk was just a walk. I would take Lincoln Street to Cassell to Kings Highway. Once I got to our house I would visit with the neighbors if they were home, Mr. & Mrs. Snyder, Mr. Crosley and Mrs. Sedam.

I also remember in the wintertime; we used to take our sleds and go just above Mr. Roberts' house on the curve on Kings Highway. Mr. Roberts' house used to be the icehouse where all the ice for town was stored. This would be heading toward the Sportsmens Club. On the right was a very steep bank and on the left the same. We would climb up as far as we could on the right bank and get on our sleds, down the slope, across the street and down the other steep bank. Lots of honeysuckle vines on those banks helped us from killing ourselves. Lots of fun. Not many cars traveled that end of town in those days.

After my dad retired from the Army, we returned home and I finished my last two years of school at Susquenita High School. I walked to the elementary school to catch the bus to the high school and walked home from the elementary school. It was always a nice walk – except in bad weather. The people living in town would talk to the kids when they walked by. You didn't have to be worried about your kids being bothered by strangers. Everyone knew each other and looked out for each other. This was in the late 1960's.

Singing in the church choir and going to my Aunt Phyl's for Sunday Brunch was another highlight. Lots of fun and family time.

I was still able to have a horse, because we had enough land and Kings Highway was at the end of town. One of my friends from school had horses and her father needed a new place to board them. Pleading and begging my father – we broke him – Nancy was allowed to board her horses in our barn. I had to share the duties of taking care of them and I was able to ride anytime I wanted.

From Centerville to Liverpool

Storyteller a Proud Great-Great-Granny Myrtle Hoffman Holman
Recorded by Debra Kay Noye

Myrtle Holman was born March 7, 1926, in Perry Valley, to Russell and Ruth (Willard) Hoffman. If you do your math right, she is 95 years old, today!

Quite the spunky lady, who is very proud of her meager upbringing, and having been born at home, on her grandparent's farm. Sometime, soon thereafter, her family moved to a small, rented farm, in Centerville. It was not a very large house, and it soon became full of children. Over the span of twenty years, her mother bore ten children.

Myrt's six sisters slept in one bedroom, on two double beds. The mattresses were "chaf ticks", as Myrt called them. The ticking was a material, heavier than sack cloth, sewn together, and then filled with chaf, after the harvesting of wheat or oats. Not the stalks or strands of wheat, the fine pieces of straw left behind in the fine dust. It would've been itchy!

Her two brothers shared their bedroom, with grandpa when he came to visit. He slept on a cot, as there was only one bed. That left, her parents' bedroom, which always had a filled crib and cradle.

Twelve in a house, that had no electric, plumbing, or heating! Water was hand pumped from a well and carried into the house in a bucket. When Myrt would need a drink of water, she would go to the bucket, and using the dipper drink directly from it. No fancy glasses or tin drinking cups.

Kerosene lamps lit the kitchen and living room areas. Myrt remembers using a Ray-O-Vac kerosene lamp. If you followed correctly, there were only five rooms in the farmhouse. The kitchen had a large wood burning cook stove. Smack dab in the center of the living room, sat a pot belly stove, that also burned wood. The heat from the stoves, heated the house. It was certainly a cramped lifestyle, but Myrtle survived.

Luckily for the family, they had an out kitchen, tucked onto the side of the house. It was a very small room, with a kerosene stove. Myrt remembers her mother cooking every day and canning the **eight hundred** jars of canned vegetables and fruits, during the summer months.

The large garden, more like a "truck patch", as Myrtle called it, kept their dinner table filled with fresh vegetables in the summer and fall. It supplied them with tomatoes, potatoes, green beans, corn, to name a few. The wash boiler was kept filled, with glass jars full of vegetables being preserved for the winter months. The jars were sealed using zinc screw tops. It was a long and tedious method of canning, regardless of whether the vegetables were cold or hot packed. Remember, there were twelve mouths to feed!

Her mother dried field corn, on a rack under the cook stove. Once it was totally free of moisture, her father took the corn, to the mill in Newport, to be ground into cornmeal, for the families use. She believes it was at Wentzel's Mill, which is no longer standing. Myrt loved her mother's corn pone, baked in pans, and then eaten with a tad of sugar, and drenched in milk.

But it was the mush, that Myrt still longs for, knowing that the cornmeal available today, just does not have the full-bodied flavor Myrtle was used to, coming out of her mother's kitchen. Water, salt and the freshly ground cornmeal cooked till the texture is smooth, and no longer granular, is how Myrt remembers mush. Put into loaf pans, or some folks refer to them as metal bread pans, the smooth mush would become solid. Sliced and fried in their home rendered lard, from butchering hogs, mush was a popular meal topped with molasses, and an inexpensive way to fill bellies. Myrt recalls the wooden barrels, filled with molasses, creating a sweet sticky purchase, from the Centerville Store. Her mother stored their molasses in jars.

Butter was not used to fry the mush, nor used as a topping, because it just wasn't available. There was a milk cow, hand milked daily, (Myrt hated hand milking), but there wasn't a way to keep the milk cold. There was not an ice box, only the **cool ground** on the basement floor. Myrtle remembers when oleomargarine, Blue Bonnet, appeared in the stores. It came in a solid block, like butter used to be sold. In the center of the white mass, was an orange dot, that when squeezed and the mixture beaten, created a smooth, yellowish, spreadable "fake butter". It became the "rage", during WW ll, and the post years. Unfortunately, it became a household staple.

Her mother made butter, in a small wooden butter churn, set upon the kitchen table, when enough cream appeared, on the tops of the crocks filled with milk. Myrtle loved the butter, on homemade bread, which her mother made several times a week, from wheat flour ground at Wentzel's Mill, after the harvest.

She grew tired of homemade **apple butter,** which they made yearly. There were apple and cherry trees nearby, which made for easy picking of apples to be cooked down into a smooth apple butter. It was stored, in open crocks, in the cellar. It didn't last long, because every child would carry apple butter sandwiches, in their school lunch box. Myrtle remembers using a cherry seeder, to pit cherries, handpicked from the local trees. Generally, they were consumed in puddin's and pies, which would've made another mighty fine meal! Myrt says, "they never wanted for food, and ate real good!"

Can you imagine, making Jello in the cool of the cellar, and eating it almost immediately. Myrt loved the very wobbly treat!

"Butchering was a fun day, when family and friends would come to help. We would eat the freshly cooked meat, right out of the boiling kettles. It was so good!" says Myrt. The broth, from the cooked meats, served as the delicious base, for making scrapple, which was thickened with their own cornmeal. Ladled, into metal pans, the scrapple was topped with the freshly rendered pig fat, which helped to preserve it, in the cool cellar. It usually didn't last too long, because it was served for any meal. Scrapple or ponhaus became a staple in the winter time.

***

The large metal **wash boiler** never got a rest! It was used, not only for canning, but to heat water for bathing, and doing the laundry. It was an important piece of equipment in every household back in the old days.

Every Monday was "wash day", so the wash boiler was filled with water, brought to a very high temperature, and then dumped into another wash tub. Her mother used a metal washboard and homemade soap to scrub the clothes clean. She saved all the pan dripping, from frying meats and mush, added them to lye and water, to create rock hard slabs of soap, which required chiseling off a piece in order to use it. Lots of scrubbing took place, before the clothes were rinsed, sometimes with bluing, in clean water, wrung out by hand, and hung outside on a clothesline to dry. It was an all-day process, especially for a family that size. The same soap was used to wash the dirty dishes, in a dishpan, after a meal.

Her mother also made starch, but Myrt doesn't recall the process. And **"ironing day"**, followed wash day. Myrt says, "ironing was a job, but you didn't know any better!" Her mother ironed everything, from bedding to blouses, and pants. She had three black, heavy sad irons, that she heated on the cook stove. Once they were piping hot, she would alternate them, as they cooled down. Smoothing out the wrinkled clothing and sheets, which were sprinkled with water to create steam, was another all-day chore.

Myrt recalls using Lifebuoy soap as a body wash.

Using a treadle sewing machine, Myrt's mother made lots of dresses and skirts, for the girls, out of the floral designed, sack cloth, feed bags, which contained chop for their cow, pigs and two work horses. The horses were used to plow the fields, and bring in the wagon loads of loose hay, and harvested crops, - not to be ridden.

The city-slicker cousins, in Philadelphia, supplied the family, with hand me downs. Shopping trips, for clothing, were made to Newport, or her mother would order from the Montgomery Ward or other catalogs. Myrt was chuckling about her mother ordering Christmas gifts from the catalogs. Her secret hiding place, above the butcher shop, was known to Myrt. She would sneak up to the second story, find the gifts, open the packages, and look at everything.

Shoes were purchased in Millerstown, from Pappy Wingert. Myrt recalls her father buying the girls high topped shoes for the winter months, because they walked to school. She did not like the new style of shoes, and would also roll down her heavy, very warm stocking once she got to school. It was the trend of the day!

In the winter, for a special treat, her father would go to the Icehouse, close to the Red Covered Bridge, and buy chunks of ice, to make homemade ice cream. The ice was stored in sawdust, to keep it from melting too fast. They had an eight-quart ice cream freezer, which required taking turns to hand crank. They ate all of the vanilla and chocolate ice cream. Remember, they did not own an ice box, and relied on the cellar to keep anything cold.

Myrt is amazed at how her mother managed to raise ten kids, cooking, washing, ironing, canning, tending the gardens, and helped to hand husk the field corn. The corn stalks would be cut down, gathered into shocks, and then each ear of corn, would have the coarse paper-thin husk removed by hand. Her mother would sit, right out in the fields, husking corn. The corn was put into feed bags, and taken to the mill, to be stored and ground into livestock feed.

"Old man Gothel" would come around, with his threshing machine, after the wheat and oats, were cut off, generally bundled, and left to dry in the fields. The threshing machine removed the kernels of wheat and oats from the straw. The grains were once again mainly used for livestock feed.

Living out in the country, in the middle of nowhere, there weren't many visitors. But there were several vendors or hucksters, who made their rounds throughout the valleys, in Perry County. A "Rag Man" would show up periodically, in his pickup truck, to buy any old rags, that might be laying around the house. He paid cash, loaded the rags, and went on his way. Myrt didn't know what may have happened to the rags.

The Rawleigh Company salesman, from Millerstown, sold spices, medicinal needs, cleaning products and supplies. Myrt remarked about Ed Soule, from Newport, coming around with buckets of salted fish.

With all the fresh homemade bread, you wouldn't think, that Myrt would be excited to get sliced bread off the Stitt's Bakery truck. "It was a treat to have bought bread!"

Gypsies were known to roam around the back roads, which made most folks very uneasy, due to their bad reputation concerning business transactions, or theft. Because of all the stories, Myrt was told as a child, she was scared to death of them. If her mother wanted her to "fly right," she would say to Myrt, "I'll tell the gypsies to come and get you!"

Hobos, also wandered from town to town, looking for work or a handout. They'd show up on the porch steps, and Myrt's mother would feed them. Since their home was targeted, for a free meal, her mother figured the bums marked the property in some way, or by word of mouth, letting it be known they were in friendly territory. During the 1930 depression, many men could not find steady work. The men traveled by foot, bike, and hitching a free ride on the railways, with what few personal belongings they owned in a knapsack.

Myrt's family spent their time on the farm, at school, and walked to the Centerville Lutheran Church, and later to the Reward Brethren Church.

School was just like home, bare bones, and nothing more. Myrt started to school in the wooden, one room Centerville school house. Eight grades were taught in that single classroom, with a coal stove providing heat. A long blackboard dominated the front of the room. Myrt recalls having to take the erasers outside and clapping them together to release the buildup of chalk dust. The "dummy bench" was used to punish students, who misbehaved or didn't do their assignments. Myrt never shared if she had a turn sitting on the dreaded bench. Of course, they used an outhouse.

Students were given tablets and pencils, and they had textbooks for reading, writing and arithmetic. Oh, they also were given homework, regardless if they lived on a farm and had chores to do after school.

The students ate lunch at their desks. Remember Myrtle got sick and tired of apple butter bread sandwiches, every day. They would get yucky, by the time lunch rolled around. Sometimes, she would convince a classmate to swap their bologna and cheese sandwich, with her. She was in heaven and relished every bite. In fact, when the family moved to Liverpool, in later years, Myrt was ecstatic, realizing she would have ready access to bologna and cheese, from the stores, anytime she craved some.

Recess meant playing games, like Tippy Hi-Over. They would take turns pitching a ball over the coal storage shed.

Her first-grade teacher was her future sister-in-law, Ruth Holman. From second to seventh, Calvin Strawser was her teacher, who encouraged her, at the end of seventh grade, to take a test, to see if she might be ready for high school. Voila, she passed, and would no longer be walking to school, because she was headed to the Liverpool High School. In the winter months, she wore long johns to school, to keep her warm, on the trek to school.

Dan Kline was the superintendent of schools for Perry County, and he would visit each school and observe the students and teachers. When he came, the students tried extra hard to be on their best behavior.

Luckily, a neighbor, Mr. Brookhart, taught at the elementary school in Liverpool, and kindly offered to provide transportation for Myrtle to attend high school. Since there were no buses, students had to find their own means to school.

The Liverpool School was divided by grades. Elementary students were on the first floor. Myrt and the rest of the thirty high school students were on the second floor, in three rooms. The main room was used for morning assembly, as prayer and a salute to the American flag were a routine way to start the school day. Classes, taught by three teachers, were held in the remaining two rooms. The principal, Mr. Klinger, also taught English and other subjects, as did Mr. Williamson. Latin and history were mainly taught by Mr. Swartz. Yes, Latin was required.

Myrt continued to pack a lunch because there was no cafeteria. She did not participate in any extra activities, at the school, which was located where the Liverpool Senior Center is today.

Myrt graduated from high school, at the age of sixteen since she qualified for the accelerated program. The policy, at the school, for sixteen-year-olds, allowed them to quit and find employment. At least, Myrt had a diploma.

The family decided to move to Liverpool, after Myrt's graduation. They lived in half of what was to become the Nipple Nursing Home, on Front Street. Because of her age, she could only find work in the Liverpool dress factory. Her mother worked there also. Her dad traveled to Millersburg, in upper Dauphin County, to work in the tool and die factory.

Myrt recalls some of the businesses, that existed in town. There was a Weis Store, Miller's Grocery Store, (Myrt worked there for thirty-six years, in her later life.), Liverpool Hardware, Jake Lutz Ice Cream and dry good store, Barnies Meat market, and Stailey's Tin Shop. Lesher's Diner was at the end of Route 17, on the edge of town.

During the war years, 1943-1945, Myrt worked at the Middletown Air Depot. She traveled with five other people from Liverpool, by car, which originated in Selinsgrove. Later, she was transferred to the Farm Show building in Harrisburg, where she was an inventory clerk, for stored airplane parts.

Her future husband spent four years overseas, in the army. His family home was outside of town on Route 17. When he came home, after the war, he could not find work. So, when they met, and got married, in 1946, Floyd did not have a job. After a time, they settled in Liverpool. They had a son and a daughter. But they did not have a tv, so Myrt went to work in the dress factory again, to earn enough money to buy a tv.

Today, Myrt sings a different tune, about that old black and white tv. She blames it, for the downfall of society. People do not visit anymore, or go "Fan Toddling", between Christmas and New Year's. That's when, they would dress up in costumes or old clothes to conceal their identity, and go to neighbors or neighboring towns, to revel and see if they might be discovered.

People were trusting, didn't lock their doors at night, and welcomed costumed strangers, on their doorstep. Not so today!

Myrt would go back, to a more meaningful way of life, but at ninety-five she'd rather entertain and share her upbringing, with the up-and-coming generations.

Growing Up at Stoney Point

Storyteller Jane Smith Dobbs

I have so many memories of growing up on our farm. Our farm was owned by my grandparents, then my father and now my sister, brother and me. My dad was born here and lived to be 93. He was very proud of that fact, and he had many stories to tell about the farm and his family.

When I was young, I thought it would be neat to live in town. But now I feel so blessed to have experienced farm life. We raised chickens and a few pigs. We would purchase 5000 peeps and raise them for fryers and roasters. It was so much fun to see and hear the peeps, but they grew up into pecking chickens. My dad had to debeak them so they wouldn't peck each other to death. The smell of debeaking was worse than hair and feathers burning.

Every summer my sister, brother and I would have some peeps that were designated as ours to feed, water and care for. When they were sold, we divided the money and it went promptly into our savings accounts. When I got married, the money was used to buy pots and pans from a traveling salesman. He also gave me a set of china dishes which I still own.

When it was time to sell the chickens, big trucks would come at night. The chickens were always calmer at night and had to be caught with metal catchers with a hook on one end. One of my earliest memories is carrying two chickens, one under each arm when I was three years old and putting them in a coop to go to market.

Every spring when the plowing and harrowing were done in the fields, we had the privilege of picking stones. More and more stones each year were put into huge stone piles. I presume that is why the area is known as Stony Point. Mountain stones are still my favorite of all varieties. My dad actually sold many of them to builders. It is exciting to think they may be used in buildings and homes anywhere in Pennsylvania.

Some silly things we did as kids was to set up a store in the wood house. Mud pies were made in jar lids. We picked leaves off the lilac bush to use as dollars to purchase goods from our store. We used the corn crib which was part of the barn as our apartments. We each had a section in which to decorate and play. We had a cat cemetery behind the barn. I was the caretaker.

Every fall we picked up walnuts from our walnut tree. My dad ran over them with the tractor tire to break the hulls. Then we had to pick up the black shells and get our hands stained black. Dad said, "Don't worry it'll be worn off by Christmas time!" The following summer we cracked the shells on the barn floor and picked out the goodies for cookies at Christmas.

My mom and dad made us wonderful treats from recipes handed down by family. Homemade marshmallows, several kinds of fudge, peanut brittle, pull taffy and a variety of delicious cookies. Sometimes when my dad would go to Hershey, he would bring back big chunks of white and milk chocolates. I loved those days and still love Hershey's chocolate.

When there was snow and ice on the ground, we made chocolate ice cream in a White Mountain ice cream freezer. My mom's recipe is the best. She had a secret ingredient, and she would not allow the ice cream to be made until that ingredient was in the can. Dad hooked up a motor, so we didn't have to churn by hand.

We made our own fun on the farm. Sunday evenings in the summer we played softball in the yard, badminton over the clothesline, croquet and rode our bikes a lot. And the Conococheague Mountain was always there to explore, sled ride on the hills and the creek to wade.

We always had a large garden. I learned to can and freeze vegetables and fruits. Of course, we had chicken every Sunday for lunch after church services. We had chicken sandwiches for supper as we watched the Ed Sullivan Show. We also watched the Lawrence Welk Show, I love Lucy, Bonanza, the Lone Ranger and Roy Rogers, just to name a few.

Butcher day was a big day on the farm. A pig or two were made into hams, bacon, scrapple, lard for cooking and baking and other delicacies. I liked eating the tongue. My dad smoked the ham and bacon in our smokehouse.

My great-grandma Johnson came to stay in the house with us kids until we were old enough to help. She would sit in a chair in the living room and I would sneak up behind her and say "Boo"! She would always jump but never get cross. (That's what they called getting upset.)

We had milk in real glass bottles delivered to the end of our half mile lane. Hall's Dairy of Millerstown put it in a metal box every week. In the summer, my dad would put the tailgate down on his Ford pick-up truck and we rode with our feet dangling down out the lane to retrieve the milk delivery. Capitol Bakers delivered bread to the house and Hall's Dairy brought popsicles and ice cream.

We bought groceries locally at Smith's Store in Blain, Adair's Store at Pine Grove and Fisher's Store in Andersonburg where we always bought barrel molasses on election day in November. Wentzel's Mill at Bridgeport provided flour for pies and the best cornmeal for corn pone and mush. It's the only cornmeal I'll buy and I like to gift it to friends every fall.

We have many cousins and always enjoy seeing them. We looked forward to our Smith family reunion at Big Spring State Park. We walked the trails and went to the cave in the mountain where once they were going to dig through the mountain for the Newport and Shermans Valley Railroad. The menu was always chicken corn soup and home-made ice cream. Many fond memories were made there.

One time when a distant cousin was visiting our farm from the big city, my brother took him into the henhouse to see the chickens. Well, the cousin got the chickens all flustered and upset. He then ran out of the building and locked the door. We laugh about it now, but my brother was not too happy then with all those chickens jumping and flying at him.

My parents worked hard to give us a good life and to keep things going because they grew up during the Great Depression when they didn't have all the conveniences we have today. We learned to appreciate home and family and to thank God for our many blessings.

Fun Stuff and Memories from Home

Storytellers Deitra Neidigh Hinkle and Christina Cressler Morrow

NEWPORT HIGH SCHOOL CLASS OF 1964

Dee Dee lived on Walnut Street between 5th and 6th Streets and Chris lived on Walnut Street between 4th and 5th Streets. When we were old enough to sled on our own, we remember our parents stopping traffic at the intersections of Walnut Street and 5th and 4th Streets. We would sled from the top of Walnut Street at 6th Street to almost the railroad tracks that were on 3rd Street. That would now be in front of the Newport Weis Market. Many a good sled was broken when sliding under parked cars. We can't recall that there were any serious accidents.

Dee Dee remembers going tobogganing in the country with friends. Paul Jones, the auto mechanic in Newport and father of our classmate, Dave Jones, transported a bunch of us in the back of his open truck. She recalls that a 500 pounds motor hit her foot and broke her toes when the truck hit a bump in the road. She says she still went tobogganing and bore the pain but could barely walk the next day.

In our teenage years, there were Saturday night firehouse dances at the former Newport Firehouse on 3rd Street between Market and Mulberry Streets. They were not held during the summer because it was too hot in the firehouse. That firehouse was built in 1956 and had an open room on the 2nd floor for the dances. Don Lorenz, from WJUN, a radio station in Mexico, Pennsylvania, was the disc jockey. We remember the last song of the night was always "Goodnite Sweetheart, Goodnite". Chris did some research and found that the song was written in 1951 and was first recorded by The Spaniels in 1953. Since then, many artists have recorded the song. We are not sure which version was played by DJ Lorenz at the firehouse dances in the late 1950's and early to mid1960's. The Newport Firehouse dances ended in the early to mid 1960's after a few years of local live bands.

Female pajama parties in the summer were great sport. During these parties, Dee Dee remembers playing games in the street, sneaking certain boys in for a short time, and playing either the radio or record player. As Chris recalls, the street games were played on the flat part of Mulberry Street where two of our friends lived. The main food was Chef Boyardee pizza, made from a box with all ingredients in it. Plus, we had snacks such as popcorn, pretzels, and potato chips. Some of the girls stayed up all night talking and giggling.

Cherished Memories 65

The View from the Back Porch
Submarines and Rafts

Storyteller Larry L Little

Growing up on the shores of the Susquehanna River presented me with a variety of adventures without getting into too much trouble. Summertime was the best, school was out, days were long and warm, and the river ran low and clear. My best friend, Steve and I lived the lives of Huckleberry Finn and Tom Sawyer. Up early in the morning with a quick breakfast, we'd be out of our homes until dark. At some time during the day, a sure bet would be that the nearby river would attract our attention. The possibilities were endless. Maybe we'd decide to throw sticks in the current and then try to hit them with rocks. Throwing rocks accurately when you're twelve is important, and the rocks were everywhere along the riverbank. On hot days, to cool off, we'd start out wading in the shallows near shore. This was our private part of the river bordered upstream and downstream by two large boulders; that we named imaginatively as First Rock and Second Rock. The water would be no more than two to three feet deep here. When we were younger (10), it was all the further in the river we were allowed to go, it was our swimming hole. Beyond the two boulders were two small islands that only became islands when the river was at its lowest stages. They were named First Island and Second Island. If nothing else, we were consistent in our naming conventions. They were actually gravel bars that had been created by ice jams sometime in the geologic past. The ice gouged out the river bottom and deposited the material in piles that became the islands. The Second Island was furthest from shore, and beyond it, was "The Hole". The Hole was the trench that the ice had gouged to create the island. It was maybe 100 feet long by 50 feet wide and relatively deep, over 6 foot in some spots. It was the deepest water for some distance around and attracted the largest fish to its cool dark depths. Between the Second Rock and Second Island, another pool had been gouged, much smaller and shallower than The Hole. Material gouged from this pool had become the First Island. This pool was about 25 feet in diameter and three feet or so in depth. In the center was a huge boulder of a rough aggregate material much different from the sandstone most of the river's rocks were composed of. I often wondered about its makeup. It would have been millions, or maybe billions of years old; how did it come to be placed where it was in the middle of my little world? This pool became our second swimming hole after we had outgrown the one between the two rocks. This pool became the site of our great submarine and raft adventures.

There was always a large pile of used lumber underneath the raised back porch. This pile contained boards of various widths, lengths, and thicknesses, the remains of construction and repair projects around the homestead over the years, from new porches to chicken pen repairs. This pile provided materials for the building project that Steve and I would take on. We decided that we needed a watercraft of our own. Boats were much too complicated so we decided that we would build ourselves a raft. Four by six-inch planks became the frame of our craft. They were nailed together on edge with large nails that I bought by the ton from the local hardware store. The planking was nailed on top of this to become the raft's deck. It was a major time-consuming project for us boys; we must have spent two or three hours putting it together. What we didn't think about was how we were going to get the finished raft to the river. We had it all assembled; it was very primitive, but it looked really neat to a twelve-year-old. A rope was tied to one end (I bought rope by the mile), which was later to serve as a tether for the anchor. We gave a mighty pull in the direction of the river, but nothing moved. It was all we could do to budge it a few inches, it was so very heavy. Being young and creative, we put our Radio Flyer wagons to use. With great effort, we lifted the ends, one at a time onto our wagons. The wagon wheels wanted to sink into the soft soil under the grass, but we were able to transport our creation to the riverbank. The wagons allowed us to pull it right into the river until it floated free. It did float, although with all the weight, it floated very low in the water. Then for the great event, as one we climbed on board our worthy craft. It went straight to the bottom; it didn't have the buoyancy to support our scant weight. A raft that didn't float isn't of much use, so it was back to the drawing board. We knew that things filled with air floated very well. In addition to floating sticks, we often targeted floating soda bottles with our rocks. With that knowledge, we pulled our raft back out of the water which required even greater effort than launching it; now that it was uphill from the water. We flipped it over to dry and headed to one of the town's gasoline service stations with our wagons. An hour later, we were back and commenced pounding again. Soon, we were launching our craft again and were elated to find that it floated like a top, even with both of us on board. What did we do, you ask? Why did we visit the service station? The answer was simple; we collected all the two-gallon oil cans that our wagons could carry. They were made of tin or some metal and had sealable caps. We arranged them in rows inside the 2x6 wooden frame from underneath the raft and nailed boards to keep them in place without puncturing them. They gave the raft the lift that it needed, and we were thrilled. The raft became the center of our river activities for the summer.

That same summer, my parents had to replace our water heater. This must have been about the same time that home insulation was discovered. The new water heater was enclosed in an insulating wrap of fiberglass for efficiency. The old heater, on the other hand was a big bare metal tube with pipes sticking out of the top of it. I guess that it had a heating element someplace, but I don't remember of any electrical connections. Anyway, I asked my dad if I could have it; I was making plans already. Steve and I drained the remaining water from it and plugged the pipe ends with wooden stoppers that we whittled out of the wood pile. It was easy to get to the river, just turn it sideways and roll, roll, roll. It was so heavy that it didn't float very well, just barely above the surface. When one of us would lay on it, it would float just under the surface like a submarine. It even had a periscope of sorts in the form of one of the pipes that came out of the side and curved to the top. We spent hours pretending that the raft was an aircraft carrier being attacked by the water heater submarine, we had great fun.

All good things come to an end, however. As the summer was ending, a passing hurricane or tropical storm unleashed heavy rains. We hadn't moved our craft to higher ground beforehand and the rising river waters washed both our craft away. The loss didn't bother us for long however, summer was over, and the river was turning cold, it was time for us to turn our attention to our next adventure.

Amity Hall from a Waitress' Perspective

Storyteller Judith LePere Armstrong

While attending college from 1970 to 1972, I worked at Amity Hall. It was a beautiful place and an enjoyable atmosphere. I loved working the weekends, especially on days that Penn State had home games. This place was a popular stop for dinner for Penn State fans going home. Boy, was it busy, but the tips were great! Much needed money for a college student!

There were 3 dining rooms on the main floor and a bar/lounge area. Kenny was the piano player who entertained in that room. Yes, this place was really upscale! The dining rooms each had their own names. The 'Squires Room' was reserved for the elite and special customers (big tippers)! The experienced waitresses worked this room. Needless to say, that wasn't me. The other rooms were the Coach and Hunt. I mostly worked the smallest room. We worked as teams, where one waitress took drink orders, and one took dinner orders. Cathy Magill Hoffman and I were the only waitresses in this room and loved letting our tables know we were in college (big tips)!!!

The chef was Walter, who not only prepared the meals but did ice sculptures for special occasions. Amazing, beautiful sculptures, done within 15 minutes with a chainsaw!

When new owners took over, the upstairs dining room was opened. What an experience that was! The 'dumb waiter' did not work so meals had to be walked up the stairs; up the crooked leaning stairs!!! We always wanted a busboy to help carry or walk behind us in case we lost our balance. Luckily, no major mishaps occurred.

In 1972, Agnes flood hit. Amity Hall flooded, I graduated college and that ended my wonderful experience at Amity Hall!

Growing Up in Perry County

Storyteller Carol Janet Gabel Ulsh

Born November 18, 1940, to Homer Thomas Gabel and Rhoda Arnold Gabel after my mother was told fifteen years earlier when she delivered a stillborn boy at home and nearly bled to death, she could never have children. Many locals called me the "miracle baby".

Growing up as an only child in rural Perry County 2 miles outside of Newport on a dairy farm, I learned to entertain myself with the help of farm animals of which I had many; kittens, dogs, lambs, pigs, chickens, cows, and horses. My mother was completely involved in milking the cows, gardening as well as working in the fields during harvesting which meant I would entertain myself with paper dolls. Since my mother didn't drive in those days, my dad was always responsible for all errands and other commitments; therefore, I got to tag along whenever possible. One time when I was around 3 years old, I wasn't permitted to tag along, but I ran after dad to the car that he was backing out of the garage. He ended up knocking me down and backing over me before he realized I was there. Fortunately, I was not injured badly. I remember vividly going with him to the Third Street Railroad Cars in Newport to pick up animal feed in printed feedbags. I was excited to be able to pick the bags that I liked best because my mother would use them to make my dresses.

When I was old enough to steer the tractor but not old enough to reach the pedals, I was placed on the tractor in low gear to steer through the fields to pick up the hay bales. Our live-in hired man for many years, Roy Tressler, would be close by to jump on the tractor to stop it since I couldn't reach the pedals. Our fields were fairly flat. I learned to drive alone on the farm by the time I was 13 and would be responsible for driving our Model A Ford truck to the chicken range to collect the eggs and feed the chickens on a daily basis. Also, many summers as a teenager, I raised and sold broiler chickens for money for my college fund. Since I never attended a 4-year college, that savings accumulated was used to purchase our first home in Williamsport, PA in 1963.

By the time I was 10 and eligible for 4-H, I was active in dairy, baby beef and homemaker's clubs. I learned more in these clubs to prepare me for adulthood than you might imagine i.e., sewing, cooking, feeding and grooming animals. I even had the experience of showing my Angus steers at the Pa. National Farm Show several times. I enjoyed judging animals, meeting and interacting with many members across the state at Penn State University, including managing money and keeping accurate records of each and every project for judging to complete projects. Florence Wolpert was my homemaker's leader every summer and Roy Snyder was leader of the animal clubs that met on a county-wide basis anywhere from Blain to Liverpool for many meetings.

My parent's priorities were always church first and they attended Wila EUB Church where they grew up and were married in 1924. Later the EUB church joined with Methodist church, and that's where I met many friends and family regularly for Sunday School (SS), church, Bible School, Confirmation classes, and many soup and ice cream festivals during the summer. Besides many family members of the T. W. Tressler family attending this church, another couple that stands out in my memory was Luke and Betty Toomey. They never had children, but always spent their time teaching and entertaining all the local kids. Betty was an excellent teacher with children's SS, teaching songs like "B I B L E" and "JOY, JOY, JOY" down in my heart with motions. Both Luke and Betty were always on the Wila Dam during the winter, to instruct and monitor the youngsters on the ice. They would have fires burning so we could skate safely after dark.

Being farmers didn't stop my father from being active in many community affairs, i.e., Perry County Cooperative Extension, where Louie Rothrock was the first Perry County Extension Director when I was born. My grandfather Nelson B. Gabel owned and operated Barnview Farm near Oak Hall School. He was on the original committee that was instrumental in bringing Cooperative Extension to Perry County. My dad became one of the first Perry County artificial breeders along with Lester Fuller. I was fortunate to ride along with him to different farms in the county when he made calls as a relief breeder. When Lester became Perry County Sheriff, my dad became full-time breeder. We sold our farm in March 1958 and moved to New Bloomfield. My parents purchased the "Beamer Clouser" property on the corner of Apple and Barnett Streets. We had "Bung" Umholtz reconstruct the 2-story cinder block building into a one-story home on that property. Beamer used mules at that time and had a so-called barn on the property, that was torn down. My mother continued farming in her garden until she was 80 plus years old. She produced many fruits and veggies for the family's enjoyment. Our outdoor wedding reception was held in that yard catered by friends and neighbors of the New Bloomfield United Methodist Church. Hazel Myers and her daughter Rosalie were in charge of the ladies who prepared and served the beautiful reception that day.

My parents were life-long members of the Grange. They attended and participated in regular meetings of Oliver Grange, that met at Oak Hall School and Pomona Grange. The meetings would rotate between Granges, county wide. These folks were front and center in restarting the Perry County Fair and continue to support it in many ways to this day. Of course, I became a member as well when I was old enough and would participate wherever possible while growing up in Perry County.

My dad was a member of the Newport Joint School Board of Directors for many years and presented me with my diploma in 1958. Since we resided in Oliver Township, I was able to attend Newport Elementary on Fourth Street. I didn't get to attend one of the one room schools in adjacent Juniata Township where my parents and many of my cousins went to school. At that time, Mrs. Gertrude Wolfe was principal and would walk the halls with her yardstick slapping it against the wall if she needed to get our attention. My first-grade teacher was Miss Walker followed by Miss English, Mrs. Barton, Mrs. Hoke, Mrs. Eslinger and Mr. Raffensberger. While in elementary school, I learned to play the clarinet and piano, taking lessons from a nearly blind teacher, Mrs. Corson on South Fourth Street.

I attended Newport High School on Sixth Street for grades 7-12. I continued playing the clarinet for marching band, followed by baritone saxophone for dance band directed by Foster Brinser. This required me to participate in many practices for football games, parades, and concerts, as well as county and district concerts. Other activities in high school included singing in the chorus where I took private vocal lessons to do solos and county and district chorus. I played on the girls' basketball team (when we only played half court) with Mrs. "Billy" Cox as Coach. I was class treasurer graduating in 1958 as 8th in a class of 66 in the Academic Course. Even though I currently don't live in Perry County, I enjoy returning to be with my classmates of 1958 for monthly breakfasts and annual reunions. Even though I considered going to PSU to study Home Economics, I ended up going to Maryland Medical Secretarial School, Hagerstown, MD. I attended for 14 months straight to complete and graduate. I become Drs. William Magill, M. D. and James Rumbaugh, M. D. first medical secretary in 1959. Their offices were located at the corner of Fourth & Market Streets in Newport.

On June 25, 1960, I married David Alexander Ulsh, son of Dr. Leonard Beaver Ulsh and Eleanor Greenover Ulsh, at St. Pauls Lutheran Church on Market Street, Newport. I actually was introduced to Dave by a mutual, good friend and classmate, Judy Neilson when I was in the 8th grade. We were married by my minister, Rev. Paul Miller, who was Dave's neighbor at 200 North Fourth Street. Betty Myers played the organ for that occasion. My attendants' dresses were handmade by seamstress Sally Black and the hats made by Martha Nickel, who had a hat shop on Second Street in Newport.

Dave graduated in May 1960 from Lafayette College commissioned a 2nd Lt. in the Army and assigned to Ft. Benning, GA for basic training. We departed Perry County in November 1960 with tears in my eyes but have had no regrets being able to experience living outside of Perry County. We returned to the county in 1976-2001 with our two children, Keith, and Joanne for more exciting experiences.

Lyons Family History

Storytellers William & Crista Lyons

Our family farms are located in the western end of Perry County at the Village of Cisna Run, Loysville, Pa. near Adair Covered Bridge. The bridge was built in 1864 and is the oldest and second longest bridge at 176 feet long, in Perry County. My great-grandfather, Alvin N. Lyons, was born May 1, 1862, in Cherry Valley, Tuscarora Township. He was a Tuscarora Township Teacher from 1881 through 1897. He taught at the Mt. Pleasant School in Buckwheat Valley, Lyons' School in Cherry Valley, Kerr's School in Marsh Run, Oak Grove School in Buckwheat Valley, and Locust Grove School in Donnelly's Mill. By 1900, Alvin had moved from Cherry Valley near Millerstown, Pa. to Madison Township and was a farm laborer. Our farm was first owned by my great-grandfather when he bought it on April 5, 1913, at a price of $36.00 an acre from Elizabeth A. Adair (husband Benjamin deceased). On a cornerstone of the barn, there is a date marked WO Au 27, 1899.

Alvin N. Lyons' great grandfather, Nicholas, was a revolutionary soldier. His grandfather, also Nicholas, was born September 14, 1795, in what is now called Saville Township. Alvin's father, John, was born in Saville Township June 4, 1823. Alvin married Elmina Paden on November 27, 1884, and they went on to have ten children. George lived in Iowa. John of Andersonburg was a farmer and a mailman. Frank of Landisburg was a farmer, bottled milk, and an insurance agent. Jeremiah (my grandfather) of Cisna Run was a streetcar trolly engineer, farmer, and an auctioneer. Ira of Blain worked for the railroad and was electrocuted at his job. Ray of Blain, Loysville, and New Bloomfield was a farmer. Russell of Harrisburg was a bus driver. Mae of Andersonburg married to Ezra Harris. Pearl of Centre married to Wilson Shope, and Mary of New Bloomfield married to Jesse Shumaker.

My grandfather, Jeremiah R. Lyons, was born May 4, 1892, and when he got out of school, he went to Harrisburg and was a streetcar trolly engineer and later worked in Cleveland, Ohio. He then served in World War 1 earning the rank of lieutenant and after returning home, married Pearl M. Gutshall on February 26, 1920. Together they had eight children, Ruth, Mabel, Helen, Glenn, William (my father), Gail, Ronald, and Elmina. Jere bought the farm from his father on March 25, 1929, for $4000.00. My father, William, was born January 16, 1932. Most all of the roads around here were dirt back then and coincidentally 1932 was the same year a new road, Route 274, was built.

The Shermans Valley Railroad ran by the farm from Newport to New Germantown and closed in 1927. Also, there was the Cisna Run Train Station in the current day pasture near the barn.

Grandpa farmed with six horses in the 1930's. He, along with his family, hand milked twenty cows. My dad's oldest sisters, Ruth, Mabel, and Helen were known as the best and fastest milkers. The milk was put in cans and was transported two-tenth of a mile to a spring house by a two steel-wheeled cart to be stored until picked up.

Grandpa grew wheat, oats, corn, clover, and timothy hay. There was no alfalfa to grow back in this day. He would use a cradle to cut around the corners and then use a McCormick-Deering binder to cut and make sheaves out of the grain. Penrose Harris came from Laurel Run with his steel wheeled thrashing machine and would set up on the barn floor to separate the grain from the straw. It was a very dirty and dusty job and sometimes they would add some water just to cut down on the dust. Penrose would also go to other neighboring farmers to thrash such as John Reapsome, Sam Kuhn, Herbert Moyer, and many others. The women would spend all morning cooking to feed the fifteen men that would help with the thrashing. The grain was stored in the barn granary, carried in by bushel baskets, one at a time.

Back in the mid 1940's and early 1950's, as darkness would fall and the men would still be working, a beacon light could be seen making its revolutions in the sky, reflecting off the fields. The beacon light was about 40 feet tall. It had a bootleg on it to show wind direction and two revolving lights along with a ladder attached to do maintenance. The light was located about two miles from our home farm in what is now Ronald and Florence Emlet's yard. Florence's father, Van Milligan, also Crista Lyons' Grandfather, provided the land for the airstrip for which he was the caretaker. The airstrip was located just west of what now is called Airport Road and ran from Van's upper farm buildings north to the fence row. There were lights along both sides of the airstrip and the Milligan children had to walk along it to make sure all the lights were working properly. The children would really get excited when they found out that a plane would be coming in. The main reason planes would land there was because they were lost and needed directions. This is the obvious reason why Airport Road has its name.

They would cut hay, let it dry, and fork it onto a wagon as loose hay. A hay fork was mounted at the peak of the barn roof, then dropped into the wagon load of hay, and then pulled up by horses (later a tractor), to lift the fork fulls of hay into the mow to be separated. Basically, all that was used was a fork, dump rake, and a wagon to harvest the hay, along with much physical labor.

In the 1930's there were some very dry years, so dry that the cows were pastured near streams and along Shermans Creek to give them something extra to feed on. In the fall after all the crops were off, the whole farm would be pastured.

When it came time to cut corn for silage, it was all cut off by hand, one stalk at a time, and put on a wagon. It was pulled off of the wagon and fed into a stationary papace cutter that was run by a belt and tractor to be chopped into silage. Ear corn was also very labor intensive, husking ears by hand, and then shoveled into a corn crib.

Grandpa also had pigs, chickens, ducks, and geese, to go along with the cows. He and Dean Shull did most of auctioneering in Perry County, started during the 1940's. Grandpa also purchased his first tractors, two Ford 8N's. He bought the 208-acre adjoining "Burchfield Farm" on April 28, 1947, for $2900.00. The farm was bought at a cheaper price because at the time there wasn't a road back to the farm buildings that was easy to travel, and all of the fence rows were all grown up and out of control. After the Newport and Shermans Valley Railroad ceased to run, the first 4/10th mile of road ran on the railroad bed back to the farm and the other 4/10th mile had to be constructed down to the house and barn. A section of the road was full of springs bad enough that grandpa fell in up to his chest at one place. My mom's father, Herman Kettering, my other grandpa, worked for the pipeline and knew an engineer that could give advice on how to make the road construction last. There was a very large pile of field rocks that was used to put on the road for a base and help make it solid for travel. They also put in some culvert tiles to make the road better. Grandpa Lyons hired David L. Comp from New Bloomfield to come and clean out all the fence rows with a bulldozer to open up the land and make it easier to farm. Thousands of feet of field tile were installed over the years at both farms to alleviate the wet spots. At the home farm, it was so wet at one place that as the ditch was dug, it was hard to keep the one-foot clay tiles in place until ground would be placed on top of it because of so much water flow. The men must have done a good job because that line of tile is still filling a spring fed water trough to this day. A lot more tile work was done at the back farm in various fields, and in later years, instead of one foot clay tile, 300-foot-long coils of plastic tile was used. Enough water runs from the tile that it feeds a water trough year-round. The overflow from the trough goes into a pond that Bob had Billy Smith build in 1999 and enlarge in 2001. The pond is over an acre in size and is nine feet deep. Grandpa was part of the first group of farmers in Perry County to utilize artificial insemination to breed his cows through First Pennsylvania Artificial Breeding Cooperative. The telephone number then was JAckson 35221, Lewisburg, Pa. and the service fee was $5.00.

A big change took place in 1952 when the thrashing machine was not needed anymore. Grandpa bought a Massy Harris 44 tractor, a John Deere 12A bin combine, a New Holland 77 baler to bale the hay and straw, and a corn picker to pick the corn. My father, Bill, and Uncle Ron started farming together in the late 1950's. A 1953 Ford Jubilee, 29 horsepower, was bought for $1600.00. Later on in the early 1960's, neighbor, Walter Goodling and his sons, Ed and Don, would come down with their harvester to chop corn silage. Later, Lee Casner, from west of Andersonburg, came to chop the corn silage. In January of 1955, Uncle Ron was a passenger in a car coming from Ickesburg to Blain on Route 17 where West Perry Farm Service (near Blain) is located, the driver lost control of the car going at a high rate of speed. Uncle Ron was thrown out and suffered many injuries including a concussion, broken ribs, punctured lung, and a severed nerve in his left arm. He was in very critical condition in the hospital for some time and was fortunate to have survived. He was laid up for eight months or more. Grandpa and dad did all the work until Uncle Ron recovered enough to help again. It doesn't matter what generation you talk about, there are always times where family members step up to help out in tough situations. 1956 was the first year of selling milk to Harrisburg Dairies in cans and in 1960 they bought their first bulk tank for milk. William R. Lyons bought the farm from his dad in January 27, 1958 and brother, Ron, bought the "Burchfield Farm" on the same date. They were known for having good milk production and were one of the first herds to be enlisted with the Dairy Herd Improvement Association (DHIA). At that time, they were one of the first three herds in Perry County, along with Alfred Albright of Landisburg and Mary Rice of Blain, to average over 600 lbs of butterfat per cow.

The Shermans Valley Railroad bed still exists on the first half of the lane to my brother's farm. In the winter of 1968, there was a chimney fire at the tenant house. A lot of cold temperatures, snow, and ice was around that winter. When the Blain Volunteer Fire Company raced to the scene, the new tanker went off the road and rolled over. Luckily, no one was hurt.

My mother, Kay L. Kettering, moved to Perry County from New Brighton, Pa. in 1948, when her father was transferred by the pipeline to Cisna Run. She was used to a big school in town and now she was attending the one room Cisna Run Schoolhouse, affectionately nicknamed "Corn Crib College". Mom liked going to school here so much better because you got to know everyone that you went to school with. The schoolhouse building was moved from Centre to Cisna Run on December 17, 1872. Dad attended the schoolhouse for seven years and because of good grades, he was told he could skip 8th grade. He attended 9th grade at Blain Union School and graduated from there three years later in 1949. Mom went to 8th grade at Cisna Run in the 1948/1949 school year and went on to graduate from Blain in 1953. The Cisna Run School closed its doors in 1949 and the Blain Union School sold the schoolhouse and one quarter acre of land more or less to Jere on April 6, 1953. Dad and mom married October 24, 1953, and went on to have five children; William, Diane, Robert, Sue, and Beth. Dad was born in the farmhouse and has lived there the last 88 years.

The summer of 1980 Uncle Ron had been dealing with arthritis for a few years and wasn't able to do as much on the farm. When I graduated in 1975 and Bob in 1979, dad decided that we could add another row of stalls in the barn to make room for 22 more cows to milk. Dad asked his cousin, Mort Loy, to head up the construction and another cousin, Boyd Kitner, was hired to do the excavating. Chuck Nyce and his mud mixer/assistant, Chester Lesh, laid the block. George Barnes sawed a lot of the lumber and cut some oak that was over twenty-six feet long for rafters. We had to dig a ditch by hand for the gutter behind the stalls because the existing wall wouldn't be taken out until later, and it was too close to use a backhoe. Dad, Bob, and I would dig with pick and shovel in the morning while it was shaded. Later dad would soak the next area to dig out, to soften the ground, for the next day. We had to dig it two feet wide and two feet deep for one hundred and ten feet long, so we worked at it for several days. When the building addition was under roof, the next job required us to use wheelbarrows to place all the fill, limestone, and concrete. It was late fall until the project was completed.

It's nice to have Shermans Creek close by unless it's during a time that it rains heavy and the water gets high. Different times over the years we would have pasture fence ripped out by high water and floating debris. Tangled up barbwire fence and posts were always a nightmare to work with. A time that stands out for me was when parts of a tree was pushed into the fence at the most western part of our pasture where it crosses over the usually small Cisna Run. I put on chest waders to cut the limbs away from the wire before it would tear down the fence. As I was working at it, my feet slipped off a ledge in the stream into a big hole that I didn't realize was there. Before I knew it, I was up to my neck in water with my waders filling fast. It was quite a scramble to get out of there. I was very happy to have Crista help me get out of those boots, full of water, soaking wet, and glad not to be laying at the bottom of Cisna Run!!

September 6, 1996, we had many inches of rain, high water, and the ground was saturated. A week later on September 12, through the night it began raining again. We did not realize how bad things were until we wanted to get the cows back in from pasture to milk in the morning. The 62 cows were trapped in water up to their knees on the other side of the now swollen Cisna Run and Shermans Creek was roaring with high water on the east and south sides of them. My brother, Bob and I, looked on helplessly as daylight broke, seeing the situation. Cows often follow their leader, when that happened, they started diving in to cross the high flowing water to get to the barn. The cows were swept off their feet as they continued into the water. The force of the water lifted them over the fence onto the road near the covered bridge. One by one they ran up the road through the barnyard gate and into the barn. Three were missing. One came up over the creek bank near Uncle Ron's house and three hours later, one came by way of Couchtown Road from Helen Bender's direction. She went about a mile before she washed onto land at a big turn in the creek at the base of the Burnt Hill Ridge. The last missing cow's remains were found by a trapper a few months later, many miles downstream where the creek divided. He brought us her neck chain. We were very fortunate and blessed not to have lost them all and now take no chances when water could get high.

Life on the farm is a lot of work, but over the years, we had lots of fun too. Uncle Ron was known as a fast runner and a great all around fast and slow pitch softball player in the 1950's and played at Cisna Run, Couchtown, New Germantown, Kistler, New Bloomfield, and Shermans Dale to name a few places that had fields. At New Germantown, he once hit a ball very high and deep. Another player proclaimed, if he would have leveled it off, the ball would have landed on the other side of the street. My father-in-law, Ron Emlet, was a baseball player for Loysville in the Perry-Juniata Sandlot League, who once struck out 20 batters in a 7-inning game in Liverpool. He hit three triples in one game and narrowly missed a 4th that went foul. My wife, Crista, apparently had some good athletic ability through her father as she excelled at West Perry in field hockey, basketball, and softball and was awarded the schools outstanding female athlete in 1974. My brother, Bob, and I, played baseball over the years. My brother was a really good all-around softball player for many years and was a member of the 1979 West Perry State Champion Baseball Team. Our brother-in-law, Jaymie Stum was considered by many as one of the best shortstops and leadoff hitters in the state during the 1979 and 1980 high school seasons.

I first played Perry-Juniata Sandlot Baseball in 1976 at Ickesburg through my good friend, Craig Sheaffer, where his father, Harry, was the manager. That was a really good team that won the championship. I went on to play at Blain who was led by player-manager, Gov Seager. The team featured many brother combinations including the Wilt's, Roy and Alan, the Reisinger's, Chip and Rick, the Swab's, Greg and C.A., the McMillen's brother-in-law, Hugh and Tom, and my brother, Bob and I. Barry Barns was a team leader along with other players such as Rob Neidigh, Dale Earnest, and Dan Rice. We won a league championship in 1978 and the playoffs in 1980. Some personal highlights were I pitched a 12-inning game beating Loysville 8-7. Winning a game against Port Royal 5-0 on 6-17-78. Greg Swab hit a 3 run HR, a triple play by Roy Wilt to Chip Reisinger, and Port Royal was limited to three hits. A game at Newport where we played under the lights to a 0-0 tie, through 6 innings before being rained out. I pitched against Ken Holtzapple and we each gave up a hit. Another game at Newport, in a one run game, Roy Wilt and I picked off a base runner at first to end the game. At Loysville, I pitched 66 pitches in the whole game, but lost 1-0 on a HR by Brent Milligan in the 6th inning. Losing a final playoff game at McAlisterville against Port Royal, when in the 8th inning of a tie game, Gov Seager was camped under a fly ball in center field, when the ball struck a tree limb, and it was declared a HR. A lot of memories from those years of baseball, but the thing that stands out the most are the friendships that have lasted a lifetime.

I pitched for Loysville the first two years that the team played in the West Shore Twilight League. There were a lot of great players on our team. Some highlights from being on that team for me was pitching our first game and beating Carlisle 6-3, winning against perennial power Mechanicsburg 6-5 in 8 innings, and beating New Cumberland 6-0, where they had 3 hits in the game, and we picked 3 runners off first base in 1 inning.

From 1998 to 2009, a group of us got together one night a year, at Doubleday Farm near Landisburg to play a baseball game. The owner had a former major league player present each week for the games. Over the years we were able to meet 19 big leaguers, talk, take pictures, and get autographs with them. Notable players that we met were Brooks Robinson, Maury Wills, Bill Mazoroski, Vida Blue, Ferguson Jenkins, John Kruk, Tony Oliva, George Foster, Jerry Koosman, Doc Ellis, Nellie Briles, Greg Luzinski, ElRoy Face, Ron Cey, Vernon Law, Al Bumbry, Willie Wilson, Ellis Valentine and John Candeleria. I've been a Pittsburgh Pirate fan since 1966, so it was really neat to meet some of them (six of these players were Pirates). We started our team with Gov Seager, Roy Wilt, Barry Barns, Ralph Albright, Ron Shambaugh, and I in 1998, and over the years we added different people to play. We always would get 10 players together including my brother, Bob, and the later years my sons, Ben and David, along with others to play each year. Another brother-in-law, Joe Karmazin, was my catcher for many of those years.

We played many years of Three Springs Church softball. Playing with friends was always fun and full of good memories and we had a lot of very successful seasons. Especially cool for me was the years playing with my brother, Bob, and my sons, Ben and David.

We were fortunate to have a cousin, Terry Brozenick, who was an avid and successful big game, waterfowl, and bird hunter who hunted all over North America. He shot a lot of game including the grand slam of wild sheep. In 1991, my brother, Bob, went along with him to Alberta, Canada, in 1994 to Texas, and 1997 to Saskatchewan, Canada. In 1992, I went along to Montana, in 1995 to South Dakota and in 1998, a trip to Alberta, Canada. My brother and I could never go together with Terry because one of us had to stay home with the cows. We were lucky to have Crista help the one who was at home with the barn work in those early years. Terry tragically died in 1999 on a trip to Alaska where he suffered a heart attack on Kodiak Island at 52 years of age. He laid the groundwork and instilled in me the desire to go out of state to hunt. Later, I made several trips to Wisconsin to archery hunt white tails and in recent years many trips to Virginia muzzle loader hunting. It's a nice getaway from the farm and many lifelong friends have been made over the years. My brother and I have enjoyed hunting at home on our farms as well.

On March 31, 1989, at the age of 57, dad suffered a heart attack and a few years later he had bypass surgery. It's now been 31 years since that, and he has been healthy throughout the years. He hasn't been able to do all the hard work that he used to do but has been invaluable to Bob and I for teaching us common sense and to do the right things. We realize that without his leadership and those before him, we wouldn't be able to do the things we have accomplished over these many years. To this day, he keeps himself busy driving Amish on local trips. Dad at 88, mom and Uncle Ron at 85, still like to mow their own yards.

We had always baled all of our hay dry and in small square bales, up to 25,000 bales a year. There were always neighbor kids around looking for work to earn money along with our own family to help unload wagons of hay. A memory that stands out was a day we had several fields ready to bale, a lot of help to unload wagons, and a good chance of rain late in the day. We were unloading and a man stopped in, saw a bale laying on the barn floor, picked it up and put it on the elevator for us. It wasn't on quite right and the bale caught on a log near the top. Before anyone could pull the plug to shut off the elevator, pieces of chain and paddles flew in all directions. It took us many hours to put it all back together. By the grace of God, we got the hay baled before it rained, and the cows milked. One other memory was a big hay day when mom's cousin, Bob Brucker, came for a visit with his wife, Marcia, and their two boys, Robby and Brian, from Camp Hill. He wanted them to experience a day on the farm. We unloaded seventeen loads that day and everyone was pretty tired. Eating supper after the evening milking, their dad, Bob said "eat up now because we are coming back tomorrow for more hay". The boys rolled their eyes and slumped their shoulders, "Oh no, no more!" It wasn't until the early 1990's that we started chopping haylage and that alleviated baling as many small bales as we use to. Neighborhood kids didn't seem to be as readily available as each year went by and we were counting more and more on our family to help unload. Daughter, Jenny, and husband, Nick, sons, Ben and David, Bob, and I were about it, for help towards the end and not all of us were there at the same time. A transition to chopping more haylage and baling big round bales has made life nicer and more efficient for getting our hay crops off and also a higher quality forage.

In 1994, when Bob and I took over the farming, we built a silo for haylage and started to do all no-till. Instead of buying a lot of other equipment, we had Dave Morrow plant corn, chop hay and corn. His business took off and he got really busy. Ed Martin and their operation was growing and they were buying bigger equipment. To help justify the expense, he offered to do some custom work for us to get things done in a more timely manner. Working together with great neighbors is a godsend in today's dairy farming economy. Merrimart (Martin's) and our other close by neighbors, Josh and Liza Loy, make Cisna Run a great place to live and work.

In January 2014, we finished the work in the morning and went home to eat breakfast. My dad called and said there was quite a commotion at the barn. I went back in to find cows laying in their stalls dead and then rushed around to shut off all the electric breakers and called an electrician. There were 9 cows dead and we turned the rest out of the barn. The electrician traced the wiring through each breaker until he found the short. A bare wire sent a surge of electric through the barn and that's what killed the cows. The problem was repaired, but the big job ahead was to get the dead cows out of the barn. Donny Bartch, Billy Rice, and Chris Comp came over from Merrimart and helped for several hours to get them out. We had to link chains together, pull the dead cows out of their stalls with the skid loader, and get them out through doorways. Then we loaded them on a dump truck and were buried in a compost pile. About the same time that this took place, a good friend of mine, Dick Metz, was going to be selling his cows. He offered for us to have first choice of his cows before selling them. That was quite an offer considering he was one of the top breeders of good cows in Perry County. Through Dick, we were able to replace our cows that were electrocuted with cows of very high quality.

In August 2016, we had a calf acting strangely, not wanting to drink, acting listlessly, and slobbering. We had the vet check her out and it was decided that there was a good chance it could have rabies. Possibly a rabid animal such as a skunk could have bitten the calf. We had to euthanize the calf, then dad and I took it to the lab on Cameron Street in Harrisburg to be checked. It came back positive! We had to vaccinate all the other calves near it and our dog, Buster. The State Veterinarian said anyone who had made contact with the calf should go for shots. My brother Bob, son David, grandson Adam, neighbor Charlie Rowe and myself all had made contact, so after the evening milking, we all went to the Carlisle Hospital for our first round of shots. We all got antibody shots in our rear ends and thighs, plus a booster in our shoulder. Over a two-week period, we had to go back 3 more times for additional booster shots in our shoulder. The hospital charged us a total cost of $92,000.00 and with the various insurance coverages among us, I had to pay over $4700.00 out of pocket. Through all of that, we were blessed to be okay.

For the most part I consider myself pretty healthy but on occasion, like anyone else, there are things that you have to deal with. On October 28, 1970, we were playing football in gym class at Blain. When I went up for a pass, I came down hard on my right arm and broke both bones. My mom took me to the Carlisle Hospital for my first experience of an operation and a cast on my arm. A few months later on my little sister, Beth's, sixth birthday, March 18, 1971, I fell down a hay hole and broke both bones in both arms. I had stepped out on the first rung of the ladder and got ahold of the hinged door too high. The door came down and so did I, nine feet onto the concrete. After a week in the hospital and seven weeks with both arms in casts, it is something not easy to forget. My mom, dad, and grandma had to help me with everything while I had those casts on. When getting a bath with Mr. Bubble soap suds, my brother would hold my arms out of the water as my grandma washed me. Carl Fuller, a teacher at Blain, came each evening to keep me up with my classes since I wasn't able to go back to school functions. Through the day, I would prop my arms on the handlebars of my bike and ride around for something to do. Somewhere around 2005, I had a cow swing her head hitting my left arm against a steel pipe and one bone was broken that time. That's enough broken arms, now I'm even on both sides. Another series of painful experiences have been kidney stones. My dad had some in the past and I started to get them too, about every two years apart for a total of six. It was painful and torture each time. I was able to pass all of them on my own except for one of them that measured seven millimeters. I had surgery with a laser to break it up into smaller pieces so it could pass. A stent had to be removed four days later which was another experience of a higher level of pain. To put that in plain words, it was like pulling barbwire out with fire flying at the same time. Two bouts with cellulitis are something not easy to forget. I came home from the barn one night with a sharp pain in my shin. The next morning there were blisters between my toes and my skin was red on my shin. The medicine kicked in right away and over a week it subsided. This happened about a year later with similar results so getting on it right away made the difference to be successful. Last but not least, many years ago, apparently a cow tramped on my right foot. I had cortisone shots over several years, but it got to be painful enough along with swelling, that I went to a surgeon. An earlier MRI had shown nothing, but an x-ray showed two toes completely detached from the foot plate. The surgery was two hours long, but it took three months for the swelling to go down to wear a shoe again. It was a long ordeal, but my foot is pain free now. Many people have gone through much worse, but these are things that I have dealt with and I am still able to continue doing things that I need to do, although it would be nice to slow down the aging process!

Sometimes people can leave an impression on your life, both how you felt about them while they were living, but also how they tragically lost their lives. Crista's younger brother, David Emlet, who at 26 years old was a fine young man in the prime of his life when he was shot and killed on the first day of Pennsylvania's firearms deer season, December 2, 1985. It happened in the dark before shooting time that morning as he crossed the field to take watch for a buck at daylight. He was carelessly shot by another hunter. His death made it hard for me to want to continue the Pennsylvania tradition of the first day of deer season or even want to hunt much around home. Crista was pregnant at the time and that's how we ended up naming our youngest son, David. A few years later, that led me to hunt out of state more readily. On July 15, 2018, my younger sister, Sue, was in an abusive marriage, unknown by us, was shot and killed by her husband at the age of 54. Sue had confided with a couple of her close friends about the domestic violence, and we also found things later that she had written. This rocked our whole families' world, and like David's death, still does. The way we lost these two loved ones has affected my overall desire to hunt, but I still enjoy my time away with the people I have gotten to know over the years. It is still hard to believe that Crista and I both have lost younger siblings the way we did.

No year ever turns out to be quite the same, especially with life on a dairy farm where so many things can happen that are totally out of your control. It can be the prices of what you buy or sell, things that can happen to your animals, and the weather. Being a dairy farmer is not just a job, but a completely different lifestyle every day of the year. You have to take one day at a time, enjoy the good, endure the bad, lean firmly on faith, family, and friends. As the year 2020 came around the price of milk was finally over $18/cwt. (hundred weight) and it was looking like we were going to have a favorable year ahead. In early March the Covid-19 pandemic hit, schools closed, restaurants closed, and the economy began to crash. On April 2, 3, and 4, all Harrisburg Dairies shippers were asked to dump all of their milk as there was no place for it to go. We ran 13,522 pounds down the drain into the manure storage. At a price of $18/cwt. the lost milk was valued at $2433.96. On June 24 we had to dump an additional 8,213 pounds. As the year progressed, we were able to sell all of our milk until December 22 when we received word again that we all would have to dump more milk. For 8 of the next 9 days, 31,240 pounds of milk went down the drain. Forty percent of Harrisburg Dairies business is schools and food service, but we became very blessed when they found a home for the extra milk to avoid more dumping. During the late Spring months, the price of milk had dropped to as low as $9/cwt. for some farmers depending on who they shipped to. If you take a 100,000 pounds of milk and the price drops $1/cwt., you lose a $1,000.00, An example would be: An amount of milk at 100,000 pounds at $18/cwt. would amount to $18,000.00 or the same amount of milk at $9/cwt. would amount to $9,000.00. We are fortunate to have bought the federal based insurance Dairy Margin Coverage (DMC) that came with a premium of close to $2000.00. We have 1.5 million pounds locked in to pay us indemnity payments when the milk price drops below the $9.50 income over feed cost figure. During these unprecedented and difficult times, the United States Department of Agriculture (USDA) developed the Coronavirus Food Assistance Program (CFAP) to help dairy farmers survive during these trying times. The federal direct payments are not considered a handout, but rather the government's recognition that our nations farmers are essential to our nation's future. These much-needed funds will not make farmers whole but are a lifeboat in uncharted waters. Bad situations with cattle happened like never before for us in these same few weeks of time. A good cow with a "tramped teat", a dry cow knocked another dry cow down that couldn't get back up, and a pregnant cow, Rebecca, due in August, with a record of 328 days in milk, 36,340 pounds, 1175 pounds of butterfat, 952 pounds of protein, injured herself that resulted in another one that couldn't get up. We sent two cows to market, one fell in the trailer, could not walk again, and the other one arrived at the plant deceased of unknown reasons. They both seemed fine when they left our farm. To add to the misery, a cow that was due to calve in four days was lying dead in the freshening pen one morning. In all, we lost five cows in a short period of time that was out of our control and unexpected. Their beef value alone would have amounted to a nice sum of money considering at the time, the dressed weight price was around $1.15/pound. If they would have averaged 750 pounds dressed weight times $1.15, each one would have been worth $862.50 or $4,312.50 for all five. That isn't even taking into consideration the loss of their calves, milk production, sentimental values, and stress! In the end, we received nothing for four of them and a bill for $105.50 to remove the one that died on the truck. Things started to turn around the next week when one of the red and white holsteins, Gwen, had a cool red and white heifer calf that we named Gail. The weather had been cold and wet into the middle of May, so no corn or beans were planted yet. The forecast didn't sound good for the week of May 18th, but it changed. We mowed hay on Monday and chopped it Tuesday for the silo. We were able to use one of Merriment's 15-foot drills on Wednesday to plant the soybeans. Chris Comp and Donny Bartch made it over with their 12-row Kinze cornplanter and planted all of our corn on Thursday. We received a little rain on Friday. The year started out wet but throughout the summer and fall the weather was very dry and the crops suffered. Usually, we have many acres of corn to shell but this year all the acres were chopped for silage. We can never say thank-you enough to Donny Bartch and Merrimart Farms for their willingness to do custom work and for being such good neighbors. They bend over backwards to make things happen in a timely manner and beat the weather whenever possible. As it is written here, you can understand how without a faith in God, it would be much harder to persevere life on a farm.

The pandemic continued to affect many people and businesses as 2020 ended and we headed into the new year. Our family farms have been shipping milk to Harrisburg Dairies since our father started in 1956. The majority of those 65 years were with Harrisburg Dairies other than a few years with a couple other markets. In recent years and especially the last year, due to the pandemic, it has been a struggle for them to find a home for all the milk its producers make. They have diverted millions of pounds over this time frame along with having their farms dump milk those 13 days in 2020. On March 26, the President of Harrisburg Dairies stopped at our farm to inform us that they are letting some farms go, including ours, not pulling names out of a hat this time, but using an internal process to determine farms to release in order to manage their milk supply without dumping. Along with the visit came a letter. The letter to its valued farm producers first put blame on the Pa. Milk Marketing Board stating that basically Harrisburg Dairies wouldn't be able to make its farmers dump their milk without being paid something for it. Additionally, even though we added no cows to our herd, the letter stated that many farms increased herd size and production, causing them disappointment, more surplus, and great expense to them to divert more pounds. The letter continues saying that since September 2020 they have seen a significant decrease in the quality of milk from several farms along with a substantial increase in farm re-inspections. Despite the considerable effort and expertise of the Farm Inspector, many producers remain uncooperative for his requests for his improvements. We did all we could, bending over backwards to satisfy our inspector, never showed disrespect, never uncooperative, spent more than $10,000 per his requests, to have a milk market, knowing full well that few if any other opportunities are available. Since September 2020 we were inspected twice with scores of 96 and 93. According to our Dairy One reports our SCC counts for the last 3 months were good at 123,000, 173,000, 169,000 and low bacteria counts. The last time our inspector was here I even thanked him for his guidance on our improvements. Our reward for all our efforts was a 28 Day Release Notice. The pre-inspection pictures that we took, in my opinion are worth a thousand words! Thankfully, a week after receiving our notice of not having a market for our milk, Maryland & Virginia Milk Producers Cooperative Association gave us the opportunity to market our milk with them. Our contract is signed and our first inspection is completed with a score of 99. When one door closes, God opens another, possibly a blessing in disguise.

We know for sure that if we did not have a strong faith in God, it would be hard to handle the things life throws at us; the loss of loved ones, hardships, and just the day to day living the life of a farmer, etc. We are members and attend Three Springs Church of the Brethren since 1996. Over the years we have been blessed by strong leadership including Pastor John Kipp, Pastor Ed Weaver, and current Pastor, Brad Bennett. They, along with those we worship with, all have the ability to instill in us a stronger walk with the Lord and help us try to live life in the right way.

I, William G. Lyons, married Crista L. Emlet September 16, 1978, and we went on to have three children: Jennifer, Benjamin, and David. We bought the farm from my father on January 1, 1994. My brother, Bob, bought Uncle Ron's farm August 29, 1991. Since then, Bob and I have been partners at the farms. We have participated in a three-year Environmental Quality Incentives Program (EQIP) where we completed sixteen conservation projects including manure storage, riparian forest buffer, and stream bank fencing, just to name a few. Also, fifteen years of Conservation Stewardship Programs (CSP) to step up our conservation practices. Things are done much differently nowadays than in the past. I'm not sure if I could stand up to the tremendous amount of hard work those before me did. I am very proud of their accomplishments and to be able to call these earlier generations family. The farm has been awarded the "Dairy of Distinction". The land was preserved by the Perry County Land Preservation Board in 2011, and more recently, the farm was acknowledged as a "Century Farm", as it has been owned and operated by the same family for over 100 years. Our youngest son, David, worked for us as much as he could and helped run a three-man partnership that hauled liquid manure for up to 30 farms, and other custom farming for nine years. We aren't sure how he handled all the long hours he put in. In 2018, Bob had both hips replaced and was laid up for a total of 15 weeks. That's when David worked at getting out of his partnership because he couldn't be two places at one time. Then I had foot surgery the end of 2019 and wasn't able to do anything for 12 weeks. We would never have gotten everything done if we didn't have David and our other family members helping us out. Presently, David, a fifth generation, works full time on our farms with my brother and me. He is valuable to us and can do anything! Our oldest grandson, Adam Campbell, a sixth generation, has become an all-around big help for us. His sister, our granddaughter, Carla Campbell, steps up and helps us out whenever needed. It is great to have our oldest son, Ben, and son-in-law, Nick Campbell, who are always there to help out when needed. We are truly blessed to be part of a family farm and wish the best to the future generations and all that they will do. As our family progresses into our second century, things look promising to continue the legacy.

Early Memories in Perry County

Storyteller Jerry A. Clouse

Although I'm a native of the Doubling Gap area, I often crossed the Blue Mountain in my youth. Both my grandfather Clouse and grandfather Warner were born in the Landisburg area. I particularly became familiar with Henry's Valley where my grandfather Charlie "Pap" Clouse was born and raised. An annual spring outing involved the entire family (Mom, Dad, Pap, my sister, brother, and myself) in hunting "mushrooms", actually morels, in the Valley. It was always fun to see who could spot the brown, cone shaped, pitted fungus first or who could find the most. Usually, a lunch had been packed, and we'd picnic either at the Sundy place, the "Old Rancher" cabin or at the Sherman's Mountain fire tower. It was always fun to run up and down the tower.

In the summer, huckleberries were gathered along the dusty roads on the crest of Bower Mountain. Of course, we were always on the lookout for snakes, and we'd try to catch a glimpse of the "bear ponds". My grandfather, who had been a foreman at the CCC Camp in the Valley, would tell the story of the man who was killed during road construction at "Deadman's Curve". Again, a picnic lunch may be had at various locations. Among these, was the "Cow Pens", near Camp Gnat, where early in the century farmers had rounded up their young cattle after summer grazing in the mountain. This spot was located along the Three-Square Hollow Road which was the main entrance into western Henry's Valley from Cumberland County. Sometimes, Dad would bring the Bunsen burner along, and we'd have a mini cookout with grilled hot dogs which was a special treat.

During the winter, sledding expeditions would take place on the mountainous roads through the Valley. We had packed our "Lightning Guider" sleds in the trunk of the car. Often, it would seem as though we were the only people in the mountain traveling the snow-covered roads. Beginning in my grade-school years, I tagged along with my great uncle Albert Clouse, my grandfather, and their friends on trips through Henry's Valley. Albert, who worked as a butcher for Marlin "Buz" Cohick in Newville well into his eighties, would pick up friends and my grandfather along the Doublin' Gap Road on the way to the Valley. These visits occurred either on Wednesday afternoons when all the stores in Newville closed or on Sunday afternoons when it was good to escape the house. I came to enjoy the old men's stories and reminiscences on the ride through the Valley where then, there were no longer permanent residents. Although I didn't know it at the time, I had become hooked on history. I went on to write my master's thesis on the stories of Henry's Valley and to become a co-founder of The Perry Historians in 1976.

Memories from Ickesburg Elementary

1957/1958 – 1963/1964   1ST THROUGH 6TH GRADES

Storyteller Polly McMillen Eby

Built in 1927, Ickesburg Elementary used to be a high school, Ickesburg High School. It remained a high school until the late 40s or early 50s when it became a grade school. My father, Perry McMillen and most of his siblings and cousins attended high school in this building. He graduated in 1934. The following are memories of my attendance when I went to grade school in this building from 1st through 6th grades.

The reading classes, in Miss McAlicher's 1st Grade class, were named after birds. I remember sitting up front, on little chairs, and looking at the perfect way to print letters, on the hard board above the chalk board, while waiting for my turn to read.

Reading Dick and Jane books and their adventures with their pets Puff, the cat; and Spot, the dog.

We worked in the 1st Grade workbooks which I still have.

Miss McAlicher loved cats so if you had a skinned knee, she painted kitty cats on it. We sat on a long table at the back of her room, legs dangled off the side, and waited for the mercurochrome to sting.

I remember that we chewed a red dental tablet in 1st or 2nd Grade, which stuck to the part of our teeth that we missed when we brushed our teeth that morning. The exercise taught us to brush our teeth thoroughly.

I was in 2nd Grade when I was in the Mayflower Court wearing a puffy white dress, with petticoat and a shawl. Tom Powell also represented 2nd Grade. The court included: 1st Grade, Deb Cook & Steve Reisinger; 3rd Grade, Marlene Sheffer & Tom Sheaffer; 4th Grade, Sally Swartz and Keith Saltsburg; 5th Grade, Ellen Snyder and Dave Powell; Special Ed, Ruth Nace and Linda Rice. Queen of the Mayflower was Kathy Shiffer and King of the Mayflower was John Shotsberger. I only know this because I have the program in my scrapbook. Gloria Zellers, 6th Grade, designed the cover called The Seasons.

In 2nd Grade I discovered that my best friend, Sue (Reisinger) Binger, who also lived on a farm and had cows, did not like white milk either, so she brought chocolate syrup to school to stir into her milk. Why didn't I think of that?

Students of 1st and 2nd Grades were not allowed to go up the wooden steps to the upper level where 3rd through 6th Grades and the Office was located. There were Safety Patrols, wearing white cross bands on their upper body, positioned at the top of the steps to keep students from sneaking up. When I was older, I became a Safety Patrol, monitoring who was allowed upstairs and who had to walk up or down the stairs again if they were caught running.

We carried our trays to our rooms, from the basement cafeteria, to eat our lunch. If you were in 1st or 2nd Grade it was 9 steps. If you were in 3rd through 6th Grade, you carried them another flight of stairs for 10 additional steps.

The awful green medicinal-smelling soap in the restroom was not a good memory.

We had several recesses which everyone looked forward to. When the bell rang, we ran outside. Another bell rang to let us know that recess was over, and the slow trek was made to return to the schoolhouse. Favorite games, when the fields were too wet to play softball/baseball, were Prisoner's Base and Dodge Ball. The boys had a baseball team, and, not to be excluded, the girls had a softball team. We also had a swing set, which probably accommodated six to eight children, and a merry-go-round that was for those brave kids who managed to hold on without falling off. The circular momentum started either by running and pushing against the inside rails or doing the same on the outside. If you pushed it from the outside, it was a dangerous leap to the seat, and then you had to swivel around, all the while hanging on for dear life.

The grandstand had assigned areas for 1st through 6th grades with 1st grade having the bottom row and ascending in grades and rows until it reached near the top. Due to its steepness, only 6th Graders were allowed on the very top rows. The grandstand was where we watched games or other school functions where the baseball diamond was the center of attention.

Ickesburg students joined the other elementary school students, in the Green Park Union School district, to perform operettas. One operetta that I can single out, we made bumblebee costumes out of black and yellow strips of crepe paper and performed on stage at Green Park Union High School. Unfortunately, I did not save any programs from the operettas.

As I told my friend, Sue Reisinger Binger, the school gave us incentives to want to succeed by simple things like the steps at the school. You were not allowed to take the wooden steps upstairs until you reached 3rd Grade. The outside concrete steps were only to be used by the 5th and 6th Graders. Lastly, only 6th Graders were allowed to be on the upper row of the Grandstand.

In the basement was the cafeteria, a large gathering space for watching science or nature movies, instrument lessons with Mr. Baird Collins, TB shots administered by our nurse, Mrs. Miller with Mrs. Glassburn assisting; and disaster drills where we stood against the wall with our heads touching and arms protecting our heads; plus various other gatherings. Also found in the basement was the Special Education

Classroom, the Custodian's room and the favorite, the candy counter! The "back steps" were used to access the second floor which came out at the Office and 3rd Grade Classroom.

A "Walker" was a person who lived in town and did not have to use the bus for transportation. They were allowed to leave a few minutes early before the buses arrived. I longed for the day that I, too, could use the front steps like the "Walkers" did, because, otherwise, no one else was allowed on those steps. My dream came true when I took piano lessons from Mrs. Alvin Fuller, who lived in Ickesburg and was also the wife of our principal. Then my sister, Perrietta (who also took piano lessons), and I joined the "walkers".

No one wanted to appear in the Office for a paddling, for we knew that if we got paddled at school, we were to expect to get paddled at home. Mrs. Morrison patrolled the school yard during recess, gathered up offenders under her outstretched arms and marched them into the Office where each one was paddled before returning to class.

Our teachers' names were 1st Grade, Miss Catherine McAlicher; 2nd Grade, Mrs. Floy Crum; 3rd Grade, Mrs. Nora Bixler; 4th Grade, Mrs. Regina Rice; 5th Grade, Mrs. Isabelle Dillman; 6th Grade, and also Principal, Mrs. Martha Morrison; lastly, Superintendent, Mr. Alvin Fuller.

Cooks were Mrs. Kathryn Kerr, Mrs. Anna Johnson

Custodian: Mr. Boden.

Musical Instrument Instructor: Mr. Baird Collins.

My favorite foods from the cafeteria were homemade sugar donuts, Mrs. Kerr's recipe, sticky buns, Johnny Marzetta, fish sticks, and peanut butter sandwiches. Our milk was in a glass milk bottle with a cardboard cap. I did not care for school food throughout my entire school years. One day, after Mrs. Kerr, one of the cooks, talked to me about not eating everything on my tray. I exclaimed, "My mother does not cook like this!" I was saying this as I looked at the government- issued industrial size cans of peas, etc. stacked up in the storeroom. That was the same room where you handed over your money to purchase a weekly or monthly lunch ticket. As an adult, I met her at a Crozier Reunion where I learned she was my future mother-in-law's sister! They were Croziers.

Most students purchased a weekly lunch ticket which was green and the ticket collector would clip the day off at the line. My family purchased monthly tickets which were red, and the ticket collector would snip off the number day of the week. All the days of the month were printed around 4 sides. I wanted to look like the other kids and have a green ticket, but Mother had four children, so once a month was enough check writing for her.

Ninety years after it was built, I looked forward to the Open House of Ickesburg Elementary building in May of 2017. It was attended by many past students who wished to tour the remodeled building. After touring the entire building, top floor to basement, refreshments were served in an area that used to hold both 5th and 6th grades, now used as an event place. As we took our seats at the round tables with past students and friends, many conversed and reminisced of happy memories many years ago. What a meaningful day.

"You don't go out and have fun until the work is done!"
MY STORY GROWING UP IN RURAL PERRY COUNTY

Storyteller Deb Reisinger Nyce
Recorded by Debra Kay Noye

Grace Shope and Robert "Dick" Rumberger Reisinger had a dairy farm, between Ickesburg and Kistler. Deb learned early on, that the farm work and housekeeping, had to be accomplished before all else. Her mother and Dad were hard workers, who instilled in her, that hard lesson, which still resonates with her today.

Deb has three brothers, Grady, Robert "Bob" and Danny, who, because she was the only daughter in the family, accused her of living a "charmed life". Surely, they were overlooking a few times when Deb filled in with the milking chores, so they could play baseball, on the Ickesburg Midget team. Thankfully, milkers were electrified, which made for easier milking, than the days of milking cows by hand. The milk was strained and put into extremely heavy metal cans, which were placed in a cooling tank, full of cold water. Deb couldn't lift the cans, but recalls that her dad and Wayne Hart, who drove milk truck, had no problem. The milk was hauled, by truck to the Sunnydale milk plant, in Elliottsburg, which was located near to where Tuscarora Hardwoods stands today. The metal cans would then be returned for refilling. Deb's mother had a pasteurizer, making the milk safer for the family's use, in drinking and cooking.

Deb and her brothers, visiting cousins and friends, would often play in the barn. One time almost proved fatal, when they were playing in the oats bin. Deb had climbed into the full oats bin, while her playmates were pulling the grain out at the bottom. This caused her to sink down into the oats and become covered. Not able to get herself out, she remembers her father came to the rescue, pulling her to safety. It is dangerous around the farm and kids need to be careful and aware, of what might happen.

Feeding the chickens and gathering the eggs, into the bright yellow rubber coated wire baskets, was an occasional chore, that Deb hated. Dealing with a hen sitting on her eggs, in the nest and not wanting to be disturbed, was something Deb really disliked! After taking the eggs to the cool farmhouse basement, her mother would then use her egg washer, to remove any debris, from the shells. The egg washer made the job simpler, than hand wiping each egg. Her mother used an egg scale to size the eggs, before putting them into "egg flats" and large cardboard boxes for shipping. Deb's Uncle Joe Bender and Ron Emlet were two of the men, she fondly remembers, who picked up the eggs for Emlet Brothers in Loysville.

In later years, her mother supplied eggs for Harry Campbell, once he bought Patterson's store re-naming it, Campbell's Grocery. It remained at that location, for many years. Back in those days, neighbors like Emilie Maxton, Millie Smith (Mrs. Glenn) dropped in to buy eggs. Of course, purchasing eggs meant a long, chatty visit, when all the news of the day, would be shared.

Household chores meant dusting all the rooms, running the sweeper, and mopping the linoleum kitchen floor. Her mother would wax the kitchen floor on hands and knees. The upstairs bathroom was heated, but none of the bedrooms, until her youngest brother was born. Then, one bedroom was heated. Deb recalls the tiny closets and the lack of closets in the bedrooms, which was typical in the early farmhouses.

There was an outhouse on the farm, but the family didn't use it, other than in an emergency! Whew!! Lucky, they didn't rely on the outhouse, because when she was pretty young, Deb accidentally burned it to the ground. Like most kids, she was curious and decided to play with some matches. Now the two-seater was used to store gardening tools, straw bales, and supplies like lime, some of which certainly ignited the outhouse's demise. The end result was the only real licking, "butt smacking", she remembers receiving from her father. The outhouse was rebuilt.

Her parents were disciplinarians. Brother Grady reportedly buried their mother's pot stick across the road, from the house, when that field was being plowed up for seeding. Having been in the service and serving in World War II, her father was one not to disrespect and he had the final say in matters.

Deb is very clear that her parents were not abusive, but there was no "gray" area, with respect to "right and wrong".

***

Cooking and baking were something her mother did, but Deb recalls peeling potatoes and making iced tea for her dad. Her cousin, Connie Barnes, who was a few years older and lived on Route 17 traveling toward Millerstown from Ickesburg, taught her how to bake pies. The pie crust recipe Connie used was one of Lenore Trostle's pastry recipes. Lenore Trostle was the Home Economics teacher at Green Park Union, and West Perry Schools. She lived on a farm, outside of Green Park.

The Saville Mixettes 4-H club taught her cooking, sewing, and camping skills. Some of her 4-H leaders were Joanne Fritz and Maryann Smith. One year, Deb, with the help of cousin, Sue Reisinger, put together an insect collection. The collection was exhibited for judging, and for others to see at the 4-H Roundup, held at the Knouse farm, outside of Ickesburg.

Myrtle Barnes would come to the farm every Christmas season, and the women would bake many batches of raisin filled cookies. But it was the smell of freshly fried Fasnachts, that greeted Deb upon her arrival home from school, that brings back fond memories. Grandmother Reisinger mixed up the traditional potato doughnut dough the night before. Bringing it to the farmhouse in the morning, the dough would be rolled out and cut into rounds with the hole in the center, made with a thimble. After rising, the doughnuts would be put into extremely hot melted lard, till they were puffed and nicely browned, on each side. Once finished, they were placed, into brown paper shopping bags containing granulated sugar. The bag would be gently shaken, allowing the sugar to coat the warm Fasnacht Day treat. The farmhouse kitchen table was completely covered in doughnuts.

Pulling weeds, planting and maintaining the family garden were not on Deb's chore list. She did help to pick green beans and roasting ears.

There were sweet black, and red sour cherry trees on the farm, which needed picking when the cherries were ripe. Her mother used a cherry seeder, so Deb didn't have to delicately squeeze the seed, from the ripe juicy cherry. The fruits, beans, corn, and other vegetables were canned and/or frozen by her mother.

Going to Knouses, outside of Ickesburg to pick blueberries (as a condition of visiting with her favorite cousins), was something Deb didn't enjoy either. Deb, Linda, Judy and Connie picked blueberries, for resale by the Knouse family. Her earnings for time spent picking, in the heat and swarms of gnats, were a whopping seventy-five cents, because her heart just wasn't into the sticky task of plucking berries, into a big, heavy bucket.

Laundry wasn't on her radar either, but she did help to iron the handkerchiefs and pillowcases. They were easy items that she "learned" how to iron, as a girl. Her father wore a soft work pant, with a small cuff at the bottom of the legs. Thankfully, they didn't get ironed, because her mother used what Deb referred to as a stretcher. It was metal and placed into each pant leg. As they dried on the stretchers, they would be creased and wrinkle free.

Deb's Aunt Marg Barnes made a lot of her three daughters' clothes, which meant a lot of nice "hand me downs". It was a "big deal" to Deb, to receive a new dress at Christmas and Easter. She was especially excited, when she received a record player one year at Christmas, and along with it, a Bing Crosby Christmas album. Chatty Kathy and Tiny Tears were dolls she received as presents, when she was a little girl.

Christmas meant going to Grandparents Elsie (Wilt) and Frank Lee Shope, beyond Adair's Covered Bridge at Cisna Run, to cut down a Christmas tree. Her grandfather raised and sold Christmas trees. Back at the farm, the tree was decorated, with colored lights and various Christmas balls. Deb's grandparents, on her father's side of the family, were Phoebe (Rumberger) and Charles Elmer Reisinger.

As a teen and member of her church's youth group, Christmas found Deb climbing into Reverend James Gold's VW van and caroling around town, and even as far as, Bob and Lenore Irvine's home, outside of Ickesburg on Route 17. Rev. Gold ministered at the Lutheran Church in Ickesburg and would plan activities, for the youth group. Every fall, Deb looked forward to the hayrides, and party afterwards.

As youngsters, Deb's Mother would sometimes take the children to the Saville Lutheran Church, which is no longer standing. They walked home from church. Often, neighbors would give them a ride, too. The church had wasps in the chapel. To this day, Deb is afraid of bees.

The tiny village of Saville, west of Ickesburg, was where Deb went to Ross Titzel's Store. The store was wooden, with high ceilings. The glass enclosed candy counter stood front and center, but what caught Deb's eye was the doll, on the overhead shelf. Titzels sold packaged goods and had a cooler with glass soda bottles. Soda was a rare treat, for Deb.

Reisingers had a black and white tv, which had three channels. Deb's favorite movie to this day is the Wizard of Oz. Walt Disney's Wonderful World of Disney was watched often, and she enjoyed the movie, Peter Pan. The family watched Lawrence Welk on Saturday nights.

Aunt Marge Barnes had a tv but could get only one channel. Deb spent a lot of time, at her home, with her cousins. It was the only place, where she would not get home sick, when spending the night. One wintry, snowy, and frigid evening, at Aunt Marg's, Deb and her cousins, Connie and George, decided to walk to Ickesburg (in the dark), to buy more ice cream. Needless to say, Deb got stuck in a snow drift, and had to be helped out. What ya did for prepackaged ice cream, back in the day! Over the years, Connie and Deb would pull many a prank and stunt.

***

Fresh fruits, like watermelon and lopes were trucked by hucksters around to the farm, in the summertime. Ice cream products were also delivered. A bakery truck brought sliced bread and baked goods, always arriving around dinner "lunch" time. Wearing a uniform, the bread man would come into the house displaying, a variety of baked items, in a covered metal container, so her mother could choose what she needed.

Even though they raised beef cattle and hogs, Deb's family didn't do their own butchering. Clair Gutshall, from Blain, who worked with her father at the sawmill, butchered their hogs. Joe Trostle, a friend and livestock hauler, from Green Park, transported the animals for her dad. Virginia and Martin Dum, from Elliottsburg, also hauled animals for them. Clair Gutshall made ponhaus and puddin' meat, and cans full of lard. Deb remembers helping to wrap the meat, with the heavy butcher paper, and sealing it with freezer tape. Her father would pickle the tongue and make pig souse. Her mother would can beef and pork sirloin, for a "quick meal", when time was short. It was tender and delicious.

Their beef cattle were slaughtered at Duke Trostle's butcher shop, outside of Loysville, behind the Tressler Lutheran Children's home, or present day, Youth Development Center. Joe Trostle again hauled the cattle. The family, again, wrapped the cuts of meat. Her mother would roast the beef heart, filled with a bread stuffing.

Ickesburg Elementary School, at the east end of Ickesburg, was where Deb spent her first six years, in school. First and second grades were on the first floor, and the basement housed the cafeteria. Miss McAlicher was a stern first grade teacher, while Mrs. Smiley was somewhat gentler. Mrs. Smiley shared with Deb's Mother that as a student, she was always in a hurry, to get her work finished, so she could go get a book to read. Who'd ever think a teacher would negatively remark, about a student wanting to read! But other subjects were obviously affected.

Deb remembers the homemade meals cooked and served in the school basement. Anna Johnson and Kathryn Kerr were the kindest of school cooks, who made a lasting impression on Deb. They were also church friends, and Sunday School teachers. She loved the Johnny Marzette, soups, and corn bread. She and her "best friend for life", Pam McMillen, enjoyed those wholesome meals together, and still talk about them!

Starting with third grade, Deb had to carry her tray of milk and food up two flights of steps, to eat in her classroom. Many trays were spilled, by students, trying to navigate the steps. Deb always felt so bad when that happened. It was embarrassing for the students.

Sixth grade teacher, and school principal, Mrs. Morrison was quite the disciplinarian. She didn't spare the paddle, in her upstairs "office," which she welded loud enough for the entire student body to hear.

Music class was a favorite, as well as singing in the chorus.

Deb remembers walking from school on an outing, to Philip Cook's home, between Ickesburg square and the movie theatre. Cooks had a pony, which was saddled, and the students were allowed to ride. When it came Deb's turn, the pony took off running, down through the field. Luckily, she didn't fall off! Mrs. Cook treated them to Oreo cookies and lemonade. It made the day special, for the first-grade class.

Her dad sold the dairy cows in 1965, and afterward raised beef cattle and hogs. He worked, with his brother, John, at a sawmill, outside of Millerstown, in the abandoned Breyer's Creamery building. He became the sawyer and they sold lumber, mulch, and sawdust. To Deb's knowledge, he was the only one, who knew how to run the saw.

When Deb turned twelve years old, her mother got her a job at the Hi-Way Theatre, in Ickesburg, beside present day, Tom Powell's Garage. She was responsible for selling candies from the glass candy counter and collecting tickets from patrons. She never worked in the bowling alley beneath the theatre. She was allowed, to watch the movies, and especially remembers Gone with the Wind. Her earnings supplemented her fifty-cent weekly allowance from her parents.

Her experience, behind the counter gave her a foot hold in the business world. Skills, such as knowing how to count out change, save your earnings, as well as spending them wisely, were important lessons, which complimented her upbringing.

But, what I noticed, was the twinkle in her eye when she spoke of her cousin Connie and the devilment they got into throughout early adulthood. Now, that's another story!!

Last Class at the Elliottsburg Schoolhouse

Storyteller Dorothy "Dee" Shiffer Wesner

I was part of the last first grade class (1953-1954) at the Elliottsburg two room school. Punk Carlin picked up the Pleasant Valley kids (1st-12th) in his woody station wagon. There weren't many of us. He dropped us off first then took the older kids to their schools.

Catherine McAlicher (Cassie) was our teacher. First and second grade were on the first floor, and third and fourth grade were on the second floor. I don't think I was ever on the second floor, so I have no idea what it looked like.

There was a big wood furnace in the back of the first-floor room. I think keeping it stoked was one of Miss McAlicher's duties. There was a wood room off to the left as you came in the door and a big pile of wood outside. If you got in trouble, you had to bring wood inside to the wood room.

In the back of the classroom, there was a sink and hand pump – no indoor plumbing. There was a peg board over the sink. When school started, you brought a mug with your name on it and hung it on a peg. Needless to say, we all brought lunches and thermoses from home. No indoor plumbing also meant outhouses. They were out back of the building.

Miss McAlicher took turns teaching each grade. We had work to do when she was on the second-grade side. We sat at a low table with 4-6 kids at each table. I can remember reading Dick and Jane books, doing letters and numbers, etc. There was a big blackboard that stretched across the whole classroom. There was a permanent chart near the middle. We took turns filling it in with numbers 1-100. I remember doing that one time and I missed a number. The second graders were whispering to me so I could fix it. I look back fondly on that.

For Valentine's Day, Miss McAlicher erected a cardboard structure with a barred window like the post office. It was decorated and maybe 8 feet long by 6 feet high. We went to the "post office" to get our Valentine mail. Valentine's Day made an impression. I don't remember much about Christmas. I'm sure there was a tree.

The playground was out back. The boys played ball. I don't remember playing back there much. I remember playing out front with other girls. There was a big, maybe pine, tree out front. I remember one of the older girls hanging upside down on the branches. I think her first name was Sue.

We went to Ickesburg for second grade and Messiah Lutheran Church acquired the Elliottsburg school. They tore it down and made it a parking lot. We were all members of Messiah so Miss McAlicher continued to be a big part of my life until I got married in 1968.

Farmer's Daughters

STORIES FROM THE 1950'S AND 1960'S

Storyteller Polly McMillen Eby

My parents, Perry and Ruth McMillen, met on a blind date! They were introduced by his sister, Lois, and her husband, the Rev. George Leukel II from Centre Presbyterian Church in Loysville. She was a beautician and a "city" girl from Marysville, daughter of storekeepers Henry and Lizzie Cox of Cox's Grocery in the same town. My father was the 6th generation on the McMillen Homestead, one mile east of Kistler on Route 17, along McMillen Road. Now it is owned by 7th generation McMillen, Clee and Caroline McMillen.

My parents' farm, what the McMillens called the Lower Farm, was one mile west of Ickesburg on Route 17, 1297 Tuscarora Path. When daddy returned from WWII, S/SGT in the US Army, Company B, 1877th Engineer Aviation Engineers in the CBI Theater (China, Burma, India), he continued farming and then brought his bride to the farmhouse that needed extensive remodeling. The only thing mother insisted on, before she moved in, was an inside bathroom!

To their union, four girls were born; two brunettes and two redheads (like mother and Grandfather Cox) named Perrietta, Polly, Pam and Phyllis. Perrietta and Phyllis were the brunettes and Polly and Pam were redheads. Included in the 307-acre farm was 100 acres of woodland which stretched one and a quarter mile long, and a patch of woods, below the house, which was situated along Panther Creek. The rectangle field was wide and one mile long. There was a large pasture above the farmhouse and two meadows, separated by our dirt lane, below the house. Farm buildings included the two-story, four bedrooms, living room, den, beauty shop, and one bath farmhouse; large bank barn; wagon shed; car shed; chicken house; woodshed and washhouse. The farm was our world! The following are my stories from my life on the farm.

Blackie and Goldie
Although we were raised around horses, we never became good riders. Safety was always daddy's foremost concern since he was raising girls. We were only allowed to ride the horses, Goldie and Blackie, with my father's presence and availability. Goldie was a palomino with a menacing backbone that was

very uncomfortable to sit on. Blackie was a dapple gray that was very suspicious of any rider on her back. We always rode bare back. Before being introduced to reins, we just grabbed a hunk of mane in our right hand and another hunk of mane in the left hand. Mostly we just rode the horses out the field lane at a slow pace. However, Blackie had other plans for Perrietta one day. Daddy was helping me with Goldie when Blackie decided to escape with Perrietta on her back. Flying through the open barnyard gate, Blackie took off with Perrietta screaming. With one leap, daddy hoisted himself up on Goldie, and behind me, as we galloped after the runaway Blackie. After a short distance we caught up with them. Luckily Perrietta didn't fall off because these horses were broad, which made it hard to dig in with your heels to hold tight.

Herding Cattle and Horses
It was usually after Saturday's supper when daddy announced that it was time to "move the horses". This was met with groans, mostly because we feared for our very lives! (Mother wasn't very happy about it either, as she had just washed and styled my younger sisters' hair for church the next day. Disappointedly she said, "Oh, Perry!") Horses, especially, are very curious and known to gallop right up to our faces. We were expected to "buck up" and move the horses or steers from the pasture above the house to the meadow below. But wait! Let's make it challenging by opening the meadow gate at the lane, move them across the lane to the meadow on the other side! At our strategic positions, we nervously waited with outstretched arms and holding long sticks. The horses charged down the hill, splashed across the creek to the four sisters who were now positioned across the meadow, at the gate and standing in the lane to keep them going in the right direction. It amazed us that these "moves" were successful!

Teams of Horses
Daddy used to farm our fields with two teams of horses, six to a team, at the same time in order to finish double rows. One team was trained to do its strip while daddy's team followed on the strip beside. This was common on the McMillen farms. His favorite horses were Tony and Red. It was hard, dusty work, but the teams required rest, food and water so, in turn, daddy got rest, too. Mother said that daddy worked harder after he got the tractor because it had lights, although they were not as effective as the lights on today's equipment. I can remember lying in bed at night hearing the tractor approach the end of the strip near the house and turning around, the tractor engine noise fading as it headed west for another round.

Gathering Eggs and Feeding the Chickens
Gathering eggs was a daily chore for all the sisters, although it was more like a treasure hunt. We grabbed the golden willow basket from the closet beside the refrigerator and headed out to the chicken house. For some reason or other, Pam came equipped with scissors one time. I was not a witness to it, but it was probably in her boredom, waiting for all the chickens to lay eggs, that she cut her hair. She never wanted to leave the chicken house until all the chickens laid eggs. She leaned against a perch and waited, occasionally getting up to pick up a tail to see if there were eggs underneath. Anyway, apparently, she leveled the scissors, or weed clipper, on her scalp and cut from her bangs back to her ponytail. Much to daddy's disappointment, as he liked Pam's long red hair, my mother immediately cut her hair short to blend in with all the short hairs on top. We had a few chickens that made finding their eggs a treasure hunt. One in particular laid her eggs under the main barn floorboard, which was discovered by climbing down the ladder to the ground floor. A couple rungs down we came eye to eye with the nest under the floorboard and in a protected pocket. It was such a surprise to find it, but now this meant that after we gathered eggs in the chicken house, we had to trek to the barn to get these eggs!

Farm Fun

Yes, we were secluded back a quarter mile long dirt lane, but it was self-contained for exploring and entertainment. I always had a vivid imagination and was all over the farm property exploring with Pam and Phyllis joining me.

A favorite place was the little woods below the house. A wooded trail led down to Panther Creek where we gathered nuts and stuffed a hollow tree for the squirrels, looked for fossils on the rock pile, stood upon a flat rock that jutted out midstream, or dammed up an area downstream that had a little island. All this play came to a stop when, either mother called us from the beauty shop, or the horses charged down the path for water.

We caught tadpoles, fished with crude sticks and strings, and waded in Panther Creek which cut through the meadows and little woods. We waded with caution after Perrietta screamed with a leech attached to her foot! I can still see her with her leg sticking high out of the water with this long black thing on her foot!

In the winter, sledding and tobogganing was just a trek up the hill, behind the wagon shed, from the house. The best sledding was if daddy made a path with the tractor because the tractor tread packed the snow. After the purchase of a toboggan, all of us could ride at the same time. No more waiting for the sled to come back up the hill for the other girl's turns. Also, having a toboggan meant we shared the fun together, all the way to the creek. Then we made the long walk back up to the top of the hill. We could only make three or four runs until we had to head for the house to warm up our frozen feet. Pam and I had a thrilling ride on the sled one time when we decided to sled on top of a heavy crust of snow. It was so thick and slippery that, not only did it hold our weight, but we also had to crawl on our hands and knees to inch up the hill with the rope attached around my wrist. I know we giggled the whole way up. It was a dangerous ride down as we could not control the steering, and the speed was great. A big pile of plowed-up snow, at the lane, stopped the sled, but Pam and I flew out over the snowbank landing in the lane. Two things I saw as we flew down the hill, the snowbank and daddy watching us from the barn bridge. I thought he would surely scold us due to the dangerous conditions, but that time we lucked out!

Another winter sport was ice skating. We didn't have a pond, but the ditch in the one meadow filled up with water and spilled over onto the flat meadow. When it froze, we had a huge area to skate.

Daddy loved to deer hunt. Our friend and neighbor, Ross Barnes, and daddy hunted together for years. A precursor to deer season was spotlighting. We piled into the 1950 Chevy and went out through the fields spotlighting. Usually, the beam was concentrated on the right side of the car going west. It was exciting to count all the pairs of eyes caught in the light. The game plan was, upon turning around at the end of the field, to try and catch the same deer as they headed to the ridge for cover. If it worked, we had deer running across our path in front of the car, watching them run and leap into the cover of the woods. Speed was factored into turning around at the end so that we could catch them escaping. The windows were down, and the cold air rushed in as the spotlight danced in the fields searching for the deer, we spotlighted on the way west. On the opening day of deer season, which was a day off of school, we were confined to the house for safety reasons, but we got excited when a shot was heard. Did daddy get a deer?

The hay holes: We were not allowed to jump across the hay holes, much less jump down the hay holes, but I did both, and I'm sure my sisters did too. Luckily, no one got hurt. There was only one particular one we used as it had a pile of hay on the ground floor which gave us a soft landing. Also, the ladder was next to the hay pile, so we ran up the ladder and jumped again and again!

Polly and the Rooster
Of course, you had to have a rooster in the chicken house. For some reason and to this day I don't know what possessed me, I liked to mimic its crowing. He would strut around at the edge of the front yard crowing followed by my imitation. One day he must have had enough and he started chasing me. Around the house we went, pausing only long enough at the kitchen door to yell for help. (We were locked out of the house because mother said "in or out" as she was tired of the screen door banging. I chose "out", so then she locked me out.) Little did I know that mother and daddy had hatched a plan, since neither the rooster, nor I, would give up the play. One Sunday, after church, the family gathered between the lilac bush and the willow tree. Daddy saw the rooster was out and told me to go out and imitate his crowing like I always did. However, this time, I was to run toward daddy who was standing there with a loaded gun! I was scared and exclaimed, "but you'll shoot me"! He replied that he wasn't going to shoot me, but the rooster! When I heard the gun go off, after running toward daddy, I knew the rooster had met its demise. I'm sure he ended up on our table for dinner.

Blizzards
Unlike today, blizzards seemed to be a common occurrence when we were growing up. It was an exciting time for us------a deviation from the norm. No school! However, it did create a lot of work for daddy. Mother had a beauty shop, Ruth McMillen's Beauty Shoppe, in the remodeled summer kitchen. The blizzard meant her customers had to be rebooked, which meant plowing the lane was a top priority. Daddy said, "these ladies have to get their hair done"! Sometimes we were snowed in for days. Poor daddy would be out in the cold, for hours, with the blustery wind whipping around his neck. His plan of attack was always to push the snow to the barbed wire fence on either side of the lane, which made room for more snow. The pushed-up snow piles around the buildings provided very high piles to climb, make catwalk-type trails along the ridges, and carve out "houses" for our play. One notable blizzard blew the snow from the fields into the buildings creating huge, high and hard-to-break-through drifts. Daddy actually got a blood clot in his calf from repeatedly using the clutch, trying to ram through the drifts. Sometimes our power was knocked out, so, to keep warm, we closed off all doors to the kitchen and huddled around a kerosene heater. Our best chili was made on top of the heater, in a large Dutch oven, as it slow-cooked all day.

Our First Bicycle
Perrietta and I earned fifty cents a week for cleaning the house, dusting and doing the bathroom fixtures. Because we wanted to buy a bike, we put our chore money in Ponds Cold Cream jars. We used to have mini visits with my Aunt Violet and Uncle Jake from Mechanicsburg, so mother asked them if they would take us shopping for a bike sometime. With jars in hand, we found our bicycle in a shop. I remember dumping all our quarters on his work counter to pay for the bike, maybe $25 or $35. How excited we were to bring it home. Daddy made a rule, though. We could ride out the lane to get the mail, but we had to park the bike at a walnut tree and walk the rest of the way. He knew if we rode the bike to the end of the lane, we would be tempted to ride on the dangerous, narrow rural road of Route 17. Knowing his eyes were probably boring into the back of our heads as we rode out the lane, we followed his instructions. A few years later Aunt Kathryn, mother's sister, gave us a small bicycle from her family, so now Pam and Phyllis used the smaller bike while Perrietta and I shared the larger bike. It was such freedom to ride our bikes, flying out the lane and going on pretend adventures.

Massey Harris Tractors
We were fortunate to have two Massey Harris tractors, the "44" and the "33". When we were old enough, Perrietta, Pam, Phyllis and I learned to drive. Daddy preferred that we drove the "44" because it had a heavier front end and didn't bounce so much in the furrows. Our job was to help daddy disk or mow down grasses, as required, when it was in Soil Bank program. It was a federal program of the late 1950's and 1960's that paid farmers to retire land from production for ten years. It took two tractors, two weeks from early morning until dusk to mow down the required acres. Daddy took the first strip and we would take the second strip following behind him. The one-mile strips proved to be very boring for me so I would sing or scold the tractor if it veered off of the row. Pay day was an exciting time for us. After two hot weeks of sunburn and long hours, we felt that we were really deserving of the fifty-dollar check! With the desktop checkbook open, and daddy sitting at the head of the kitchen table, he prepared to reward us. With a mid-air practice Palmer-method swirl, he brought his pen down to the check and signed his name in a flourish. Since it was August, the pay came at a particularly convenient time, as we used the money to buy school clothes for the following month of school opening.

Helping on the Farm
I remember wagon loads of corn being pulled by the tractor and parked horizontally with the wagon shed. Perrietta and I shoveled corn from the wagon to the moving elevator which took it to the corn crib. It was so tempting to want to jump onto the moving paddles, but daddy was very strict about safety, and so we never had that thrill. Heaving heavy hay bales from the wagon to the elevator was another job. If we were not dropping bales onto the elevator, we were positioned at the top of the ladder, in the mow, to receive the bale and walk it to the adult who was in charge of stacking.

Picking stones had to be our least favorite chore. It almost felt like punishment for being under mother's feet. First you had to hold up the heavy wagon tongue and line it up to the tractor's hitch that, somehow, daddy perfectly aligned. When in position, we grabbed the huge pin and dropped it through the hole which successfully hitched the wagon to the tractor. Our ride on the wagon to the fields was the last ride we had for a long time. Once we reached the fields, the dusty, clumsy walk began. With daddy perched high on the Massey Harris, he picked out large stones just in case we missed them. We dutifully ran to pick them up and throw on the ever-moving wagon. My first ever large stone that I picked up had a snake curled under it. Daddy didn't believe my yelling until he got off the tractor for a look. It was a long walk to the stone pile as our fields were one mile long, and the stone pile was 7/8ths of the way out. We disliked the stone pile as there were so many tent caterpillars hanging from the tree branches. At the end of the field, we rested under the walnut trees along the field lane. Our reward there was a long, cold drink from the green water jug with the porcelain liner.

Baling hay was always on hot days. Our bales were set to a large size which made it hard for young girls to grab by the binder twines and walk them back to the end of the wagon for stacking. After a while daddy got off the tractor and stacked the bales for us. We never realized, until we handled neighbor Fritz's hay bales, that the bale size was adjustable. Fritz's bales were smaller and so easy to carry, however daddy said he had a reason for having larger bales.

We also helped to bag oats and wheat, lying under the wagon for shade, but perking up when we heard the tractor and combine approaching. A thunderstorm came down on us several times during that job. We scrambled for cover under the wagon, which was in the middle of an open field. One particularly nasty thunderstorm, daddy built us a little fort of hay bales for cover and protection as we returned from the fields.

Mowing the yard, hand-pulling weeds and washing two cars were additional chores. The car washing and weed pulling was inspected by daddy after the job was finished. We walked beside him to learn where we missed a spot on the car or if the weeding was done correctly. He taught us how to do it the "right way" the first time. That was the Army Sergeant in him!

The Barn
Of all the animals we had on the farm, the least favorite was the pigs, especially if they were given free roam. I always thought they would eat me, so I kept my distance. This fear was reinforced when I saw Dorothy, of the Wizard of Oz movie, fall into the crowded pig pen.

We had a few milking cows for our use, but my sisters and I never had to milk them, nor did we ever learn the skill.

The barn was an exciting place to explore for kitties when we knew the pregnant mother cat was no longer pregnant. As much as we hunted, we never discovered their hiding place. The barn also held other adventures like watching the cattle chew their chop with chop dust all over their nostrils, helping to put hay sections in the feeders, the unpleasant smell of silage, but the pleasant smell of hay and chop and the warm moist smell of the animals. Sometimes a newborn foal was in the stable with its mother. Daily we worked with the foal until it would soon come up to us where we were perched on the stable side of the feeder. Holding out our hands, it sucked on our fingers until we noticed teeth.

It was here in the barn that I learned a new expression. I was probably bored and goofing off in one of the alleys. Daddy was moving the big wheel barrel full of chop, when he called to me, "girl, you'd better walk the chalk line", but for most of my life, I thought he said, "walk the chop line".

Play Time
Unlike today, our play was homemade, imagined, or imitated. The see-saw was just a board perched on a stump laid on its side which worked fine until we see-sawed off the stump. As I recall, we were constantly placing that board back on the stump to continue playing. Daddy made our swings from three poles, ropes, and boards. It gave us hours of playtime from swinging sideways to wrap around the pole and then wait until it unwound, to climbing the rope to the top of the pole and returning back down, hopefully without getting splinters in our fingers. This skill came in handy in gym class. Only the farm girls, Sue Reisinger Binger and I were able to climb the rope to the rafters. Sue is my lifelong friend who lived on the other side of our ridge on a farm. We also had a homemade sandbox and later a tractor tire which served as a sandbox where we sat on the rim and stored our toys underneath the rim for protection. Our trusty tricycle, wagon and wheel barrel took us everywhere around the house and to the barn. The little enclosed porch off the kitchen was the perfect place to playhouse; hang up clothes, talk on our play phones and work with our little refrigerator and stove as we played "house". Later we moved to the washhouse where we also played "store", collecting mother's empty boxes and waiting patiently for the prized Calumet Baking Powder can.

The Farmhouse
How fortunate we were to be raised in a large farmhouse. For a family of six it was spacious enough for all

of our needs. We had a typical farmhouse kitchen which was big enough for cooking, dining and clothes washing. Before the kitchen was remodeled it had an old coal/woodstove with a water reservoir on the one end, a two-burner/one iron plate on the other end, a shelf that ran across the top, a drawer for the ashes, and an unused doorless oven. We used the oven to warm our cold feet when coming in from sledding-----just pulled up chairs and sat with our feet in the oven. I remember mother drying corn on large sheets on top of the stove, but I don't remember what other foods were cooked on it. There was a huge, divided wash sink behind the cook stove that also disappeared during the remodeling. Perrietta and I used to sit on either side, when we were toddlers, for our baths. Pam lost her carnival goldfish down one of those drains when we changed its water.

Heat was provided by an oil burner in the living room and tv room. The cook stove heated the kitchen. There was no heat upstairs except for what little heat came up the floor registers in our bedrooms from the oil burners directly below. (We could lift the top of the register off and view the room a foot below us through a protective metal grid. It was tempting to step down in to it, but I knew I would probably fall through. However, it was fun to imagine, and it was a great place to eavesdrop on conversations below.) To stay warm, we slept between flannel sheet blankets and piles of heavy comforters. The weight of the comforters kept us firmly in place on "our side" of the bed. Although there were four bedrooms, one was kept for the hired hand or for "company". Mother and daddy had their own bedroom and my sisters, and I shared the remaining two bedrooms, a double bed in each room. We only had one bathroom. Flooring was wood with rolled linoleum on top so that the floors were cold in the winter. An electric heater was turned on in the bathroom so we could bathe and dress in the warm. In the morning we draped our clothes over the oil burners to warm them while we ate breakfast.

In the late 1960's the kitchen was remodeled, and we got an oil/hot water furnace with baseboard heat for upstairs and downstairs. What a luxury! Gone was the cook stove and double sink in the kitchen and the oil burners in the other rooms. (I must add here, that although we had that cook stove, mother always had an electric stove.) With the extra space mother had room for the washer and dryer, and daddy had a sink and built-in medicine cabinet for shaving. The kitchen was paneled, the refrigerator recessed in the wall and cupboards painted turquoise, mother's favorite color. The work was done by Tom Lyons.

Large attics in farmhouses were common. Ours was a large T-shape with the bottom of the "T" being interrupted by the staircase. There were three windows, one at each point, which were permanently sealed, making it freezing cold in the winter and stifling hot in the summer. It was too uncomfortable to play up there, but we did have the daring adventure of jumping across the open stairwell at the steepest place, knowing full well of the danger it posed. I do not know about my sisters, but my ankles were weak as I jumped across the span. To me it was just like jumping down the hay hole, although there, there was a pile of hay at the bottom to cushion a fall. No accidents to report from our play in the attic.

Musical Hobby for Church and School
My whole family sang in the choir at Centre Presbyterian Church in Loysville. Daddy sang bass; mother, alto; Perrietta and Phyllis, soprano; Polly and Pam, alto. Mother was also a talented pianist. We used to provide the entertainment for The Women's Association with mother playing the piano and my sisters and I singing, "I Believe" and "He". We were baptized, confirmed and attended church and Sunday school at Centre. Polly was married to Gary Eby, at Centre Presbyterian Church, while he was attending Corpsman School at Great Lakes Training Camp, Waukegan, IL during the Viet Nam Conflict.

All McMillen sisters played musical instruments and sang in the school chorus. Perrietta played both alto and tenor saxophone plus bass clarinet, I played the alto saxophone, Pam played the glockenspiel, and Phyllis played the flute. She was the smart one because it was lightweight to carry out the long lane, which was almost a fifteen-minute walk. Gym class and band day, ironically, were on the same day so that you not only carried a stack of books (before backpacks), but also a gym bag and a bulky instrument, too.

Friends
Raised on adjoining farms, Sue Reisinger Binger and I have been life-long friends. Imagine, she taught me how to ride a bicycle by just putting me on it and sending me down the gravel-lane hill! Without a lesson, and through sheer terror, I balanced the bike without even thinking about it. The only problem was that Sue forgot to show me how to stop it, so I ran the bike in circles around the barn bridge until it slowed down enough to get off. That was the only lesson I needed to ride a bike as I could get back on and balance it immediately. I decided, years later, to visit her knowing that she was just across our ridge, relatively speaking, as I was soon to find out. Crossing our ridge took at least twenty minutes. I thought I would come out on the other side with her barn below me, but coming out of the woods, it was to the west in a distance, at least another twenty-minute walk! What a surprise! As I recall, either my mother or Sue's mother took me home because I know I did not retrace my steps!

Neighbors
In closing, I would like to add that living on a farm required depending on your neighbors for support and bonding. We were fortunate to have, as our close neighbors and friends, Myrtle and Ross Barnes. Myrtle came to our rescue many times; when mother got her finger stuck in the electric mixer beaters requiring Perrietta to dial Myrtle's number, which she was able to do because she had just learned her numbers. Myrtle had to go out to the fields to find daddy to come help. Another time, mother's water broke and Phyllis was delivered at home. Again, Myrtle was called upon to straighten up the bedroom afterward. At the time, my sisters and I had the measles. With the commotion of the doctor and daddy going up and down the steps, I woke up and with curiosity and went to the bathroom to get a drink. Their bedroom was connected to the bathroom, so I peeked inside from my stool at the sink and spied a bassinet. I walked right in, measles and all, and looked down upon my youngest baby sister, Phyllis, and said, "ohhhh, a baby". I loved babies. (I just have to add that sister Pam was born in our 1950 Chevy in Dauphin enroute to the hospital! Perrietta and I were born at the Polyclinic Hospital. Obviously, mother's childbirths got quicker with babies three and four!)

Other good neighbors were Byron & Freda Weibley, Brownie & Joanne Fritz, Gene & Beattie Fritz, Dick & Grace Reisinger, Boots & Mable Reisinger, Glenn & Millie Smith, Harold & Helen Swartz, Wayne & Anna Weibley, Bertus & Helen Smith, Lincoln & Elizabeth Reisinger, Ellsworth & Emily Maxton, Ross & Dorothy Titzell and Homer & Emmie Simonton.

Tell your story. It is invaluable!

An Eye for the Future

Storyteller Penny Rudy Nicholl

I live in a house that was built in 1871. I have been told that it was one of the first houses built in Loysville. My husband's grandparents, William and Grace (Wilt) Nicholl lived in the house, located in the center of Loysville, for many years. My late husband and I completed renovations, during our years in this house, but much remains the same. Upstairs a big old door with a click latch type handle opens to a set of stairs that led to the attic. Many items were stored here during the years and some made their way downstairs. These items hold stories, from the past that I hope will be passed on to the future.

Grandpap Nicholl was a man of many talents. He served in the Army and was a schoolteacher at one time. He was the janitor at the elementary school in Landisburg, which was located where the Landisburg Fire Company is now. He also worked at the Tressler Orphan's Home, which is now the Youth Development Center, in Loysville. Grandpap was a very interesting, intelligent, and inquisitive man.

I have become the keeper of many of their things, that simply came along with the house. A set of grandpap's schoolbooks he used, while teaching in a one room school house, near Blain, have been proudly perched on my floor to ceiling bookcase, for over 40 years, along with current novels.

A set of pink flower dishes, that were grandmas, and recently used in a tea party, hosted by my granddaughters, are stored in my kitchen. Her set of glasses adorned with a variety of flowers painted on them are contently displayed in the corner cupboard. They originally were purchased with jelly in them.

Their family bible with a heavy, huge black cover opens to reveal a list of family events and family member's birth dates. It also holds sentimental snippets into the family's past. There is the Certificate of Naturalization of Andrew Nicholl, when he arrived from Ireland on April 11, 1905. There is a telegram from the Army about a son being treated at Walter Reed Hospital. A receipt from a store that used to be located, where the bank in Loysville is now. A newspaper clipping, of a letter, written by their son Harold Nicholl, while he was serving in the military, stationed in Italy, dated July 22, 1944. Many personal important papers that held dear meaning for the family, and has provided a snapshot of how life was, and how it has changed. Has it really changed?

All of these possessions make me smile and feel at home in this old house. There is comfort, in knowing about the past. Recently, I have been doing some "spring cleaning" and was going through items. Deciding what to keep, and what to donate is tough, as each item has some type of value or adds joy to daily life.

I ran across an old sewing machine cabinet, that most definitely, was Gram Nicholl's. I hesitantly pulled open one of the small drawers in the cabinet, finding some sewing items, and little spools of thread and needles. Stuffed in the back of the drawer was a crumpled ball of paper. It looked like a white napkin rolled in a ball. I pulled the ball of white paper out of the drawer. I could tell from the weight, that something was wrapped up in the napkin. I slowly opened the napkin to find a blue circle resembling an eye, staring back at me. It startled me at first and then I realized, it definitely was an eye. It was Grand-pap Nicholl's fake glass eye. I knew he had a glass eye, but I did not know that it was kept in the sewing cabinet drawer!

I smiled, as I remembered the glass eye story, my late husband had told us.

There was a feed mill, that operated directly across the road, from grand-pap's house. It is still in operation today and known as Kreider's Mill. This was also a train station stop, for a train that ran from Newport through Loysville to Blain. Grand-pap frequented the feed mill, but I can't remember why he did that. He didn't have any animals to feed. He would catch the train to Newport sometimes.

Perhaps, his visits were just for some conversation with others in town. Anyway, this particular visit did not go as planned. Back in those days, the feed mill would become overrun with rats, looking for a meal. Since there were no "pest control" companies, that would come around monthly, and control the rat and mice population like there is today, the feed mill operators were responsible for handling the pesky mice situation, on their own. The operator, at the mill, had decided that evening, he would simply shoot the critters. Now I don't know, if that was legal back then or even if it is legal today. Let alone, a smart thing to do.

But the operator and some town folk…I am sure they were young men looking for excitement, decided to chase the critters and shoot at them. They had loaded some guns with bird shot. Now you must remember that I know nothing about guns, so I don't know what kind of gun uses bird shot. Apparently, these town folks knew.

So, while they were shooting bird shot upstairs, grand-pap decided, that he would walk over to the mill, and see who was around. You can probably guess, where this is going…. a glass eye, young men shooting bird shot, a mill full the mice, and grand-pap looking to exchange some conversation.

Grand-pap heard the noise coming from upstairs and started climbing the steps. Just as he got to the top of the wooden creaking staircase, some one shot at a mouse or rat. The story got bigger each time the story was told, and well you guessed correctly…. grand-pap took a direct hit of bird shot in his eye. Thus, a glass eye kept in the sewing cabinet drawer.

My husband never told us anymore of the story. Although, the critters got bigger with each time, the story was retold to my young children. He never said what doctor grand-pap went to, or what hospital, or how the eye was removed, or any details. By the time I had married my husband, grand-pap had passed away.

My husband and I spent years raising our kids, working, and living in grand-pap's old house. That old sewing machine cabinet, which held such a treasured possession, survived many renovation projects, had been moved from upstairs to the basement, and is in definite need of refurbishing.

My husband passed away seven years ago. The story, with all the details remains somewhat a mystery. I will wrap the eye up and tuck it safely back in the top drawer. The mysterious details will remain in place. All I can really confirm is, that grand-pap did have a glass eye, and it along with its history, will stay in the drawer, to be found by one of my grandchildren sometime in the future. I hope when they do find it, they will think of all their grand-paps and smile.

WILT SISTERS FROM ALINDA

Storytellers Connie Lupp and SueEllen McElhiney
Recorded by Debra Kay Noye

The sisters are still on the farmlands at Alinda originally owned by their grandparents, Clarence Kirby and Myrtle Mae (Reber) Wilt. Although they never farmed, they have fond memories of the Wilt homestead.

They grew up in Landisburg along with their brother Jim. Their parents, Richard and Martha (McAllister) Wilt moved several times within Landisburg borough before building on the farm. Being around their grandparents on the farm shaped their lives and has them longing for the old days.

Grandmother Muzzy, as she was nicknamed, was the backbone of the family who influenced them the most. Noted as being a great cook, she sure knew how to provide for her family.

The sisters began by reminiscing about winter butchering days on the farm, which was spearheaded by their Pap and Muzzy. It was definitely a family affair that also included friends and neighbors, who couldn't wait to taste Pap's scrapple. Connie said he had a secret to making his scrapple, which often got him an invite to other farms to oversee their scrapple making.

There wasn't a written recipe. Years of experience and personal taste guided Pap. After he used his special gun to put down the hogs, he gave instructions how to butcher the hogs by carving out the hams, bacon, shoulders, loins, and ribs. They trimmed specialty cuts of meat producing random chunks to be cooked with water in the cast iron meat kettles till they were fork tender. The wood fire under the heavy iron kettles kept them boiling for hours. Most of the cooked meat was turned into scrapple.

Making scrapple, Pap used a lot of cooked meat that was finely chopped with nice fat, especially head meat which is tender and full of flavor. He wasn't stingy on his use of salt and black pepper. A small amount of roasted cornmeal, probably from Wentzel's Mill at Bridgeport near the farm, was used as a binder. Connie thought that maybe he would use a little more rendered pig fat, liquid lard, in his scrapple. Once the thick concoction was cooked and flavored to Pap's satisfaction, it was ladled into metal loaf pans or bread pans. Sometimes the scrapple, once it settled in the pans, would naturally form a surface of lard. Generally, more would be added to the top sealing it so it would be preserved in the cold cellar or washhouse.

Scrapple was sliced fairly thick then pan fried and eaten for breakfast. Fried long enough it will become crispy on both sides with a soft interior. Topped with King Syrup molasses or apple butter, scrapple along with eggs and homemade bread made a filling start to the day. Of course, scrapple in the winter months was served for any meal.

Sue was salivating over the memory of eating freshly cooked hog liver. Cutting the whole liver into bite size pieces, she would then dip it into salt popping it right into her mouth. The texture was soft and tender, as long as it wasn't cooked too long.

Puddin' with fried mush and molasses was another favorite breakfast meal. The puddin' was made from the cooked meats and liver, which gave it a signature taste. It was ground, seasoned with salt and pepper, and generally recooked. Muzzy would also put the puddin' into loaf pans and top it with lard to seal. Some folks also canned the puddin'.

The sisters just can't find anybody that makes scrapple and puddin' as they remember as a child. Often times, the ratio of cornmeal outweighs the meat and the cornmeal isn't added properly so it clumps throughout the faux scrapple. The puddin' ends up tasting like a harsh blood liver sausage!! The look on their faces describing the locally sourced scrapple and puddin' was that of a kid who hates spinach and red beets!

They enjoyed munching on the cracklins, which is produced by compressing rendered hog fat. The fat is trimmed from the meat and cut into uniform pieces to be put into iron kettles to melt over a wood fire. They were cooked till you couldn't squeeze much more liquid from them. Ladled into the metal lard press, the handle was turned allowing the metal plate to compress the fat particles into a solid cake. The liquid lard would be strained through cheese cloth into metal lard tins holding at least five gallons. Once solidified you had yourself some mighty fine pure white lard which according to the sisters made the best flaky pie crusts and fried mush. The cakes of cracklins were removed very carefully because they would be very hot, just like freshly popped corn. The smell and crunchy chew were like no other treat!! They would break off pieces and munch away knowing it might be another year till they would be able to enjoy it again.

Butchering wasn't all fun according to the sisters, because they had the chore of cleaning the hog intestines so they could be used for stuffing the sausage. They would turn them inside out scraping all the debris, aka pig poop, from the intestine walls. Using knives, it was a tedious job, because they had to be very careful not to nick or puncture the walls. Holes would expand under the pressure of the sausage being forced into them and they would burst.

Right back to loose sausage, which could be used along with raw potato pieces to stuff the cleaned hog stomach. Muzzy took care of cleaning the stomach which entailed having to delicately remove the lining. The cooked filled stomach would be served with chopped raw onion. Baked right the stomach would be soft and chewy. Otherwise, it would quickly become like shoe leather!

There was a smokehouse on the farm where the sugar-cured hams, shoulders and bacon were hung on metal hooks and smoked for days. The smoking and the salt-based cure ensured that the meats would be able to hang in the cellar or washhouse throughout the winter. Often times mold might form just like on aging cheeses and it was simply washed and trimmed before cooking and eating. They would save a smoked ham for Easter dinner.

The tongue was generally pickled or eaten with the other delicacies of the day. Some of the meat was cut into chunks small enough to fit into a canning jar. It was first cooked in salt water then carefully transferred to the canning jars and topped with the cooking liquid. They used metal lids and rings to seal the jars. They didn't use rubber jar rings with glass tops. The sealing process took hours. Connie still remembers those meals of canned pork pieces being rolled in a little flour and fried in lard. The gelatinous cooking liquid was used for making gravy. To Connie, it was one of the best meals!!

The sisters still make mush, but Sue back in the day liked it fried crispy topped with puddin' and King Syrup molasses. They were not used to eating a bowl of mush straight from the kettle, like some folks (this author) who add molasses and butter or milk. The water, salt and cornmeal are cooked till the cornmeal no longer has a toothsome bite and is thick like porridge. It is poured into bread pans where it will become solid enough to slice. The thinly cut slices are sauteed in lard or butter till they are crispy on both sides. The aroma of roasted cornmeal used for the mush is like no other food smell.

***

The sisters attended Mt. Zion Lutheran Church outside of Bridgeport. They recall generations of the same family attended; Albright, Nace, Johnson and Kellers were a few mentioned. Each family took turns cleaning the church. They enjoyed hayrides sponsored by the large youth fellowship. Bible School filled their summer for two weeks. Their mother was a Bible School teacher. Sometimes, they would go to a church camp in the Johnstown area.

They didn't attend the one room schoolhouse on the lower street in Landisburg like their brother Jim. Their first six years in elementary school was in the Landisburg Elementary School where the Landisburg Fire and Ambulance Companies are today.

May Day Dances were an activity they looked forward to dancing around the may pole holding onto streamers which eventually became one giant woven braid. They wore their best clothes and recalled a favorite blue dress designed by seamstress Chia Rice from Barkleytown. Mrs. Ben Rice made all of their clothes, dresses, blouses, skirts, coats. She didn't use a bought pattern. She would take a large piece of brown paper the height of the girls and hold it up to eyeball a size needed. The dresses she made had buttons or a tie in the back to make it more form fitting. The dresses were beautiful and lasted through the hand me down process. Shoes were bought at Dutrey's in Carlisle, and shopping excursions took them to Pomeroy's in Harrisburg and York.

***

They named their least favorite teacher first. Mrs. Miller was nicknamed the killer, who would lock students in the closet if they did something wrong! Connie recalled spending time in the closet because she wouldn't eat her red beets at lunch. Mrs. Miller's weapon of choice was a wooden ruler which she used regularly. She whacked students with her ruler if she didn't like something being done. Lefties were particularly sought out and whacked for writing left-handed.

Mrs. Rice taught second grade and had Sue stay inside after lunch because she needed to improve her penmanship.

They gushed with praise for Robert Owen, a teacher and principal who allowed them to dance. They obviously learned from him, and Toots Stambaugh, and Mrs. Gobretch, their first-grade teachers, who obviously loved kids.

Grades six through twelve were spent at Green Park Union High School, which later merged with all the schools in the western end of Perry County to form the West Perry School District. Connie later taught elementary students in the West Perry Schools. Sue became a physical therapist often working within the county.

***

The family had a television by the time they were in fourth and fifth grades. What they really enjoyed on a regular basis in their teen years was the famed Hi-Way Theatre in Ickesburg. Connie recalls seeing Gone with the Wind for the first time. They didn't talk about bowling in the theatre basement, but they did go to Rheams Roller Rink outside of Millerstown to roller skate. The school would take busloads of students to the popular rink. They shared their parents were excellent roller skaters.

After school they would walk to their parent's grocery, hardware and paint store, Wilt's Self-Service Store on the square of Landisburg. They were responsible for stocking the cooler with soda pop and sorting the glass bottles returned for deposit. The bottles were taken back down the rickety stairs to the basement and placed into the proper wooden case for return to the distributors. The store sold Coke, Pepsi, 7-Up, orange, ginger ale and root beer.

They were given what Connie referred to as grease pens, with soft textures, to mark items in black with the proper price.

They are proud of the fact they learned how to count and handle money. Making change was figured out in your head. Responsible for sorting the coins and bills, this chore enabled their father to do the nightly deposit.

Wilt's Store was one of three in Landisburg. Sweger and McGowan also sold grocery and hardware items.

When their parents purchased the store, the Landisburg post office was housed in the back. Dean Wilt, their uncle, was the postmaster. He also helped out in the store. Melvin Sweger was also an employee.

They recall Doc Matunis shopping at the store with his many children in tow. Once when he finished shopping, he left without taking a head count. Sure enough, they had to call to remind him that one child remained with them.

Dale "Pickle" Rice would hang out at the store threatening to tickle the girls till he would get their gizzards. And, in later years, upon seeing the girls would remind them, he saw them when they were in diapers.

Donna Fosselman would patronize the store daily for her Pepsi. Buying a pint of ice cream and a Pepsi, the oldest Crockett boy would peel back the cardboard exposing the ice cream and he would proceed to enjoy it all.

Their mother also worked in the store, managing it herself once their father sought other work. They decided to sell the store in 1967/68. Their mother also liked to hunt deer and would go along to their camp along the Laurel Run at the base of Doubling Gap. There she would shoot pistols for sport.

The sisters tell the story of their parents going hunting in their International Pick-Up Truck. Their mother was sitting in the truck with her deer rifle when their dad inquired if she had the safety properly secured. Well, no sooner did he say about the safety, when the gun went off shooting a hole through the truck's floor boards. Luckily no other damage occurred.

The family did enjoy venison made into burger, deer bologna and jerky. At their camp which was originally co-owned by Mutz McNaight, barber from Loysville, they would have Sunday picnics and open kettle soup boils featuring corn or ham bean. Dick was known to make a special soup after butchering which included pigs' feet, potatoes, cabbage, corn, and lima beans. The soup would be topped off with fresh diced onion and served with slabs of homemade bread smothered in barrel molasses. "A mighty fine meal" according to the sisters.

***

The holidays meant new clothes. Easter was celebrated with new dresses, bonnets and patent leather shoes. An egg hunt would be enjoyed after returning home from Sunrise Services at King's Gap. All the Wilt family would gather at Christmas. The girls would receive candy, oranges, and other treats in baskets. Some of which were sponsored by the church. The Fourth of July and Memorial Day meant large family picnics.

They spoke of bums or vagrants traveling through the county looking for work. If they stopped at the farm, Muzzy and Pap would feed them, giving them odd chores, and allowed them to sleep in the barn. They recalled their grandparents speaking about gypsies roaming the county.

The sisters wanted to make sure to mention that they also helped with the farm chickens. They were responsible for collecting the eggs and gently placing them into wire baskets. Sue absolutely hated the henhouse with the scurrying chickens who were known to defend their eggs in the nest. Once they collected the eggs, they wiped them clean for Muzzy, who used the egg scales to determine their size. They were boxed accordingly and sold to the neighbors.

Sue delighted in talking about using chicken catchers which were long sturdy wires attached to a wooden handle. On the opposite end was a curved hook, if used correctly would easily snag a chicken leg. You would pull the chicken to you and grab both legs. This was the first step in preparing chickens for a chicken dinner. They laughed as they talked about their Pap who would whack the chicken's head off and toss the flapping chicken in their direction. Next was to scold the chickens in kettles or buckets of boiling water. This allowed the feathers to soften right down to the quills and made for easier plucking. Because chickens also have some hair, they are singed over an open flame. The chickens were scrapped to loosen any remaining debris and the innards removed. They enjoyed many a pan-fried chicken for their summer picnics and Sunday dinners.

Their family like so many others in Perry County primarily lived off the land. The apple orchards on the farm provided apples for yearly apple butter. Once the apples were picked, Muzzy would cook them down and use a giant sized foley food mill to puree the apples into apple sauce. The washhouse was prepped for apple butter making in copper kettles in the open fireplace. Special wooden stirrers were manned by the girls to keep the apple mixture from scorching or sticking to the bottom. The copper kettles were best for even cooking and less chance of scorching. You needed to keep the wood fire regulated under the kettles. They know Pap added cinnamon and other spices but added very little if any sugar. They relied on the natural sweetness from the apples. It wasn't apple butter until the grandparents declared it thick enough. What a delight on homemade bread, pancakes, scrapple, and ice cream. Muzzy would jar and can the apple butter.

Asked if they ever used sassafras in the apple butter, they said not, but Sue made sassafras tea. She would dig up the roots, clean them off, and boil them. She sometimes added sugar enjoying the tea hot or cold.

***

Another business in Landisburg that they favored was run by their aunt, Mrs. Max (Gladys) Wilt. Gladys Restaurant was right beside the family store. Having never learned to drive, she would rise early each morning, walking to the restaurant so she could open by 5 a. m. It was a small establishment seating in booths or at the counter slightly more than twenty patrons at a time. A pool table was tucked into the back room and if you started a fight, you were immediately kicked out.

Gladys was known for solid home cooking. Larry Baum reminded the sisters that he could buy the largest hamburger and platter of fries for fifty-two cents. Sue demonstrated the size which resembled a large meat platter. Soups were homemade as well as the pies. Local children would drop off pumpkins at the back door for Glady to make into pumpkin pies. By the next day there would be fresh pumpkin pie for everybody's enjoyment.

Connie and Sue grew up within a family and community that groomed them for the future. Likewise, they left their mark on those they met along the way and strive today to preserve their legacy by sharing with their grandchildren and fellow Perry Countians.

A Perry County Hero

Storyteller Harriet Berrier Magee

This story definitely needs to be told. It is about one of great heroes of Perry County. His name is Alexander Kelly McClure from Madison Township. This man lived at the door of history his entire life. For example, he knew every President from Franklin Pierce to Teddy Roosevelt.

This story is centered around our Civil War President Abraham Lincoln. On January 1, 1861, McClure received a telegram from Lincoln requesting that he come to Springfield, Illinois to meet with him regarding the formation of his cabinet. A "red flag" came up when Lincoln's selection of Simon Cameron for Secretary of War became known. Lincoln remembered a message he had received from McClure, during the election concerning this matter, and how it would create much dissension among the politicians of the day.

Now, I think, this is a **giant request** of Lincoln, especially without the existence of an Air Force 1. But McClure boarded a train headed to Springfield. When he arrived, it was 7 p.m. He sent a message to Lincoln announcing his arrival and that he had but four hours to meet with him as he needed to depart Springfield for Pennsylvania at 11 p.m.

In 1892, McClure published a book called "Lincoln and the Men of War" and in his book he impeccably describes his meeting with President Abraham Lincoln.

The story goes this way. "I hastened to Springfield. I went directly from the depot to Lincoln's house and knocked on the door. I doubt whether I wholly concealed my disappointment at meeting him. Tall, gaunt, ungainly, ill clad, with a homeliness of manner that was unique in itself. I confess that my heart sank within me as I remembered that this was the man chosen by a great nation to become its ruler in the greatest period of its history. I remember his dress as if it were yesterday, snuff colored and slouchy pantaloons, open black vest held by a few brass buttons, tattered evening dress coat with tightly fitting sleeves to exaggerate his long bony arms, all supplemented with awkwardness that was uncommon among men with intelligence. Such was the picture. We sat down in his plainly furnished parlor and were uninterrupted for four hours and little by little, as his earnestness, sincerity and candor were developed in conversation, I forgot all of the grotesque qualities which so confounded me when I first greeted him. Before a half hour had passed, I learned not only to respect him but indeed to reverence the man. He surely was the person to lead the nation."

In this story you had two opportunities to learn of Alexander Kelly McClure and secondly, to be introduced to President Abraham Lincoln.

McClure has made many contributions to the history of the United States. We truly owe him many accolades for his many accomplishments.

An historical marker has been placed in Madison Township in his honor. It is located along Route 850 near Fort Robinson.

My Story - Growing up in Loysville

Storyteller Galene Guiles Weller

It Takes a Village…..
Until recently, I never realized just how much this phrase applies to my early years.

Born in 1956, and raised in Loysville, Perry County, Pennsylvania, was really a blessing to me. An only child, of working parents, the village took care of me. My Dad, Archie Guiles, worked for Sheaffer Chevrolet, as a mechanic, and body and fender repair man. I would ride along with him in the tow truck, to pick up wrecked vehicles. It was always fun to watch him restore them, and how good he could make them look again. My Mother, Janet Sloop Guiles, worked at Reeves Hoffman Crystal Plant, in Carlisle. She worked in the clean and etch department.

Dear "Old Mrs. Stahl" told my mother that I was a fussy baby, because I was hungry. "Get that child off of formula and give her some good cow's milk." That began a growing spurt, that I'm not sure ever quit.

Milk was delivered door to door, in those days, and in our case, by Halls Dairy out of Millerstown, Pennsylvania. By three years of age, I figured I could do a lot to help my mother, including bringing in the ice-cold quart bottles of milk, from the milk box on the side porch. It didn't matter that Mr. John Hall, who was delivering one fateful morning said, "Good morning Missy, now you wait for your mother to get the milk, OK!" I didn't say a thing, but I must have had a look on my face that told him, I wasn't going to listen. He didn't get to the neighbors, before the sound of broken glass, and my mother yelling could be heard. Mr. Hall raced back to replace the broken bottle, telling my mother, "Oh that can happen to anyone. These bottles are slippy." He winked at me and went on his way. Needless to say, I didn't get any milk out of the milk box for many years to come.

Our closest neighbors were either grandparents or childless couples. The grandparents would call my mother, when their grandchildren came to visit, for me to play with them. The childless indulged me in conversation. "Mutz" and Helen McKnight lived next door. He was one of the two barbers on our street. I would sit on a small wall, between our two properties, and talk to Helen when she sat on her side porch.

I was told not to go in their yard, and for some reason listened, until Helen called my mother, asking if I couldn't come sit on the porch with her. "Mutz" would join us when he didn't have customers. He would tell me hunting and fishing stories and bring me a sweet treat or T-shirt along home from his hunting trips to Cross Fork, Potter County, Pennsylvania.

Miss "Tilly" Reapsome lived on the other side of us. She was a tiny, incredibly energetic little old lady. She cut her grass, with a reel push mower, and her yard was perfect. There were no weeds between the cracks of her brick sidewalk out front, or in her large vegetable and flower gardens out back. I think that is where my love of gardening sprouted. I would watch her, and occasionally she would sit down on a little bench by her back cellar door, and we would talk about plants.

Next to "Miss Tilly" was Homer and Grace Evans. They were a special couple. My parents rented half of their house, before they bought the house, I grew up in. Homer was the other barber on the street. They didn't have any children, but Grace would mother all the children, that came in with their parents to get haircuts. Homer would tell stories, while cutting hair, and Grace would play simple games and read stories to the children, to occupy them. I would always go with my dad to get his hair cut, and was always glad, if I happened to be the only child there. I would have Grace to myself, when she pulled out her reading books to read to me. My favorite was the "Three Billy Goats Gruff". Grace would change her voice for each character, in the book, and no matter when she read the story to you, the characters sounded the same. Homer usually gave each child a nickel, when they left, saying "save that for when you grow up".

When my bank got full, my mother took me to the First National Bank of Loysville and Mr. Merle Miller, the banker, helped me open a savings account. As I got older, I was allowed to walk to the bank myself, and deposit those nickels. I learned to collect soda bottles, for the deposit money. When manufactures coupons started, I would clip them for the items that Mother would shop for at Robinson's Grocery Store, at the west end of town. Mrs. Robinson always gave me the money, for the coupons, instead of taking it off my mother's bill. Occasionally, she would give me the coupon money, even if we didn't purchase the item, but they did carry it in the store. They had a much bigger selection of items, than the smaller corner store, in the town square. Robinson's Store taught me economics and good business practices, since we shopped there all the time. I'd save up for a magazine or candy and, of course, to help that savings account.

I'd save labels off canned goods, to send for small toys. My first fashion doll came from saving Lux dish washing soap labels. We would get S & H Green stamps for purchases too. We would paste them in a book and redeem them, for items in the S & H catalog. My sheet and towels for college, came from the S & H catalog, as did some things after I was married.

Ben and Fanny Sheibley owned the corner store on our street, and that is where mother would send me for a loaf of bread or sugar. She would call the store and let Fanny know, I was coming. She watched me cross the street, and then Mrs. Sheibley would watch for me to cross safely back across, and I'd walk home. Wow! Thirty-five cents for a loaf of bread.

Neighbors helping neighbors.
My friends and I would walk around town at Halloween dressed in whatever costumes we put together, and usually a plastic mask of some kind on our faces. That corner store was a great place to Trick or Treat, because you could pick whatever candy bar you wanted, out of the candy case. Such hard choices to make,

the big Hershey bar, Three Musketeers or the coveted candy necklace? Seemed to me that the case was so big and had many more choices, than the smaller selection of staples on the other shelves.

The other end of our street was where I spent most of my time growing up. Three different families opened their doors to keep me when my mother returned to work. Don and Margie Rice, and Leroy and Sara Rice had children of their own and they were always fun to play with. We even played evenings and weekends together, went to church at Tressler Memorial Lutheran, and later to school together. Starting school, in the two-room schoolhouse, at the end of the opposite street, (Now the Loysville Community Building) Mrs. Lenora Duncan was my first-grade teacher and Miss Carrie Bell Hench taught second grade. Miss Carrie Bell directed the children's choir at church.

Raymond and Isabell Shuman also kept me. They had no children and Isabell's parents, Mr. & Mrs. Showers, lived in half of their house. It was like another set of parents and grandparents for me.

I called her Mommy Bell. We would garden and cook together. I loved making jelly with her. I think crab apple was my favorite, maybe because we would go pick the crab apples and then make the jelly. She'd always watch her soap opera in the afternoon, when I would come home from school. Good old General Hospital! She taught me to crochet, but I never reached her speed or ability to complete complicated designs. I'm happy to say, I still have several pieces she made and I now own her dining table, where we shared many meals. Homemade chicken pot pie was my favorite. I helped to kill and clean the chickens, make jelly, and grow African violets; just not as good as Isabell could.

There were others throughout town that babysat me at times and other families that I played and went to school with their kids. It was a safe, quiet little town where everyone knew each other, and looked out for each other. You didn't worry about staying out at night catching lightening bugs, that you chased from one yard to another.

You tried to help out where needed, and knew in return, you would be looked after too.

Growing Up in the 50's and 60's – My Story

Storyteller Sue Reisinger Binger

I was born in 1951. My parents were hard-working farmers, having taken over the family farm in the early 1940's. For nearly ten years, my parents remained childless, until my brother was born in 1949 and two years later, I came along. This was a time of great transition. The Second World War was six years in the past, but the Korean Conflict was just beginning. By the time my brother and I were born, my parents had modernized our farmhouse with electricity and phone service.

I was quick and agile as a child and apparently a handful for my mother. Having no sisters, I learned at an early age to keep up with my older brother. Stories from my mother have me climbing onto a forbidden hay wagon and falling to the ground, knocking out a front tooth (luckily it was still a baby tooth) or climbing high into the tree in our backyard so my brother (who was not so agile) could not get to me when we would have an argument. I can remember that at a young age, I could crawl out the upstairs window of our two-story brick farmhouse, slide down the roof onto the adjoining washhouse and shimmy across the tree branches to that same backyard tree. Later, I would climb to the rafters in our barn and jump into the piles of grain stored on the barn floor. I am thinking that my logic to these antics had something to do with my need to create my own adventures. My brother was off doing brother things and as the oldest child on a farm, he often shouldered the burden of the farm chores. So, having no other companions, I created my own excitement.

Our farm was isolated, being located on a dirt road in a hollow, just southwest of Ickesburg. Our closest neighbors were almost a mile away. Until I became school age, I had very limited contact with other people or the outside world, as my parents were very busy trying to survive on a family farm in the early 1950's. Being shy, I would hide when a stranger would stop at our house and my mother would find me either in the basement or out back in the aforementioned tree. I never hid, however, when my Uncle John and his family came to visit. My four cousins were always full of fun and we would play Hide and Seek, Prisoner's Base, and other active games until well after dark when our parents would insist it was time to come inside.

During the summer, my parents allowed me to stay one week with my Uncle John's family. They lived about a half mile from the Millerstown community swimming pool. Every day we would quickly complete our chores in the morning and shortly after lunch we walked to the pool. My oldest cousin was in charge (she being three years older) and we would cross the neighbor's lawn, walk along the berm of the road for a short distance, take a back dirt road for most of the remainder of the walk until we crossed the highway just before arriving at the pool. After swimming for the afternoon, we would repeat the walk home. Imagine doing that in today's world!

There were few outings or vacations. However, one year when I was about 5 years old, my mother and my Aunt Francis decided to take a trip to the seashore. This was my first vacation, and I was excited! My father stayed home to milk the cows. My uncle did not accompany us either. My aunt drove her station wagon with my mother, my brother and I, along with several of my cousins and our beach gear all crammed into her vehicle for the long ride to the shore. This was long before the seatbelt laws were passed and I can remember the children all jockeying for a seat. I was the youngest and ended up sitting happily on a cousin's lap for the entire trip. Once there, we stayed in a cabin and would jump back into the station wagon to make the trip to the beach and back. I was a child with blond hair and fair skin and my only real memory of my first time at the beach was how much pain I had from the blisters on my back due to a severe sunburn! I think perhaps it was a bad experience for my mother, because we did not make the trip ever again. That was the closest thing to a family vacation that we ever took.

At an early age, both my brother and I were expected to "pull our weight" as part of the family. On the farm, all hands were needed, both small and large. My mother had hundreds of chickens that produced a large quantity of eggs. The eggs needed to be graded and boxed by size before they were shipped to our supplier. We had a large egg grading machine in the basement of our house. My job was to put the eggs on the machine where they would roll by gravity downward until they landed in the proper slot that graded them by size. Once graded, my brother boxed each size appropriately from extra-large to small. At the time, I was too small to reach the roller, so I had to stand on a block of wood. This job took us at least an hour and sometimes more each day. I have to say that the occasional egg would slip from my hand and land on the cement floor causing quite a mess. I got pretty good at cleaning up broken eggs! Later, I progressed to feeding the calves and cows. I found that I acquired my father's love of animals and farming, and I could often be found at the barn where I would cuddle with my many furry friends that consisted of cats, dogs, and calves.

Food was always plentiful at our home. Our meals were always cooked. Breakfast was our first meal of the day after spending three or more hours in the barn. Dinner was the largest meal of the day and was served at noontime. We usually had a hired man who ate and, for much of my early childhood, lived with us. Our evening meal was a smaller version of the noon meal and was not served until all of the outside work was finished. This was usually about 7:00 at night. We butchered a pig and a beef annually, so meat was a large part of the meal. My mother and a neighbor would also butcher some of her laying hens once a year. We had a very large freezer. My mother maintained a large garden and I spent many summer days preparing peas, pickles, carrots, green beans, red beets, corn, and strawberries for canning and freezing. We canned peaches, sweet cherries (my favorite), and pears from the local orchards that delivered their fruits on the back of a pickup truck. We had a bakery truck that stopped once a week with bread and baked goods. Sometimes my mother would allow me to pick a sweet treat just for me, so I would always wait anxiously for the truck. The ice cream truck would stop every other week and my mother would fill our freezer with boxes of delicious ice cream and popsicles. About once a month, my mother and I would make to trip to the Newport A & P store for the few additional items that she needed in the grocery line and to collect the Green Stamps that came with her purchase. It was my job to paste them in the Green Stamp book when we got home. Eventually we would collect enough to cash them in on some wish item that would otherwise never have been purchased.

School changed everything! My mother took me to the big town (Newport) to buy new shoes and five dresses (one for each school day) at Benny Carl's clothing store. Oh, how I loved my Buster Brown shoes! My mother drove us a mile to my neighbor's house (which was also my cousins' house) to board the school bus. My brother and I rode that bus to our elementary school in Ickesburg where we had one classroom for each grade 1-6. There was no kindergarten. My life-long friend, Polly, also rode that bus and together for the next twelve years we shared our lives on those rides to and from school. I always marveled at her life because she had three sisters to share her adventures with. We found that, as the crow flies, her house and mine were within walking distance if we hiked over the ridge that separated us. We spent many great times together. I was always invited to birthday parties at her house and with so many sisters, the parties were always very lively. We played beneath the willow tree beside her house and to this day I have a great fondness for willow trees. Polly's mother was a hairdresser, so I made regular visits to her house for haircuts. She would come to my house too and during one of her visits learned to ride a bicycle without the training wheels on our barn hill. Stopping was another matter entirely! This was before helmets or even shoes were required as riding gear. Several years later, we both took a leap of faith as teenagers and allowed her aunt to pierce our ears for us. And all of a sudden, we were grown up!

As I grew up, the world changed. My first memory of a phone was a black rotary dial with a party line. Each family had a different ring, but rest assured that your conversation was never sacred, for there was usually a neighbor listening in to the conversation. And if you talked too long, or a neighbor needed the phone, you would hear the clicking noise made repeatedly by that neighbor clicking the receiver. I remember the day we got our first television, black and white of course (color was many years away). It was big and heavy, and we rearranged the furniture in our living room to place it at just the right spot. It had three stations and a tuner on the top of the TV to turn the antennae that had been mounted to the top of our house roof. Only one station was clear, but you could still see and hear the other stations through the "snow" that covered the picture screen. On weekdays, I would come home from elementary school and run to the barn to do my chores quickly so that I could be back at the house in time for the Mickey Mouse Club. Saturday found me glued to the living room floor as I watched the Saturday morning cartoons. By my early teens, I viewed the assassination and funeral of President John F. Kennedy and shortly thereafter the assassination of his brother, Robert Kennedy and Civil Rights leader Martin Luther King. By my high school years, we would eat our supper while listening to Walter Cronkite report the latest body counts and battles of the Vietnam War, as well as the protests associated with the war and the Civil Rights marches happening in the South. But I also was privileged to watch entertainment greats such as Red Skelton, George Benny, George and Gracey Burns, Andy Griffith, and Lucille Ball. I tried to subdue my excitement as my entire family watched the greatest English invasion of all time (known as the Beatles) one Sunday night on the Ed Sullivan Show. My mother did not seem nearly as impressed as I was!

Before we bought our first television, the radio was our news and music medium. Our radio was about the size of a dresser bureau and was located in a room adjacent to our kitchen. The only music available was from the local radio station, WJUN, that played country music. My father in his younger years had played country music in a local band – "Three Strings and a Boot". So needless to say, we listened to country in the house and also in the barn where we had another radio in the cow stable. I loved to hear my father yodel along to the old country songs as they played on the radio. By the time I became a teenager, transistor radios had become the rage, and rock and roll had replaced country for me. My first record albums purchases were by Leslie Gore, the Supremes and, of course, the Beatles. We had no live stream or apps to listen to music, for we had no computers or i-pads. Record players and radios were our music sources.

After a shy beginning, I became a very social person. I participated in our local 4-H club, where we learned the skills deemed necessary at that time to become a young woman – sewing and cooking. Although I liked sewing and cooking, I liked the 4-H animal club better and raised and showed my own cow at yearly "round-up". In 1964, my 4-H club made a trip to the New York World's Fair by train. At the age of 13, my friends and I viewed in wonder the exhibits that appeared at the exposition. This was the origin of "It's a Small, Small World" by Disney. I can still sing the tune and imagine myself as a young teen staring in awe at the animation created by Disney for the Pepsi Company.

I participated in the school band and my instrument of choice was a clarinet. Marching band had heavy, hot uniforms that we wore not only in the winter, but for all of the local parades in the heat of summer. Dedication was required to be a band member, but there was never a lack of students that participated. In high school, I also chose to become a cheerleader. Practice was after school and then we would ride the activity bus to our drop off point. Mine was Patterson's grocery store in Ickesburg. There I would wait until my mother could break away from the farm work to come and pick me up. While I waited, I would buy myself a cold "pop" and maybe a couple of pieces of penny candy from the enclosed glass shelf that sat on the checkout counter.

For anyone that grew up in the Ickesburg area, no account of our youth would be complete without including the Hi-Way Theater. The Hi-Way was built by my uncle, Ken Reisinger. It was a combination movie theatre, bowling alley, pool hall and soda fountain. My parents bowled with a group of their friends in a bowling league, so from a young age, I spent a lot of time there. My brother and I would watch the movie that was playing upstairs in the theatre while my parents bowled downstairs. Afterward, we would be allowed to have a cherry coke or orange soda from the fountain and sit in a booth until the bowling was finished. The juke box was constantly belting out tunes, mostly country but with some rock and roll slipped in. As I got older, the Hi-Way became the place for every teenager in the area to hang out. Many of us were by now dating. I met my future husband in the 9th grade and by our high school years we spent many Friday and Saturday nights together at the Hi-Way. We could watch the latest movie first and then go downstairs to spend the remainder of the evening with friends. I became a pretty good pool player! Some of the luckier teens owned their own cars and the Hi-Way was the place to show them off with pride. Loud motors were the "in" thing and you just weren't cool if you didn't have your motor revved in order to lay some rubber in front of the Hi-Way when you took off!

I started my first "real" job (with pay) at the age of 13. My uncle owned a restaurant and store just a few miles from my home. We also served soft serve ice-cream. To my great delight, in addition to my meager pay, I could have all the ice cream and milk shakes that I desired. To this day, I love milkshakes, so you can imagine that I made the most of that part of the deal. As I became more skilled at my position, I graduated to making our fresh French fries and other delicious food. I can still remember the beef bar-b-que recipe. I worked there throughout my high school years.

My graduation year was 1969. It was time for us to face the world - a world that was in turmoil at the time. As with all graduations, friends hugged and cried and wished each other a great life. Some headed for war, some to college, some to already established job situations, but all of us into the unknown world called the future. And what an amazing future it became! We could not have predicted a world of computers and cell phones and I-pads. Looking back, each phase of life is a wonder, one to live fully, but also one to share with future generations. We can only move forward if we know where we have been…….

Thank you for the opportunity to share my story!

Perry County Hero's Life During WWII

Storyteller Jeff Dobbs

This is a story about Leo Dobbs and his life during WWII. He was born February 7, 1925 to J. Earl Dobbs and Laura Ann (Weibley) Dobbs. J. Earl was a minister and had charges in the Bedford and Somerset Counties.

Leo was always a jokester from an early age. He also acquired a taste for music and picked up the trumpet, which came in very handy in the future. He was also one to naturally help the less fortunate and would always help or would root for the underdog. Which seemed to fit as he got older and was drafted into the army in 1943; exactly one week after graduation from high school. United States had entered WWII when the Japanese bombed Pearl Harbor on December 7, 1941. United States had already been involved indirectly by supplying Britain with equipment and supplies, but now American boys and girls were going to war. So, by 1943 every boy was doing something for their country.

After graduation from Bedford High School Leo was drafted one week later. With Leo being an only child and his father being a Minister, J. Earl could have Leo placed safely in the Army so he could never see combat. However, Leo said "NO, there is no difference between me or any other 18 or 19-year-old boy being called to save the world." And save the world they did. The country had one mission, to defeat evil.

During basic training Leo relayed this story. One of the recruits was said to be "crazy". Other men would pick on him and make fun of this individual. But Leo didn't. He would help him. Every night, someone's shoes would be urinated on but Leo's shoes were never urinated on. Eventually the man was discharged on a Section 8. Leo always said "Just how crazy was this man? When so many of these men had to see and endure so much by the end of the war."

He also conveyed a story of a recruit who got caught chewing gum in formation. A big NO NO. The recruit had to dig a hole 6 x 6 and 6 feet deep, using his helmet. But it wasn't long until the soldier was allowed to use a shovel to finish the job. Then he couldn't use the ground from that hole to fill back in, he had to dig another 6 x 6- and 6-feet deep hole to fill his first hole, then use the ground from the first hole to fill the second hole.

He also told the story of being on "KP" duty (kitchen patrol). "You learned to peel potatoes correctly, if too much potato left on the peeling you had to peel the peelings."

Leo was in the 100th Division for a short time. He enjoyed being part of a dance band as he played the trumpet. Leo said "Being in the dance band was like royalty. No "KP" duty." He had relaxed times, but all good things do not last. The army came along with what Leo described as "the stupid IQ test". Leo's company of men, approximately 140-150 were given the IQ test. The top 6 of every company tested were sent to a new army program. ATSP (Advanced Training Specialized Program). This was a 4-year college program designed to be completed in one year. Everyone in the program had an extremely high IQ. The program had 1,000 participants at the start and zero graduated. Everyone flunked out. Some lasted longer than others. Leo was a number one whiz kid. But when he got past the numbers, he struggled and flunked out of the program which brought him to the 82nd Airborne.

The days of being treated as royalty of a dance band were long gone as were the days of being a college student. The reality of war was about to grip Leo and would live with him for the next 76 years. Leo would never attend a fireworks display. He would never be a hunter. He valued life. All life, in whatever form. He never wanted anything to suffer. For life in itself is precious and no day is promised to anyone.

Leo became a glider man. He was 82nd Airborne 325th glider infantry 1st battalion company C. He was a 60mm mortar man and an excellent marks men with a M1 rifle. Gliders were only used in WWII. The most common glider that the US used was the Waco CG-4. Approximately 14,000 gliders were built. They carried 15 men plus their equipment. They could also carry a jeep, a small trailer or a 75mm howitzer. They usually flew being towed by a C-47 plane, at 600-800 feet above the surface. They were made of wood and metal tubing as the frame was covered in fabric. Gliders followed the paratroopers into battle. In theory, there would be a secure landing zone for the gliders. In reality, landing zones could be overrun by the Germans and the gliders would land in hell.

Glider men carried with them 2 first aid kits. One strapped to their helmet and one in their pack. They were the only troops to have 2 first aid kits as standard equipment. Glider men were an elite type of soldier. Alongside paratroopers, rangers, and special service force. They carried in their equipment usually 90-100 pounds. Standard weight of equipment was 70 pound minimum. Then you added extra ammo and gear that you knew you needed. Basically, you carried everything you could. Most important was your weapon, ammo, and water.

Training was extremely tough. 25-mile marches were common with a full pack. Leo said "You learned early on when you got a break you didn't sit down. Because if you did, you could not stand back up. But the 25-mile march was not so bad, what was a killer was the 2-hour sprint to and from the start/finish line." Many men were transferred out because they could not physically do the training, and even more were transferred out due to lack of making grade on marksmanship with a rifle. Airborne and glider troops had to be very efficient with weapons. You had to know your weapon, every part of it. Tearing it down blindfolded and putting it all together again. That became so automatic, Leo could very easily disassemble his M1 and put it together blind folded very quickly. Leo caught up to the 82nd airborne in England after the Normandy invasion. Somethings changed for glider troops. They got hazard pay and an additional $50/month. They also got issued jump boots. A very coveted part of their uniform.

In September 1944 Leo had his first taste of combat. In operation Market-Garden, the allies invaded Holland and the Netherlands. September 17, 1944; the 82nd Airborne was dropped on landing zones with the mission to secure and hold bridges at Grave and Nijmegen. The 325 Glider Regiment was scheduled for September 19, but due to heavy fog each day, the glider men did not get in flight to the landing zones until September 23. They lifted off around noon time for the exceedingly difficult 4-hour ride into Holland.

You did not wear your helmet. The weight of your helmet could snap your neck with a sudden drop. Instead, the helmet was used for men who could not hold their breakfast as many men did not. Once you crossed over enemy lines you tried to sit on your helmet as plywood and canvas did little to slow down enemy bullets and flak.

Almost all the men attended a church service before leaving and all men started praying when bullets started to go through the gliders. Company C was in serial no. 16. Forty gliders were in this serial. Out of the forty, only 18 made it to the landing zone.

Landing in a glider was an adventure all its own. In reality, it was an attempted crash landing. One reason why glider men got 2 first aid kits. If you survived the landing, you now had to survive the combat.

Market-Garden was designed to be a 3-day operation. Which was already behind schedule the very first day. The backbone of the German Army was hurt in Normandy, but it was not broken. The Germans had pulled back, refitted, resupplied, and were ready to fight. The allies had stumbled into a stalemate. The 101st and the 82nd obtained their objectives. But the British landing in Arnhem had a rough go of it. Of the 10,000 British Airborne troops that landed in Arnhem only approximately 2,700 men were able to return to friendly lines.

When you were airborne in WWII, there were no rescue plans and no way to pull you back out of a bad situation. You were surrounded by enemy that had one goal and that was to kill you.

Leo, like all glider men drew 3 days of c rations plus a fourth day of emergency rations which was one pound of Hershey chocolate bars. However, it was 8 or 9 days before supplies caught up to the 325th. Fortunately for Leo, he was near a pear orchard and that is what he lived on for several days.

You only got out of your fox hole at night. Fox holes were about 30 inches deep and usually had water in the bottom. You never got out of fox holes in daylight as that would be instant death. The German line was only a few hundred yards in front of them.

Leo recalled one German solider that had what the troops called a bad moment (BM). Leo said the young man popped out of his fox hole dropped his pants and squatted. We gave him the dignity of relieving himself. Then when he stood up and pulled his pants up, we opened up on him. Leo said it looked like his body was dancing in the air as bullets blew through him. Probably every M1 rifle within 500 yards emptied into that body.

What the 82nd airborne did in Holland after the first few days, was repulse counterattack after counterattack. Airborne troops were never intended to be defensive troops, but they ended up defending what became known as Hells Highway which is the supply route of all the allied troops in Holland.

In what was intended to be a 3-day operation for the 82nd was actually a 2-month combat time. The 82nd was relieved on November 17, 1944. Leo spent 55 days in combat in Holland and one instance he and another trooper got pinned down in a sugar beet field by a German sniper. Fortunately, the sniper had missed on his very first shot. Leo dove into the sugar beet field. At full height sugar beets are usually 15-18 inches tall. Leo put his helmet on his finger and raised it up into the air above the plants. P-I-N-G went a bullet off his helmet. Leo said that's the day the earth got 4 inches flatter because he was pushing down that hard.

Leo also relayed a story of one time when he was to lead a patrol. He moved forward from his fox hole and motioned for the rest of the patrol to move out. Just then the Germans sent an illumination artillery shell. Everyone got back in their fox hole, but Leo was too far out. He dove behind a tree stump. The Germans had seen him and opened up with a MG-42 machine gun. He said if he had a newspaper, he could have read it from the light of the tracers going just inches above his head. He could never understand why they never dropped a mortar on him. But they just fired that machine gun for what seemed like hours. The MG-42 machine gun had a firing rate of 1200 rounds per minute. Leo eventually was able to shimmy on his belly back to a fox hole.

Holland was Leo's baptism to combat. He didn't like it and the worst was yet to come. In Holland Leo was the hunted and Leo was the hunter. Something he would be until the war was over. After leaving Holland, Leo's unit was trucked, after they walked the first 20 miles, to Sissonne, France. The 82nd airborne got much needed rest, hot meals, and showers.

While in Holland, getting a shower was a luxury. They got replacements in Sissonne; men that were going to single handedly whip the Germans. But when the bullets are coming your way, those type of men realized that talk is cheap and bravery under fire was a lot different than boasting what one was going to do.

On December 16, 1944, the Germans under the command of Von Rundstedt attacked through the Ardennes Forest in Belgium. In what became known as the Battle of the Bulge. Very nasty fighting followed. The 82nd airborne was alerted on December 17,1944. On December 18th they were in line to stop the German attack. The 82nd was to go to Bastogne, but they were ahead of the 101st so the 82nd was diverted North to Werbomont.

The 101st gained fame as the "battered bastards of Bastogne". They were in hell. But at no time was the pressure on the 101st anything like the German attack was on the 82nd, which was exerted by 3 SS divisions. The 82nd had rolled into the path of the first, second, and ninth panzer SS divisions. The 82nd and the SS, did not take prisoners. There was a lot of hand-to-hand combat, complicated by freezing temperatures and lack of supplies. This is where the 325th made a recruiting statement for decades to follow.

The seventh armored was in full retreat, and on their heels were the Germans. A tank was in retreat when it came upon a loan infantry solider from the 325th who was digging a foxhole. The solider looked up at the tank commander (which happened to be Will Rodgers's son), and said "Are you looking for a safe place?"

"Yes", answered the tanker.

"Well buddy, just pull your vehicle behind me. I am the 82nd airborne and this is as far as the bastards are going." Can you imagine a tank being told to get behind a lone glider man digging a foxhole? That was the attitude of the 325th glider men, they didn't run, they were there to fight, so they fought, and they fought hard.

Leo said "That is exactly how far the Germans got. They never pressed farther than that line, that the one lonely 325th glider man started." In the Bulge Leo experienced extreme cold. Nighttime temperatures below zero and daytime temperatures around 20 degrees. Men froze to death. Rations and water were hard to come by. Snow was knee deep and sometimes waist deep, and Germans were plentiful.

On what Leo and his unit thought was Christmas Day he was successful in sneaking into a village and stealing a chicken. Him and three other men used a helmet to boil water to cook the chicken. However, they moved 4 times before they got the chicken cooked. He said you didn't have to worry about the chicken going bad because as soon as you took it out of the water it was frozen again.

They used snow to melt for water to cook the chicken in and by that time they were using snow for drinking water. They had no other water and using snow was the only source available, and like the Germans, there was a lot of it.

Leo also relayed this story many times. When they got a chance to fall back and get a hot meal and supplies, they picked up new replacements. One of these was very boastful. One of the types that were going to single handedly win the war. So, when they got back to the front line, they were ordered to do a patrol. The snow was nearly waist deep, and they were to find enemy positions and enemy strength. They headed out into no man's land. At some point, this one loudmouth that was going to whip all the German army, cracked. He went down, paralyzed from fear. He couldn't move and was a total mess. The other men on the patrol decided to leave him, with the idea that with any luck, he would freeze to death before the Germans found him.

But one man said "come on boys, we don't leave anybody behind. I'll carry him if you guys carry my equipment and his". It was so cold, and the wind was blowing and the snow deep, but they got the new replacement and all the equipment back to their lines.

Another patrol they ran, Leo was rear guard. Rear guard was not an easy job. While the rest of the patrol was in front of you, your job was to make sure the enemy didn't come in behind you, trapping you. It also meant if your patrol got into trouble, you had to rescue them or cover their retreat.

As happened, the patrol was to check out a small town of just a couple dozen houses. Well, the town was full of Germans and the patrol ran into trouble. Leo heard several gun shots, and saw his guys on the run. Leo waited, holding his ground, watching his buddies run past him, and around the corner of a house came a German in pursuit. Leo squeezed off one round. The man went down and no other Germans appeared. Leo said "after thinking about it, I should have waited another 2 or 3 seconds. Maybe more would have showed themselves and I could have gotten a couple more". Every man on that patrol got back safely. Nobody killed or wounded.

Leo also told of friendly fire. His unit was fired on by American artillery in which 5 rangers and 20 glider men were killed. Also, another friendly fire incident, in which his platoon moved into a small town. The American commanders did not believe that an American unit had pushed that far forward, so they had the town shelled. And the next night, the Germans realized that they didn't have anybody in that town, so they shelled the town. Leo said after being shelled by the Americans the first night and the Germans the second night, not a single house was standing, but nobody in the platoon was hurt or killed.

Leo also told a story of when they were on the front line and the Germans were giving them an artillery barrage. Leo and one other soldier were in a two-man foxhole. All of a sudden, another soldier several yards away popped out of his foxhole and sprinted to the foxhole Leo was in and jumped in. This made three men in a two-man foxhole. The soldier said he had a real bad feeling about that foxhole over there. It wasn't five minutes when an artillery shell made a direct hit on that foxhole! Leo and the other man with him told the third guy to let them know if he got a bad feeling about the foxhole, they were in.

On January 5, 1945, Leo earned the purple heart medal. While in a foxhole, during an artillery barrage, a phosphorous artillery shell exploded about tree top level. Leo got hit and phosphorous rained down on him. Some burned into him just below the belt line of his stomach. Leo was able to get to a field hospital which was nothing more than a small barn. There were wounded everywhere. Leo got a report filed but he never got treatment. The doctor had run out of morphine days ago and was amputating civil war style. There were a pile of arms and legs laying outside the barn. Leo couldn't take the screaming of the man having his leg sawed off so he left. Leo got married in 1951, and that wound was still seeping a yellow puss like liquid that his wife discovered and took him to the family doctor where he finally was able to get it healed.

On Christmas Day, the 82nd was ordered to retreat. (This is why the chicken they were trying to cook took so many times to actually cook it.) Retreat was an unknown concept for the 82nd. They believed that there was only one way to go, forward! To retreat represented failure, and no one in the 82nd wanted to give up ground, but an order was an order.

Only later did the men learn that the division to their left and the division to their right had been pushed back several miles and the 82nd was within hours of being surrounded. Knowing this did not sit well with the men of the 82nd. After all they were fighting three different SS divisions in some of the hardest and bloodiest battles. The 82nd stood their ground, why couldn't the other divisions stand and fight?

Anyway, the 82nd pulled back to a defensive line. They dug in at the village of Vaux Chauvanne. The ground was frozen hard, but foxholes had to be dug for the Germans closed the vacated gap very quickly. And in the early morning hours of December 26th, they attacked Leo's company. A battalion of Germans attacking a company. Roughly 1,000 enemy troops were descending on approximately 140 men.

Company C was under a brutal attack. The sky was lit with tracers. The outpost was quickly overrun. The Germans got into the outskirts of the village. One soldier of the 325th had a finger bitten off in brutal hand to hand combat. Leo and the others of the 60mm mortar units went to work. They fired around 500 mortar rounds into the attacking enemy. This made a decisive turn in the attack. This helped break the back of the 2nd SS panzer division. It is said that after this attack, the 2nd SS lost its bite and dash. An element pushed into Gavin's 82nd and got a severe mauling from the glider men of the 325th.

On the 27th of December, the 325th got 370 replacements. Within a few hours, most of these green non-experienced men were dead or on their way back to the states, wounded. Leo said you never made friends with the new guys, their survivor rate could be measured in hours or a few days at best.

Also, with the new replacements on the 27th came much needed winter clothing and overshoes. On December 30th, Leo's unit got pulled off the line for a short break. On January 1st, 1945, they got a hot meal. The first hot meal since December 18th. It was their Christmas meal. Turkey and hot coffee. For a brief moment, the men could relax and think about home and be mad at the Germans for attempting to break out in the Bulge, because by early December, everybody thought the war would be over by Christmas, but that was not to be.

Sleeping and living like hunted animals in the bitter cold and snow, hungry and eating snow for water was an inhuman experience. Again, Leo said they were the hunted, and they were the hunter. For a couple days, Leo's battalion was regimental reserve, giving the men time to sleep and get supplies because on January 4th, they were on the attack.

They took the village of La Chapelle. On the 5th, they took the high ground between Abrefontaine and La Falise. In the afternoon of the 5th, Leo's unit was ordered to hold so other units on their flanks could catch up.

This is when Leo was wounded during an enemy artillery barrage. His unit held on the 6th, but on the 7th they were back in action, pressing forward. They took the village of Menil, Gernchamps and Brux. On the 10th, the 325th was pulled off the line and trucked to Pepinster Belgium. While there Leo had his picture taken with three other men of his unit. A picture that Leo valued very much. That picture as was told by one of the men on the picture to his family, that got in contact with Leo's family, after Leo passed, was a picture of four of the five remaining men that entered the Battle of the Bulge in a platoon of fifty-two men. The others were either killed by the enemy, killed by the extreme cold weather, wounded, or missing in action.

For many years, Leo stayed in contact with one of those men on that picture, they would talk on the phone sometimes all night long. Mostly if one had memories or attempted to watch a war movie, then they would call each other and talk for hours. Leo watched *Saving Private Ryan* and he also watched *Band of Brothers*. But he would watch ten to thirty minutes at a time and then he would wait several weeks before he would watch more.

On January 10th, 1945, the 82nd Airborne got a statement to them from their commander General Gavin. It was recorded in the book, "Let's Go", written by Wayne Pierce, company commander.

In it General Gavin wrote:

To the Troops of the 82nd Airborne Division. This date brings to an end a period of arduous and intensive combat unparalleled, I believe, in American History. Called upon most unexpectedly, you moved, within a space of hours, to the northern flank of the overpowering German drive into Belgium. Shortly thereafter you advanced into German positions with the mission of extricating what was present of three U. S. divisions then engaged in the vicinity of St. Vith. Your advance enabled you to cut off the armored spearheads of the German 1st SS panzer division. The spearhead of this division in your sector you destroyed. All efforts of the 1st SS panzer division to relieve this spearhead were also dealt with severely and driven back. On the south flank of the division's advance, the German 2nd SS panzer division was beaten off in repeated determined and costly attacks. The U. S. 7th, 106th and 28th Divisions were wholly or in part withdrawn through the Vielsalm bottleneck into the area of our division. Covering positions were held and these divisions were again withdrawn farther to the rear. From this covering position, upon orders from the Commander of the 21st Army Group, Field Marshal Montgomery, you withdrew in excellent order to a defensive position along the TROIS PONTS-ERRIS-BRA-MANHAY LINE. Here you met and repulsed the powerful and costly attacks of the German 9th Panzer Division and the 62d Volks Grenadier Division, who were attempting to continue the northern advance. When finally permitted by higher headquarters to resume the offensive, you completely destroyed the German 62d Volks Grenadier Division, elements of the 18th Volks Grenadier Division and the 3rd Parachute Division in addition to a number of odds and ends. You inflicted upon the Germans a great loss of men and equipment and you captured over 2500 prisoners. In the offensive you attained the objective assigned and seized Their du Mont overlooking Vielsalm, thus placing the First U. S. Army in an excellent position to resume the offensive. These accomplishments, gained under most trying conditions of winter warfare, are a vital contribution to the ultimate decisive defeat of the Wehrmacht. I have received numerous commendations for your combat behavior in the past few weeks and these I have transmitted to you. I would like to add my own to you for a splendid soldierly job superbly done.

James M. Gavin
Major General, U. S. Army

In Pepinster, Leo got himself in a pickle. They had a curfew, but officers didn't. One night while passing a night club, Leo and the soldier with him observed officers in the club. These were not airborne officers. Leo said, "what is good for the goose is good for the gander". He and his buddy entered the club and approached a table where the officers were seated. Leo asked why the regular man had a curfew, but officers didn't? To which a Major stood and started to berate Leo for entering the club. Leo claimed he didn't know how it happened, but the Major ended up on the floor with Leo on top of him. Other men pulled Leo off and the Major wanted Leo's name and dog tag number. Leo held up his dog tags and said to the Major "you are so scared you can't read my dog tags, so I'll tell you my name and number".

The MP's showed up and hauled Leo off to the brig. Leo's buddy that was with him that night ran to where the company commander was and explained what happened. The company commander went to the brig and got Leo out. He said that PFC Dobbs is the company bugler and was needed in the morning for roll call. Leo always smiled when he told this story because he was the company bugler, but he had an assistant. And he said" I never blew the bugle. I always had my assistant do it".

On January 26th, the regiment left Pepinster. On the 28th, they were in bitter freezing cold and waist deep snow, attacking the German border. At first resistance was light. This was the famed

Siegfried Line. Full of pill boxes and dragon teeth. The rifle squads of Leo's platoon got demolished on the Siegfried Line. They were attacking without tank support and the Germans opened with everything they had.

Leo told this story with tears rolling down his cheeks. Men were literally blown to pieces. And a buddy of his had shrapnel in his knee and could only take two or three steps and fall. The man made it back to cover and Leo said he could always remember Wally trying to run for cover.

The Siegfried Line was very tough. Leo said the hardest thing you'll ever do in life is to listen to men burn to death. They had to use flamethrowers and burn some of the pill boxes out. The Siegfried Line was one of the toughest battles the 325th faced.

By February 8th, the 325th was off the line. Leo's birthday was the 7th. He turned 20 years old and he said if he remembered right, the high temperature on his birthday was zero. Another hot meal. Life was good. They even got hot showers. Although if the water ran out before you were done, you had to stand and shiver until more water was heated, but they would take that compared to having to kill or be killed. And by that time, most of the German soldiers just wanted the whole thing to be over. The next mission for the 325th was to cross the Roer River, but that order was rescinded and the men of the 325th cheered.

At some point, General Jumping Jim Gavin, commander of the 82nd Airborne division, had told Supreme Allied Commander Dwight Eisenhower that when it gets too hot for the other divisions, to call the 82nd. Gavin stated, "it's just getting warm for my boys".

Leo actually got to talk to General Gavin in Holland. Jumping Jim as he was known to his troops, was well known for being in the front line with his boys. Encouraging them and the boys had an immense amount of respect for Jumping Jim. One reason why the Germans feared the 82nd. The 82nd is credited with taking more prisoners than any other division. The 82nd stood toe to toe with the best German divisions and gave no quarter.

Leo's unit was back in Camp Sissonne, France. Perhaps the war was over for them. Many hoped so. They witnessed death and destruction and the inhuman treatment that mankind could have toward other human beings. Leo saw children fight for scraps or maybe a bite of grease in a garbage can. They had heard stories of some of the concentration camps that existed, and they were about to experience one with their own eyes.

On March 30th, the 325th was back in the line. They did mostly mop up operations and defensive positions. Enemy strength was weak and enemy morale was very low. The common German soldier knew what the outcome of the war would be and nobody wanted to be the last man killed.

All through April the 325th only did patrols with very little action. On May 1st, the 325th crossed the Elbe River. This would be their last attack of the war. Company C would lead the attack but there was no resistance. Instead, they met civilians and German soldiers walking toward them. They wanted to get behind American lines. Civilians carried what few possessions they had on their backs. Some pushed wheelbarrows and some had small carts but most just carried what they could. German soldiers still carried their weapons, but they had no intent of using them.

The Russians were pushing behind them and they knew if the Russians captured them, they would be executed. Just as the civilians knew they would be robbed, beaten, raped, and then killed. The Germans and the Russians had an extreme hatred of each other and when the Germans were having success in Russia in the early years of the war, they did some of the most atrocities of the war to the Russian civilians. Now the Russians were going to get revenge and even the score.

On May 2nd, General Von Tippelskirch, Commander of the 21st German Army surrendered to General Gavin of the 82nd Airborne Division. Approximately 144,000 men were taken prisoner by only 10,000 men.

The 325th pushed into Ludwigslust Germany. There the 325th found Wobbelin concentration camp. Bodies piled high from starvation. American medics were moved in and did their best to save the living, but for many that were still breathing, it was too late. They could not be saved.

The towns people of Ludwigslust said they had no idea that the concentration camp was starving people. General Gavin did not buy their story or their excuse. So, on the park grounds at Ludwigslust, General Gavin made it mandatory that the towns people dig graves for the dead. They buried 200 bodies that had been starved to death. It was also mandatory to be in attendance for the ceremonies.

Leo was part of the group of soldiers that over saw the graves being dug and that all towns' people were in attendance. He said that after the graves were dug, they pushed some of the towns' people in and started to throw ground on them. They buried no one, but they certainly made sure that the towns' people knew they meant business. Leo said that is a memory that you can never erase from your mind. The stench of rotting flesh and the ghostly look from the bodies deprived of food so they would starve a slow death.

The fighting was over. The war was over. No more combat. Leo was on occupation duty in Berlin. Couple things happened there that Leo talked about. World War 3 almost started there. In the Russian sector beside the American sector, two Russians were celebrating and fired their pistols. The soldiers of the 82nd fired on them. Leo wasn't sure but thought both Russians were killed.

The Russian commander went ballistic. General Jumping Jim Gavin came down to the area. The Russian via a translator said that his men were just celebrating and when a Russian celebrates, he fires his weapon as an exclamation point. General Gavin's reply was that we are the 82nd Airborne and when shots are fired near us, we shoot first and then ask questions.

His suggestion to the Russian commander was to tell his men not to fire any weapons. Leo said after that, no more shots were fired from the Russian sector and nobody in the 82nd got in trouble for shooting the 2 Russians.

Also, one time on patrol, Leo and the soldier with him witnessed a man being kicked out of a restaurant. Leo and the other soldier were able to ascertain from the man that he used to be a soldier and the people in the restaurant were ashamed of him because he lost the war and would not allow him to eat. Leo and the soldier with him felt sorry for the man. He was just regular army, fighting for his country just as Leo had done. These two 82nd men marched the man back into the restaurant and the man got to order anything he wanted on the menu. And eat for free! No charge.

Leo was able to return to the U. S. in January of 1946 with an honorable discharge. He received many medals and he had a lot of memories. Some he enjoyed and a lot of memories he wanted to forget. But they stayed with him for the rest of his life.

Leo passed on to heaven on June 30th, 2020, at the age of 95. A week before his passing, he was dreaming and still fighting that war 75 years later. The price the men of the 325th Glider Infantry paid was high.

Some like Leo had memories that would not go away. They lived with battle scars, mental and physical. Leo's feet were frozen, his ears were frozen and his left hand was frozen. He was deaf in one ear. But you never knew. He never complained about anything.

After seeing and living what he went through as a nineteen- and twenty-year-old man, he had no complaints. And he always stated, "The American people have no idea how fortunate they are. Life is so short. Life is promised to no one, and what you have is so precious."

No man that served will forget the ones who never returned. The men of the 325th came from all walks of life. United in a life and death struggle, they overcame fear, sadness, hardships and with a M1 rifle, they beat back the evilness of Nazism.

They believed in patriotism, honoring their flag, their country and their family. Just a few short years ago, Leo was talking about our country, and he started to cry. Tears rolled down his cheeks. Football players were kneeling instead of honoring the flag when the National Anthem was played. He said the country we have now is not the country that he fought for and so many died for.

He said our country will soon be lost. If anyone would ever refer to Leo as a hero, he would say no he wasn't. He was just an American kid serving his country and doing his job, just like all the other eighteen- to twenty-year-old kids were doing. They were saving the world. If you want to see what real heroes look like, go to Europe, and visit all the cemeteries. When you see all the white crosses, you will be looking at all the heroes. Because the heroes are under them.

After the war Leo returned home, but it wasn't easy. For years, if a plane flew too low, Leo would seek shelter. He eventually learned that the planes would not strafe him. He also, at the sound of a loud noise, dove flat on the floor or ground. The bang of a rifle shot could send him back to 1944. He never attended firework displays. He spent most Fourth of July's and New Year's Eve's in the house, so others could celebrate.

For the next 74 years Leo built a beautiful life raising four children, three boys and one girl with his beautiful wife Marcella of 68 years.

Memories of Growing up in Liverpool in the 1960's

Storyteller Julie Shumaker Harvey

Labor Day celebrations at the Liverpool Ballfield –

For several years in the 1960's, Liverpool held Labor Day celebrations at the ballfield on Pine Street. Lots of good food and games but the biggest draw was the greased pig races and the banty chicken races. The town kids (mostly teenage boys) would chase after a greased piglet. I think the prize was the pig – but I'm not certain about that. The pig would run wherever it could. I don't believe there was a fence.

For the banty chicken races, if I remember correctly, they would release several chickens and the kids would chase and catch them. The chickens would run all over the place. You never knew where they would go. But it was fun to watch all the chickens scatter with little kids chasing after them.

Like other small towns in Perry County, Liverpool Fire Company would have a carnival every year. Sometimes there would be fireworks. It was held at the ballfield which was just one block from my house. Growing up, my best friend lived catty cornered from me. Her name was Jack Arnold. We would go down and watch the carnival people set up the rides. We would walk to the carnival every night, and since we lived so close, if we had to go to the bathroom, we would just run home! I'm not sure what they did for bathroom facilities back then – did they have porta johns??? I do remember how exciting it was to see all the ride tickets that my mom purchased ahead of time at Miller's grocery store.

One year, as we were walking back from watching the carnival guys set up the rides and games, a mama skunk and several baby skunks went under a porch. We thought it would be a great idea to catch the baby skunks. We ran home, got a trash can, and set off to catch them. Needless to say, we did not catch any, but we did manage to get sprayed by them. When I walked in my house, my mom made me exit immediately and go to the shed to undress! I was mortified! But I never tried to catch baby skunks again!

Riding bike – My friend Jack and I used to ride bicycle out in the country to what is now Red Bridge Road. There is a small creek that follows that road. We would play for hours in that creek, catching whatever we could. One time, a leech landed on Jack's arm – yuck – so disgusting. But we just kept playing. Our mothers never worried about where we were, or what we were up to. When we knew it was about supper time, we rode back into town.

Speaking about supper time – all the town kids knew what time it was when the church bells chimed 5 times – time to go home for supper. Another tell-tale sign it was time to go home was when the streetlights came on. The fire siren rang every day at noontime – so everyone knew when it was lunchtime!

Jack and I used to roller skate all over town, too. The roller skates that fit over your sneakers and you had a key to tighten them! Hours upon hours of skating and stopping and picking apples off the Stailey's apple tree – hoping not to get caught. Or picking cherries off my uncle's tree. We would skate to my grandma's house or Jack's grandma's house, or down to my cousin's house. You could walk along the street and name everyone that lived in each house. There weren't any strangers. And you always felt safe.

There were many times we would have a pick-up softball game in the field beside our house. Nothing organized, just a bunch of kids passing time on a hot, summer day playing ball. At night we would play Tin-Can-Alley. The can would be set up on the sewer lid under the streetlight. Someone would be "it", and someone would run and kick the can. All the kids would scatter and hide. The person that was "it" had to run and get the can, put it back on the sewer lid and go in search of all the kids. When he (or she) would spot someone, "it" would run back to the can, put their foot on it, and yell "I see" (and yell out their name). That person then had to come sit on the stoop until someone could kick the can before "it" could. It was always fun, hiding in the dark yards and alleys.

In the summertime, we used to make tents out of blankets and sleep out. Sometimes we would build small fires and roast marshmallows. (Although I don't think our parents knew we did that). We would also run all over town in the middle of the night, hoping to not get caught by the town cop!

One year, at Halloween, instead of soaping windows, we decided to knock over outhouses. Liverpool had water and sewer at that time although it was still fairly new, so there still were plenty of outhouses in peoples' back yards. Needless to say, we gave Joe Newton (the town cop at the time) a run for his money. I don't believe any of us were caught (there were probably about 6-8 of us) but Joe certainly did use up some gas that night searching for us in his cop car. One outhouse we tipped had a concrete floor. It took all of us to heave-ho and it made a very loud crash when it hit the ground. We scattered so fast but weren't caught!

Wintertime meant ice skating at the creek beside what is now Chris's Pizza, or we would go down to Wallis's Pond and skate. We would have a big bonfire made with tires (that would never fly now) and skate for hours. We would also sled all day long (and I mean ALL day long). I was lucky enough to live at the bottom of Democratic Lane when it was still a dirt road. There rarely were any vehicles on that road. We would climb to the top of the hill and, if we were lucky enough, we could get to Front Street in one ride. We had runner sleds and we would hook our feet into the sled behind us and have a sled train, sometimes with up to 10 sleds! Most of the kids in town would sled down Keyhill (which is Race Street), but since we lived at the bottom of Democratic Lane, we would sled that one. It was usually all the kids from the upper end of town.

Growing up, my mom and several of my aunts would take all of the kids down to the ferryboat to swim. It wasn't the campsites it is now, but there were swings for the adults to sit and swing while the kids swam and played in the river. When the ferryboat came over, you had to get out of its way. There was a big rock just off the shore. It had a name, just not sure what it was called. I was always scared to swim to it because it seemed so far away. My sisters and cousins would. I was usually the chicken! My grandma, Ruth Hoffman, ran the snack stand with lots of penny candy. It had a foot board for the kids to stand on so they could see in the big window to look at all the candy. Sadly, it was swept away in the 1972 flood.

Memorial Day Parades were big in Liverpool when I was growing up. As a child, I would march with the Daisies or Girl Scouts. We would pick flags from our garden, wrap them in tinfoil, and march up Keyhill to the cemetery for a ceremony. We would then place the flowers on the graves of veterans. As a teenager, I was in the marching band and we would march up over that hill to the cemetery for the memorial ceremony. And back then, we had to wear wool suits for marching band. Sometimes, it got very hot!

The elementary school was a block from my house and we would walk to school every day. The cafeteria in Liverpool Elementary was really the gymnasium and the lunches were made from scratch by 2 ladies – Mrs. Freed and Mrs. Sheaffer. If you were learning to play an instrument, lessons were held in the basement of the school. Barner Swartz was the band director.

And because I have such wonderful memories of growing up in a small town surrounded by people who loved me and I loved – I am trying my darndest to make memories like I cherish, for my grandchildren. They don't live "right around the corner" from me, but they aren't too far away. I try to get them together with their cousins at least once a week. I hope they look back and say, "remember when. . .." and smile!

Carson Long Military Academy New Bloomfield

Storyteller Judith Lepere Armstrong

Growing up on the campus of Carson Long in New Bloomfield was wonderful. My parents were Joseph and Anita Lepere. I had 3 siblings: Joe Jr, Pattie, and Ellie. The freedom we, as children had, was unmatched by today's standards. My father started working at Carson Long in 1945. He taught Latin and Russian. Carson Long was owned by Edward Holman (whom we referred to as Daddy Ed when we were with his grandkids). Our parents would strangle us if we didn't call adults by Mr., Mrs. or other titles. His wife was Helen (Nana). Carson Holman (Spike), wife Martha, also owned the school. Our family was very close to the Holmans and their home, called The Maples. As children, we LOVED riding the elevator, playing old records in the formal sitting room and coloring napkins. In those days, napkins were designed with flowers, butterflies and designs.

The campus was a military school for boys from grades 6 to 12, running from September to June. The summer was the time for us kids to have the run of the campus. We had the gym, library, ballfields, tennis courts, backboard (when you didn't have anyone to play tennis with, you hit the ball at the board and the ball came back). We played in the woods collecting sap and then we would try to boil it down. Yes, we had matches and lit fires (small ones). Boy, we were lucky not to burn down the woods. We spent all day outside and never needed a watch to keep track of the time, because we knew the time by the chimes that rang every 15 minutes. When the chimes rang for the hour, we all stopped playing so we could count the number of gongs.

We once had a green grape battle with teams. I say once because when we got caught, we were punished. Two reasons, we picked all the green unripe grapes from the vines, thus ruining any chance of using them.

Second reason, one team was on the rooftop of the garage. The adults thought it was dangerous! By the way, ANY adult could reprimand us! We got lectures and told to stop, and we knew that when we returned home, Mom would know and real punishment followed.

We also played with knives. One game was called 'chew the peg'. I don't remember the details but if you lost you had to chew a piece of stick (the peg) out of the ground with your teeth.

Imagine, playing with matches, knives and climbing roofs! We lived dangerously.

Not all our time was on the campus. We had the run of the town. Before the swimming pool was built, that area was a swamp. We would slosh in the water collecting frog eggs and tadpoles. We knew our mailbox combination, no keys to open the little door. We got our mail quite often, by ourselves. We also went to the grocery store alone for little things. Then there was the ice pond where we skated in winter and explored in summer. Again, no adults! To get to the pond we had to go through the graveyard. Thank goodness we didn't go at night! When it rained, we went to Clouser's Hardware Store and helped bring in items they had lined on the sidewalk. We got a dime each time for helping.

Then off we would go to Carmichael's to get penny candy.

Our parents knew everything we did in town! Yes, our town was full of tattle tales! But that kept us all in line! Growing up in New Bloomfield gave me such wonderful memories!

Perry County Farm Girl Gives Up Milking Stool

Storyteller Linda "Rocky" (Dum) Rock

I was raised a farm girl, outside of Green Park, and still live on part of the farm yet today. My parents were Glenn E. Dum and Hulda L. Dum. We didn't have tv, computers or cell phones. Our phone hung on the wall. You'd talk into a mouthpiece attached to the wall phone, with a listening device put up to your ear. The phone lines were all party lines, meaning more than one household shared the same line. You'd hear the other household's ring. They were our neighbors and you could hear their conversations. Our ring was one long and two short bleeps. Our phone numbers were only three digits, like R12 which was ours.

We had two work horses, Prince and Dolly. I remember one spring day when Dad got them out of the barn stable to do some work. He didn't tether them and when he went to grab the harness, they took off running out the dirt road. I was so upset, I started out after them. Dad stopped me. He said they'll be back. Sure enough here they come. Well I guess, father does know best! Those draft horses were ready for work. We didn't ride them.

We made hay with an old hay rake. It took loose hay to the back of a wagon, with someone taking a fork full to the front. Someone would stomp it down till we had a full load. We'd take the wagon to the barn to be unloaded.

At the barn, we had a large horseshoe shaped iron fork that was attached to the roof along with two ropes. The pronged fork with its locking mechanism was hooked onto the hay. One of the ropes was attached to the horses, and they would pull the hay over into the hay loft. Somebody would man the second rope opening the jaws allowing the hay to drop freely into the loft. It looked like jellyfish falling from the sky. So pretty!

Being raised near a small town, you went to a small school. Your class may have ten to twenty students. You knew everyone by name. My first couple of years in school were at the two-story school in Elliottsburg, which currently is a parking lot for the Messiah Lutheran Church. We got our water from the house next door, owned by Jane Dyer and we used an outhouse. There was a wood fired furnace for heat.

Grade three through sixth, I went to Landisburg High School. The cafeteria was in the basement. You went down the steps to get your tray of food, and then back to the classroom. We ate at our desks. You could always hear somebody tripping up the steps and loosing lunch. They'd watch their sandwich and fruit roll down the long steps.

For fun once a month, for ten cents we'd go to the Yankee Movie Theatre in Landisburg. In the summer, the one room Green Park School had a summer playground. You could meet your school friends and have a Saturday full of fun. Walking home we would stop at Ed Garlin's Store and Post Office, for penny candy. The older men met there to solve all the troubles of the world. They always sat in front of the candy case blocking our view of the sweet treats.

The store was located in Green Park at the intersection of the short-cut road back to the school. The store was on the left side of the house with the post office in the back. Walking inside, the candy counter was to the left, groceries in the middle, and barrels of pickles and crackers to the right.

My sister went to the one room Green Park School. Her teacher was Helen Briner. One day school mates Bill and Ed Kennedy, who lived on a farm in Green Park, told Lucille, they had puppies for sale. At lunch time, the three walked to the farm, to see the puppies. My sister came back to school with a puppy for a big price of ten cents. His name was Ten Cent Tippy and he was going to spend the rest of the day in the school trash can. Well, that didn't work! Miss Briner decided the class could play with the puppy the remainder of the day. He was the best groundhog hunting dog we ever had.

When I was ten years old, I joined the 4-H Dairy Club, but I didn't have a registered calf. While I was at school, my dad went to Kruger's Dairy in Carlisle and bought a registered Guernsey calf. I found my surprise when I went to the barn to do my chores. I named my 4-H project Jenny.

Back then the 4-H Roundup was held at various farms throughout the county. The Knouse family started hosting the Roundup at the present-day Greenwood Nursery, near Ickesburg. After the county show, if you won a blue ribbon, you went to the district show. There you would show your heifer competing against several other counties at Center Hall or Beaver Springs. You stayed in area homes during the show. Sure made a lot of friends.

When the Perry County Fair started again, in 1971, we housed our animals in a tent. The Roundup or show was held in the dirt parking lot.

In the 1960s, some of the members went to the Farm Show to compete with their animals. My mother and I stayed at the Farm Show all week, in the women's dormitory. To get Jenny ready for the show ring, I brushed her coat and tail. Then I bathed her with baby shampoo to soften her thick hair. I also used bluing to whiten her legs. Tar soap was used for really tough stains.

After Jenny dried off, I'd brush her again and trim her hooves. It was hectic with all the other animals being groomed at the same time. I had to keep a tight hold on Jenny's halter, so she wouldn't become skittish from all the unusual activity. I practiced leading Jenny every day, so she would respond well in the show-ring during the crucial judging.

The judges looked for a straight back, good muscle development, and firmness of the udder on the dairy cows. They noted cleanliness, well-trimmed hooves, and temperament.

The 4-Her was also judged. I had to wear a white uniform, complete with a skirt. I, too, was judged on cleanliness, showmanship, and how I fitted Jenny's halter. Dairy cattle were shown walking backwards. I also had to present my 4-H records, which documented my daily activities of feeding, watering, and brushing Jenny, as well as training her to lead. Of course, I also milked her daily once she came of age and started producing milk.

Back then, there wasn't a milking parlor in the Farm Show building. You had to take your own equipment to hand milk your cows. I took my special milk stool made by a cousin in school shop class. Relaxing on my stool in the Farm Show dairy barn, I was approached by two men who inquired if they might use the stool. I asked for what purpose. They said they needed it for Governor Lawrence to use. I told the men ok but gave instructions that he needed to sit in the middle of the wobbly stool.

Well, he didn't get the message and Governor Lawrence fell on his backside, as a photographer snapped a picture. After wards, Governor Lawrence received an award.

A few weeks later, at a news conference, my sister and I presented our cantankerous stool to Governor Lawrence. My mom helped me to write my speech. Our wobbly milking stool is now in a museum.

The following year at an American Guernsey Breeders Association luncheon, I was surprised when they presented me with a handmade milking stool. Of course, I had to give another speech!

My grandparents, Joshia and Grace Dum, got the first tv in the family. Once or twice a week, all the aunts and uncles along with their kids would go to my grandparents to watch tv. Some of the shows I liked to watch were the Cisco Kid, Roy and Dale Evans, and the Lone Ranger and Tonto. I also listened to them on the radio. The men would watch wrestling broadcast from Hershey.

We had homemade cakes with churned vanilla and chocolate ice cream. The women visited and caught up on the local news. All the kids played games, like hide and seek, Red Rover, and Catch or Tag. Always seemed as though the smaller kids would end up being it. Sure worked up an appetite for bowls of ice cream.

At Christmas, the kids put on a talent show. We sure had lots of fun!

Perry County Living in the 1940's and Beyond

Storyteller Frances Ickes Owen
Recorded by Debra Kay Noye

Who ever heard of hand-picking bugs off the farmer's crops, and pulling the wild mustard, just to earn a few coins, to spend at the local carnival! Well, Frances Ickes Owen did just that, and spent her money on cotton candy and caramel corn, at the Bloomfield Fireman's annual 4th of July Carnival.

Fran had a great time at the carnival, but not so great catching bugs and putting them into small containers, which held kerosene. There was no escaping that fate. A Campbell family lived, in what was to become the John Adams stone farmhouse, outside of New Bloomfield. The farm still has a pond and barn, right along Shermans Valley Road. Campbell farmed the land, and he hired Fran and her siblings to debug the fields. This was before spraying with insecticides, became popular. It was a daunting task! And, no wonder, she fell asleep, before the traditional fireworks display, on the eve of the 4th of July celebration!

At that time, the Ickes family was renting, from a Dromgold, that owned a farm across the road, from the Campbell farm. Fran lived back a long dirt lane, in a stone farmhouse. One day, to the surprise of the Ickes children, a long black snake, came slithering down the steps, from the upstairs bedrooms. They were petrified, but their dad calmly opened the front door, and the snake went on its way. Her dad told them, it probably had crawled up the side of the stone house, into the attic, and was venturing through the house looking for a way out.

Fran first lived, on what the locals refer to as "the back road to Duncannon", outside of New Bloomfield. Her parents rented a tenant house from Libby Roth.

Picking sweet cherries, into empty syrup buckets, was a fun job. Fran, Sadie, William, Richard, and Ronald would ultimately have a cherry battle. Their mother had them wash off all the sticky, juicy mess, in the creek, which ran through the property. The kids knew, they'd be enjoying cherry puddin', for lunch that day!

The creek also provided them, with ice in the winter. They took advantage and used the ice, to keep their hand cranked ice cream cold. It would've been an easy chore, because each child could take a turn. Wonder, who licked the ice cream beaters?

Pulling taffy candy was another winter treat. Fran remembers her mother's brother coming to the house, to make taffy. Into a deep pot, her mother would put water, sugar and/or molasses, a *little* vinegar and butter, and a pinch of baking soda. Fran recalls the mixture was cooked till somewhat stiff – hard ball stage. The candy was allowed to cool enough, so their buttered hands wouldn't get blistered from pulling it. The men rolled up their sleeves, to avoid getting the buttery sticky candy, on them. Each person would reach into the pot, pull out a handful of candy, stretching, twisting, and turning it over and over, as they moved away from the cook stove. The idea was to have a candy rope, which could be cut into bite sized pieces, before it hardened completely. It was easy to store in the cool months, but with a large family, it probably didn't last long! To Fran, the taffy tasted similar to butterscotch. It was one of the few treats, and simple joys of life, back in the early days.

Fran, at present day 81, lived through rationing, during WW ll. That's when premium food items and goods were directed to the war effort, instead of to the family dinner table and wheels on vehicles. Butter was one of those food items. That's when "fake butter" was born! According to Fran, her mother would buy, what she described as a solid block of white shortening or lard. In the center of the block was a round orange button. When the button was pushed or squeezed, the orange coloring was released. Each child would then take a turn squishing the shortening, to mix in the coloring. They pretended to be churning butter. The outcome looked like present day margarine. Fran and her siblings loved creating the "fake butter", as much as they enjoyed eating it on bread. It was also used in baking. When it would harden too much, in the wintertime, her mother would place it on the back of the cook stove.

The heavy cast-iron cook stove was the most important piece of equipment, in the home, that helped to keep the family fed, and warm through the cold months. Fran enjoyed growing up, learning how to cook, on the durable stove, that when she got married, plans were to use one, just like her mother. However, due to the extreme weight of the cook stove, the floor needed to be braced, which was not doable. She says, freshly made potato chips, using the cook stove are the best!

Fran recalls the **warming oven** with doors, on the top of the stove. It came in handy for keeping Sunday dinners warm, till they walked home from Pine Grove Church of God.

Her mother, like so many women, did not drive. But most importantly, they needed to conserve gasoline consumption, so her father could get to and from work, at the state Highway Shed, in Bloomfield. This was, during the WW ll war effort, when gas was rationed. The family walked everywhere!

A **water tank** fit on the side of the stove. It heated water for cooking, washing dishes, and bathing. There wasn't any indoor plumbing. Everybody had to run outside to the outhouse when nature called.

Fran recalls, every summer the outhouse had to be cleaned out. Yepper! As Fran describes, "there was a cesspool, in the ground, on the back side of the outhouse. The back trapdoor, of the outhouse, would be opened up. Buckets were used to remove the waste."

Oh, yeah! The Sears and Montgomery Ward catalogs served a dual purpose, at Fran's home. It was their Charmin of the day – toilet paper.

The children got first dibs on the catalogs, when they arrived, in the mail. Soon, they were writing down their Christmas wish list, for their mother. She in turn, placed a mail order, from the catalogs. Fran and her siblings would eagerly await the mail delivery, knowing they would not be allowed to peek or open the packages. But they wanted to make sure, packages did arrive!

One year, there was a wind-up toy train, that choo choo'd along on a small track. Metal tops were pumped up and down to spin. Fran especially loved the Little Golden Dictionary book, and the Night Before Christmas, because she enjoyed reading. Her mother would make dolls, for the girls. Often times, she used the same plastic doll head, and fashioned new clothes. To the girls, it was a brand new, beautiful doll.

Carmichael's Store, on the square in Bloomfield, had an employee, Flossie Shatto, who would fill bags of hard candies, for the children.

Every Christmas, the church would have the children memorize and recite lines, for a Christmas play. Now, Fran enjoyed going to church, but was very shy and 'backward', as she put it. Christmas celebrated, at the church, was something she did not necessarily look forward to, at all.

However, she did look forward to snow, when their bachelor neighbor, Frank Sheaffer would come by, with his two big horses pulling the open sleigh. The sleigh bells signaled his arrival. All the kids would pile into the sleigh, and off they'd go, for a ride around the countryside, on the snow-covered township roads. Back in those days, only the main roads would be plowed and cindered. Fran's dad was one of the highway workers, who would stand on the back of the cinder truck and throw the cinders off onto the plowed roads.

Fran's mother stayed behind, to prepare, what became a traditional dinner after the sleigh ride. Frank Sheaffer and the children were treated to chicken and dumplings, which warmed them up after the wintry sleigh ride. Of course, the family knew chicken and dumplings was Frank's favorite meal.

There were no school buses, so Fran and her siblings walked to school, regardless of the weather. Fran walked from current day, Pine Grove Road, where she lived, to Airy View, a one room schoolhouse. Airy View is currently the headquarters of The Perry Historians, a Perry County historical organization, whose focus is genealogy. Airy View is located, east of Bloomfield, off Route 34.

The students wore snow suits and boots, and walked on unplowed roads, to get to school on time. They arrived cold and often times wet. Girls even wore snow suits, over their dresses. This was way before slacks or jeans were permitted and became the fashion.

All eight grades were taught at Airy View. Fran remembers no more than twenty students attended the school, at any given time. She enjoyed school, where she learned all about history and writing. Frank Fry, from Bloomfield, was the teacher. The children listened and obeyed Fry, who had a single arm. Fran indicated, they might have been just a little scared of him, because of his special challenge.

Fry made Friday a special day, for the students. No, not because it was the last day, of school for the week. It was 'potluck day'! Each student brought a food item, to be added to a kettle, which sat on top of the wood stove, which was the only heat source, in the one room school. Fry would then cook everything together, creating a soup or stew. The students would enjoy their special lunch with toasted homemade bread.

Other times, each student was instructed to bring an empty soup can. Frey would punch two holes, in each side of the can, near the top. Then, he put a sturdy stick through the holes, creating a handle. Adding some water to the can first, he added an egg, and the can was set on top of the wood stove. The students enjoyed their soft-boiled eggs, on toasted bread. To them, it was a feast made in heaven.

Fridays, in the spring, also meant hiking to the nearby pond, on Ed Haines' farm, to pick water cress, for their teacher. He enjoyed eating water cress.

When the students weren't preparing for the weekly spelling, and math bees, they could be found outside, playing their favorite games. Fran remembers playing the harmless game of Red Rover, Red Rover, Let Frances Come Over! However, Tipp-High-Over was not so harmless. The students would be divided into two teams. One team would be on the east side of the school. The second ream would be on the west side of the school. The idea of the friendly competition, was to pitch rocks over the school house roof. The opposing side was supposed to try and catch the falling missiles. If you caught a rock, you were to yell out, Tipp-High-Over! Fran did not indicate that anybody needed any medical attention, due to participating in the friendly competition. Just imagine!

Fran's older brother, Bill, was told by the teacher, that he didn't read right! Well, Bill became so angry, he threw the schoolbook, into the burning wood stove. He sure got a licking, when he got home, because not only did he do wrong, but his parents had to bear the expense of replacing the book. As Fran says, "Books are precious!"

Fran's brother, Ronald, was deaf and attended the Pennsylvania School for the Deaf, in Philadelphia. The family included him in all their activities.

By the time Fran went to fifth, and sixth grade, her family was living on the Dromgold property, outside of Bloomfield, and she was bused to Center school, at Gilbert Adam's farm. The school was known by many names, such as #2, and Darlington's. Fran describes the school, as being out in the meadow!

Seventh and eighth grades brought many transitions, into Fran's life. It was the first time, she experienced having to change classrooms, for various subjects. This was in Bloomfield. Sounds simple enough! The Bloomfield Firehouse stage served, as Fran's homeroom. Off she'd go, regardless of the weather or time of year, down the alley by the firehouse, to attend classes in the now empty store fronts of Carmicheals, and Barton's. The stores were located in the vicinity of the current day Perry County Chamber of Commerce headquarters..

The Lutheran Church, on High Street, also hosted student classrooms. Fran says they had a piano.

Fran only mentions two teachers, Mrs. Campbell, and 'Puffy' Rice. She couldn't recall Rice's proper first name but described how she got her nickname. "If a student would cause her to be upset, Puffy's face would become bright red and puff up!"

As a freshman in high school, Fran was teased a lot, by her fellow classmates. It was the debut, of black and white tv, and the popular show, Francis the Talking Mule. There were constant references, about Francis to Fran. She took the kidding in stride reminding them, her name was spelled Frances, not like Francis, the talking mule.

Fran recalls Saturdays, when Roller Derby, was on tv. Her mother demanded peace and quiet in the home, when the rough and tumble show was being aired.

***

The clothes Fran wore to school were usually home-made, hand-me-downs. Her mother went to Barton's Store, to purchase material and sewing supplies. But she also, fashioned old feedbags, into dresses, skirts and blouses. The sackcloth came from her grandparent's (Merrill and Leah Seidel) farm, near Blain.

She looked forward to visits, from her Uncle Bob, who was a career military man. When he came home, to Perry County, he always brought along parachutes, and gave them to Fran's mother. She turned the silky material, into shorts for the children. Fran loved her new shorts. The way they felt, and the fact, that they lasted a very long time. She was quite proud of her new clothes!

Fran wore shoes to school, but if it rained, she carried them so they did not get wet or muddy. She realized, she needed to take extra care of her shoes, because they had to last. Shoes were very expensive. Otherwise, Fran and her siblings, run barefoot, most of the year.

Her mother used a White Treadle Sewing machine, not only to make their clothes, but new haps each winter. All year long, all the old, well-worn clothes were saved, to be cut into patches. The patches would be laid out on the floor, and the children would use heavy thread, to tie them together. Once the patchwork top and underside were complete, her mother would use worn out haps as a filler. They were thick and very warm.

Fran and her siblings shared two beds, while her parents had their own. They took turns getting that new hap, for on their beds. The thick layers of straw were replaced, each year, in the mattresses. Her mother made the mattress covers, from blue ticking. It was a heavy, rigid, blue striped material, that wore really well. So, between the layers of straw, the heavy haps, and body heat, the family was snuggly warm, in the unheated upstairs.

The nearby spring provided water, for cooking, bathing, cleaning, and washing clothes. The kids would carry water, into the house, to be heated, on the cook stove, for washing the family's dirty clothes. Fran's mother used a hand-crank, wringer washer. (Got to remember, they did not have electricity, and used kerosene lamps for lighting.) When her mother felt the clothes were clean enough, they were hung outside on a clothesline, to dry, regardless of the time of year. The telltale singing, by her mother, "When the Roll is Called Up Yonder", automatically signaled to the kids, that she was hanging up laundry.

Air drying clothes, generally meant, there were few wrinkles. To eliminate wrinkles, Fran's mother would sprinkle the clothes with water, roll them up, and let them like that over-night. A flat sad-iron was heated on the cook stove, before she unrolled the damp clothing. When ready, she would take the iron gently over the clothing, and the resulting steam would erase the wrinkles.

By now, we know Fran's mother liked to cook, but she had other purposes for some of her bowls. Spring and the end of school meant it was time to get a haircut. Her mother allowed the children's hair to grow all winter, as an extra layer of warmth, on their heads and shoulders. She did not take them to the local barbershop. Instead, she decided upon the proper size mixing bowl, for each child's head. Placing the bowl, on their heads, she trimmed their hair, following the bow's rim.

Fran's mother did not keep the hair, for any use. But she does recall, finding long strands of horsehair, in the plastered walls, of her home. Her mother decided to wallpaper, and there were several holes in the wall, which needed fixing. That is when, the horsehair was discovered. Once the wall was repaired, the children helped their mother mix up flour and water, to create a paste, which was applied to one side of the paper, before being placed against the wall. Fran's mother soon discovered; the walls were very crooked. It was not an easy task.

***

To feed a family that size, or any size for that matter, back in the 1940s – 1950s, required a large garden. What wasn't consumed, on a daily basis, Fran's mother canned. She used wire and glass topped jars, with rubbers, to seal everything from green beans to meats. A huge canner would be placed on the cook stove. The jars were put inside the canner, which was filled with enough water to cover the tops, of the jars. The water would be brought to a boil, then allowed to simmer, for hours. The canning process took an extremely long time.

Venison and other wild game were also canned. Fran's grandparents raised hogs, so her mother canned any pork product, that wasn't smoked. Without electricity, refrigerators, and freezers, the families wooden ice box came in handy. The ice man delivered ice weekly, but Fran's mother didn't always have money to pay for the important commodity. The ice man would cut or shave off a piece of ice, to fit onto one of the ice box shelves. Sometimes, he'd chip off chunks of ice for the kids to suck. That was a treat. Soon after the ice man would leave their property, Lebo's Meat truck would arrive selling a variety of freshly butchered meats. Lebo had a butcher shop in Bloomfield.

Uncle Orie Ickes lived not too far from them when they lived outside of Bloomfield. He would bring his mules and plow up the garden. His farm was also a source for fresh milk. Fran and her siblings would walk to Ories, and hand milk one of the cows. Using a milk pail or bucket, they carried the raw milk back to their house. Otherwise, they probably wouldn't have had fresh milk.

Fran's parents made sure they kept some potatoes, to be used as seed potatoes for the following year. They used lime to help boost the potato crop but made sure it did not touch the freshly cut potato eyes. The kids would run along dragging a chain over the rows, to better distribute the fertilizer.

Turnips, white potatoes, and apples were kept, in burlap bags, and hung in the basement steps, to keep from becoming damp. She also dried apples.

Her mother also liked to keep tomatoes, at the end of the season, till they ripened. She would hang them upside down, in the basement. The family ate lots of fried green tomatoes, too.

They raised chickens for eggs and meat. The kids were allowed to have a pet chicken, which they named and tended. They would make tents out of feed bags, to keep them safe. Of course, the pet chicken eventually graced the dinner table. The pet's owner was not required to eat chicken that night.

They did not have pets. Their hunting dog was not to be coddled. The kids were allowed to feed it and that was it. If a stray cat came around, it was allowed to stay for a while. One time, a cat showed up and crawled into the family car. Her dad drove off to work for the day. When he returned home, to his surprise, out jumped the cat never to return.

***

Fran's life was centered around her family, going to school, and attending church. Otherwise, she and her family remained at home. The evenings were filled with listening, to the battery-operated radio. Their dad enjoyed the radio show, "Green Door" – who's behind the green door?

After walking to and from Sunday School, Easter was spent at home, with their dad rolling the hard boiled, Easter eggs down through the yard, and hiding them. The family had colored the eggs, by using boiled onion skins.

It was a treat to attend Pine Grove's Strawberry festival, in June. The church members would prepare soups, sandwiches, and strawberry shortcake, to be sold and enjoyed. They would attend the Saturday social, after all the cleaning, including hand scrubbing the kitchen floor, was accomplished.

***

If the children had issues with their teeth, their parents would take them to see Doc. Adams, in Bloomfield. He sure knew how to pull teeth, as Fran found out. The discomfort afterwards, was enough for Fran to miss going to the Bloomfield Fireman's 4th of July carnival.

Fran remembered a doctor making house calls when anybody was sick. He brought a bag full of medicine. Pharmacies did not exist, back in those days. Often times, he would apply a plaster or poultice, for treating colds or coughs.

Entire families were quarantined if a family member contracted polio. So, when Fran became stricken, her father could not stay with the family, because he was the wage earner. After work, he would bring them food and leave it on the porch.

Fran was taken to the Harrisburg Hospital, where she was treated. She underwent spinal taps and had to stay for twelve days. During that time, her parents did not visit, because they needed to conserve gasoline. Luckily, her roommate's parents visited and were kind enough, to spend time with Fran as well. She ended up wearing a metal brace on her right leg, for a period of time.

Fran is a walking history lesson! She is proud of her upbringing, and having spent her entire life in Perry County!

Growing up in Tuscarora Township in the 1950's

Storyteller Patricia Kerr Brodisch

My home was in Tuscarora Township, just across the Juniata River from Millerstown. The old iron bridge over the river and the bridge over the railroad didn't line up, making it difficult for big trucks to get across.

The main line of the railroad had four tracks then, along with a freight office and a siding. It was fun to watch all the trains go by.

My parents were John F. Kerr and Florence Forry Kerr. My father had a construction business that included building houses and commercial buildings for clients, such as The United Telephone Company of PA and Gulf Oil. He made use of the railroad siding since he bought rail carloads of lumber for his business. In my memory, the lumber always arrived when the temperature was highest.

I was an only child but had neighborhood children and cousins to play with. With rode our bikes in the summer and went sledding in the winter. I had a small playhouse that served as a place for us to gather. We attended the Methodist Church in Millerstown. I was a Brownie and Girl Scout, 4-H club member, played the clarinet in the band and accompanied my mother in the summer to shop in Harrisburg at Mary Sachs, Pomeroy's, and Bowman's department stores. My mother also got me started on collecting antiques and items of Perry County historical interest, an interest that continues to the present day.

I attended first and second grades at the two-room school in Donnally Mills, now part of the Donnally Mills United Methodist Church, which my father built. We had no indoor plumbing, so we used outhouses for bathrooms and hand pump for drinking water. When the country schools were closed, we then went to Millerstown for third through twelfth grades.

The area had lots of businesses. There was a Breyer's Creamery that had a nice park behind it for picnics and bike riding. Secrist's Mill and Long's Hatchery were there too. Hall's Dairy is still there. Early on, we even had a veterinarian, Dr. Meiser. And, of course, the lumber sheds for John F. Kerr, building contractor are still there, though no longer used.

My parents are gone now, but my next-door neighbor, Vicki Cox Cameron and I are life-long friends.

My childhood was always interesting, fun and filled with really nice people.

Special Memories of Buckwheat Valley

Storyteller Shirley Burd Reisinger
Recorded by Debra Kay Noye

Shirley Burd was born at home in "Swamp-Poodle", at Donnelly Mills. The family moved to a typical thirty-five-acre, country farm, when Shirley was months old. The farmhouse was modest, with no indoor bathrooms, until 1957. A wood stove served a dual purpose, for cooking and heating, because there was not a furnace. The wooden ice box sat on the out-porch, "shanty", and ice chunks were delivered right to it. This was how foods were kept cold, all year long, prior to refrigerators.

Her first-grade teacher, Harry Bixler, who was also her Great-Uncle on her mother's side of the family, marked on Shirley's report card that, "she was mischievous and whisper". There was no explanation, from the man, whom everybody assumed was the wealthiest person in Raccoon Valley, between Ickesburg and Donnally Mills, at the time. However, his remarks rang true on many occasions.

Shirley recalled packing her school lunch of butter bread served with hot chocolate. In the summer months, for lunch, Shirley's mother served her home canned tomatoes cold, with butter bread. Times were austere.

Her father, John W. Burd, raised cows, pigs and chickens, in his spare time. He was a painter by trade, school bus driver on the side, and worked out his days delivering gas for J. P. Russell, of Millerstown.

One day on the farm, mischievous Shirley and her older sister, Doris, decided they would lend a helping hand, with tending the chickens. They managed to distribute a fifty-pound bag of chicken mash, into the nests of laying hens, clogging the water fountains, and over-filling the feeders. It was a feeding bonanza for the chicks! Their hard work was not appreciated by their father, who used Bridal Bush switches across their legs.

The bags, that contained chicken mash, and other animal feed, were fashioned by her mother, into clothing, for the girls. Everything was repurposed, due to lack of money, to purchase new items. It was a farmer's way of life, despite the depression.

The vehicles traveling on the dirt highway past the farm, kicked up a lot of dust. But was even worse, when Mr. Brown would drag the road, in an attempt to level out the ruts, and remove large stones. Adventure-some Shirley would jump onto and ride the rolling equipment, without regard for her safety, or becoming extremely grimy.

***

The mailman, L. L. Hoverter, always retold the story, of how one day, when he opened the Burd's mailbox, a cat came flying out, right through his mail car, and out the opposite window. He thought he spied Shirley, Doris and Sandra hiding behind a nearby tree, but never confronted them about the prank. Later years, he would remind Shirley, about the frenzied cat in the mailbox.

***

Tragedy struck when Shirley was eight years old. Her mother, Dorothy Rice Burd, passed away after an illness. Her dying wish, as told to Shirley's father, was that the sisters, would always remain together, if he could not continue to raise them at the farm. He kept that promise.

Reverend Victor B. Hann, the director of the Methodist Home for Children, in Mechanicsburg, reached out to Shirley's father. The Burd family were members of the Walnut Grove Church, which was a Methodist charge. They agreed that the sisters would go to the home, until one of them graduated from school. Then, they could return to the farm to live, with their father and younger brother.

As the sisters adjusted to the children's home, they were allowed visitors, once a month. The Saturday visits took place, in a monitored setting, from 2 p. m. to 4 p. m. Luckily, they were allowed a vacation, with their father, once a year for three weeks. Shirley recalls packing her vacation clothing, which were documented by the home. All the clothing had to be returned, in good shape. As fate would have it, Shirley's shoes became soaked, while visiting the farm. In an attempt to dry them, Shirley put the shoes on the oven door. That failed, ruining her shoes. Her father had to purchase new ones, before her return to the home.

Shirley experienced a well-rounded upbringing at the home. The personnel were strict, and there were many rules to follow. Each child had chores to do, which would enable them to know how to survive on their own, in the future. Shirley came away, from the home, with a wide knowledge of housekeeping! And, having grown up, with fifty-two brothers and sisters!

The boys at the home, would work on the farm. There were two cottages of girls and very young boys. Older boys lived in a separate cottage. They enjoyed meals, school, and special activities together.

They were not allowed to walk on the grass, unless removing the ripple. The well-maintained grounds were spotless, to impress the benefactors and visitors.

Methodist churches would host the annual "Harvest Home", every fall, at the end of the gardening season. The fresh produce and canned goods would be brought to the home, to help feed the children. Shirley, to this day, will not eat Spanish Rice, as it was a staple in her diet.

She enjoyed her first Pepsi, when the children walked to Shiremanstown, and received a small stipend to spend. Shirley kept that bottle top, with its cork underbelly, to remember the essence of that very special treat!

The sisters were bused, by the home, to the Mechanicsburg school. They returned back to the home for lunch. They ate, cleared their lunch dishes, and made sure everything was in proper order, before being bused once again to school.

Their routine care involved marching to the local dentist. And as a 'rite of passage,' had tonsils removed by Dr. Heikus.

Swimming lessons were held for three weeks every summer.

Christmas day at the home consisted of Rev. Hann arriving at each cottage. He would take the youngest child and mount them on his shoulders. Then, he would instruct the child, to pull down a sheet, shielding prying eyes, from piles of gifts. Each child had a pile of ten gifts, which included thank you notes. They were required, to write thank you cards, to the people, who donated the various useful gifts. There were few toys or gifts a child would wish for at Christmas time.

***

When Shirley's oldest sister graduated from high school, in 1957, the girls were allowed to return home to their father. Her older sister got a job, to help support the family.

Shirley, a junior, continued her education at Greenwood High School, in Millerstown. She also returned to Walnut Grove Church, which was her family's church. Her grandparents Hiram S. and Elsie Sowers Burd, were also members. By then, the church had a large youth group, and Shirley became active with them.

Shirley's grandparents, on her mother's side of the family, were Laura (Bixler) and Harry S. Rice.

What few luxuries existed; Shirley cherished. She remembers attending the Millerstown Fireman's Carnival, and her father buying her a plastic pinwheel, which went round and round, with the slightest breeze. She never received an allowance, but she pulled her weight when helping out her family.

Living way out in the country, without any means to go anywhere, Shirley could not participate in school or extra church activities.

Having been brought up in the church home, where she learned respect, teamwork, a strong work ethic, and faith in God, Shirley put her upbringing to good use, and her mischievous nature survived.

Just Another Kid from Wila Tech

Storyteller Larry Reisinger
Recorded by Debra Kay Noye

Larry Reisinger may have started life, on a farm in Eschol, but his roots are deep in Wila. His father, Franklin F. Reisinger, had been in the Army, serving in Northern Africa and Italy during WW ll. After four years of service, he returned home to get married and begin farming.

He has few memories of the farm. However, not unlike his wife, Shirley, who was a prankster and dare-devil, Larry handled life the same way. On the farm, there was a straw mow in the barnyard, that reached to the second story of the barn. His visiting cousin decided to step off the second floor of the barn, onto the straw mow, without mishap. Of course, Larry followed his cousin's example. However, he jumped and barely touched the top of the straw. Larry landed on the ground, with the wind knocked out of him. "I knew, I was dead!" Larry said. Needless to say, Larry did not jump out of barn floors again.

He was five years old when the family moved to "Wila, absolutely the greatest place to grow up"! They lived smack dab on the town square. Actually, Wila was more of a village, with a total of twenty houses, plus a church and general store. It was a close-knit community, where everybody looked out for one another. That included keeping tab on the kids. Even before Larry could reach home after a hard day of riding bikes with lots of kids his age, his mother, Helen (Campbell) Reisinger, knew what he'd been up to.

His father worked at Toomey's Mill, located near the Wila dam. Owned by Luke, his mother Vera, and his sister, Edith Toomey, the mill made animal feed, primarily for hogs, chickens, and cows. Farmers would bring their harvested field corn to the mill to be ground and bagged.

Toomey's Mill was also noted for milling fine wheat flour, which was used in baking and cooking. Larry proudly possesses flour and feed bags from the mill, a remembrance, of his enjoyable days spent at the mill with his father, and Luke Toomey.

Albert Baker, Bob Zaring, and Ralph Ehrhart were also employees at the mill.

Luke Toomey was Perry County's Representative in the Pennsylvania House of Representatives. His wife, Betty, worked at Shiffer's Store in Newport. They adored children, having none of their own, and Luke doted on Larry. He gave Larry fifty cents, nearly every time he came to the mill, and asked him to go to Lyons Grocery Store, just up the street. He always instructed Larry to purchase Mail Pouch Chewing Tobacco, which was a whooping forty cents. The remaining ten cents allowed Larry to treat himself to a hand-dipped, Sealtest ice cream cone, from the four lidded ice cream freezer. Larry says, Luke probably had a gigantic stash of Mail Pouch, because he sent Larry to the store quite often.

Toomey's and their dog, Jaggers (the ugliest dog, Larry has ever seen) were the town's godparents, who always kept a watchful eye on the "Wila Tech" crew. In the summer, the kids swam near the dam. In the winter months, especially in the evenings, they built bonfires using old tires, so they could see to ice skate and play fierce matches of ice hockey, with local rivals. It was hard to beat "Wila Tech". He wore the title, like a badge of honor.

Larry remembers Toomey's were the first in town to purchase a color tv. It was so gigantic; it took up the entire end of Toomey's living-room. The Reisinger family did not possess any tv, but their neighbors had a black and white. Larry especially liked to watch "Covered Wagon Theatre" on Channel 8, on Saturday mornings. In an effort to get an invite to watch the show, Larry would stand outside hollering and yelling, till his wish came true.

Since the Toomey's were politically active, they had various political posters, in their yard, from time to time. One in particular caught Larry's attention. It read, "Pat for First Lady." He asked Toomey, who Pat was. He was surprised when Toomey told him, she was the wife of the Republican presidential candidate, Richard Nixon.

***

The one room school, Oak Hall, which is now the Oliver Grange in Juniata Township, was where Larry started his education. In the middle of third grade, all the small, one and two room country schools, including Oak Hall and Wila, in the Newport area, were closed and the students were bused to Newport Elementary School in Newport. Before school started for the year, in August, his parents would take him to Colonial Park, in Harrisburg, to buy clothes for the upcoming school year. It was a big event for Larry. His mother would pack bologna sandwiches and iced tea, for them to enjoy, while sitting in the store's parking lot.

In high school, he thought he might like to wrestle, but instead was asked to become the team manager. For the next four years, the Newport wrestlers were undefeated, in the Blue Mountain League.

Ken Whisler was the demanding coach, who stood out, with his trade-mark bright red socks. Larry shouldn't have laughed when the coach, while making a point about an upcoming match, whipped his arm around and his wristwatch flew off, and slammed into the wall. That cost Larry many extra laps, during that week's practice.

Larry graduated from Newport High School, as a commercial student. He had no real plans after graduation, other than seek employment. But as Larry says, "that God moment happened", when he walked into Elizabeth Lyons Grocery Store, in downtown Wila. On that day, his life-long friend since grade school, Tana Lyons, was in her mother's store with her older sister, Alice Jean. Conversation started and Alice Jean, who was a senior at Elizabethtown College suggested to Larry, that he might want to apply to Elizabethtown College. Tana, following in her sister's footsteps, had already been accepted. This inspired Larry to apply, and he ultimately graduated, along with Tana, from Elizabethtown College.

***

Taking his father's 1953 Ford, Larry drove to the Newport Theatre, where Steckley's Pet Store once stood, in Newport. He was so nervous and scared, on his **first** date, that he forgot to turn off the motor, when he entered the movie theatre, with his date. Much to his surprise, the car had been running for two hours.

***

Elizabeth (Lib) Lyons became the sole proprietor of Lyons' Grocery Store, when her husband, Dean, died of cancer in 1960. Alice Jean and a brother, George, also succumbed to cancer. Lib ran Elizabeth Lyons Grocery Store till she retired.

The store was the center of Wila's activities. Even though it was closed on Sundays, Lib would open the store, after the traditional Sunday afternoon, town baseball or football games. The thirsty players would come in to grab an ice-cold soda, like Nesbitt's Orange, Root Beer, or Pepsi, from the soda cooler filled with ice.

Larry remembers a metal milk box on his front porch. Harrisburg Dairies driver, Nearhood, would put glass bottles of milk, in the milk box. The milk was processed at the creamery in Duncannon.

To earn money to purchase baseball cards and special treats, Larry had a paper route. He delivered the daily newspaper for a whopping five cents. Friday, he delivered the Grit for ten cents. Twenty-five cents bought the Sunday paper. He would collect the monies for the newspapers, at the end of the week. Larry made sure he would arrive at Mrs. Cloward's house on collection day, just in time to watch wrestling on tv.

As the story goes, Mrs. Cloward had sheep, that strayed from their pasture. Larry and his friends as they were riding around the area, found the sheep, and brought them back to Mrs. Cloward. She was so grateful, she rewarded each of them twenty-five cents. Seems the kids had a hankering for more money and the next summer, concocted a scheme to swindle Mrs. Cloward. They went and told her that they had found the sheep out of their pasture again and returned them safely back. Unfortunately, they did not realize Mrs. Cloward had sold the sheep, the prior fall. Larry sheepishly apologized, for his bad behavior.

Every summer, the church would hold a huge festival, serving up chicken corn and ham bean soup, barbeque and hot dog sandwiches, and home-made ice cream. It was the highlight of the year and brought many people to the small community.

Larry attends to this day, Walnut Grove United Methodist Church, between Markelsville and Eschol. It is a country church, which had a large youth group, when Larry was growing up. However, he made sure he was back home from Sunday youth activities, to watch "Bonanza", at 9 p. m. on tv. Church was where he met his future father-in-law and brother-in-law, becoming life-long friends.

Walnut Grove Church always treated the children to an orange and a box of Catherman's Candy at Christmas. One year, Larry was in the church's Christmas program. Santa arrived and greeted the children. Much to his dismay, Larry recognized the voice of his father, and the Santa mystic was gone from his young life.

***

Larry, at around ten years of age, helped his grandfather build an outhouse on their Wila homestead. He was proud of the outhouse, and the craftsmanship of his grandfather. It was kinda like his grandfather's legacy, after he passed.

When Larry sold his parent's property in Wila, one of the conditions of the sale, was his being able to remove the outhouse. He relocated it to his wife, Shirley's family farm. As he says, "Only in Perry County, does a real estate deal hinge on who gets the outhouse!"

***

Larry's grandparents were George and Sara (Vance) Campbell, and Jacob and Pearl (Rhoads) Reisinger.

***

Fresh out of college, Larry was approached by Norman Pressley, a member of the Perry County Republican Committee. He shared with Larry that, the Republican Party was starting a Young Republican Club in the county, and would he like to become involved. That is how Larry became a founding member of the Perry County Young Republicans. It also began a life-long friendship with Fred Noye, now a former Representative of the Pennsylvania House of Representatives.

His county-wide activities caught the attention of Sam Wagner, who was part of a group attempting to restart the Perry County Fair. Sam asked Larry if he would like to join them.

Well, it's been a fifty-year journey, in preserving the Perry County Fair, held at the fairgrounds outside of Newport. In those fifty years, he only missed three nights of the fair. He has been a director for forty-five years and held the office of treasurer for many of those years.

It wasn't easy putting together the fair. In the beginning, it was a lot of blood, sweat, tears – and a whole lotta' dust! Vendors were set up in a single row, around the dirt track used for pony sulky races. There were no pole buildings, to house animals or displays.

Larry recalls, he and his dad helping to set up a huge tent, and while driving a stake to hold the tent fast, they hit an underground hornet's nest. They decided that stake was in the ground deep enough, as they proceeded to run!

The fairgrounds had to be leveled, because after all, it was an open farm field. It needed to be fair-goer friendly.

The free entertainment were local country and gospel groups, such as the Heffelfinger family, of Newport.

Larry eventually became responsible for "Band Day" at the fair. Each of Perry County's four high schools participated in a friendly competition. Each school is awarded a rosette and cash award, for participating.

***

Larry has left his footprints, through-out Perry County. Regardless of his accomplishments, his love for Wila and the Wila Techs, remains true. Oh yeah! He cherishes that outhouse, too!

A Flood of Memories

Storyteller Bradley Halter

The winter of 1961-62 stands out in my mind, as a record setter, for cold and snow. I believe it was this winter, that we had one whole week of snow days. Spinning Wheel Road, in Watts Township, was closed until late February or early March, when it was cleared with a bulldozer.

As a child living in New Buffalo, along the Susquehanna River, I always watched for the river, to freeze over. This winter did not disappoint me. Both the Susquehanna and Juniata Rivers froze solid. When the weather changed, and the spring thaw began, the ice began cracking up, sometimes with loud bangs, and then slowly began moving southward. When the ice reached the Clarks Ferry Bridge and the Duncannon Bridge, it piled up against the piers, and the flooding began. But this year was different!

The ice had frozen to depths of six feet, in some places. Great chunks were carried up on the river shores, by the rising water, from melting snow and rains. With unstoppable momentum, the ice cut down trees, shrubs, and anything in its way. Summer cabins were smashed. At least one large house disappeared under the ice.

The story is that a man, who was inspecting the chunks of ice, left on the shore, found a tunnel-like opening, and went inside. To his surprise, there were the remains of a house and furniture, buried under the ice.

The ice slowly moved under the bridges, and joined together to form an ice dam, about thirty feet high across the mile-wide Susquehanna River, below Duncannon. There the ice stayed, and the waters kept rising. But then, was it a coincidence, that at around the same time, a prayer group met to pray about the situation, the ice jam began to break! Flooding was already serious, but greater disaster was avoided, when the river water could freely flow again.

This scenario of freezing, thawing, and flooding is not unusual, for those of us fortunate enough to grow up, in the vicinity of two beautiful rivers. I left this area many years ago, but the memory of the winter of 1961-62 has never left me.

Bradley Halter now lives in the Philippines.

Growing up in Liverpool, PA

Storyteller Patty Campbell

Growing up in the small community of Liverpool, Pennsylvania holds many precious memories for me. Memories of an era long ago that I will forever treasure. I was born in 1953 in an area just outside of Liverpool, Pennsylvania known as Oriental. My parents were David and Joanna Fisher Knouse. I was seventh in line of a family of nine children. Mom and dad named me Patricia Jean. At a young age, I became seriously ill with pneumonia. Making it necessary to place me in an oxygen tent, I was taken to Sunbury Hospital. After weeks of hospitalization, I was finally allowed to return home. At the same time as I was returning home, my sister Darlene contracted pneumonia and she needed to be hospitalized in Sunbury Hospital. So, I was placed temporary with my Aunt Hulda Fisher Kiser and her husband Sam Kiser. The temporary turned into a permanent home here in Liverpool. I would be raised like their daughter. A wonderful relationship was established. I have often commented it was like I had two families. I always loved my biological parents and siblings as well.

Originally, we lived just two houses from Jack Long's little store on North Front Street in Liverpool. As a kid, Jack would treat me to huge Hersheys vanilla ice cream cones. They seemed enormous to a little kid. The serving counter was pretty high. I recall I had to stand on tiptoes to receive my ice cream cone. Jack was a long-time family friend of Uncle Sam and Aunt Hulda.

Aunt Hulda often shared memories of attending the POS of A (Patriotic Order Of The Sons Of America) fair at Oriental; which was sons of civil war veterans. Jack would take Aunt Hulda and her sister Dot to the fair. They would ride in Jack's rumble seat. The roads were dirt and most of the time the ladies were pretty dusty by the time they reached the fair.

Today Jack Long's store is the Shine Coffee Company. I will never forget my first trip back inside the newly renovated building. My son Scott took me there. It was like a step back in time. There was the original counter from my childhood days. Tears of joy filled my eyes. It was like meeting an old long-lost friend. The counter had found its way back home to Liverpool, Pennsylvania. Many thanks to Jans and Deb Roush for its restoration.

Though I was very young, I recall "Hurricane Connie" hitting Liverpool. The trees bent over and broke in the strong winds. The flagpole in front of our house swayed wildly in the storm. Bob Regester's garage was next door and their sign got damaged. During the height of the storm, my beloved sister Connie was born and named after the hurricane. I recall extreme happiness learning I had a baby sister. For the most part, Liverpool escaped with minor damages. Other towns were not as lucky.

Some of my early memories were playing with the neighborhood kids! What fun we had! The Matter, Willard and Lindquist children all stopped by. Saturday nights found us watching Lawrence Welk on the old black and white tv. Uncle Sam Kiser made me two wooden sticks and I pretended to help lead the band. Then he would dance with me to the old-time songs. It was great fun and to this day I enjoy Lawrence Welk.

Aunt Hulda was a marvelous cook. She did things the old fashion way. Wonderful home cooked meals with delicious desserts. I learned to cook from her. She made wonderful potato salad, pepper slaw and warm lettuce with bacon dressing. Her pumpkin pies were so delicious! We grew a lot of our vegetables in our own garden. Fresh onions, tomatoes, lima beans, and green beans. I miss not having a garden today.

Holidays were filled with wonderful memories. We had a real tree cut from my homestead woods. The tree was placed in an old crock filled with coal. It was adorned with handmade paper chains and ornaments. Blue electric lights glowed in the night and candles flickered in each window. I had a small tree of my very own in the hallway that I decorated with old ornaments from the 30's and 40's. There were tiny old metal bulbs in various colors and a very old metal star sat on top of our tree for decades. A fragile old angel was always on our tree. I still recall the smell of the fresh pine tree.

Easter was also special. One year, I received three peeps as an Easter present. One was yellow, one pink and one blue. I had them trained like household pets. They followed me everywhere. I recall the sad day Uncle Sam told me they were too big and had to be relocated to my parent's farm. I am sure they eventually found their way back to our dinner table!

For generations, our family reunions were held at Crows Ferry, below Liverpool. Ferry rides for only a few cents were quite exciting. Often church services were held in the old bandstand. Delicious food would be placed on long tables under the pavilions and families came from miles around. We would even swim in the cold Susquehanna River. There were games and fun for all! Family was very important in those days.

How I recall our neighbors Edna Ebberts and Madge Stailey. Edna lived in the next house north of mine. She always kept her table set with beautiful blue chinaware and blue goblets. She always had fresh flowers adorning her table. Aunt Hulda always told me to sit quietly so as not to break anything. Edna gave me two beautiful old watches; one from the civil war era and one an old Elgin watch. I still treasure them to this day.

On the north side of Edna's home lived Madge Stailey. Madge ran Liverpool's first telephone exchange. Madge's home was a grand old hotel back in canal days. Its rich history is a vital part of our town's history. Madge often sat out front dressed in pearls and costume jewelry. She was always a fashionable lady.

As a kid I often visited with them on their porches. They always seemed to tolerate my many questions. Pop Wallis often stopped in front of our home with a treat in his pocket for me. He had a cocker spaniel named LulaBelle that I loved to pet. Pop Wallis always wore a big, brimmed hat and had a fancy pocket watch he used to show me.

On the south side of our home was Aunt Ada Kiser Regester and her husband Bob's home. Bob ran Regester's garage from this location next to Jack Long's store. Aunt Ada treated me just like a real niece. Ada had two sisters, Elizabeth Kiser Knouse and Sarah Kiser Kerstetter. They often stopped at our home to visit. They were sisters of Uncle Sam, and I grew to love them all!

The Kiser family were early residents of Liverpool. Their grandparents Leonard and Sarah Beigh Kiser were well respected. Leonard was a boatsman on the Pa Canal system. He also was in the Civil War. I have in my possession his Civil War artifacts.

Uncle Sam had a brother John Kiser. John ran the lookout tower during WWll. It was located near Liverpool cemetery where many residents took turns watching for planes.

Around 1959 we temporarily moved to Pfoutz Valley. We moved into one side of the historic old Pfoutz Valley store and post office, said to be haunted! It was a huge home with many cold, drafty rooms and many bumps in the night. My grandfather Clell Fisher had recently passed away. We moved in the front side of the house to care for Grandma Chestie Shadel Fisher. Her name alone was humorous, but it was indeed her correct name. I'm sure she was teased often in school. Grandma Chestie ate the same breakfast of Wheaties and Postum every morning. On her kitchen counter sat a hand-painted cookie jar, always filled with Oreo cookies for her many grandchildren.

Saturday nights would find grandma Chestie on our side of the house. We had the old black and white tv. Gunsmoke and Red Skeleton were her favorite shows. We made homemade root beer and dishpans full of fresh-made popcorn.

About every two weeks we would go grocery shopping. I recall of snuggling in the backseat with grandma Chestie. I recall the fresh coffee smells at the A&P store in Newport. Grandma Chestie would always get me some kind of candy. I recall she bought everything she needed at the 5 and 10 cent Store in Newport as well.

Her parents, the Shadels spoke little English. They were of German heritage. Pa Dutch was mostly their method of speaking. Grandfather Clell Fisher made beautiful furniture despite being totally blind. He played the fiddle for dances at the Pollyanna dance hall near Liverpool. Carrying an ear of corn in his pocket, after each set he put a kernel in his opposite pocket. That way he knew exactly how much they owed him. They paid him for fiddlin' per each square dance set.

I recall a very heavy snow in the winter of 1959. We used old car hoods to sled and pieces of cardboard. From our front window we could see large bonfires on Byers Hill across the fields. John Byers always helped the youngsters to enjoy the steep hill by his home. Huge sledding parties were held at his farm in Pfoutz Valley. Then hot chocolate would be served. Such kind folks were John and Viola Byers.

I started first grade while living in Pfoutz Valley. The big yellow bus would transport me to Liverpool Elementary School. Later that year, Grandmother Chestie became very ill. A stroke paralyzed her left side.

I slept with her in case she needed anything during the night. I still have the old bell I would use to alert Aunt Hulda. Sadly, Grandmother Chestie passed away. I vividly recall the undertakers carrying her out in a black body bag. It devastated me seeing her leave. I recall Aunt Hulda telling me she went to heaven.

While cleaning in my upstairs I came across a few funny items of my grandparents; Grandma Chesties gallstones in a bottle and Pappy Fishers old false teeth. Seems a gall bladder operation was a big deal in early 1900s. HaHa! I started to throw them away, but instead wrapped them up for my family to find someday! They will have a little laugh when they find them! Both my Fisher grandparents are buried in St James cemetery, not far from where they lived in Pfoutz Valley. The cemetery is located along Rt 235 - Liverpool Rd. Today the church is known as The Church of The Living Waters.

We returned to Liverpool in 1960. Uncle Sam and Aunt Hulda purchased the former Gamby home on South Front Street which was built in the 1800's. Today, almost 61 years later, I still live in that same old home and have the same neighbor, Ken Stailey. Ken is one of the last original descendants of the founders of Liverpool. John and Eve Stailey were his ancestors.

I grew up with Ken Stailey's children. What fun we had playing tag and hide and seek! We also played a unique game known as tin can alley which involved two teams, a ball, and a vegetable can. We had so much fun making tents out of blankets and putting baseball cards in the spokes of our bicycle tires, which made them sound cool! Jack's and marbles were two of our favorite games too. I recall making stilts out of vegetable cans and using binder twine to maneuver them along.

One time we played on a tree on the cemetery hill. We called it our horse while playing cowboys. Having no idea what ivy poison or sumac poison oak was, I learned real fast never to do it again! Dr. Minihan said I was one of the worst cases of two poisons he ever saw! What a mess I was. I didn't sit really well for a while after that!

I was game to try anything. An elderly neighbor, Ellie Zaring, had me help rid her house of skunks. They had camped out under her porch. Wow did that smell! She had me jump up and down on the wooden porch to scare them. When they came out, she doused them with water. Well let's just say my skunk extermination business ended that day when I got home! Aunt Hulda was none too happy with the way I smelled!

My sisters often visited me in town near carnival time. We loved to go to the carnival held on the ball field by the Liverpool Elementary School. It was a huge treat going on rides such as the ferris wheel and the octopus. We would earn money by doing chores and save it for the carnival. At that time, food and drinks were much cheaper. Soda was 10 cents a bottle and hot dogs were about the same. Hamburg and french fries were about 25 cents. Money went a lot further back in those days.

Christmas meant going to see the displays in Pomeroys and Bowmans windows in Harrisburg, the state capitol. We would ride to work with Uncle Sam. He was a Capitol Policeman at the Education and Forum Building. I will never forget my excitement at my first ride on an escalator. What fun that was at Pomeroys! Then I got to see santa at Joe The Motorist Friend. Of course, I always told him I was well behaved. HaHa!

Memorial Day was a special holiday in Liverpool. People would return back home to visit. Our Sunday School classes would take part in the parades. We would be given lilacs to place on the veterans' graves. Every veterans grave was marked by an American Flag. After the parade, everyone in town would head up the hill to the cemetery. Under centuries old cedar trees, the deceased veterans names would be recalled by military members. Then the eerie sound of taps would be played. Tears flowed from everyone's eyes!

Everyone in Liverpool decorated their homes patriotically. Flags waved from every house. Front porch swings and chairs were filled to capacity as people watched the annual parade. Lemonade quenched the thirsts of parade participants. Everyone came home to their "beloved" Liverpool.

Liverpool had supplied many men to the Battle of Gettysburg and the Civil War. Many never to return! Each war men and women from Liverpool served proudly. Many dying on that far distant battlefield!

Liverpool Elementary was the school I attended. I have many warm memories of those six years. Teachers taught us respect and honesty. We learned the Pledge of Allegiance to the American Flag. I was taught from the Bible and learned Bible verses in grade school.

We played outside at recess regardless of warm or cold weather. Jungle gyms, merry go round, swings and see saws were our playground equipment. Many a bloodied nose resulted from falls, but we took it all in stride.

We were survivors of many childhood illnesses. Sadly, we lost a very dear classmate Jane Yetter. I think that loss made me realize how precious life really is. I missed her terribly. Seventh grade I attended Greenwood High School in Millerstown. Here I would grow into a teenager and learn my greatest lessons. We learned how to cook and keep house in Home Economics. Our teachers tried very hard to instill in us good values. I realize now how much they cared. I made many new friends and now, 60 years later we still stay in touch.

I recall my first crush on a boy at our high school dances. Then came proms and graduation. After graduating, I went to work at PennDot and spent the next 30 plus years working for the state. For a shy Perry County young woman, the city actually kind of frightened me. I wasn't used to a big city.

It was shortly after graduation in 1971, I met Bill Campbell from Snyder County. Bill had just returned home from the Vietnam War. We were married on September 23, 1972, in Good Shepherd Lutheran Church in Liverpool. I would spend the next 34 plus years as his wife, till his passing on May 20, 2006. They were good years. I miss him very much.

The Vietnam War left many veterans emotionally scarred. Bill and I both became involved in many veterans affairs in Perry County and traveled to volunteer at the Lebanon VA Center.

We had our son Scott Campbell in 1973. Scott and his wife Heather gave us three beautiful granddaughters, Lexi, Hayley, and Peyton. I love them all beyond measure!

Today I lead a very quiet life on South Front Street in Liverpool. I have lost many family members, including my husband, parents, some siblings, and most aunts and uncles. My close friend Mike helps me so much in maintaining my home. We enjoy a wonderful companionship and friendship.

In 2001, I became interested in genealogy and local history. I dedicated my life to doing research in Perry, Juniata, and Snyder counties. My dear friend Kathy and I recorded many cemeteries in these counties. We still remain close Christian friends some twenty years later.

Growing up in Liverpool, Perry County has been a wonderful experience. I look back over my lifetime and I realize I grew up in a special era. We felt safe and secure. I think back of all the changes I have seen over the years in Liverpool. It's kind of amazing.

Recently many of us have been personally touched by covid. Our dear sister Connie passed in January of covid. We miss her so much. But one thing will always remain constant, our town was founded on Christian roots. We are survivors! The love of God, family and country will always be first in my life.

Today my pace has slowed. I'm somewhat limited in climbing those cemeteries anymore. About six years ago I started a Facebook group called Liverpool Reflections, to record Liverpool's rich local history for future generations to enjoy. It has grown into a labor of love. I try to include an inspirational reading every Sunday. My faith is very important in my life. Perry County to me will always be home! My beloved town of 'Liverpool' will forever be in my heart.

Cherished Memories

Storyteller Steve Hower

The 1960s was a wonderful time to grow up here in Perry County. We had no cable TV, computers, cell phones, or other such entertainment such as it exists today so we were always busy doing things, mostly outdoors.

The winter months seemed much colder then. I can remember days when the temperature dropped well below zero degrees, sometimes as low as -15, and occasionally even lower.

We had a milk box down by the road in front of our house and the "milk man" from Hall's Dairy near Millerstown would come by in the mornings and place the bottles of milk inside the box. We always had to check the box when we got off the school bus in the afternoons since our parents both worked during the day. By afternoon on these cold days the milk would freeze and the bottles would sometimes break inside the box. I guess you could say it was just an accepted loss.

It seemed as if there was always snow on the ground throughout the winter months and we would spend our days sledding, building snow forts and having snowball fights. One year my parents gave me a new sled for Christmas. It was a "Lightning Guider" that was manufactured right here in Perry County at the Duncannon sled factory. I still think it was one of the best gifts I ever received!

Once the ice became thick enough on the local ponds we would go skating and if there were enough of us, we would have some pretty competitive hockey games. The kids from Centre Presbyterian Church, our church, located several miles from Loysville would sometimes play hockey on a farm pond just up the road. It was great fun.

The school we went to, West Perry, rarely canceled classes due to the weather conditions and the snow would certainly create challenges for the bus drivers. Our driver was a really nice man named John Smith. The kids all liked him but unfortunately John was tragically killed one weekend while cutting down a tree, so for a while his brothers, Clyde, who we all knew as "Gene" and Dale, both farmers, took over the bus driving duties. Eventually Dale became our regular bus driver and I have a lot of fond memories of this man.

One night it snowed really hard and the roads were in bad shape. Like most of the drivers then Dale kept the bus at his home and that morning he took the time to put chains on the bus tires for better traction. Some of the roads in our area at that time were unpaved dirt roads and that morning these hadn't been plowed. Since school hadn't been cancelled, Dale was required to drive through the snow to the homes in these areas where children would be waiting. As I recall, we arrived at the school about two hours late that morning and as soon as Dale opened the bus door the assistant principle stepped on the bus and said, "Take them home. All classes are cancelled." The kids on our bus were all aware that Dale had a temper at times, but I don't think we had ever seen him that angry.

As I mentioned, Dale was a Perry County farmer. He lived on the north side of Limestone Ridge near Elliottsburg and he was our school bus driver. That was all I ever knew about him until I paid him a visit one afternoon in November 2015. He was 98 years old then and was as spry as ever. I hadn't seen him in many years and as I sat in his living room that day, I noticed some military documents and medals on the wall. When I inquired about his service time, he told me of his experiences while in an Army unit as they fought their way across Germany to defeat the Nazis during World War II. I thought it strange that I had never known that about him and I was saddened by this ignorance.

I'm sure that every Perry County resident during that period was affected by the war and I'm certain that like Dale, there were many other county residents who had also returned home after the battles to live among us without even their own neighbors knowing what they had endured.

As I was leaving Dale that day, he asked me to return soon for another visit but sadly he passed away only a few weeks later. I will always remember with fondness my bus driver who lived quietly with his family on a farm just down the road, and I will forever cherish my memory of our final visit.

Growing Up in Perry County, PA

Storyteller Vickie Rudy Johnson

I grew up along Erly road, approximately midway between the hamlets of Mannsville and Erly, smack dab in the middle of a myriad of playmates, in spite of the fact that we lived miles from any suburbs on a paved road. Playmates included my three brothers, one sister and neighbor kids, some of whom were cousins, or cousins of cousins. We set out in the morning, ate lunch at somebody's house along the way, and often didn't return until dusk.

We played in the woods, building forts, and swinging on monkey vines, playing hide and go seek, building dams in the creek, and playing foursquare, jump-rope and baseball in summer. Or at somebody's house playing dress up dolls or jacks, string games and board games like Monopoly and checkers.

Winter meant building snow forts and sled riding (sometimes on old car hoods), snowball fights, and ice skating on someone's pond. Another winter treat was making homemade ice cream with raw milk from Geesaman's farm and eggs from Tilly Weaver before we had our own chickens, chiseling ice out of the local creek (really just a no-name run) before we had a large chest freezer.

My parents, Marlin and Ethel (McNaughton) Rudy, bought an acre or so of property and built a small house, adding onto it and doubling its size by the time I was 11. But I can remember the well in the front yard with a pump and the outhouse in the back yard before we had indoor plumbing. Mom had a wringer washing machine (which I managed to get my arm caught in occasionally) and we heated the water with a small electrical heater submerged in the water. Our clothes were hung outside on the clothesline and froze in winter before they were dry.

Summer we were busy with our garden. Almost everyone had one and we were no exception. A bus from the school would pick-up those who signed up for swimming lessons at the New Bloomfield pool, but we had our garden chores to complete before we were allowed to go. This included picking rocks, which I always thought was our best crop, freshly "sprouted" after spring rains. Potatoes, corn, green beans, beets, pumpkins, cucumbers, watermelon, radishes, lettuce, peas, and carrots are some of the vegetables we grew. I don't remember broccoli or asparagus, probably not my parent's favorites.

Mom canned these vegetables, as well as fruit from local orchards such as peaches, pears, apples, and cherries. She also canned the venison my father hunted, and we consumed squirrel, turkey, and ringneck pheasants, often in potpie with homemade egg noodles and our own potatoes. She didn't like rabbit, groundhog or the eels my father caught when gigging (they looked too much like snakes for her taste), but we ate a LOT of ham and green beans or chicken potpie, sometimes from the chickens or pigs we raised and butchered. I wouldn't care if I never had another meal of ham and green beans, but chicken potpie is still a favorite family dinner made with homemade egg noodles, diced potatoes, deboned chicken and broth seasoned with parsley, salt and pepper, and sometimes onion and carrots.

We picked blackberries, raspberries and blueberries from wild vines and bushes and wild strawberries from a local field for a summertime meal of strawberry shortcake with milk and sugar. Years later I worked with a lady from High Point, NC who thought the wild strawberries were poison and was amazed to find out you could eat them!

We also boarded horses and Mom bought a horse named Bucky, who she liked to ride. We learned how to feed and care for these animals, since this was part of our chores as well. Riding became an enjoyable but challenging past-time, learning to duck and hang onto our finicky horse, who apparently had been able to dismount the former owners by running under tree limbs and clotheslines and liked to live up to his name.

We attended Pine Lawn Chapel Sunday School at Erly and later Pleasant Valley Brethren in Christ church. Sunday school picnics and Bible school were always fun and great fellowship, along with the youth group activities. They supplemented the school years at Ickesburg elementary, West Perry Middle School in New Bloomfield, and the high school at Elliottsburg.

We had Halloween parades with the students in costume marching from the school through the town of Ickesburg. There were class trips to the Barnum and Bailey Circus where we saw Doug McClure who played Trampas in "The Virginian" TV show and to a local shale bank near a classmate's house in Eschol to gather fossils. I still mourn the box of rocks Mom disposed of from under my bed while cleaning one day.

School started for me at age 5 and I remember sitting near the window feeling melancholy and crying for my Mom on rainy days. Nothing has changed in that regard! The first time there was a fire alarm drill I left my seat by the window, ran out the classroom door and was waylaid by the teacher halfway across the parking lot. She explained that we had to line up and exit together, which was slowly and methodically. I figured it should be every kid for themselves and not waste any time.

School was rarely closed for snow. Bus drivers simply put snow-chains on their tires and occasionally all the high school boys got out to help push the bus out of a ditch. It wasn't unusual for the snow in our driveway to be piled higher than our six-foot tall father.

What we didn't grow for ourselves could usually be obtained locally. Little corner stores carried groceries and hardware, tobacco and clothing and most had a gas pump as well. We had Urich's at Mannsville and Rice's at Erly; Beanie's near Ickesburg and Skyline Corner on Middle Ridge Road. We would walk or bike to Mannsville and Erly, and within 15 miles in Newport a Weis Market and Woolworth's Five and Dime carried all the necessities.

Our doctors, Rumbaugh and Magill, were also located in Newport. Dr. Rumbaugh used to call me his little lightning rod, since I was struck by lightning inside our screen door when I was about 4 or 5 years of age. I was playing between the metal washing machine and a metal storage cabinet in Mom's laundry area when the bolt reached in the door to the metal. Other than a round red ring on my tummy I was uninjured, but I couldn't move and Mom had to pull me out. Needless to say, I'm not a fan of thunderstorms to this day.

I don't recall that being as painful as the large wooden splinters Mom had to dig out of my thighs and backside from the elementary school merry go round. After retrieving our food trays from the basement cafeteria and eating our lunch, we could spend recess on the playground or ride the merry go round. It was a challenge to jump on, hold on, and keep down the food you just ate as someone bigger and stronger pushed it faster and faster, usually by running along inside and then hopping on. The carnival merry-mixer had nothing on this ride!

We had two cooks, Mrs. Campbell and Mrs. Kerr, whose husband was also the janitor. Their food was delicious and balanced meals, although I don't recall price. Popsicles could be bought for a nickel, although Mrs. Kerr was kind-hearted and sold this five-year old one for a penny once.

Some years ago, we took our granddaughter to lunch at Bear's Den in Ickesburg after attending Grandparent's Day at Blain Elementary. Afterward we stopped at the Ickesburg Elementary building, which then housed a flea market, so my granddaughter could see where I had gone to elementary school. It seemed to have shrunk, the rooms so much smaller than I remembered. Lonelier without the bustle of children and teachers. Teachers like Miss McAlicher (first grade); Mrs. Smiley (second grade); Miss Bollinger (third grade and left-handed like me); Mrs. Rice (fourth grade); Mrs. Dillman (fifth grade and the one who told us that President Kennedy had been shot); and Mrs. Morrison (sixth grade, principal and paddle wielder, not that I ever got paddled).

It's been nostalgic roaming the hallways of my brain looking at these childhood memories. I hope it's been an enjoyable trip for you too!

Pleasant Valley Memories

Storytellers Patricia Dunkleberger Kretzing,
William G. Dunkleberger, Flo Dunkleberger Loy
Recorded by Debra Kay Noye

At almost every turn of the conversation, at the forefront, were their paternal grandparents, Scott and Cora Bender. They lived on a small farm outside of Elliottsburg, on what is now known as Briner Road. The oldest of four siblings, Patricia (Pat) recalls the family living with their grandparents till she was three years old. (Diane Dunkleberger Ulsh, the second eldest, passed away in 1984, at the age of thirty-seven.) The Dunkleberger siblings loved and respected Scott and Cora, who were the kindest, gentlest, and giving grandparents. They spent a lot of their youth with them.

When their parents, Glenn and Betty Dunkleberger went to housekeeping in Pleasant Valley, just like most homes, there were no frills. There was electric, but no bathroom or heating system. The Sears catalog in the two-seater outhouse, helped to pass the time.

A single kerosene heater, with a water tank for humidification attached to the rear, stood in the living-room. There was no heat upstairs in the bedrooms. They recall going upstairs to grab their pjs, then running back down to warm them in front of the heater. Once they were toasty, back upstairs they went to jump under lots of blankets, haps (extra heavy home-made blankets, that Pat still possesses today) and quilts. The morning arrived with them bringing their clothes to warm by the heater, before dressing for the day.

It was not unusual for ice to coat the inside of the single pane glass windows during the winter months. When Bill turned fourteen years old in 1964, that is when a furnace was purchased from Hair Brothers and Myers, on the sharp curve on South Carlisle Street in New Bloomfield. That was a game changer, a real luxury.

Flo liked the old kerosene heater, because she would warm chocolate candy bars received as gifts at Christmas time, on top of it. She would open up the wrapper, just enough to see how far it softened. It was an extra special treat, in a simpler time.

There was a telephone hanging on the kitchen wall, it was a party-line where you picked up your receiver and the operator would say "number please". Of course, it was the local source of gossip, since you could hear all conversations, if you so desired. Bill remembers his grandparents phone number 71J1, since he probably called them quite often, before riding his bike over the ridge.

William and Bernice Bernheisel were maternal grandparents. Like most rural Perry Countians, back in the fifties and sixties, you kept close to home with your immediate family and church family. They were your social group – the ones who kept you safe and taught you life's lessons.

Dunklebergers were confirmed and attended Messiah Lutheran Church in Elliottsburg. They looked forward to the two weeks of Bible School, taught by church mothers, every summer. They were allowed to ride their bikes to Bible School, down over the hill, past their grandparents, out the township road and then past the Sledzinski farm, where the barking dogs came out to greet them. Like all eight- and ten-year-old kids, those dogs were very mean and scary, so they avoided biking that way again. There was always a picnic and ball game at the end of the two weeks. The following Sunday, participants presented a biblical play based on the Bible School theme to the church audience.

They had the opportunity to go to church camp, known as Perry Retreat, at Doubling Gap, across from Colonel Denning State Park, in Cumberland County.

Bill Kennedy, church member from Green Park, whose family owned a fleet of school buses, would transport them to Sower's (Rheams) Roller Rink near Millerstown, or Rainbow Rink in Cumberland County. They obviously enjoyed roller skating.

Even at young ages, they helped out with the church's fundraising efforts. The church family would prepare soups, sandwiches, and desserts for a yearly supper. Pat and Flo acted as food servers (waitresses). Pat remembers, all too well, spilling soup on a diner. And Flo was equally embarrassed, when she spilled coffee down over an unsuspecting supper guest.

Church pageants were a highlight of the Christmas season, that included lots of singing. Everybody was involved in one way or another. The Dunklebergers looked forward to the traditional Christmas orange and small box of candy presented to each child, by the church.

Even the school bus drivers, Brant, and Ard Kretzing, would treat the children on their bus route to an orange.

Christmas meant the traditional pine tree in the back woods would be cut down by Bill and their dad, to be dragged to the house and decorated with antique ornaments and bubble lights. They seemed to delight in the memory of the bubble lights! Their stockings were filled with golden coin candies and an orange. Santa Clause brought new clothing and a few toys. All their clothes were store bought.

They would play their favorite games, Parcheesi and Chinese Checkers and listen to WWVA – Wheeling West Virginia on the radio. John Buck, from New Bloomfield, installed their first black and white tv. There was only one blurry, snowy channel.

Holidays meant spending time with their grandparents, at the foot of Limestone Ridge. Flo remembers when the traditional Easter basket hunt had them discovering melted chocolate bunnies. Scott and Cora would hide the Easter baskets between their barn and the abandoned, local cemetery. Once they got up on Easter morning, they would be treated to an Easter egg hunt around their home. Their parents would hide colored eggs anywhere imaginable.

Few extravagances were allowed and certainly no allowances. They were expected to willingly do chores and help out when needed. In turn, they were clothed, fed, nurtured, and loved by their family. According to Bill, Flo never had to do chores! It was obvious to him, that she wouldn't have received an allowance, had there been one. Pat confirms, "Flo got away with murder!" Of course, being the baby of the family, Flo smiles and reminds them she helped to dry dishes and bring in the hay from the fields.

Bill was quick to describe 'hay making', using old methods -- no baler twine yet! Their mother would drive the tractor, which was hitched to a large wagon, through the cut hay fields. Everybody would use pitch forks to throw the loose hay onto the wagon bed. Gramps, Scott, would tramp-down, flattening the hay, to allow for more to be added. Once the wagon was full, it was taken to the barn, where their dad manned the gigantic hay fork, which was extended from the barn roof. The claws would enclose the loose hay and by the use of roping, their dad would maneuver the claw over the hay mow and release the hay. It was a lot of hot, hard work and extremely hot in the mow. They needed to make sure the hay did not get too hot, because it would combust and probably burn the barn to the ground. If cut hay would get wet from rain, salt was spread among the loose hay, in hopes of preventing a fire.

Mowing the lawn was another story entirely, as they remember using the rotary reel, which was pushed by hand.

It seems their mother was the workhorse in the family, as she gardened, cooked, cleaned the house and made sure their clothes were laundered. Their dad worked outside of the home, in New Bloomfield, at the local division of the Pennsylvania Department of Transportation.

She used a wringer washing machine with two tubs to do laundry every Monday. Blocks of hard laundry soap were bought. Pieces of soap were chipped off the block to be added to the hot water. Doing laundry was a laborious task, back in the old days. The clothes were hung out on the clothesline, regardless of the weather or time of year. They related finding their clothes frozen solid to the clothesline. Even the trousers, which were put onto leg stretchers were frozen.

Their mother made her own starch, which was used quite liberally in those days. We would sprinkle the liquid starch on the washed and dried clothing. Then, roll each piece of clothing into a log shape. The next step was to iron most of the clothing. It was an all-day job.

They remember having a very large garden, which their mother tended. She planted and raised peas, green beans, carrots, broccoli, lettuces, tomatoes, sweet corn and potatoes. Pole beans would be planted at the base of the wooden teepee trellis, because they required a place to climb.

What they didn't eat fresh out of the garden, their mother harvested, and canned or froze. The potatoes were dug and stored in the wooden bin, in the cellar, for use throughout the winter. Potatoes were a staple in their diet.

However, their mother dried some of the sweet corn. After husking the corn, she would cut it from the cob and along with a small amount of water, would toast it on the stove top, in a large rectangular metal pan with sides. Constantly stirring and adding more water as needed, was the key to not scorching the corn. Burnt sweet corn is not edible and smells awful.

The process took forever, it seemed, as the corn lost all of its moisture. It would be allowed to air dry further, before being stored in glass jars. The memory triggered smell-a-vision, as they longed to experience that unique preservation of sweet corn, once again. The dried corn was reconstituted, before cooking in a cream sauce for Thanksgiving dinner. It was a delicious, special treat, they looked forward to enjoying, according to the siblings.

Their dad loved creamed lettuce, which was served cold. The fresh lettuce was dressed with a mixture of cider vinegar, sugar, a touch of salt, mayonnaise, and fresh cream. They remarked, "it sure cut the saltiness of the pan-fried, home-cured ham"!

Fruits were also preserved, by their mother. She had a rhubarb patch and a black raspberry patch, at one end of the garden. The berries were made into raspberry puddin' and served with milk and sugar. This would also make a meal. Puddin', in this case, is a loose batter with the berries gently folded in and baked.

Their mother also made raspberry custard pies, in a home-made, lard crust. Flo particularly seemed to enjoy the raspberry dumplings. The raspberries would be cooked with sugar and water till softened. Then, after making a biscuit dough, rolled up like cinnamon buns, she would drop it onto the simmering raspberries. The dough would steam and become fluffy, similar to making sauerkraut with dumplings. Only the end result is definitely sweeter.

Butchering was an all-day job, at the home of Dick Ulsh off of Erly Road, between Elliottsburg and Ickesburg. Dunklebergers would transport their hogs to Ulsh's property to be butchered. The process began, once a 22 rifle was used to shoot the hog between the eyes. They were then put into troughs, of scalding, hot water. Everybody would grab a small metal pig scraper and start to remove the hairy bristles from the skin. Ropes were used to flip the hog around in the trough. Once that laborious chore was accomplished, the hogs were hung on iron metal meat hooks and cut into portions.

Their mother would can the pork tenderloins. The hams, bacon and shoulders were cured with Morton Home-Cure, from the blue box. They were not smoked, which meant salt needed to be reapplied over the winter months, to prevent spoilage. That is why, Bill shook his head at the memory of eating ham that was way, too, salty for him.

The meats were hung in the cellars' meat room on meat hooks or placed to rest on meat benches. Some might be wrapped in cloth bags. When their mother would need ham for the creamed lettuce dinner, she would simply use a hand meat saw to slice off as much as she needed. That in itself was a strenuous task.

The fresh, uncured meat was wrapped in freezer paper and freezer tape was used to seal it. Kept froze, the meat would last a year.

Their mother would stuff the pig stomach with cabbage, potatoes, and sausage. They also enjoyed eating the warm cracklins, which were the result of squeezing the rendered fat chunks to produce lard. Lard was used to fry most everything, from eggs, potatoes and other meats and made the flakiest pie dough. They claimed foods fried in lard and cured bacon, didn't hurt their Gramps, because he lived to be one hundred and one years of age. And he enjoyed smoking cigars!

Ulsh made scrapple from the odd pieces of meat and organs. The freshly cooked kettle meat was not eaten, by the family. Instead, all of that goodness, went into the meaty scrapple. "Everything, but the oink, was used", Bill said. Instead, Vivian Ulsh made the most delicious vegetable soup for lunch, according to Flo. Pat nodded her head, that was the highlight of the day.

Their beef cattle were butchered by Duke Trostle, who lived behind Loysville, on a farm. The fresh liver would be taken home to be hand-sliced, and wrapped, for the freezer. Their mother would fill the heart, with a bread stuffing, like she would a turkey for Thanksgiving. But she was sneaky with the beef tongue. It was not a favorite of the kids, so she would hide it among slices of roast beef, on the meat platter. Obviously, they caught onto her trick and avoided the tongue, which was chewy.

Their diet of pork and beef was supplemented with wild game when Bill would go hunting with his dad. They would come back to the house with squirrels and rabbits. When their Gramps would come to hunt rabbits, behind their house, the kids would watch out the windows to see if he was successful.

They raised chickens for eggs, which they sold to Bender's Eggs. After gathering the eggs in wire baskets, their mother would use an egg-washer to clean off all the poop and dirt. The round, galvanized egg washer, contained water, which would swoosh the dirt off. The eggs were then graded, by use of an egg scale and placed into the proper sized cardboard boxes, for shipment.

Home-made butter was churned by their mother in a wooden bowl or dough tray, as she used a wooden paddle, to continually beat the cream, until it formed a solid mound. She probably salted it.

When they needed odds and ends, like a loaf of bread, they would go to Urich's Store on the corner of Mannsville Road. It had a single gas pump in front of the store. The owner would use a grabber to get things, like a box of cereal, off the top shelves. Pappy Kretzing and Charlie Brunner, generally could be found loafing out front. Charlie would always tell the kids, "If ya fill a five-gallon bucket with water, he could catch a fish"!

Capital Bakers, of Harrisburg, delivered bread to their home, and they recall a cat jumping into the back of the bread truck. Bill Fleisher delivered milk, in glass bottles, right to their front door from Hall's Dairy, outside of Millerstown. Ed Fisher, a driver for Loysville Feed Company, delivered chicken feed. The chicken feed or mash came in burlap bags. The oyster shell and grit were in fabric bags. The oyster shell and grit were fed to the laying chickens to produce a harder eggshell.

School meant traveling on school buses. Pat went to first and second grade at Airy View, one-room school outside of New Bloomfield on Route 34. She had a wonderful teacher, Milly Sanderson. Pat would eat her packed lunch, before going out for recess. She also went to the Jericho School and New Bloomfield Elementary, where the current New Bloomfield Borough Office and Post Office are located. When the one-room schools closed and the school district consolidated, she attended Perry Joint.

Her least favorite teacher during her elementary years, was Herman Heston, who would become extremely upset when students didn't know the answers to his questions. He was known to carry a book around the classroom with him. The book was used across the backs of students when they couldn't answer his questions or snickered, at others. Pat was scared to death of him, but remembers the day fondly, when Heston fell off the piano stool as he was playing the piano. Seems a student sought revenge and loosened the piano stool legs.

Frank Fry, Sam Murray, Mary Jane (Bolze) Collins and Joanne (Rice) Reed were teachers, that influenced Bill. His elementary years were spent at Bloomfield-Centre. Till eighth grade, he went to Perry Joint and through all the consolidations, he graduated from West Perry School District.

His school buddies were Ron (Speedy) Fry, Fred Frey, and Patrick Zerance. He denies doing anything out-standing in school, but his sisters reminded him that he played the drums for a stint and was the chairman of the prom committee.

"I cried every day and wanted to go home!" Flo said. Thank goodness, Miss Joanne (Rice) Reed, her first-grade teacher, had patience galore! Her elementary years were spent at New Bloomfield.

She met Kathy (Sheaffer) Reighter on the school bus when she was in first grade. They are still friends to this day.

Pat had a box of receipts, that she kept through the years. Upon graduating high school in 1962, she purchased her first car. She went to N.E. Black on West Main Street, in New Bloomfield and bought a used car for $665.

Her second car, a Chevy II, was purchased for $2425.25 in 1963, from Carl Sheaffer, owner of Sheaffer Chevrolet in Loysville.

When she needed a survey for two acres of land, Earl D. Palm and Sons charged $45, compared to astronomical fees upwards of $5000 charged today.

Yes, they lived in leaner times, but the love in their home was abundant. Having had a meager upbringing, by their parents and grandparents, the Dunkleberger siblings appreciate how they were raised. It was a time, where family and church community shaped them, with love and understanding for the future. They smile with joy and pride, while bantering about the good ole' days!

My Story - Growing Up on Meadowgrove Road

Storyteller Heather Lynn (Little) Reed

I was lucky enough to grow up on Meadowgrove Road in Newport.

In the summer, my sister Shawn and I would don our green gum boots, grab our empty drywall buckets, and newly emptied whipped topping containers and make our way down the bank to the creek that ran beside our house.

We would spend hours slowly turning over rocks to find crayfish or salamanders. We would chase minnows downstream and into our buckets. The creek was our playground, our unofficial 'touch tank'.

Multiple attempts were made by us to create a 'swimming hole' by damming up the creek. These attempts were always thwarted by exhaustion from the summer humidity and usually ended with a splash fight... aka water battle.

The creek played a major role in my childhood memories. We laughed, played and even shed a few drops of blood in that creek.

No matter where I go, Meadowgrove Road will always be my home.

***

Heather's parents – Russell Eugene Little 'Hodge' and Barbara Ann Coldren Little

Grandparents - Jean Irene (Livingston) Little and Harvey Donald Little

Margaret Olive (Palmer) Coldren and John Coldren

Sister - Shawn Ann (Little) Reeves

Growing up in Beautiful Perry County

Storyteller Jane Neely Stambaugh

For over 60 years my roots have grown deep into the fertile soil of Perry County. The small dairy farm where I grew up was purchased from my mother's grandfather, Sam Morrison by my dad's grandfather, William Henry Neely and has remained in the family for over 100 years. When I married, I moved onto my husband's family dairy which has traced its linage through Perry County's past for over 200 years and here is where we raised our two sons with a new generation already enjoying the life in this very special place of American soil.

Everyone certainly has special memories of their youth but now-a-days with the loss of family farms it seems important to preserve some snippets of life from this segment of our country's history.

My dad, Howard was the only sibling of 7 children who stayed on the farm. So, after his service in WWII, he purchased it from his dad, Ira. Later, my dad met my mom, Hilda Morrison who had grown up on a farm near Andersonburg and they began their lives together on what my Dad called Sunnyside Farm – the farm being nestled on the south side of a hill hidden from Shermans Valley Road and bordered on two sides by Bixler's Run and Shermans Creek. This is where my memories began.

My older brother and sister, Fred and Sue, and I had another special blessing in that our paternal grandparents lived in a house about 15 feet from ours. What could be better than that! Our Grandma Neely was a kind, hardworking, love-of-life, gentle soul. We had a hunting dog named Brownie and every Spring she would bring a couple baby rabbits in from a field to Grandma. Grandma would have us get a cardboard box and fill it with fresh grass for the baby bunnies. She would heat milk in the lid of a peanut butter jar on her wood fueled kitchen cook stove and used a medicine dropper to feed each one, holding them in the palm of her hand with her thumb and finger gently around their necks. She kept them toasty warm under the kitchen stove and not a one perished in her gentle care. Grandma loved animals as much as she loved us. It was commonplace to see her move snakes to better surroundings, trap a blue wasp under a glass, slip a piece of paper under it and free it outside. When Fred would bring his horse to her kitchen door, Sugar would thrust her head in the door to get Grandma's treat of a sugar cube. If Fred would have let her, I'm sure the horse would have walked right into the kitchen and Grandma wouldn't have minded. I watched as Grandma split wood for her cook stove, place wood chips in her apron to start the fire and prepare all her tasty meals on it. Once a year she picked the first of the Spring dandelion greens and topped them with hot bacon dressing. Oh, so good! As a child, I spent countless hours beside my Grandma in her rocking chair - something I love to do with my grandchildren now. Such special moments to share whether talking, singing, or just in peaceful motion.

Now my mother's father, Luther Morrison, visited frequently to help Dad on the farm. I only recently came to the realization that it must have been nostalgic for him to help on the farm that he also spent time on in his youth before the Neely family bought it from his dad. He and my grandma lived in Loysville after they sold their farm in Andersonburg. They had an outhouse that could still be used even though they had indoor plumbing, but we kids thought it fun to use it at times. One time I stayed overnight and was fascinated by the way the traffic lights came through the venetian blinds and moved around the room as the cars passed by. The only time we ever had lights shine in our bedroom was when someone was spotting deer on Hidden Valley Road and the light happened to flash by from so far away.

There was always work to be done on a farm, so we had no family vacations. Our 'vacations' were day trips. Early summer was our yearly trip to pick sweet black cherries near Newville. We picked our own and could eat as many as we wanted. That was great fun but then we had to spend hours canning (preserving) them when we got them home – not so much fun. In mid-August, our other yearly trip was to Sandoes Orchard for peaches. The best part of this day was being able to buy the fresh doughnuts at their fruit stand. Again-the downer was canning the peaches when we got home. But my favorite day was what we called 'putting away corn.' In our family sweet corn was the highlight of the year. When the sweet corn was ready, we seriously had it for breakfast, dinner, and supper. We might have a tomato sandwich or a hamburger along with the corn but all we cared about was the corn. We would make pyramids of the cobs, seeing whose would be the biggest by the time we were full. Of course, then we had the BIG day when we froze the bulk of the corn. For that, Dad would use the bed of the pickup truck or a couple trips to the corn patch with the tractor and scoop. The day would start early with picking the ears, then back to the shade of the walnut tree by the house for husking and silking. Now silking was my least favorite job. The silk is the shiny, thread-like fibers that grow as part of the ears of corn. We used a vegetable brush to remove the silk from the ear because who likes those fibers to get caught in your teeth when eating your roastin' ears as we called them. After that it was into the kitchen to blanch each ear and then cutting the kernels off the cobs. Finally, the bagging and into the freezer it went. Everyone helped with the whole process and were rewarded by eating as much as we wanted along the way. The worst part was finding worms and smut in an ear. If you never saw smut before, it is a fungus that usually grows in place of the kernels. It is usually white or gray and fleshy to the touch. How disgusting!

Summer also meant making hay. Dad ran most of the equipment with Mother running the baler at times. We kids helped mainly on the wagon and at the barn. We did not have the modern machines at that time. Our hay was either baled on the ground – for steep hills or on the wagon. If it was baled on the ground, Dad would drive the tractor around the field with a flatbed wagon in tow and Fred, Sue or I would throw the bales on the wagon and one of us would stack it. There was a special way to stack the bales so they would be 'tied' together without coming loose and falling off as they were stacked in higher layers. If we were on the 'flat' (bottom land), we could use a hay hook and pull the bales out of the baler onto the wagon and stack them. That eliminated the extra step of picking them off the ground on the hilly fields. But here are the worst parts of haymaking: the sweat bees stung, the pine flies bit, the salty sweat dripped in your eyes, the heat of the hayloft and inhaling the dust when the bales dropped off the elevator in the mow was almost suffocating. One fun part of hay making was riding on top of a loaded wagon down the old lane and grabbing sassafras leaves to chew on the trip to the barn. There was another fun experience, but it was during the boring winter months. Fred was an excellent tunnel maker in the hay mows. He started out by rearranging bales to make passageways through the mow, but he progressed, each year making them more intricant. He even used boards so larger rooms could be formed. Sue and I enjoyed Fred's hard work, but our Dad did not, especially if he moved some bales and fell into one of the tunnels. But it sure gave us something fun to do on cold winter days.

Picking stones off the fields after Dad plowed and 'worked down' the ground was not anyone's favorite activity. It seems to be unheard of with the lack of plowing these days. Back then it was a necessity if you did not want to break up machinery. We walked alongside a flatbed wagon, picking up middle to big sized stones and throwing them on. The best part was throwing them off, usually bending over and throwing them between our legs into the fencerow, although sometimes a few managed to hit someone else in our frenzy to get the job done as quickly as possible.

To take a break from the summer heat, we cooled off in the creek. Fred, Sue, and I would don our oldest sneakers, follow the cow path through the pasture to the swimming hole, sniffing the peppermint along the way. If we were lucky, the creek had a bit of coolness on a hot day but if not, at least it was wet. Sometimes we did this after finishing up a day of hay making and could wash off the worst of the sweat and dust. If we had one, we would take an inner tube to relax on. We searched for crayfish among the stones and tried to avoid the water snakes.

A couple times during the summer, the three of us would raid the pea patch. We would do this after dark in the glow of the nightlight. We would grab a big bowl and head for the garden. We would pick as many peas as we wanted, sneak up onto the front porch and shell and eat the peas raw – no better way! Our mother always wondered why her peas never produced well although I'm sure she had an idea!!

Really hot summer nights we spent on the front porch. The farmhouse was brick and like an oven after a few steamy days so we would head for the glider until the house cooled down. There we had a great view of the land from the house to the creek. We would watch the lightning bugs emerge from their hiding places in the corn and blink up into the night sky, listen to the frogs croaking by the creek, and the cows lowing in the pasture. Such a peaceful time of day.

When Dad built a new milk house, he let us take over the old one as our playhouse. We spent endless hours there doing what kids do best – using our imaginations. When our Aunt Mae visited from Harrisburg, she enjoyed playing with the 'three birds' as she called us.

The fall was a hurried time to get things ready for winter – the last of the crops in, canning or freezing the vegetables from the garden, cutting winter wood to feed the giant wood furnace in the basement – the list went on and on. One job that had to be done was picking walnuts. At that time, we did not have plastic or rubber gloves available and if you know anything about walnuts, the hulls stain whatever they touch. After collecting them from under the trees around the farm, we scattered them on the lane by the garage so vehicle tires could smash most of the hulls off before we had to gather them up. This was the worst part –

trying to pick up the walnuts without getting the 'juice' on your hands. It did not matter how hard we tried, no matter what kind of work gloves, the stain seeped through the gloves onto our hands and it took forever for the stain to wear off. With all that fuss complete, there was still more work to do. You had to crack each nut and walnuts have a hard shell. We used a hammer and many a time my thumb got in the way. Ouch! After that, you had to use a small 'pick' which had about a half inch long and curved with a pointy end. You literally picked the nut meat out of each section of the shell, usually in small pieces and some smashed but finally you had your prize – tasty walnuts. After all this effort we were rewarded with our favorite - walnut cake. Very delicious!

Winter brought its own set of chores – plowing snow, frozen water lines, power outages. But when the important jobs were done, we did have time for fun. We had many hills available for sledding. Unfortunately, some ended with electric fences, so we had to jump off before we reached the fence. That held its own excitement! Another activity that my dad thoroughly enjoyed was ice skating. We had a lot of choices – Bixler's Run, Shermans Creek, the dam across the road at Waggoner's Mill. I learned to skate in my brother's hand-me-down hockey skates. Dad loved to hook his hockey stick in my blades and pull me around the ice which stretched my ability to stay on my feet. Dad loved playing hockey and got together with the guys from the church who liked to play on the ponds, dams, and creeks in our area. Younger ones like me would go along and skate on the fringes of the game, trying to avoid the players and the puck.

Although snowstorms made chores more difficult on a dairy farm, it offered adventures for us. One year after a blizzard and with no electricity, our neighbors had no heat, so Sue and I carried a kerosene heater up the center of Shermans Valley Road to their house. There was no traffic, barely enough plowed for one vehicle to make it through, but I thought it was so cool to walk right up the middle of the main road.

Our family are members of Centre Presbyterian Church and my Dad's great grandfather was a minister there. In fact, Rev. William Burchfield retired from Centre church and spent his retirement near the town of Centre. Interestingly, my Dad's mother, who lived on the farm with us, was sent to Perry County as a young woman to care for this elderly retired couple, her grandparents. That is how my Dad's parents met- when Mildred Nelson moved from Brockway to Perry County.

When I was growing up, churches and schools were not closed as quickly as they are now even though we did not have front wheel and all-wheel drive vehicles. So, we did not miss many days of either school or church. For example, one snowy day when we were still using our extremely steep 'old lane', my dad had to attach a chain from my mother's car to his tractor to hold the car back from sliding the whole way down the lane and across the main road. All worked as planned and off to Blain school she went with the 3 of us in the back seat. A few times when church was called off, we were so excited but not for the reason you may think. We had church at home. Our mother played hymns on the piano, we collected offering, and I do not remember who had a sermon, but we thought it was great to have our own church service!

Now I cannot end these memories without a word about milking on a dairy farm, can I? When in the barn, our cows were secured by a chain around their neck that was attached to the front of their stall or were secured in head locks. We used Surge Belly milkers hooked up to a vacuum pump which sucked the milk out of their udder kind of like a vacuum cleaner. A surcingle, which is like a huge belt, was placed over the cow's back to hold the bucket milker off the floor. We wiped the teats with a sponge dipped in iodine water to sanitize them. Then we gave each teat a couple squirts to check for mastitis before placing the inflations (individual rubber 'cups') on each teat. After that the vacuum sucked the milk into the bucket. When the cow's udder was empty, the inflations were removed, and the teats were dipped in a cup of iodine solution. The bucket of milk was then taken to the milk house. The lid, with attached inflations, was taken off the milker and the milk was poured into a strainer that sat on top of a milk can. Here the raw milk ran through a paper filter in the strainer and into the can. When the milking was over, the can had to be heaved over the 3-foot side of the cooler and lowered into the ice-cold water it contained. This cooler looked like a huge chest freezer with a motor on top to keep the water very cold until the milk truck transported the milk to the dairy. When we were older, we switched to a bulk tank making the milk cans obsolete.

My sister and I avoided milking since Fred was the oldest and a boy - until he left for college in North Carolina when I was in 8th grade. Sue and I got a quick lesson from Dad and we were on our way. Sue played sports after school, so she took the morning milking and I helped with the evening shift. I got the hang of it quickly and Dad said I was the best milker of the 3 of us. When Sue went to college 2 years later, I milked with Dad in the morning and evening. I had long hair at the time and did not have much time to get ready for school after the morning milking, so I wore a shower cap to the barn. It worked well until one day I forgot to put it on and did not have time to wash my hair before school. I was so embarrassed in art class when someone got a whiff, and everyone wondered where that smell was coming from. Fortunately, I do not think anyone figured it out and I never made that mistake again. I remember one year it was the 1st day of school and during the summer we did not milk as early. So here we were back on a schedule that we had not shared with the cows. They were out in pasture, before daylight, in the fog and when Dad called them, they were extremely slow to come to the barn. Dad called his cows in with, "Here Whitey, Here Whitey" - Whitey being the name of our lead cow. I was certainly frustrated waiting for the herd to meander in. I was able to get a quick shower and Dad drove me to the end of the lane to catch the bus but what a way to start the 1st day of high school.

The 2 most unpleasant parts of milking for me were hunkering down beside a hot cow on a hot day right after a rainstorm and having the dirty water run off the steaming animal onto me. Yuck! Another experience was getting smacked in the face with a cow's tail. And if that was not bad enough - when the tail had just gone through fresh manure before hitting you in the face. Words cannot describe…

These are just a few cherished memories of growing up in this beautiful land that God has created and shared with us – Perry County – the place I call home!

Nicknames of Duncannon and Marysville Residents

1930s – 1980s
Recorded by Joe Mutzybaugh, Harriet Magee and Clarence Clouser

Allander, Clyde "Badger"
Allander, Willis "Chick"
Allen, William "Bunk"

Barton, Warren "Bart"
Belton, Carl "Farmer"
Barrick, Ramond "Dutchie"
Balsbaugh, Robert "Charley McCarthy"
Bornman, Dan "Decon"
Bolden, Paul "Boob"
Boyer, Kenneth "Pineapple"
Boyer, Carl "Farmer"
Boyer, Charles "Jukey"
Bender, Collier "Tickly"
Britcher, Mark "Flute & Itch"
Britcher, Bernard "Bones"

Collins, Ralph "Racky"
Carpenter, George "Jucky"
Cummings, Charles "Pecksy"
Cromleigh, Robert "Abe"
Cummings, William "Fatty"
Conklin, Merlin "Toar"
Carns, J. Harry "Moony"
Charles, John "Chick"

Allander, Roy "Dude"
Allander, Ellis "Nip"
Arter, Patrick "Pig Iron"

Billow, Charles "Boozer"
Blaine, William "Billy Nighthawk"

Brightbill, Lerue "Tiny"
Bornman, Homer "Toady"
Belton, Harry "Irish & Andy"
Boyer, Samuel "Stiffy"
Bender, Stanley "Skeet"
Barninger, Walter "Sleep"
Bolden, Paul "Boob"

Clouser, John "Chick"
Clouser, Clarence "Jiggs"
Cromleigh, Calvin "Budd"
Cromleigh, Gilbert "Scratch"
Collins, Elmer "Pickles"
Crouse, Stewart "Slim"
Crull, Edgar "Paddy"
Campbell, Percy "Pud"

Carpenter, Harold "Tuff"
Charles, Nelson "Sam"

Cummings, Lindley "Jim"

Downs, Charles "Dummy"
Dudley, John "Wib"
Dodrick, Daniel "Tucker"
Dodrick, Eugene "Hard Head"
Dromgold, Lynn "Drummy"
Dodrick, John "Peffer"
Dodrick, Walter "Hershey"
Deitz, Truxton "Tuds"

Dudley, Harvey "Benedick"
Dudley, Joe "Sharky"
Dodrick, George "Porky"
Dodrick, Gerald "Red & Red Eye"
Delancey, Lawrence "Hookem"
Derrick, Harry "Red"
Doyle, James "Doc"
Dersham, James "Red"

Evans, Chester "Zebby"
Ellenberger, Kenneth "Deets"

Evans, Issac "Ike"

Fry, Earnest "Toots"
Fry, Lucien "Vicks"
Flickinger, Neil "Pete"
Froggett, Dave "Bud"

Fry, Clyde "Pinky"
Franklin, Marshal "Punch"
Fritz, Ross "Tarbelly"

Gamber, Jon Howard "Tags"
Griffith, Elwood "Huff"
Gusler, Willard "Strap"
Gamber, Charles "Billy Goat"
Graff, Glen "Deacon"
Gandy, Maynard "Muskrat"
Gilbert, Henry "Hoot Owl"
Graff, Daniel "Dandelion"

Griffith, Alfred "Tink"
Gilbert, George "Chubby"
Gusler, Nelson "Do Die"
Gamber, Charles "Pank"
Gandy, Dyson "Goose"
Gilbert, George Sr. "Baldy"
Gross, Lake "Ting-a-ling"
Guyler, Raymond "Ramey"

Hennessey, Clarence "Spike"
Hunter, Elmer Jr. "Pud"
Holland, Nelson "Runt"
Holland, Stanley "Stink & Geronimo"
Harp, Elmer "Babe"
Hammaker, Ellsworth "Buzz & Hawkeye"
Hammacker, Elmer "Pete"
Hockenberry, Charles "Boots"
Hoffman, Ronald "Jucky"
Hiltner, Merle Jr. & Sr. "Pete"
Hollenbaugh, Betram "Hulley or Boo"
Hamilton, Clifford "Pete"
Hess, William "Bay Rum Bill"

Hunter, Charles "Pickles"
Hunter, Elmer Sr. "Pie"
Hetrick, Eugene "Beans"

Hammaker, Winfred "Windy"
Hamilton, Frank "Judge"
Huss, Dyson "Dice"
Hamilton, Maynard "Tater"

Howell, Melvin "Skinny"
Hetrick, Guy "Geezer"

Jones, Clifford "Jumbo"
Jones, Sherman "Tick Tock"

Kiner, Russell "Kinter & Kissy"
Krick, Vernon "Buck"
Keel, Charles "Chick"
Keene, Harold "Haddy"
Kluck, Harold "Danny"
Kulp, Stanley "Teenie"
Keel, Lester "Bones"
Kisner, Foster "Boone"
Koltrieder, Earl "Gunnea"

Lukens, William "Flag ears"
Lowman, Charles "Jadda aka Jatta "
Lusk, Howard "Pluge"
Laird, Wilber "Knute"
Lightner, Warren "Bucky"
Lewis, George "Skinner"
Liddick, Jacob "Happy Jim"
Lower, Harry "Rummy"
Liddick, Charles "Jukey" Leedy, Custer "Cussy"
Lauster, Fred Sr. "Fats"

May, Charles "Humpy"
Manning, Walter "Shoocker"
Miller, Gerald "Egghead"
McNeil, Kenneth "Punch"
Miller, Landis "Scoop"
Morrison, Stanley "Yum"
Miller, John "Whitey"
Mutzabaugh, John "Gomer"
Mutzabaugh, Thomas "Clook"
Morrison, Donald "Bert"
Morrow, Alvin "Mutt"
Mullen, Harold "Buzzy"
Moody, John "Teabag"
Miller, Clyde Jr. & Sr. "Soddy"
McGuire, Harold "Mickey"
Morris, Clarence "Kid"
Miles, Walter "Ditty"
Mumpher, Leroy "Bean Belly"

Johnson, Alfred "Whitey"

Krick, Lloyd "Jake"
Krick, Roy Jr. "Chappie"
Kline, John "Spook"
Keene, Sherwood "Sherb"
Kisner, Harold "Gink"
Klinepeter, Ralph "Sid"
Kline, Charles "Boo"
Kiner, Alvin "Hook"
Knaub, Elmer Jr, "Pokey"

Light, Frank "Catty"

Laird, Ray "Sadie"
Liddick, Alton "Biddy"
Lepperd, Charles "Hitler"
Lewis, John "Warpy"
Lowe, Fred "Bat"

Morrisey, Lee "Doc"
Meck, Warren "Shorty"
Malseed, H. Ward "Pumpkin/Punk"
Maneval, Herbert "Sputter"
McKelvey, Warren "Smokie/Smoke"
Morris, Gerald "Scribby"
Mutzabaugh, Ellis "Muskrat"
Mutzabaugh, Melvin "Sporty"
Morrison, George "Shimmy Show"
May, Milton "Hooker"
Mullen, Karl "Cug"
Mullen, Clyde "Klick"
Morris, Charles "Chunk"
Morrow, Edwin "Piggymo"
May, Edward "Brownie"
Maxwell, Carl "Bud"
McKelvey, Charles "Yuckel"
Mader, George "Tater"

Noye, Charles "Bumps"
Noye, Charkes Sr. "Butch"

Potter, Victor "Goat"
Palmer, Charles "Tilly"
Peck, Merle "Smoke"
Peterman, George "Shake"

Reynolds, Robert "Crackers"
Reed, Clarence "Peck"
Reed, Nelson "Mossey"
Reighter, Emery "Bummy"

Smith, Donald "Dice"
Smith, Chellis "Doc"
Smith, Charles "Chink"
Sanderson, Paul "Iggy"
Sload, Kenneth "Red"
Sterner, John "Horny"
Simpson, Donald "Satchel"
Snyder, Emerson "Skin"
Shuman, George "Peck"
Stansfield, Harry "Slick"
Shover, Marlin "Popey"
Snyder, Robert "Rattlehead"

Tayler, Floyd "Sam"
Thompson, Earl "Squirrely"
Thompson, Edwin "Young Squirrely"
Toland, Charles "Bones"
Toland, John "Skeet"

Ulrich, Russell "Matty"
Vogel, Harry "Bus"

Weaver, Lloyd "Doc/Mooney"
Weldon, Gordon "Gumshoe"
Weldon, Clarence "Teenie"
Wagner, Oscar Jr, "Sonny"
Wright, William "Wimpy"
Wright, Orville "Roddy"
Wolford, Keith 'Big Foot"
Wolpert, Melvin Jr. "PJ"

Noye, Floyd "Soupy"
Ney, Irvan "Bud"

Pines, Robert "Shorty"
Puff, Gilbert "Gilly"
Pressler, William "Cheesey"

Roth, Harry "Butch"
Reed, Oscar "Barney"
Richter, Elwood "Pier Pont"

Smith, Robert "Moat"
Smith, Charles "Butter"
Simonton, Earl "Katy"
Sload, Ivan "Mickey"
Seiler, George "Slick"
Sterner, Peter "Turko"
Shaffer, Gary "Frog"
Spence, Albert "Abby"
Sheets, Stephen "Pappy"
Shultz, Wilmont "Bud"
Sieg, Thayer "White Eagle"
Stidfole, Edward "Hap"

Thompson, Millard "Zip"

Toland, Ellsworth "Hungry Sam"
Toland, Russell "Peetie"
Toland, Thomas "Elk"

Ulrich, Howard Jr. "Tub"

Weaver, Jack "McCoy"
Weldon, Lester "Bugs"
Weldon, Arthur "Sparky"
Wagner, William G. "Judge"
Wright, Walter Sr. "Waxy"
Wright, Harry "Scoopy"
Wolpert, Melvin "Red"
Wentzel, Orville "Orley"

Even the ladies had nicknames back in the day!!

Achenbach, Helen "Weezy"

Bender-Smith, Helen "Till" Bender, Verna "Toots"
Bornman, Violet "Bunchy" Boyles, Florence "Poky"

Clouser, Naomie "Skipper" Cummings, Sarah "Dickie"

Dowdrick, Doris "Sid"

Holland-Bealor, Ruth "Pearl" Holland, Borcheding, Thelma "Till"

Krick, Alice "Fat" Keel-Krick, Thelma "Tea Kettle"
Kiner – Morris, Rita "Peg"

Mader, Mignon "Noni" Myers, Margaret "Mommy"
Mutzabaugh -Ricupero, Helen "Chook"

Noye, Marie "Nuncy" Noye, Alta "Nannaw"

Smith, Isabelle "Bill" Snavely, Ruth "Sniffy"
Shope-Ellenberger, Alice "Doppy" Summy, Charlotte "Jim"
Skivington, Blanch "Tubby" Sterner, Mary "Wild Bess"

Robinson's Store and the Western End of Loysville

Storyteller Dean Robinson

My name is Dean Robinson and I was born in 1945, to Harry and Irma (Furler) Robinson, between Cisna Run and Couchtown, in Perry County. My dad's parents were Lawrence and Carrie (Smith) Robinson. My mother's parents were Warren and Mabel (Moore) Furler.

My grandfather Furler operated the store at Couchtown. He and my dad built the grocery and hardware store, west of the square in Loysville, in 1946, operating Robinson and Furler till 1951. We also had a Gulf Gas Station. Gas was delivered by Graybill's from East Newport. Jim Turnbaugh later bought the gas business and delivered gas to our store.

My dad bought out my grandfather's share of the business, in 1951, so he could retire. My dad built the brick house beside the store, for our home. My grandfather built the one next door.

My dad operated the store with my brother Carl helping out until 1956, when Carl went away to school. I then started working in the store, selling groceries, household goods, hardware, and gas. At that time, there were some older men who were real characters coming into the store to spend the evenings. I remember Ben Barclay, John Swarner, Stanley Weller, Paul Ritter and George Ickes. Plus others I can't remember. They would have disagreements one day, and be best friends the next, loafing around the storefront.

One time Mr. Barclay and Mr. Ritter fell out. Mr. Barclay would always come to town with his tractor and plow the snow for people. Well, it snowed and Mr. Ritter got up very early and drove his tractor fitted, with a plow, into town. He plowed **all** of Mr. Barclay's customer's driveways **for free.** Just to spite Mr. Barclay so he would not make any money that snowy day!

I worked in the store and went to school (hating school all the time), graduating in 1963. I bought the store from my dad in 1968 and ran the store with the help of my parents until I married Ellen (Naylor) in 1975.

Some of the vendors for the store were Kling's Meats of Elliottsburg, Trostle's Butcher Shop of Loysville, Juniata Dairy of Duncannon, Rakestraw's Ice Cream of Mechanicsburg, Kessler's Meats of Lemoyne, Valley Pride Bread Company of Newville, and Harrisburg Grocer's to name a few.

Ellen and I operated the store until I leased it to Bill Campbell in 1988. By that time, my wife and I were both working for the postal service.

Campbell ran the store until 2011, when he leased it to Rick Kuhn for TnT Bargain Boys. Mary Morrison bought him out in 2014, closing Morrison's Grocery in 2017.

Jan Smith, Ed Hughes, Sam Martin, Harvey Maneval, and myself were setting up at the Carlisle Flea Market, selling antiques, used equipment, collectibles and household goods. We decided to move into the empty store building for the winter, creating Robinson's Bargain Store, which is still operating, Thursday through Saturday.

The building, next door going west of Robinson's Store, was built for the Farm Bureau. They moved from Cisna Run in 1950. Farm Bureau became Eastern States and then Agway, selling animal feed, farm supplies, and seeds. When Agway closed, they sold the building to Frank Latchford, who operated a trucking company, a short time. He sold to Howard Turner and Jim Burhnam, for a paint store and auction house.

The next owner was Jeff Heikenfeld, who ran a full-time auction house, Jeff's Auctions. I set up the auctions and cleaned up afterwards. I got a lot of my flea market items, from the auctions. Heikenfeld retired and sold the property to Leon Leid for a grocery and fresh produce store, Leid's Market. Dennis Kistler bought the buildings behind the store for a butcher shop.

The property that existed to the west of Leids, was Paul Shover and Sons who built and ran a Massey Harris dealership, selling farm equipment, in the early 1950s. Later the building was leased to Norman Clark of Honey Grove for an International Tractor dealership. The dealership selling farm equipment, closed and was torn down. Today Shermans Valley Senior Apartments, a senior housing complex, exists at Powell Lane, in Loysville.

Beyond the senior housing, was Gutshall's John Deer building, built in the 1970s. Selling John Deere farm equipment, they closed and sold to Lee Dobbs, for a produce store, Dobb's Produce. He sold the building to Perry Power, which today operates an outdoor equipment and repair shop.

Across the road from Robinson's store, Mary Kell built a house in the late 1950s. East of Kell, Wilbur Gutshall built the Sunbonnet Restaurant in 1961. George W. Goodling, chief assessor for Perry County, built a house west of Kell, sometime later. A cross the street from Perry Power is Enck's Sunoco Gas Station. It was started by Carroll Enck, and was sold down through the years to Bob Enck and now Barry Enck.

I started Robinson's Towing Service in 1967, operating it until 2015, when health prevented my working.

I started Robinson's Store Racing team in 1963, racing at Silver Springs Speedway. We ran hobby cars, then sportsman, and later early model modified cars. Drivers over the years, included Wayne O'Hara,

George Garlin, Bill Clouser, Gene McAllister, Glen Comp, Dave Erney, Rick Boyer, Bob Boyer, Phil Carlin, Ken Newswanger, and me. In 1975, we went to Port Royal and raced with the late models. Dave Suchy, Sam Gipe and Sam Landis were the drivers. In 1982, we quit racing.

Robinson's businesses have sponsored a bowling team, since 1958. From 1963 – 1987, the team was called Robinson's Store. Robinson's Towing sponsored the team from 1988 – 2015. Robinson's Bargain Store took over in 2016 until present day.

I have been in the last forty-seven national tournaments. The team won the Tuesday Night League at Perry Lanes in New Bloomfield, many years ago. The bowling alley is now closed. I won the Dutchman Tournament, in Lebanon, in 1976.

My how the landscape, in Loysville, has changed, but I'm glad to be back in the building that my dad and grandfather built. Seems like old times, once again!

Life in New Bloomfield, PA

Storyteller Judy Metzger
Recorded by Steve Metzger

My name is Judy Metzger, I am 81 years old and was born and raised in New Bloomfield. Since 1958, I have lived in Newport on the same corner of 5th Street in East Newport.

My parents were Charles and Lucille Sheaffer Wallace, they were married the year I was born and after that we lived in New Bloomfield throughout my entire childhood. My dad was drafted when I was very young and served in the 87th Armored Field Artillery Battalion. His group was part of the second landing force at Normandy and helped to secure France and Europe from the Axis.

After the war, my dad took a job driving truck for a company in Carlisle, delivering new cars to Dodge and Chrysler dealerships. Ironically for several years we didn't even have our own car. I think I was 10 or 11 before he bought a used car and even then, my mother needed to learn how to drive. He would bring his car hauler home and I remember climbing on it like a jungle gym as a kid. The first truck I can remember him driving hauled four cars. He was excited when he was able to get the newest model of truck which held five, one over the cab.

When he would come home, he would usually cut the corner at the monument in the square and avoid circling it with the car hauler. Of course, there was a lot less traffic back then and many times when he would come home, it would be late in the evening and no one ever said anything to him about it.

We lived in several rented houses in town through the years. The first I remember was a house on High Street, a couple of blocks from the school. From there we moved to a small, but more modern house on Oak Road, not too far from where the pool is today. We were living across the street from the butcher shop when I got married and for a while before that, we lived in part of the big brick house beside the funeral home. It was not unheard of for my dad to leave for a 2-week haul and come home to find that family had moved.

Since we always lived in town, I attended the town schools, not a one room country schoolhouse, although we still usually had only one teacher per grade. First was the elementary school, which was on

High Street across from the fire house. The high school at that time was located where the post office and borough office are now on McClure Street.

The new school, what is now New Bloomfield Elementary, was built to be a high school originally and elementary classes were moved to the McClure Street building for more space. By the time the baby boomers were all starting school and moving on in grades, there were so many students that classes were held all over town, wherever there was space and I recall one year our classroom was the stage of the fire hall.

New Bloomfield was never as big of a town as Newport. There were no large manufacturing plants, other than a few small sewing factories and of course there was no railroad stop. There were still several stores, 3 or 4 new car dealers and a few diners. Of course, Book's Drug Store was on the corner of the square.

Life was much simpler in those days. People had much more modest needs and we must have been able to find what we needed because it was a very rare occurrence to make a trip to Carlisle to shop. It was not even common to go to Newport for our family.

The two biggest things New Bloomfield was known for county wide, were the courthouse, which wasn't near as big back then, and Carson Long School. My mom worked in the cafeteria at Carson Long for a few years. It was one of the only times I can remember her working outside the home, but she was always in the kitchen doing something. She put up many, many jars of canned goods each year, baked, and cooked all kinds of things. It's no wonder that after she was a widow at a young age and she needed to work that she almost always took a job at a restaurant or lunch counter in a department store.

Maybe it was because she had first-hand knowledge, or maybe it was just paranoia, but Mom always told me and any other kids from town not to associate with any of the boys from Carson Long School. They were apparently not allowed off the school grounds too much, but they would come downtown to get their hair cut or to visit the drug store for a soda once in a while and most of the town kids were all given strict orders to not be friendly with them.

There were no trains on the old Perry County Railroad Line and the station down where they are building the new fire house was empty. I recall walking out the railroad bed with my grandmother Annie Arndt Wallace to visit her sister Elsie who lived about a half mile outside of town, across the road from Comps Schoolhouse.

My grandfather, Leonard Wallace, worked at Frog and Switch in Carlisle. I spent a good bit of time with them growing up. I hardly knew my Grandfather Bill Sheaffer because he lived in Harrisburg with his second wife until I was older. My Grandmother Pearl Sweger Sheaffer died when my mother was just a baby and she was mostly raised by her grandparents Foster and Susan Sheaffer, but I never knew either of them.

I was a teenager when the old Perry County railroad Station was torn down and the Ford garage was built. The first cars I remember seeing in the showroom were the new Thunderbirds. The men who built it and ran it were Homer Weldon, Frank McBride and Ed Dyson. It was called DWM Motors at the time, but the name and owners changed many times over the years before the building was abandoned and eventually torn down to make way for the new fire station.

Out on West Main Street there was Norm Black's Buick garage and Cupp's had the garage across the street from the news office that sold Hudsons and Kaiser/Fraser models. No one can forget Raffensperger's Dodge, where the bowling alley was.

I remember when I was little, getting my bangs clipped at Stoops' barber shop. It was funny because both my dad and Mr. Stoops were nicknamed Red. When we had a little extra money, we could go to see movies in the old theater near where the Veterans' Building parking lot is now. There were a few little grocery stores around town, even a small Weis store right down the street from Book's pharmacy, but we always did most of our shopping at the A&P store.

Being a truck driver, my dad was on the road a lot and when he was home, he enjoyed spending time with his fellow veterans at the VFW. When he finally decided to build a house, he chose a lot right next to the VFW and it seemed like he was almost always there when he wasn't at work.

I met my future husband while I was still in high school and neither of us could wait to get married and start our life together. We drove to Hagerstown, Maryland on my eighteenth birthday. A lot of people back then left the state to avoid the blood tests and red tape required to get married locally. That was over 63 years ago and neither of us would have done anything different if we had the choice.

As soon as we were married, Ray and I put a modest house trailer on a lot that his dad bought, across the street from their home in East Newport, one of the last vacant lots in the neighborhood. A number of years later, after my father-in-law's death, we bought the lot from his mother and built our house right there.

The summer we started to build, both Ray and I started new jobs. He started with the liquor store and I transferred to the Newport branch of the Eileen Hope dress factory. We did much of the work on our house ourselves. We had the block walls laid and the frame of the house built and completely finished the inside as we wanted, as time and money allowed. I spent many nights drilling holes for electrical wires that Ray would mark before going into work himself. My mother-in-law would keep me company while I stapled insulation, painted walls, and varnished trim and hardwood floors.

I was very fortunate to get along well with my mother-in-law. Not only did we live directly across the street from one another, but we both worked at the Eileen Hope dress factory in Duncannon before the company opened a branch in the old Snap-On building here in Newport. We transferred there together and I worked there until 1970 when my son was born. My mother-in-law worked there until she retired a few years later. She then volunteered to become a babysitter when I went back to work.

For many, many years she and I shopped together. Friday night was our regular night to go to the grocery stores and there were plenty to choose from in Newport. For a change of pace, several times a year, we would go to Harrisburg, Carlisle or even Lewistown to shop.

After the flood in 1972, I was asked by our neighbors to help clean up the flood mess from their stores, which were located on North Second Street in Newport. They were Jack and Millie Wagner who owned a shoe store and the Sears catalog store, right next to each other.

It wasn't long after the flood cleanup, probably the next holiday season, that the Wagners offered me a job in the Sears store. I worked there, serving customers and mainly as the teletype operator even after they left the area and sold the store to another couple. Long before computers, all customers' orders had to be entered into the teletype system and sent to Philadelphia to be filled.

After typing in the order, in just a couple of days, the items would be trucked in from the Philadelphia warehouse and customers could pick up what they wanted right here in town without driving to the city or waiting for the mail to arrive. Before there were catalog stores from companies like Sears, Montgomery Ward and J.C. Penny, orders would be mailed to the company and the customer would have to wait for parcel post to deliver their item to their home. This sometimes took weeks or more.

Now, everyone orders their items to be sent directly to their homes from catalogs, Amazon, or eBay and even though we might complain, the processing time is rather fast compared to what it was in the old days.

There have been a lot of changes to the little towns in Perry County since I was a girl. Some are good, some not so good, but life has progressed and will continue to change.

Life & Times in Perry County Growing up in Newport, PA

Storyteller Ray Metzger
Recorded by Steve Metzger

My name is Ray Metzger, I am 83 years old and have lived in Perry County my entire life. For over 80 of those years, I have lived in the same neighborhood, on Fifth Street in East Newport, near the First Church of God.

My parents were married in 1934 and went to housekeeping in a house on High Street, Carver's Hill in Duncannon. They were renting from Allen and Isabelle Michener at the time. Their son, James Michener owned the funeral home on High Street in town that is now Smith's. The Micheners became good friends of the family in the years we lived there and they continued to be friends of my parents for years to come.

Dad (Arthur Metzger) was a mechanic and an upholsterer. He and his brother worked for a time for the Lesh brothers who had a Chrysler and Graham-Paige dealership in Everhartville, outside of Newport. Bob Maguire, who was raised not far from where my dad grew up, and a good friend of Dad's, offered him a job when he opened the Ford dealership along the Little Juniata Creek in Duncannon in 1935. Living only a few blocks away from the garage, Dad took him up on his offer and worked there until he went to work for the PA Dept. of Highways several years later.

In the days before unions and not being a civil service worker, my dad's job was what was called a patronage job. That meant that his job was conditional upon which political party was in power in Harrisburg. I recall a few times over the years where he stayed up late listening to the news for election results, concerned that his job with the state might not be available for four years. This rarely happened and when it did, Bob Maguire made sure he had work as a mechanic at his garage.

I do not remember much of our life in Duncannon. In 1940, my mother (Arletta Barkley) learned of a house for sale in East Newport. It was not far from the schoolhouse she attended as a child and she talked about seeing it being built and dreaming of living there one day. Fortunately, my parents had saved enough money to purchase the house and we moved just before I turned 3. I remember my parents saying they waited to move until the day after election day in the fall. Dad was a strict Republican and would not do anything that may have caused him to not be able to cast his vote, especially in a presidential election year.

The neighborhood, on Fifth street in East Newport, had 2 houses when I was growing up. Not far away was the Church of God and on the far side of it, sat the old schoolhouse which was by this time converted to a residence. By the time I was ten or so, an aunt of my mothers built a house across the side road from ours. She moved in from Boston and always had a bit of an accent, even though she was raised in Wila.

A few years later, Stew Gibb moved to Newport from Carlisle to open the ice plant in the old spool factory on Bloomfield Avenue. He built a brick house on the opposite side of 5th street from our house. I used to like to look in the windows of the ice plant and watch the workers maneuver the gigantic blocks of ice that were cut and sold so people could maintain their ice boxes before refrigerators.

Even though they had a small lot, my parents treated our home like a miniature farm. We were right at the edge of town but there were enough empty lots near us that there was space to spread out, at least until the lots were sold, and nothing was sold during the war years. We had chickens for eggs and several times my dad would put out a large pen of meat chickens. The chickens would be butchered and either canned or taken to a rented cold storage locker at the ice plant. He would put out a large truck patch every year and planted several fruit trees and grape arbors around the place.

Mom canned fruits and vegetables that were grown and even meats on occasion. There was a time when we raised rabbits. Someone, probably a grandparent, had given me 2 rabbits for Easter one year and before long we had a lot more rabbits than we bargained for. Dad was an avid hunter. He hunted all kinds of wild game, rabbits and squirrels, birds and of course deer.

Our house had electricity and an indoor bathroom. However, the water was Newport town water, which was notoriously pumped right out of the Little Buffalo Creek, the same creek that much of the sewage from East Newport went into. Understandable, my dad decided to drill a well before we even lived in the house as soon as he was able. The well took weeks to get up and running but it was well worth the wait to have our own clean, fresh water.

My mother never worked outside of the home until after my dad died but she was always busy doing something in the kitchen, helping a neighbor or relative or making her own dresses. She was an excellent seamstress and made nearly all of her own clothes, though she hardly ever made any for my dad or I.

Newport itself was a busy town. There were several sewing factories, the Forged Steel plant, the passenger and freight stations, a few feed mills, the ice plant, clothing, and furniture stores, 4 or 5 new car dealerships and more little grocery stores and gas stations than you could shake a stick at.

From our front porch, the stacks of the old Marshall Furnace could be seen, even though it was long out of operation. The only thing I can recall being made there was the grit for shingles was ground from the slag piles around the old furnace itself. Of course, the main line Pennsy (PA Railroad) wasn't far away. There were 4 tracks at the time and smoke from the stacks of the steam trains could be seen. Their chugging and whistles were often heard, especially on a damp day. When the railroad began using the quieter and cleaner diesel engines, it took a while to get used to the lack of the train sounds.

Of course, today the old passenger station by the river bridge is in a sad condition. It was quite nice in its day for a town like Newport. It was also very convenient while it was operational. The regular trains no longer stopped at Newport by the time I was in high school. For my senior class trip to New York city, special arrangements were made for a train to stop and pick everyone up. The train took us right to the big train station in New York.

Not too far away from my home, just across route 34 and the Little Buffalo creek was the stone quarry. Regular blasts to loosen the rock were put off. A large hole, or several of them, would be drilled and filled with explosives. When they were set off, this caused a rumble and boom to be felt all over town and a plume of dust to settle all over East Newport. One time a piece of rock about the size of a large coconut dropped right into our yard. A house not far away had a large rock go through their roof and end up in their attic. People knew that whenever the blast whistle went off, it was not a good idea to not be out in the yard.

When I was a teenager, an accident occurred at the quarry just as I was leaving for school one morning. A huge piece of rock, many tons, which had been loosened by vibrations from the blasts and weather came off the side of the hill, straight up above the stone crushers. I can still see the place where it came from to this day. A man who was operating a piece of equipment jumped under it to escape but still ended up having his foot crushed so bad that Doc Ulsh crawled under the dozer and amputated it right there in order to free him from where he was trapped.

The Forged Steel Vacuum Grip factory was one of the biggest manufacturing plants in the area and was not far from our house. Many hours a day the rhythmic ka-chunk, ka-chunk, ka-chunk of the punch presses could be heard pounding the pliers and wrenches out of hot steel. The vacuum grip pliers were produced there for many years and a lot of people still have and use them regularly. The design was so popular that one of the biggest tool companies in the world, Snap-On sought out and bought the company in order to secure the patent. They operated the Newport plant for a number of years and a pair of pliers that say both Snap-On and Newport, PA on them will bring a good price with collectors at local sales.

Generally, we could get anything we needed simply by going into town, most times on foot. A few times each year, no more than 2 or 3, my mother and I would take the train to the city when it still stopped in Newport. From there, we would shop and then meet up with my dad at the garage after he got off work. Dad worked at the PA Dept of Highways garage on State Street in Harrisburg. He would take his own car to work those days rather than carpool which he almost always did.

For the longest time, my dad was the only mechanic who could do upholstery work at the highway garage, so he spent most of his time repairing seat covers on the work trucks and occasionally doing body work or general mechanical work if needed. There was even a time when he covered chairs for the state Senate chamber. We had a chair in our living room that was covered to match from a piece of the leftover material. Upholstery was something that came natural to him and he enjoyed doing it. He even took on jobs for people around town and covered seats for school buses on the weekends and evenings.

I didn't go to a one-room school like many people my age. Living close to town, I spent my first school years at the 4th Street Elementary School, and later Newport High School. At the time, the high school building was simply 12 or so rooms. Now the school covers the entire block. There was no cafeteria. We all took our lunches with us every day and ate in the classrooms, the auditorium or even outside if the weather was nice.

While there were a few bus routes, I never rode one. It was long after my retirement that I ever rode on a school bus. The buses were for those who lived in the far reaches of the district. It was nearly a half mile to the elementary school and almost a full mile to the high school from my home and until I got a driver's license, I walked it every day.

When I was young, kids would collect soda bottles and turn them in for cash. Most of them had a one cent deposit, a few were even worth 2 or 3 cents. To find a handful of bottles and return them to one of the many stores, a kid could buy a nice sack of penny candy. One of the best places to get candy was Max Walker's store on 4th Street in East Newport.

In those days, garbage wasn't collected in plastic bags and hauled to another county, many miles away for disposal. There was a dump about a mile south of town where the town's garbage was taken. Many bottles could be found there if you were lucky enough to get to them before someone else picked them up. Of course, they were mixed in with ashes, rotten food, and all sorts of other garbage. The dump was on the way to my Grandparents' house (Clarence and Gertie Barkley) so I would usually stop my bike on the way back from their place and try to find a nickel's worth of glass for some candy.

During the war years people also picked the dump, gathering up tin and scrap metal to turn in to help the war effort. Of course, there was a lot of junk that was totally worthless, and it always seemed that there was a fire going in one corner or the other to dispose of the things that would burn. When I drive by that hollow, I wonder if the people who have houses built on top of the old dump are aware of what they are living on, and their wells go down through, the town's old landfill.

My dad's parents, Oliver and Lizzie Metzger, lived down in Mahanoy Valley, Miller Twp. We rarely took a trip down there and my Grandpa Ollie died when I was in first or second grade. After that, my grandmother moved to town and rented an apartment above Lesh's store on the square in Newport. She had a habit of hanging out in one of the local restaurants or stores and talking to anyone about anything. This went on until a couple of the shop keepers asked my dad to try to do something because she was starting to annoy customers.

Another favorite past time of fellows in the 40's and 50's was to take a flashlight and a .22 to the dump after dark and shoot rats. Some of them were over a foot long, not including the tail. There were plenty of them and it was good target practice. No one had any objections either because no one wanted to see the excess dump rats begin to overrun the town.

When I graduated from high school in 1955, I got a surprise visit from Mrs. Michener, my parents' old friend from Duncannon. She came with an offer to send me to mortuary school and hire me on the spot to work at her son's funeral parlor in Duncannon.

Of course, I was seventeen with other ambitions and I wanted no part of this deal! It seemed like such a morbid and depressing business to be in. My mom must have sensed how I was feeling. She left Mrs. Michener down easily by telling her that such a job would probably not be a good fit for me. I suffered from terrible allergies and being around all the flowers which are typically associated with funerals would not be healthy for me.

Like many young guys my age I had planned to work at the plier factory when I got out of school. After the buyout by Snap-On, continual labor disputes and other troubles, Snap-On simply cut their losses and moved the plant to Wisconsin where they were headquartered. The company had secured what they desired, which was the patent on the vacuum grip tool handles, so they had nothing to gain by staying in Newport. The loss of the factory was a huge blow to the town and several of the local businessmen banded together to try to attract another large manufacturing operation to town. They even approached the board of Ford Motor Company to begin making certain components of Ford cars here. Needless to say, that never happened.

There were plenty of other places to work, though. One of my first jobs was working at Alcorn Lincoln-Mercury. The original garage was built for Ralph Lesh Sr's Chrysler dealership around 1950. My grandfather, Clarence Barkley, who was a night watchman at the Snap-On plant, helped when they were building it. Mr. Lesh would gather up men from around town to do labor work and pay them by the day. It was a good way for them to earn cash for a good day's work and for some to supplement their usual income.

In 1955, a man from York County bought the building from the Lesh family and opened the Lincoln-Mercury store. It was managed by a man named Roy T. Rossey. Rossey made it his goal to see that any young man who wanted one got a great deal on a new or almost new Mercury or Lincoln. He felt it would be an excellent form of advertising. I bought a couple of new cars while I worked there and never overpaid on any of them. Some were sold at such a good deal that it was no doubt the dealership lost money on them. There were many other young men around town who got great deals too.

My primary job at the dealership was to recondition cars that had been traded in. This meant to make them look as new as possible with shiny, polished paint and to clean them, inside and out, over and under, so that they were spotless. In some cases, it also meant that odometers were "re-set". This was not necessarily illegal, although it was unethical, even in the 1950's.

At that garage, we had one old mechanic who would retreat into the restroom for long periods of time. He would occupy the only toilet in the place that the other employees in the shop were allowed to use and wouldn't come out for love or money or until he was good and ready. A few of the younger fellows decided that old Ben must have developed a habit of falling asleep on the throne and needed a wake-up call.

A pair of tacks were secretly driven through the seat, two wires hooked up to them on the underside and run around the corner toward a nearby electrical outlet. The bathroom wasn't very well lit. The man was given what was felt to be a sufficient amount of time to complete his task and the cord was plugged in! The door came right off the hinges with an old man on top of it, his pants still at his ankles, cursing a blue streak.

The Lincoln-Mercury dealership didn't last long and by the spring of 1957 it was gone. For several years after that I worked at the Capital Products storm window factory in Mechanicsburg before taking a job at the liquor store in Newport where I worked for over 30 years, the last 15 as manager.

Growing up in Oliver Township

Storyteller Steve Metzger

My name is Steve Metzger and I have lived in Oliver Township, just outside of Newport my entire life. For the past 23 years, I have lived in a house that has been in our family, purchased by my great-grandfather over a century ago. I have always been proud of the thought that my kids are the 5th generation of our family to live where we do.

Along with her working a full-time job most of my first thirty years, my mother worked very hard to take care of our home. Her normal chores included the typical cooking and dishes, washing with a wringer washer until I was about 8, and ironing almost everything afterward. Our house always seemed spotless, with thorough cleaning and dusting done weekly and the windows were never left with spots on them, inside or out.

Even so, it was not unusual for my mom to take a shovel or hammer into her hands. When major projects were done, they were usually done as a family, with everyone working together. And a good estimate would be that 98% of the paint and varnish on the inside of the house was put on by my mom and when growing up color changes to the bathroom walls were frequent.

Dad did plenty, too. He showed me from a young age that if a job was worth doing, it was worth doing well, and doing yourself. In my 50 years, I have never seen my father hire a plumber, electrician, or any other kind of handy man. Very rarely, would he take his car or truck to a garage for repairs other than the annual safety inspection. Of course, I have followed this pattern as well, sometimes tackling jobs that were a little out of my league, but still getting them done one way or the other and learning in the process.

One of my earliest memories is seeing my dad rebuilding the brakes on a pickup truck and there was never anything he did that he didn't explain how to do and give me a part in doing. As he learned to do things by watching his dad, I learned from him, with plenty of hands-on experience.

I have followed his example and have always tried to include my son when things need to be done around the house. He has taken interest in helping me whenever there is upholstery work to be done. I am not anywhere near as proficient as my grandfather, but just like him, I seem to be one of just a handful of mechanics who are willing to do it. I guess it's truly a family tradition and I hope my son can handle the work someday.

To me, dad could fix anything and usually he did. It was nothing for friends, neighbors or even my mom's boss to ask him to work on one thing or another. Being an avid hunter, he loaded his own ammunition and often did the same for friends and relatives. I suppose his influence is why I think that with enough time anything can be done, given the right motivation.

Unfortunately, I never knew either of my grandfathers, both being gone long before I was born. I often wish I could have just one conversation with them to ask them a few questions. Of all the time I've spent with people 40, 50 or more years older than I am, the one talk I can't have is the one I would surely get the most from.

I spent a lot of my time growing up with my grandmother. She lived right across 5th street from us and growing up it was a rare day that I did not go directly to her house after school, until one or both of my parents got home from work. She retired about the time my mom was offered a job in town and it was just a natural match for me to be with her.

I suppose it was spending so much time with a grandparent that gave me a healthy respect for my elders. When many kids would have been bored, I enjoyed listening to conversations between older people and did my best to remember odd bits of information that I heard. My great-grandmother came to live with her when I was about 11 and after that, it seemed like there was often someone dropping by for a visit, many of the people already in their 70's or 80's.

At the start of the coronavirus pandemic, I thought of how I heard them talking about the funeral processions and horse drawn hearses making several trips a day up the ridge road to the cemetery during the Spanish Flu. Their family spent her first six years not far from the intersection of Middle Ridge Road and 6th Street and saw it firsthand.

After her family moved from town, she grew up in the house I now live in. It is a modest house, but my wife and I both feel that if my great-grandparents could raise their two kids there, why can't we? Needless to say, there was no electricity or indoor plumbing all those years ago and the house was a bit smaller. They kept things cool in the spring house or in crocks in the cellar, which had a dirt floor. Fortunately, these things have all changed over the years.

My grandmother attended the East Newport school and shared many memories of things that happened during her school years. Like the time a young man, her classmate, pulled a captive mouse from his overall pocket and released it in the classroom, just to cause a ruckus. This only lasted until it got too close to Grammy, who was not phased in the least, and she systematically dispatched the rodent with a well-placed swat while many of the other girls squealed and jumped onto their desks.

One thing that has always stuck with me is her recollection of watching workmen dig out the cellar of the old Marshall mansion in East Newport. During the excavation, a few pieces of jewelry and a couple of handles were found, leading to the conclusion that at one point there was a burial ground on the lot, long before the mansion was built. Try as I may, I have never been able to find any official record or mention of this anywhere.

It came natural to me to be curious about my family's past and local history. When I began researching my family tree some 15 years ago, I would come across tidbits of information and would have an "aha" moment when I would recall something I heard discussed when I was just a kid. I enjoy learning about the olden days and try to picture things, like the way the town looked 70, 80, or 100 years ago.

I do not recall the 1972 flood, but definitely remember all the celebration of the American Bicentennial in 1976. One thing that sticks out to me is how the parade actually came down through East Newport, out Fourth and back in Third Street. We were able to watch it from the hill overlooking Wentzel's Mill. The only other parade I remember coming down that street was during the Newport Sesquicentennial celebration in 1990.

Towns change and evolve over time, but it seems during the last several years, there has been a large change to Newport. Even during my teen years, the square was busy, particularly around the pizza shop, on most nights. The restaurant on North Second Street seemed to always have someone coming and going and I've never found a cheese steak as good as theirs. I stoked the coal-fired boiler in the basement of that building for a few years. In the cold months, it was nothing to shovel 5 or 6 hundred pounds of rice coal into the hopper and then turn around and remove the ashes from the other end each and every day.

Many of the other businesses I remember growing up are gone: the Hy-Lo store, where I would sometimes stop to buy a roll of film or pick up a couple of simple supplies for school; Welfley's pharmacy, where my parents always got their prescriptions filled and bought all kinds of medical related things; and Reisinger Furniture. I remember stopping in there one time to ask Mr. Earl Lesh for a look at the mummified remains of some kind of animal he found under his porch. He had it placed into a glass fronted display box and would show it to anyone who asked. It was probably nothing more than some poor, unfortunate, stray cat or maybe a wayward raccoon or opossum but to me as a little kid, it might as well have been a dinosaur or some exotic creature.

My first job was at the Sears Catalog store where my mother worked. I was the young, strong back who helped customers load their large purchases into their vehicles, rearrange the washers, dryers, stoves, and other appliances on display in the front of the store and keep the warehouse tidy and organized.

Eventually, I was assigned to come in to receive the daily shipment from the company warehouse each morning. The truck arrived anytime between 5 and 6 a.m. I learned to do more than labor work and by the time I was a senior in high school, I had taken on the task of daily cash accounting and making bank deposits. At the time, I had thoughts of being a CPA and this was good, practical work experience.

One thing I'll always remember was getting a pick-up ticket from the front counter for a customer who was coming to the warehouse door to pick up a four-drawer filing cabinet. I loaded it up on a handcart, took it up the dock, opened the door and there stood the man, dressed in his tweed jacket and sweater vest, standing beside a Volkswagen Beetle! It goes without saying that he left without his filing cabinet and returned the next day with a pickup truck.

After some schooling on the accounting subject, I decided that working at a desk was not for me and found myself working at the Ford dealership in New Bloomfield. Like my grandfather and father before me, I was working in a garage that handled Ford products. Short of notary work, over the years, I did every job possible in the place. I worked in the office for a short while, held a sales license, an inspection license, reconditioned trade ins, serviced cars, worked as service advisor and at the parts counter. I can still remember much of the way to look up parts and do occasionally bring my memories to practice, especially when working on someone's older or classic car.

Still, my favorite thing is to use my hands and work out a mechanical problem. Just like dad, I try to find a way to fix anything. From a glass butter churn to the century old pump organ in Mahanoy Church and many things in between. Over the years, I have restored or repaired all kinds of different items. Of course, along the way, there have been all phases of auto repair or restoration. From simple jobs to seat covers, to a complete frame off restoration, there is very little I have not been willing to take on. Even in his 80's, dad still likes to see some of the jobs I work on and lend a hand if need be. I am always glad for his help and suggestions.

Storekeepers Daughter to Accomplished Vocalist

Storytellers Jane Hoffman Roush and Debra Ann Roush
Recorded by Debra Kay Noye

Starting life in Bloomfield eighty-six years ago, Jane Roush recalls little about the town, because she moved by the time, she turned three years of age. Her father, William Edgar Hoffman, was a clerk, in the local A & P Store, situated west of the town square. Her father would have walked to work, because they lived in the original Seibert House, on North Carlisle Street, not too far off the square. Today, the house, which is within sight of the former Carson Long Military Institute, is referred to as the Joyce Patterson property. It would have been a short, pleasant walk through the town square to the store.

Even back then, the grocery store chains promoted and rotated key employees and her father went to work at the Millerstown A & P, as the manager. Again, he could walk to the store, because the family moved to the very end house on the corner of School Street in Millerstown. The grocery store was located, where the original firehouse stood, which was beside the current day United States Post office.

Through the years, the A & P moved across the street, where the new firehouse now stands. As the store and business grew under her dad's management, he was offered a position in Altoona, which he declined.

It was at the Millerstown store, that Jane recalls her father telling the story of the molasses barrel mishap. Evidently Charles Miller, a store employee, did not keep an eye on the huge wooden molasses barrel as instrusted. It overflowed creating quite a sticky mess, which he was responsible for cleaning up. That sure created a spectacle, and a lot of ribbing on Charles' part.

Jane's recollections of WW ll and rationing, brought to mind, her father commenting about sugar being scarce, in the grocery store. Otherwise, she said they always had plenty to eat. In her home, they had electric, plumbing, a heating system, modern stove and a cook stove. Her mother would cook mush exclusively on the cook stove. Jane enjoyed eating it straight from the kettle with butter and molasses. Frying the mush to be eaten in the same manner, was something that Jane really enjoyed. There was a twinkle in her eye, as she spoke fondly of such a fine meal. Even though, her dad worked at the grocery store, they had milk delivered to their home.

During WW II, her parents volunteered with the local Civil Defense, and Jane would go with them to the tower, to watch for enemy planes. The wooden tower was built on the hill, beyond the road to the old cemetery. It would've enabled anybody to look out over the town.

***

Jane's mother grew up in Newport and graduated from Newport High School. She became a nurse, upon graduating from the Methodist Hospital Nurses Training, in Philadelphia. When she returned to Perry County, she was employed by the Perry County Red Cross. Jane recalls her mother telling about delivering food and necessities to county residents. She was sent to help wherever it was needed.

When they moved to Millerstown, her mother, Marie Magnuson Hoffman, performed "home health nursing", right in their home. People would come for advice about health issues and receive minor treatments.

Later, she became the school nurse for the Greenwood School District, where she served for twenty-five years.

***

Jane attended elementary school at Millerstown. She wore dresses or blouses and skirts to school, which were purchased from stores in Harrisburg. The students packed their lunches and ate them at their desks.

School was important to Jane. So much so, that when her father purchased a grocery and hardware store, in Ickesburg, in 1949, they did not move there, till the following year. By then, Jane was a sophomore, playing basketball, and a member of the Greenwood High School Band and chorus. She wished to finish her education at Greenwood, so her mother drove their old Dodge car from Ickesburg to Millerstown, every school day.

Jane received her high school diploma from Greenwood, but not without mishap. One wintry morning, as they approached Lehman's Hill on Route 17, the car hit an ice patch, in front of the little country Marsh Run Church. Blessings must have been sent their way, as nobody was hurt, and the car did not receive any damage. Riding with them was a lady, who worked at the Millerstown Moose and was transporting dishes. Not one dish was damaged or broken!

The Greenwood High School Band participated in the Harrisburg Christmas Parade, and Jane played her cornet. Everybody became very cold. However, the cold caused the valves of the various instruments to freeze. To remedy the situation, Jane applied more oil on her cornet.

Christmas at home, meant setting up her brother's train set. William Andrew Hoffman, who attended the Ickesburg School, loved making Christmas extra special with his train display. Jane recalls the Christmas tree having paper chains and bubble lights for some of the decorations.

She received a watch, clothing, and dolls, as Christmas gifts. One year, her dad decided to play a joke. He gave out boxes of coal, to the surprise of the recipients. However, underneath all that black, sooty coal, was money. Christmas was one time of the year, when her entire family could spend the day together, since the store was closed. They also spent Sundays together as a family because businesses were not open on Sundays.

Her church gave out oranges to the children, and Jane performed in the Ickesburg Lutheran Church cantatas.

While living in Millerstown, as a school student, Jane remembers seeing western movies at the movie theatre, which was located where the Juniata Valley National Bank is current day. In fact, it was a popular date spot, for Jane and her future husband. Bob Delancey ran the old reel-to-reel projector, at the popular theatre.

She recalls roller skating at Rheam's Roller Rink, outside of Millerstown.

Doctor Harold Gelnett made house calls. The dentist, Dr. Roy Gelnett, had his practice in the house by the VFW.

***

Ickesburg was quite the contrast from living in Millerstown. It was isolated, at the foot of the Tuscarora Mountain. A self-contained community, with two grocery stores. Patterson's Store was located directly on the town square. For entertainment, the Hi-Way Theatre, not only showed movies, but had a bowling alley and pool tables in the basement. Debra, Jane's daughter, remembers seeing Sound of Music, taking along her Liesel doll, which was a spin-off of one of the movie's characters. The theatre owners would hand out free passes to the town's businessmen, as a way of promoting the new movies coming to the screen.

Hoffman's Store was a short distance south of the square, on the left-hand side of the road. Her father sold Atlantic gasoline and kerosene, as well as groceries and hardware. Mohler's Gas Company, of Newport, delivered the bulk gas to the store. Back in the 1950s, the store owner pumped the gas and kerosene for the customer.

The groceries were separated from the hardware and paints. Jane recalls weighing out nails, with the assistance of Thelma Johnson, who was a store employee, as well as a neighbor, directly across the street. Ralph "Dip" Johnson also worked at the store, when needed. He and his wife, Anna, also lived across the street, with their daughter Vivian. Jane and Vivian became best friends, as they waited on their front porches, for their dates to arrive on Saturday nights. The store was a family affair for more than the Hoffman family.

They hand dipped four flavors of ice cream, into cones, for customers to enjoy. A metal cooler in the back of the store, filled with cold water, kept the bottled Coca Cola and Cream Soda cool, for a refreshing bubbly drink.

Mail Pouch chewing tobacco was kept behind the counter. But, the sacks of potatoes, fresh watermelons, and lopes, were placed on a green bench outside the front door of the store. Nobody ever stole any of the items, that were placed for sale. Jane's observation of the customer back then, was that people were trustworthy and respectful of other's property. The green bench resides, as a memento, in Jane's basement today!

Her dad kept a running tab for folks, who just needed that helping hand. But he was duped out of $100, when he loaned Pappy Cramer the money to buy a horse. Unfortunately, the horse died, and so did the chances of being repaid!

In other acts of kindness, her dad would offer a cold soda to Willy Snyder, as he made his rounds selling the local newspapers. Willy was physically challenged and pulled the newspapers around town in a red wagon. He was probably ready for that cold soda on a hot, dusty day. He'd sometimes hang out with the loafers, who sat around outside and chatted about the weather, who died and when the next church social was coming up.

Swift and Company delivered meats to the store, as did Kessler's Meats from Lemoyne, in Cumberland County. Her father would also travel to Millerstown, to purchase fresh meats from Butch Bortell's Butcher Shop. The store had a slicer, and her father ground fresh hamburger. Local farmers would bring fresh lard, from their butchering of hogs. Jane's father would buy the farmer's bulk lard, and when a customer desired any amount, it would be weighed out and put into a paper container, for them to take home. Farmers also brought scrapple, which was resold.

PA & Small Company, of York, supplied the bulk of the groceries, which they delivered to the store for resale. Jane recalls her father spraying the produce, such as lettuce, celery, and peppers, with water, before covering them for the night. Middlesworth Potato Chip Company stocked the store shelves, with bags of chips. Jane points out that back in those days, the company owners, of Middlesworth and Kessler's Meats, would stop by the stores, to personally meet the store owner. They developed a good working relationship, which benefited all businessmen.

Holsum Bread Company delivered freshly baked bread and bakery products. Jane recalls her dad always rotating the breads and rearranging them after a customer squeeze tested the stock on the shelves.

What store back then wouldn't be complete without the customary penny candy counter. As a youngster, Debra Roush, Jane's daughter, loved the nonpareils. Tootsie Rolls and Mary Janes were another penny candy favorite of many a youngster, peering into the glass candy counter.

Jane's mother sold the store after her father died, in 1970. To Jane's knowledge the store remained for only a few years afterwards, until it closed for good, and was converted into apartments.

***

Hoffman's Store, their home, and the old Band Hall were connected, side by side. Jane's bedroom was over the store. The Band Hall, was once a center for entertainment. Several musically talented locals gathered, to play marches, and other musical arrangements. The barber, Piney Wallet's wife, Melva, played the clarinet and piano. Kenny Orris, a music teacher, also played the cornet. There were others, who joined in from time to time. The band was an outlet for Jane's musical talents. She also sang in the Ickesburg Lutheran Church choir, along with Thelma Johnson.

After high school graduation, Jane went to Lebanon Valley College and studied music education, from 1953 to 1957. Upon graduating, Jane was hired as a Greenwood vocal music instructor, mirroring her mentor, Barner Swartz, the longtime Greenwood instrumental music instructor. It was a match made in music, and an honor for Jane to teach alongside Swartz.

Her first teaching stint, at Liverpool and Millerstown Elementaries, lasted a year, because she married her high school sweetheart, Darwin Dewayne Roush, in 1958, in the Ickesburg Lutheran Church. Darwin decided to join the Army, and they moved to Fort Knox, Kentucky. While in Kentucky, Jane was hired by the school, in the small town of Elizabethtown, to be a substitute music instructor. The school had never had a music teacher.

After two years in the armed services, they returned to Perry County. Darwin "Dar" resumed working for John Kerr, in the construction business. He had worked through his high school years, during the summer break, learning the construction trade from Kerr. Kerr's business was just across the bridge, west of Millerstown on Route 17.

In 1960, Dar and Kerr laid the brick for the house Jane has spent her life in, on School Street. Dar finished building their home. When John Kerr retired, Dar went to work for S & A Homes, in Mifflintown. It was on a workday, in 1981, that Dar was killed in a head-on collision, in the Lewistown area.

Their daughter, Debra Ann, was born in 1962.

Jane resumed her teaching career at Greenwood, even teaching vocal music education at Liverpool Elementary, before it closed. She directed the students as they performed an operetta, where they sang and had speaking parts. She also taught a year at Lack Tuscarora School, where she directed the students, in a minstrel show.

Jane became involved in the local Lions Club minstrel shows. In the shows, the participating performers would be black faced and a single performer would be an exaggerated white face. The program would be full of jokes, a lot of ad-libbing, singing special musical selections, instrumental numbers, and dancing. It was a lot of fun, and Jane even tried to tap dance. The shows were presented in the Greenwood High School auditorium, and the Hi-Way Theater, in Ickesburg.

Millerstown's Methodist Church benefited from Jane's musical abilities for fifty years, as she filled the role of choir director.

Jane's mentor, Barner Swartz, formed the Greenwood Community Band, in 1977. Band members were from all over Perry County and beyond. Jane and Debra participated, by playing their cornets. The band became very popular, and were invited to play at local carnivals, and in the Bandstand in the center of Liverpool. The band performed a lively fall concert each year, in the Greenwood High School auditorium. Jane was a member of the gifted group for more than forty years. She loved the chance to use her musical talents and enjoyed the comradery of fellow musicians.

It's too bad, the Ickesburg band hall was long gone, because Jeanne Fry, of Bloomfield, and Jane formed a friendship, that led to performing together. They met at Eastern Star and discovered they both enjoyed singing. That was fifty years ago! Jeanne sang soprano, while Jane sang alto. Josephine Hench, from Bloomfield, accompanied them on the piano. The ladies were known as the "3 J's". They were called upon to sing at weddings, church, and Eastern Star events.

***

Once Jane resettled in Millerstown, the business climate had changed. There were new businesses throughout the town proper. Bortell's Meat Market, where her father bought meats for the store, was located towards the river, beyond current day Bark of the Town, dog grooming. Doctor Johns was new and had his office on Greenwood Street, across from the Methodist Church. Sweger's Red and White Grocery Store took up the corner on the square, where JoJo's Pizza is current day.

L & M Pharmacy sat directly across the street from Sweger's Store, in the stone building, going east. They also had a popular soda fountain.

Ice cream seemed extremely popular in Millerstown, because Clair Coates and the Wileman sisters, both sold ice cream, sodas, and grocery items, across from the Presbyterian Church.

Bill's Gulf Station, owned by Billy Roush, pumped gas.

Homer Kepler kept the fellas looking well groomed, after they stopped in for a trim in his barber shop, off the square. Jane's mother got a new do from Darla Duncan. Nancy Sweger's Beauty Shop, at Old Ferry, was Jane's hairdresser.

***

Businesses have come and gone, in Millerstown. The landscape has definitely taken on a new look, and a new attitude has crept into town.

Jane is thankful for the friendliness of the townspeople, through the years, who were eager to help out in times of need, which still continues in Millerstown today.

Those were the days! Now, honestly, if you know Jane, she can sing a heck of a lot better, than Edith Bunker, on the tv sitcom, Those Were the Days.

My, How Things Have Changed!

Storyteller Gary Eby

Growing up in any small town is an evolutionary process. It is like starting out as a fry fish that evolves into a fingerling. When a small fish is caught it gets thrown back in, hopefully becomes more mature. Over time, that little fingerling becomes the prize fish, highly sought after by the experienced angler. And so, it is with a young boy.

With that in mind, follow the sequence of growing up in Bloomfield, not so long ago in the late 1950's and 1960's.

When I was first able to ride my bike from a small farm within view of the town, my main route was a narrow uneven endless concrete slab known as "34" (route). To me, it seemed to have more tar holding it together than concrete. The furthest I could initially travel was Ralph Tressler's Service Station. It was there often times my Dad was "hanging out". "Hanging out" is an art form that I learned at a young age. More later.

My real destination was the planing mill, caddy-cornered across South Carlisle St. It was a noisy beehive of activity. The yard was always full of rough lumber that was hauled down from Northern PA to be milled into lumber for construction. Today, lumber yards and box outlets receive lumber already pre-cut into standard lengths and thickness. The type of equipment this mill had, are few and far between where one buys lumber today. Back then, a small inventory of standard cuts was kept on a few piles in sheds, but the major needs of a contractor were ordered well ahead of time, and cut to order, kind of like an old-fashioned butcher shop, which is pretty rare today as well.

My wake-up call, six days a week, was hearing the dust collector starting up at 7AM. It would run continuously all day except for the one hour for lunch. The steady hum of the motor was easily heard a mile away, interrupted only by the hammer mill of the feed mill that was across the street.

In my youth, the lumber mill was a destination because they had a large wooden box of scrap lumber of all sizes and shapes. Depending on my current project, which could be anything from a cart to pull behind my bike to a tree house, these scraps always came in handy. If the pieces were too large or too many, Dad could haul them home on his pick-up.

As my parents' trust grew with making journeys safely back home, my horizons were expanded. Vehicle volume was much less then. Barnett Woods Road (back then it was known as the back way) across from my home was a dirt road then, and not a real good one. And what horizons they were! It gave me access to the town dump. Always interesting stuff there. Most late Saturday afternoons Bussy Thebes, the owner, would light it off to allow it to burn over the rest of the weekend. The dump was a former sand pit. To make more room it was allowed to burn. Once in a while, it would catch some tree roots on fire that consequently lead to a brush fire surrounding it, bringing the fire company out to extinguish, much to Bussy's dismay! I always looked forward to a dump run with my Dad and brothers in the '51 Chevy pick-up. There was no recycling back then. When things exceeded their normal useful life, it went to the dump. Glass, plastic, metal, and of course dead chickens. Just beyond was the school ground.

Every Sunday afternoon, the "school ground" was the place for friends to "hang out". "The gang" was made up of town kids like me. It had an unwritten hierarchy. Your skills in sports, or in my case, your size, determined your position. Being big and slow would put me as an outfielder. When summer changed to autumn, I would be a lineman for touch football. You had to be two hands above the waist to be declared down!

We never had enough kids to play "regulation" baseball, so we would adjust rules accordingly. The first thing you did was drop a catcher. The pitcher had to cover home on a play, and the at-bat team supplied a player for the routine returning balls. The next level was dropping an outfielder. The hitter had to designate left or right field and if a ball was hit to the opposite field, it was an automatic out. Another was a designated pitcher that pitched for both sides and was not allowed to hit.

The only strikes were a swing and a miss or foul balls, unless a batter was taking advantage of the rule, in which case a general consensus vote was taken that the batter had to attempt the next pitch, or you were out. We would never play a full nine innings. Someone always would have to leave at certain times, due to having to do chores. This would inevitably mean a total realignment of teams if we were to continue.

Beside myself, here is a list of the regulars that would gather, along with nicknames if they had one: My brother Dave (Boog) Eby, Lester (Bub) Wagner, Randy (Y. A.) Little, Dennis (Fink) Finkey, Dave (Big D) Delancey, Dave (Buck) Kingsborough, Stanley (Stan) Kingsborough, Fred Smith, Lynn (Fuzz) Fry, John (Robbie) Owen, Larry (Butch) Cupp, Steve Sutch, and others that age has erased from my memory. Sometimes some of the younger kids played as well such as Jim (Yogi) Swenson and Dave (Cazzie) Russell.

After our time on the diamond, some of us would adjourn to the bowling alley, Perry Lanes. The bowling alley was a recycled car dealership that the business aggressive Raffensperger family transitioned into a mecca for bowling, which was the latest sports crave, kind of like what golf has become in today's past time. In the former showroom was a pool table surrounded by snack vending machines built into the wall. One could get everything from a sandwich to ice cream from these machines that is, if you had change. Raffensperger family members maned the bowling alley. Marlin usually had the Sunday "watch" sitting at one of the small tables armed with a fly swatter, a pack of cigarettes and the Sunday paper. None of us had change since we had just gotten our allowances the day before. After getting up a couple of times to get change and to replace nickels and dimes that machines would eat, he would always announce last call which indicated that this was our last chance or leave and find another place to "hang out".

I well remember when Perry Lanes opened around 1960. This was one of many bowling lanes that were opening across the county. Brunswick, which supplied the equipment and designed the interior, had a nationwide drawing. Bloomfield's own Madeline Darlington was the grand-prize winner. Some of her prizes included a Thunderbird convertible, a mink stole and a swimming pool which she traded for cash. I guess I remember because, as memory serves, she never bowled a game in her life!

Summers were always special with opportunities to make money doing odd jobs beyond the chores assigned to me on our farm. Local farmers were always looking for help baling hay, since this was prior to kicker balers. It took a certain skill to stack bales on flat wagons that would withstand the hilly terrain to avoid having it upset. Experienced bale stackers were a premium. The pay was not great, but oh what food was shared at mealtime!

There was keen competition to get out by early spring to touch base with lawn mowing customers and to see how much Steve Sutch would undercut my price (Excuse the pun). All of us depended on extra money to buy a swimming pool pass and to save for our dream car when we graduated from our second-hand bicycles.

Speaking of the swimming pool, it was quite a popular "hang out" when it first opened in the early 1960's. The pool was built just above, what was then, the high school, and a little cinder block building that was big enough to sit in, which had a telephone. This was an outpost for Civil Defense volunteers to watch for overhead aircraft through a pair of binoculars. The silhouette of the aircraft would be called into, I don't know to who, with the description. My mother volunteered from time to time, and if the weather was nice, I was in tow. This was the time not long after WWII and the start of the Cold War which at times had the older generation on the edge of their seats. Little did I know that my toy dump truck and steam shovel was already excavating the area for the pool!

It was a wonderful addition to the community and afforded yet another past time for a pre-teen kid that had enough ambition to pedal the journey. Further, what a vast improvement for Lena Stoops to teach swimming lessons, which was better than when she started in Shermans Creek, then later the asphalt swimming pool at Tressler Orphans Home, better known to us as TOH.

There was no such thing as "adult swim." Everyone was all in from 1-9PM Monday through Saturday. The pool closed at 6PM on Sundays. Most of the adults would show up late in the day or evening to veer away from the obnoxious noise and splashing of us kids. A special treat was sitting on the edge of the diving well awaiting Bill Downs Sr. to launch off his back roll cannonball from the high dive. He would aim himself to just inches from the walk so that we could get the full effect of the mega splash. About once a month through the summer, there would be a splash party, which was lots of loud music with a record player, and once in a while there would be a start-up band with large aspirations of performing on American Bandstand show up. It was indeed quite a novelty to swim in a lighted pool! It was a great place to be on hot summer days, plus, you just never knew when those special girls, who all of a sudden got my interest, showed up, sometimes in a "two-piece"! Little did I know, the confidence I got swimming and diving would come in handy when I enlisted in the United States Coast Guard.

I never backtracked on the way home on my bike. Every once in a while, I would stop off at Hen Miller's shoe shop. Henry was a special friend of Dad's. He was always happy and often singing a tune as he sat at his workbench located at the end window. The light from the window helped him a lot, as it was a cluttered dark shop. The only time he didn't sing is when he had a mouth full of nails when putting on a heel or chewing on his cigar. Then he would revert to humming. He was also the Patriot News local distributor. There were always precarious stacks of unsold newspapers along the one wall. Henry was always looking for guys with a bike, like mine, to run a paper route. That's where you could find some of my gang Saturday mornings, out collecting for what was delivered from the past week or month. Didn't matter anyway, as Saturdays were always busy around the chicken houses. Always pens to clean or feed rooms to tidy, and worst of all, cleaning water fountains. Also, the final packing for Monday's egg route in town had to be finished.

The Monday evening egg route was a total of about 150 dozen. Ninety dozen went to Carson Long. The balance was delivered door to door to our "regulars" or "call ins". This would be my first lesson in customer relations and learning how to count change.

Selected nights were scheduled for "camping out" at the Carson Long soccer field. The logistics were perfect. It was secluded enough that when we were up all night discussing our own version of the facts of life and the possible virtues of the town girls, we would disturb no one. Camp out nights would not be complete without a visit to the bench on the square between the bank and the stop sign across the street from the "deli". It was here we would be sitting to pass judgment for all that drove up to the stop sign. There was never a shortage of "cool" cars pull up that would always oblige when we asked them to "lay a patch". Then there was the occasional out-of- towners asking for directions. Whether they knew or not, we were always eager to give directions, that after they thought about it, made no sense, but they always thanked us! We spent so much time at "the bench" that we were given the designation of "Brothers of the Bench". As a matter of fact, that's what we called our short-lived softball team!

Endless supplies of snacks could be procured across the street at Arden Shambaugh's delicatessen, or as we called it, "the deli". I will always remember Steve Hoffman working endless hours behind the counter. Unlike a lot of kids our age, every spare moment he was not studying or practicing his trumpet, Steve was earning money to eventually put himself through college. None of the rest of us had that ambition at the time. The deli was small with limited seating, which lead to the controversial sign that hung from the ceiling that warned patrons "No Loitering". The proprietor assumed folks in a small town did not know what loitering was, so there was an explanation in smaller letters that stated, "Loitering means NOT spending money".

Friday nights were reserved for going to the movies, regardless of what was playing. Saturday night at the movies was not for us, as that is when Carson Long took over the theater. Tradition held that during the school year it was the town kids vs. Carson Long. It was all about the attention of the few available girls of dating age. There is something about a guy in uniform.

You must understand that most of us that went to the Perry Theater were not going to see the movie. Rather, it was just the place to be. The "Brothers of the Bench" had no problem with coming up with the 75 cents to get in. That was just to get in the door. Of course, there was the popcorn machine in the vestibule. It had a noise of its own when you stuck in your dime for it to dispense the product into a bag you held under the spout. The candy vending machine was strategically located, pushed into a corner that found you standing over the return vent to the heating system, so that when you were fumbling for a nickel in the dark, coins that dropped out of your hand would go into the vent. Those coins were taken out of circulation until the theater owner would take the cover off to retrieve them for an additional windfall profit! The fact that the theater owner had a strict policy of not allowing bringing your own goodies, because of his little monopoly of stale products, only enticed us more to smuggle in a hoagie and Pepsi from Harper's Store across the alley. The regulars had their regular mohair seats. There was a row mid-theater, that had over the years, become unbolted from the floor and when you leaned back, it would allow you to put your feet on the row in front of you, which put us in a recline position.

When the movie would get a little slow, or our legs went to sleep, the empty Pepsi bottle rolling contest would start. The aforementioned empty soda bottle owners would go to the back row, lay the soda bottle on the side and let it go to see how far it would roll down the slanted floor before hitting the legs of seats. If our conduct would get out of hand too much, "Whitey", the proprietor who was also the projectionist, would come down from his perch upstairs. Of course, when asked to leave, we denied having done anything inappropriate. He would never go beyond the threat for fear of us not coming back which would, in the end, affect his bottom line!

Did I mention that growing up is a series of evolutionary changes of responsibility and maturity? I never really liked playing baseball, mowing lawns, or going to the movies. I don't even swim much more anymore. I guess I got my fill of it in the Coast Guard. None of those boyhood past times have bled over to modern days. The common thread that has passed on is "hanging out".

So, the next part of my growing up to hang out, and to this day still is, was the local fire company. At first it was not the 'burning' desire to jump on a fire truck. It was earlier than that by a couple of years. It was the carnival. When I became involved, it was far more primitive than now. By this time the carnival was held on the ball field, now the borough grounds south of the elementary school, now the borough building. The carnival covered a narrow strip which ran from where we were playing baseball behind the bowling alley, to the end of the lot. I have more than one time recently walked these grounds reminiscing about a simpler time during my "Wonder Years."

At the head of the midway were the rides. The Ferris wheel stood where our home plate was. For a long time, that was the only adult ride. There would be a couple of small rides for young kids, but that was it. Down the right side would start the lineup of "fakers" that traveled with Garbrick Amusements. There would be the hit the block with a sledgehammer to see how far you could raise the striker up the slide to ring the bell 15 feet up. If you did, you won a cigar. Next was the shooting gallery. That was a self-contained unit mounted on a trailer where you take the attached rifle and shoot targets for different prizes. Next was the wooden milk bottles. It would be two wooden milk bottles side by side with one balanced on top that were on top of a barrel. You got three balls to clear all the bottles off of the barrel to win. I can still smell the heavy canvas that served as the throwing area to keep the balls inside the pitching area. It was there that I got my first experience of being paid to help. The owner of the stand was always looking for a kid with endless energy to reset the milk bottles back on the keg and retrieve balls. If you were lucky, he gave you a dollar for a couple of hours work, and soon spent.

Next was the pizza guy. I am pretty sure it is the same guy that still sets up at the carnival. Back then, pizza was still a novelty. People don't believe me when I tell them that even into the early 1970's, the nearest pizza shop was in Carlisle across from Dickinson College!

Next were the ping pong balls to win a goldfish. Up until just a few years ago, the lady that ran this concession was still setting up at the carnival.

Next was the nickel pitch. Glasses were put in the center of a ring and you threw nickels to get one inside to win the glass. Paul Comp, who ran the stand, would always tell me when I graduated into this stand, to never put out more than two matched glasses on the stand at a time. That way, throwers would spend more as they would have several sets started!

Somewhere among those stands were the horse race wheel and watermelon wheels which were always popular.

Down at the lower end was the soda stand and the food stand. This was the way of spreading the crowd from one end to the other.

Going back the other side, was the bingo area with Earl Rempher calling. Great care was taken to shop with Harrisburg wholesalers through the winter months to purchase prizes. There was quite a display of prizes that one could redeem winning tickets that were issued to winners. If there were two winners of a game, you were issued a half win ticket. Prize categories were broken down by the amount of win tickets you had, redeemed before you left the grounds, so you wouldn't have to lug them around. Playing for money was not heard of then. There was an array of other stands usually sponsored by other organizations. The one I remember the most, that always had a nice crowd, was by the town ball team. They had a perimeter set up, and 20 feet away was a display of toilet seats where different volunteers would stick their heads through and you paid 25 cents for three tomatoes to throw to hit them. Oft' times local politicians or other well-known people would volunteer, which brought much enjoyment and line up of willing "pitchers". Next would be the penny pitch. It was here that I got my first "gig" helping the fire company. Maurice "Shuey" Shumaker was the referee to determine if a penny was in the square to redeem.

It seemed that everyone worked their way up to stands with more responsibility. By the time the carnival moved to the middle school, now the elementary school grounds, I was well on my way having graduated to the nickel pitch for glasses. Then, I got targeted as the go to guy if we were trying a new stand. It started with a dunking tank, and my fortitude of parading around the grounds in one of Ruth Dum's dresses to promote our new attraction. That was good for a couple years until Carnival Chairman, Paul Comp, wanted me to work with a new fad called the funnel cake. That was good for a couple of years until Jim Harbold recruited me in the inaugural poker stand. My latest gig is the cake wheel. I guess I'll die there!

Back to the "old carnival". The next spot on the carnival grounds was the entertainment area. The high school band had a night, then a wagon was brought in for the county western group the following night. The carnival was only 3 nights back then, still in conjunction with the 4th of July, so the last night was fireworks. For many years, Bloomfield was the only carnival that had fireworks, so it was quite an attraction. I always aspired to be on the fireworks committee, but by the time I "came of age", it was subcontracted out due to insurance liability.

Next might be a few more "fakers", then, at the head of the grounds, was Harold Greany's ice cream trailer.

The rest of the grounds was reserved for parking, which required experience to get as many cars parked as possible. My, how things have changed! A good carnival back than would profit about $5,000. Now days the goal is ten times that to make budget!

Growing up just beyond the south end of town at the time, I knew that if the siren blew a long, two shorts, and a long, the fire trucks would be responding to the East or the South of town. That would bring me out on the driveway to watch for them driving by. If in fact the signals indicated a 50-50 chance of them coming my way, it would be confirmed if I could hear the first piece of apparatus, the '49 Mack engine rounding the curve at Hair's Store, and down shifting to climb the hill. They would soon be coming! Upon shifting into high gear at the top of the hill, here they came, all the guys standing sideways on the rear bumper and holding onto the rail with one hand with the wind blowing up their pant legs. No turn out gear then. In the winter, they would have their fire coats on, but never a helmet.

The tanker was a converted hook and ladder. It would be along a bit later, as the tractor was parked out back, downstairs. It came up the alley, was backed into the truck bay upstairs, after the engine left, to hook onto the ladder portion. The underbody had the water tank that held 800 gallons of water. This was all well before the expansion of the fire house in the early 1970's. It was also well before a central dispatch. When you had an emergency, you called the operator, and she would reach over and blow the siren. The first person reaching the fire house, would call the operator, who would reveal the big secret of why she blew the siren and gave directions.

It was when I turned the magical age of 16 that I graduated from the "Wonder Years". The old Barnett barn built in the 1820's, on Barnett Woods Road, burned one hot summer night. It was then I decided I would join the ranks of the volunteers. Besides that, my new hang out, when I could, was going to work with my Dad at Wentzel's feed mill in Newport. That would afford me the opportunity to earn yet more money for the future. My first pay checks! My Dad's right-hand man was Harold Spotts, who encouraged me to join up and become active. I was inspired, because, after all, he was the President of the organization! Those were exciting times. The fire company became recent owners of a new tank truck, replacing the make-due tanker. Boy, wouldn't it be great to be a driver! That was the beginning of my new "hang out" of friends. Many have accompanied me on this 54-year journey with this group, yes, including Harold Spotts. I continue to hang out with these guys and now gals. I have gone to lots of parades and celebrations, some pretty interesting fires where I have been lucky enough not to have been hurt, seen some very tragic accidents that still haunt me, and have called an endless number of bingo games. And now my "brothers and sisters" that I have evolved with, are about to have a new $3 million "hang out". My, my, how things change!

This "hanging out" evolution has not been without challenges. Just ask my best "hang out" partner for the last nearly 50 years, my wife!

And so, this ends my sojourn growing up in Bloomfield. I haven't gotten very far in life. I'm still here hanging out!

Perry County Boy– Born and Raised!

Storyteller Jim Kain

I grew up in Wila, a childhood never to be duplicated. All homes were open to us kids as though it was our own. We road our bikes wherever and all day long – just be home for supper. We played wiffle ball, softball, football, and basketball.

In winter months, when Luke Toomey declared it was safe to ice skate on Toomey Dam, we spent many a nights skating by the bonfire of old tires. Our ice hockey team was unbeatable! We rode our sleds down Fosseman Hill.

Every Sunday in warmer weather after church and dinner, kids and fathers would gather at the softball field and play all afternoon. After Sunday ball playing, the Lyons family would open up their store to serve ice cream and soda pop. Most congregated on the store's porch benches or nail kegs.

Fosselman's barn floor was kept cleared so we could play basketball. We had to avoid the hole in the floor for hay release to the cows which added to the challenge.

The church's annual ice cream social was a big deal! Church members made and sold many flavors of ice cream. There were homemade soups and sandwiches available at the well-attended event.

Wila had some celebrities like Representative Luke Toomey and several good high school athletes who went on to play college ball.

Wila was one big family during those years, never to be duplicated in today's world. I smile when I try to remember all the good from growing up in Wila.

The View from the Back Porch

A BUZZARD IN THE HOUSE

Storyteller Larry L Little

No, this story title isn't misspelled. It's not about the buzzer in the house; it's about the Buzzard in the house. The Buzzard in this case was the name of the pet parakeet I had when I was about 12 years old. This was during the late 1950's. My father worked for the Pennsylvania Railroad doing track maintenance. Track maintenance work would be sharply curtailed during the winter months, and he was usually off work for several of the coldest. During this time, my mother would look for part time work to help feed the family. For several years, she worked at the local Kresge's Five and Dime Store. The first year that she worked there, she was assigned to manage the pet department. Mother enjoyed the job; she sold pet supplies as well as small pets such as turtles, fish, and parakeets. Because she did such a good job she was invited back to this job whenever father was off work.

Parakeets were popular pets during these years and the store received regular shipments to re-stock their cages. Buzzard was one of these birds. When a shipment arrived, any injured or sickly birds were discarded and only the healthy caged for sale. When Buzzard arrived, he was not active like the other birds and was determined to be sickly. Mother, being kind at heart, could not just discard these birds; she would bring them home and try to nurse them back to health. Buzzard was a great success story, within a few weeks, he was flitting around his cage, eating well and chirping to beat the band. As I recall, we had as many as five parakeets at a time, but Buzzard was a lone bird when we had him. Buzzard was obviously very young, a light blue color with white markings around his face.

Being twelve and curious, I was taken by the constant activity and began spending time by the cage. To this point, Buzzard had not been named; I came up with it one day after watching an old western and then going to talk to the bird. My twelve-year-old humor thought it was a great name for him, so it stuck. Buzzard liked the attention and began coming to the cage bars whenever I talked. I heard someplace about training a parakeet to talk and whistle by repeating a phrase or whistle. Within a few days, Buzzard began mimicking my phrases. There was "dirty old bird" or "hello" or wolf whistles or his name "Buzzard". Once he got started, he would mix and match as he saw fit, it might be something like "hello dirty old buzzard" with a whistle at the end. The more he chattered, the more time I spent with him, it was great fun.

After a short period of time, Buzzard would start looking for me and come to the bars to get attention from me. One day, I decided to take him out of the cage to play with him. I carefully opened his cage door and put my hand slowly in front of him. He quickly climbed onto my finger and I pulled him out. He took a long look around the room, looked at me and took flight. It was a wild, although constricted, gyro to all corners of the room and back again. He would land on a window curtain rod for a second and immediately launch himself. After a short while, I held out my hand and he flew immediately to land on it. It was the beginning of the next phase of our relationship. We would play every day and I taught him new whistles and phrases. I would be careful that all outside doors and windows were closed before taking him from the cage and he would sit on my shoulder as we went from room to room.

Invariably, in the evening, the family would be sitting in the living room watching the only TV in the house. Buzzard would be on my shoulder or nearby as the evening progressed. At some point, he would decide it was time to turn in, fly back to his cage, climb to his favorite perch; tuck his head and go to sleep.

The more Buzzard was out of the cage, the more interested he became in family activities. He loved to sample what his people were eating. His tastes ran from such things as bananas, oranges, even raw onions but he especially loved potato chips and pretzels. He also acquired a taste for Pepsi Cola. If somebody had a glass of soda, he would fly to them, land on the hand holding the soda and try to steal a sip. I made a discovery on the workings of the Parakeet mind this way one day. I had an empty soda glass but with a few drops on the bottom. Buzzard landed on my hand for a taste but couldn't reach to the bottom, so I laid the glass on the table. He alit next to it and crawled inside for his treat. After he had his fill, he wouldn't just back out of the glass the way he went in, he would have to turn around in the bottom of the glass to walk out. It was amazing to watch but the bird would turn his body 180 degrees every time. For a moment, his head and tail would point in the same direction, we all laughed at his antics.

At Christmas time, I would set up a platform and my Lionel trains. Buzzard sat on my shoulder as I ran my trains around the oval set, cocking his head to get a better look. One day, I decided that maybe Buzzard would like a train ride, so I stopped the train and sat him on top of the engine. I started moving the train slowly and watched his reaction. At first, he had trouble maintaining his footing but soon learned how to grasp a molded protrusion from the top of the engine. After several trips around the track, I slowly increased the speed. Buzzard loved it and thereafter would fly to his perch on the engine whenever I ran the train, it was his spot.

Today, I'm amazed at how smart Buzzard was and how unaware of the uniqueness of that intelligence I was. I found that I could direct Buzzard to fly to specific people. He would be perched on my shoulder where he always was. I would pick a person in the room, point at them, look at Buzzard and say, "Buzzard, go kill". Buzzard would look at where I was pointing, march down my arm and fly to the person selected. Of course, he wouldn't kill them, just walk up their arm to their face and give them a parakeet kiss. I would then signal return by motioning with my pointing finger and he would fly back to my shoulder and do his welcoming dance.

We had Buzzard for several years but as with all creatures, he grew old, his feathers thinned, and he couldn't fly as well or often. Still, he enjoyed our company and chattered all day long from his perch. One day, he was quiet and sat on his perch, not eating or moving, noticeably ill. This continued for several days and each day he grew weaker. We covered his cage with a towel at night to protect him from drafts and on his last day, when I uncovered him, he looked at me and spewed all his favorite words and chirps while bobbing his head, apparently glad to see me. I went to breakfast but when I came back, he was gone. I am convinced that he hung on that last night just so he could greet his family one more time. It was a very sad day in the household as we laid him to rest. Today, I've come to the realization that Buzzard's time with the family instilled in me a love and compassion for all life in this world.

No Prissy Miss! Growing up in Andersonburg

Storyteller Mary Jane Nesbit Kint

From near Andersonburg, between Loysville and Blain, comes tales from Mary Jane Nesbit Kint.

I'm the oldest of the Nesbit family, followed by Jim, Sara, and Goldie. Words from my mother had required me to set a good example which Goldie says I didn't do.

From my grandfather, Pappy Rice, I learned to chew Mail Pouch Tobacco, spitting fairly far and not becoming sick. Mother was always ready to wash my mouth out with Lava Soap. I got the same treatment from saying words Pappy used!

I failed at kitchen work, but sure could wash eggs, clean stables, and crack a wagon whip. Like lots of local families, we had a small dairy herd, raised cattle, pigs and two houses of laying hens. I learned the art of milking at an early age. To train calves to drink milk from a pail, I put my fingers first into their mouths, then I stuck their heads into the pail. I did this till they learned how to drink on their own.

We got up early, milked the cows, fed the animals, and ate breakfast before we went off to school. Jim and I shared garden work, especially planting, by being given sticks of different sizes, like two or three inches, to make sure the seeds were planted far enough apart. Peas were planted two inches apart in the rows. Green beans were planted three inches apart. Mom covered our rows checking our efforts.

One evening we deciding we'd had enough of planting, so we dug a huge hole under the grape arbor and buried all the seeds and onion sets. Well, later when things were not growing in said rows, mom discovered our planting secret. Trouble came when we got home from school. No smack! We were taken to the crime scene. New rows appeared and very carefully we redid all that planting, by separating sprouting seeds, from that secret hole.

Never could please that woman! Jim was busy telling her it was what Mary told him to do. Always ready to place the blame he was!

We had a large strawberry patch. We picked and sold many. We had lots of great strawberry desserts. There was also homemade strawberry jam made for on pancakes and homemade bread. We had peas to shell, beans to pick and tons of weeds to pull.

Mother canned and froze lots of veggies and fruits for the winter months. Trips were made to the mountains in search of wild huckleberries to pick. They had a distinct taste, less sweet and smaller than a blueberry. You had to keep an eye out for copperheads and rattle snakes among the limestone rocks on the Conococheague Mountain.

Several neighbor women and mom took trips around the farm fields looking for all sorts of berries to pick. They found wild raspberries, wild blackberries, and dew berries. They were canned. Many fruit pies and batches of homemade ice cream were made. Raspberry was my favorite!

We had black walnuts and hickory nuts. They were cleaned of their shells, cracked open, and the nuts were picked for sale and our use.

We butchered many chickens and ducks, which we froze. We sold many fryers. Ag teacher Bill Koons and mom had the thought of getting a tool to caponize roosters. I never understood how that was introduced into his class, but it took place on our farm. When ordering peeps, we received one hundred male chicks for every box of hens. Jim and I were soon able to operate!

Hog butchering was a big event that required help from relatives and neighbors over a period of several days. Scrapple, pudding and sausage was exchanged with them for helping. Mom always reminded us that deer meat was needed to be mixed into the ground pork sausage, stretching the yield. The sausage had a distinct flavor. We never let her down.

We'd have deer steak fried at midnight for a special treat. We had our fair share of squirrel potpie and fried rabbit too.

Mom would mix up the sugar cure for the hams, shoulders and bacon which would then go into the smokehouse for a hickory and apple cure. Great stuff!!

A fish truck visited on Fridays and mom purchased fish which was a treat from all the regular meals we ate. To this day, I enjoy fish over having a steak!

Summer found us swimming in Shermans Creek. The guys used larger stones to dam up the water hole to make a deeper spot. We rode bikes. I had my horse to ride, doing lots of trips into the woods, covering the areas Pappy had taken me to many times. The horse would tire of this and simply take me home.

We always had plenty of company for Sunday dinners. Jim and I cleaned and dressed four frying chickens on Saturday mornings for the Sunday feasting. One time, I expressed my feelings by letting the diners know that Jim and I did not appreciate having to do all that work just so they could empty the platters of fried chicken.

Several people even tried to make a lady out of me, by dressing me in a dress. That would never do!! However, my mom sewed many of my dresses and even some jeans. Many winter evenings quilts were put together. I never got into hand stitching quilts. Mom sewed graduation dresses for Sis (Janet) Harris and Genie Shields. Her mother gave me my first perm as payment for the dress. Sis spent lots of Sundays at my house.

There was always some prank being played!

Young Ken Morrow and Jim dropped rotten eggs down a hole in the barn floor onto the feed man delivering cattle feed.

Sara and Goldie greased the draw bar and steering on Dad's tractor. Oops!!

Goldie cut off one of Sara's pigtails. Mom cut off the other and Goldie's pretty curls. They were placed into a box with my pigtails. Later in life I gave my sisters their hair and we had a good laugh. They also had other stories to share.

Halloween found us walking to Andersonburg where the loafers guessed who we were. and we were treated to a candy bar. We visited Earl Fisher's Store and Guy O'Dell's Garage. Later, we walked into Couchtown. We always told great scary stories at Halloween.

Thanksgiving and deer season were the next events. Many relatives came to hunt. One season, someone killed our old Jersey cow which made mom quite angry.

At Christmas time, Jim and I went out to cut down a jack pine or cedar tree. We were not allowed a white pine because it was valued for its lumber. We would decorate it with strings of popcorn and cranberries, buttons, and acorns dipped in aluminum paint. To decorate a tabletop, we used bowls filled with pine cones and teaberries. I loved to eat the wild teaberries we harvested from the forests.

Candy, cookies, and fruitcakes were made and Pappy added home brew to the mincemeat. Pappy's home brew was kept in wooden barrels in the basement. He made dandelion, pear or cherry wine. Some were also distilled and very potent!

There were youth events at St. Paul Lutheran Church, between Cisna Run and Andersonburg. Luther League was an important part of our lives. The group gathered at Shermans Creek or neighboring ponds to ice skate. We had bon fires roasting hot dogs, toasting strange looking marshmallows and soda. To play ice hockey, we used tree limbs and old brooms as sticks. An empty soda can became a puck. One time my cousins brought a huge truck tire to burn. We went home with blackened faces and smelly clothes.

Christmas meant lots of family gatherings with homemade ice cream, lots of food, taffy pulls, popcorn and peanut brittle. We used hickory nuts if no peanuts were to be had. Two and three freezers of ice cream would be made in vanilla, chocolate, raspberry, or walnut. Mom played piano and dad danced with me. We played checkers, Uncle Wiggley, cards, and later Monopoly. That Jim cheated and there were lots of fights.

Back then, our hay wagon was much like the Amish wagons of today. We used a four-horse hitch with two sets of two. I sat on a saddle on the horse closest to the left of the wagon. Off-side horse was a beautiful sorrel which was blind at an early age. Two grays in front were driven by the rider, which was me, and voice commands from Pappy on the wagon. Hay was picked up by hay loaders behind the wagon. They would use hay forks to load the loose hay onto the wagon. I felt very much "big stuff", when I helped with hay making. We carried an empty King Syrup quart molasses bucket filled with drinking water. This usually came with cookies as a treat.

Family and neighbors helped make hay. One time when Louie and John Moose, who both chewed tobacco, were helping, Jim and I played a trick on them, which they probably never realized. Washing up before lunch, they would always put their wads of chew on the back wall of the house. Jim and I switched the wads around wondering if they would ever notice.

To feed the hay crew, a huge dinner was fixed by Gram Rice, Aunt Lucy Stahl, Lottie Shannon and Della Kessler. A royal farm feast of hand made and rolled pot pie with fixings was scoffed down by all the helpers. Because we had lots of chicken, chicken pot pie was often made. Aunt Haddie would come the day before and mix up the pot pie dough, rolling out enough noodles to cover a ten-foot table. I was given the playful chore of flipping the noodles over so they would dry evenly. It would make several huge kettles of belly filling goodness.

Supper that night was what was left over, once we milked, fed the animals, rubbed down the sweaty horses, and cleaned the sweat from the harness so they'd be ready for the next chore.

If we cleaned off in the creek, we still faced a bath since the cows used the creek for a bathroom – per mom. Then off to bed. After riding the workhorse all day, I'm lucky my short legs ever got back together again!

After hay making, it was wheat and oats harvesting using a threshing machine which traveled to each farm. First was the binder cutting the stalks of oats or wheat. Jim and I gathered the stalks together into shocks, tying them together so they would stand up straight to dry in the fields. Mom came along to boss. Seems she was everywhere! Threshing and harvesting crops was labor intensive because modern farm machinery did not exist.

We usually got hired by neighboring farms during threshing season, at the rate of seventy-five cents an hour. I was told by one farmer he'd pay me fifty cents because I was so little. I was so hurt. I told dad who promptly set him straight by saying I might be little, but I worked just as hard as the big boys. Sure made me feel good and I got my seventy-five cents.

Being the only girl to hit the swimming hole, mom said I couldn't go with the boys because they went swimming in the raw. However, I rode my horse to the damned-up creek and took their clothes, putting them on the nettle bed. Lee Harris could sure hit some high notes!!

Jim and I introduced the straw piles to the "city cousins" and taught them to feed ear corn by hand to the pigs. In the summer, cousins would come and stay, helping mom to pick cherries in the back pastures. One such day found Wilma and mom up a black cherry tree with Davie the bull underneath pawing and snorting. They were yelling and throwing branches at him to go away. Now, I was to have called them by eleven o'clock, but I was in the barn playing with my calf. I ran to Pappy and he said to give them some time that they would calm down. I was already in hot water! He got on his horse going to their rescue. I became quite good at using a cherry seeder that afternoon!

When Jim and I were born, we were each given a heifer calf which became part of the dairy herd. Each of their offspring either joined the milk cows or were sold. Money from the sold calves was put into our savings accounts at the Bank of Landisburg's Blain branch.

Our dad worked as a sawyer at a sawmill owned by Lawrence Hoovetter from Millerstown. Dad drove off on Sunday late afternoon to go to the job site at Huntingdon. He boarded with a family, returning home Friday evening. His work left us without a car for the week. Pappy rode his horse to Andersonburg most evenings to spend time at Fisher's Store. He bought anything mom or gram needed and some candy for we kids.

Mom washed on Mondays and baked four to six loaves of bread along with a pan of sticky buns. Tuesday was ironing day and the rest of the week was doing all the other chores. Friday evening when dad came home, we were treated to movies in Landisburg where Ken Rice, mom's cousin ran the Yankee Movie Theatre. Saturday, we visited Rice relatives. Sunday, we attended St. Paul Lutheran Church, coming home to a big dinner shared with relatives. Supper was either potato or tomato soup with browned smoked sausages from butchering, and lots of cakes and pies.

Summer ends with the Blain Picnic where all of our hard-earned money could be spent. We rode the ferris wheel and other rides. Played the games of chance like the ring toss and paddle wheel. There was a wide variety of foods, including homemade ice cream.

The final event for the summer was the Centre Church picnic, known for homemade ice cream and kettle soups. It was more of a home coming where people sat and chatted.

Jim and I had to still set an example for our sisters, Sara and Goldie. They came along much to our surprise, in the mid-fifties. We were excited over the arrival of Sara, but by the time Goldie came, not so much! Those two presented many lifestyle changes for us. However, they tell a much different story.

I always think back to dad being introduced to farm life when Pappy died. We now had tractors and new ways of doing things around the farm. We learned a lot of new lessons. I passed my driver's test on the first try. Then dad took me to the garage, handed me a tire iron and told me if I could drive, I needed to be able to change a tire. What a let down!!

Looking back, I gain understanding of many things that Pappy Rice taught me. He had me draw a row of cow butts on our blackboard. Then suggested I show the Ladies Aid Society my artwork, much to everybody's surprise. That was my first art lesson!! Later, Miss Buck, a local artist and teacher, introduced me to a different style of painting.

I relate these stories to my art class at the Blain Senior Center, which I started upon retiring in 2008. The ladies are close to my age with the same upbringing, so we have a lot of laughs together. My family has found it interesting that we have come so far and done so many different things. Life was good and still is today!

The Night the Barn Burned

Storyteller Linda Martin Gilmore

For all of his days, my father William Martin remembered the night the barn burned. The year was 1934; he was eleven years old. It had been a hot July night. He and his brother Paul and four sisters, along with his parents Edward and Nora Martin, had attended vesper services in the evening.

They were living on the family farm just east of Andersonburg, Pennsylvania, on the main road through the valley. The farm had already been in the family for more than fifty years. Here Edward and most of his nine brothers and sisters were born and had grown up. When Edward bought the farm about 1919, the barn was decades old. The farmhouse, on the other hand, was relatively new, built in the year 1900.

Edward set about making changes. When chickens began disappearing from the chicken house east of the barn, he built a new one much closer to the farmhouse. The pig pen, though, remained where it always had been, sitting in front of the barn. Perhaps his neighbors thought him progressive. Edward purchased his first tractor in the 1920s even while most local farmers still depended completely on horses and mules.

Every morning and every evening, the family milked their nine or ten cows by hand. By the time of the fire, William's older brother and sisters were helping in the barn and working in the fields. At eleven William also was well old enough to do his share of a day's work. He often remarked, "We walked behind a plow all morning, came in for lunch, and then went back out and walked behind the plow in the afternoon." This was their life in the 1930s.

Like many of their neighbors, they also possessed a strong faith. Every Sunday they walked the mile to St. Paul's Lutheran Church and worshipped with their friends and neighbors. They prayed with them for God's help in time of need and sickness, and they prayed for God's providence.

The night of the barn fire, their faith was sorely tested. Shortly after they got into bed, they heard the rumblings of a strong thunderstorm. Soon great bolts of lightning were flashing, and thunder was booming. Their windows would have been open, likely sheltered with screens. If anyone had been asleep, he or she was no longer. Suddenly a bolt struck very close to the house and actually dazed Nora.

Edward tried to rouse Nora, but in the dark of the night when he looked out of the bedroom window, he thought he saw flames from the barn. Had it been struck by lightning? He alerted Paul and together they ran out to the barn and for a short time tried to put the fire out themselves. When the last of the flames disappeared, they breathed a huge sigh of relief.

Nonetheless, the flames came back, and Edward knew they needed help. They had no phone, so Paul had to run the half mile up to Andersonburg and pound on someone's door. He made the call to the New Bloomfield Fire Company, the closest one, and the firemen were soon on their way in their brand-new fire pumper.

But it would be at least thirty minutes before they arrived as they were seventeen miles away. In the meantime, the next-door neighbor was the first to show up. Others drove up and down the valley to pound on doors and wake up families. Fathers and older sons crawled out of bed and came to the Martin's to fight the fire.

The flames were relentless, and the barn was soon fully engulfed. For a while Edward and Nora feared the house also would catch on fire. The wind was blowing embers toward the house. Having recovered from her daze, Nora sent all four girls to the end of the lane with the car and instructed them to stay there. She wanted them to be a safe distance from the fire. These many years later I realize that my father never said where he was on the night of the fire. Likely he was also with his sisters at the end of the lane.

When the fire pumper finally arrived, it was too late to save the barn. Fortunately, the firemen were able to save the wagon shed and other farm buildings. By dawn, the embers of the barn were dying and the many neighbors who had helped fight the fire all night were leaving to go home to their own chores.

Even Edward's cows, saved from the fire, were waiting to be milked. Edward and Paul had been able to get the cows and the machinery out of the barn before the fire took a complete hold on the barn. But they were not able to save the grain or hay stored on the barn floor. The firemen had confirmed that the barn had been struck by lightning.

They next day Edward and Nora and all of the children faced exhaustion. But they were not alone. Those first few days saw a stream of visitors who came to look at the pile of smoldering timber and offer sympathy and their help. The monetary loss of the barn was calculated to be about $6,000. They had some insurance but not enough to cover the cost of rebuilding the barn.

Still, they were farmers. What else could they do? They went to the bank and borrowed what they needed. Clean-up began immediately. Everyone pitched in. William guided the mule as it dragged burned timbers away from the mass of debris. Paul postponed his plans to join the Navy and stayed home to help rebuild the barn. Nora cooked a mass of food every day to feed the work crew and neighbors while they rebuilt the barn.

The barn rose. Its construction was not the same as the Pennsylvania barns with the recognizable overhanging barn floor that had dotted the valley for decades. This new barn was built with a straight front, better suited for housing milk cows. The roof was angled, providing more room in the hay mows. Workmen placed the granary right inside the barn floor within easy reach.

And every Sunday they walked the mile to St. Paul's Lutheran Church, thanking God that though they had lost the barn, the family was safe. Neighbors had given them gifts of hay and grain, and they were able to purchase what they needed.

They were resilient. By July of 1935, one year later, the new barn housed the nine or ten cows and grain and hay on the barn floor. But surely on the night of July 15, everyone lay awake, remembering the night the barn burned the year before.

An Entire Life Time in Perdix

Storyteller Franklin Delano Reidlinger
Recorded by Debra Kay Noye

When Franklin Reidinger's great-grand-parents, who were German brewers, migrated to America, they brought with them a sense of civic duty, and community pride. They settled elsewhere, before finally putting down roots on the Susquehanna River Island, in Dauphin County, across from present day Perdix. They had traveled by flatboat, up the Susquehanna River, landing on the Indian inhabited island.

Able to live peacefully, his great-grand-parents started farming the fertile island. Raising vegetables for a living, the family used their flatboat to transport the produce, across the river to Perdix. From there, the produce would be shipped to Harrisburg, on the Pennsylvania Railroad. His family would also travel by horse and buggy, on the dirt Kinsey Road, over the Cove Mountain, to Marysville to peddle their crops.

His grandfather was born on the island. Eventually, he bought untouched land, in and around where the present day Perdix Firehouse stands. After clearing the land, he built a log cabin, using the harvested timber. He continued gardening, and planted apple and cherry trees, starting an orchard. He accomplished all this, while working for the railroad.

Perdix, by that time, had become a "summer get-away" for well-to-do Harrisburg businessmen and their families. Both sides of the one-lane dirt road, were lined with small cottages, owned by the Harrisburg elite. They would ride the train, from Harrisburg to the Perdix passenger train station, because it was much easier than navigating the one lane road over or around the mountain. There were a few pull-offs along the route, but in most cases when two cars met, one of them had to back-down the road, to allow the other car safe passage. Instead of a stone or concrete retaining wall, on both sides of the road, a wall of large locust posts, was placed to keep the mountain stone from collapsing onto the road. It was not very effective.

Besides, the train from Market Street to the booming Bungalow town, took only twenty minutes. And the invigorating walk to your cottage was short. The area was likened to a wellness resort, "where good health sits on your doorstep"! Boating, bathing, fishing, hiking the outdoors and local entertainment, were readily available in the swank Perdix Heights.

The cottages were seasonal and closed up during the winter months, because the road was not plowed or maintained, during the snowy winters. However, A. C. Young, of Harrisburg, in selling the lots laid out in Perdix, stressed that the cottages were also a great investment. Franklin's father was the local representative for Young and showed prospective buyers lots, as well as cottages to rent. To purchase untouched front road footage on Hi-Point Road, at the foot of the mountain, investors paid seventy-five cents per foot, and that included having the land timbered, and the logs ready for building a log cabin.

***

Theories on how Perdix got its name
According to stories told to Franklin as he was growing up, Perdix's name originated with the railroad. In railroad terms, a mile of telegraph wire was known as a dix. The section of telegraph wire running to the passenger station equaled one mile. In this case, mile post 114 to mile post 113 was the distance. The conductor would yell out Pre-Dix coming into the passenger station. Over the years, it became pronounced Perdix.

Second theory also makes sense, because most settled areas, were named after businesses or their owners. In the 1900-1920s, a Bone Mill, owned by Harrisburg Fertilizer Company, existed across the railroad tracks on the river side of Perdix. It was straight down from the firehouse and closed in 1929.

Franklin, a mere five years old, can recall the wooden mill using the water from the nearby small stream, to operate the grindstones. They would grind animal carcasses into bone meal, to be used for fertilizer. The manager of the mill was named Perry Dix. Surely, the mill used the railroad to ship their products. When the train conductor would approach the freight and passenger stations, to identify the area, he would call out Perry Dix! People hearing the name called out, obviously abbreviated it to Perdix.

Anyhow, the name Perdix stuck!

***

His grandparents, Sara Bertha (Smith) and Horace Reidlinger, decided to open Reidlinger's General Store, across the road, from where they lived. (Horace's sister Nellie married Sara's brother Lem.) The store, which was a very rustic, wooden building on raised posts, burnt down. The attached dance hall also burnt, when someone lit an oil lamp in preparation for the anticipated dance hall activities, for the evening. The lamp exploded, causing flames to spread rapidly. The gas pump in front of the store, also ignited. Luckily, no one was harmed, but the businesses were a total loss, amounting to two thousand dollars.

It was rebuilt with a concrete foundation, on the opposite side of the one-lane, dirt road. The new store and dance hall was again wooden.

When the new two lane, paved Route 11 & 15 was being excavated and built in 1938, they closed their general store for a bit. The cottages were also closed and there wasn't local traffic, on the torn-up roadway. Reidlingers wouldn't have been able to restock their store shelves. It was a bleak time.

The family lived above the store, as was the custom, back in the day. Franklin recalls looking out the living room window, above the store, and watching the dusty construction. After the completion of the miracle highway, the store was then relocated, and moved back twenty feet, before reopening in 1939-1940 with gas pumps, beside the present-day fire house.

At that time, his father was an accountant, so his mother tended the store and pumped gas. Customers would bring two-gallon containers to be filled with kerosene, for their home's kerosene heaters. Most homes did not have furnaces, especially the cottages.

Franklin recalls as a child, his home always had electric and indoor plumbing. Sadler's Coal of Marysville, delivered coal, by truck, for the coal furnace, which heated the house and store. Most of the coal, was transported, by train from coal mines, in northeastern Pennsylvania. Coal was also dredged in the Susquehanna River, at Marysville. It is hard to determine, where Sadler's coal supply may have come from, since there was a train station in Marysville.

Benfer's Meat Market, of Marysville, supplied fresh and smoked meats to the store. Meats were delivered, held on ice, because refrigeration was not yet available. Ice was delivered to the store daily, by Lee Baker. He would put the ice blocks into the store's ice box.

Groceries for the store were ordered from Harrisburg distributors and transported to the Perdix railroad freight station, which was a hop, skip and jump, from the passenger station. A panel truck, selling Jewel Tea home goods, came around to the store on a regular basis. Coffee and tea were a few of the items available, as well as everyday household products.

Being enterprising, the Reidlingers placed tables and chairs in front of the store, for patrons to relax, chat and enjoy a Hershey's Ice Cream cone or a cold home-brewed birch beer, root beer or orange soda. Franklin's mother used a cross-cut saw, cutting pieces of wood for the fire, under the copper kettles, she used to brew the soda mixtures.

He remembers her using yeast to activate fermentation, in her special brews. It would give the sodas a natural zing! She probably cooked sassafras bark and/or root, and other herbs, along with a small amount of sugar, then adding the yeast, when brewing root beer.

Birch beer was made, by tapping birch trees for their distinct tasting sap, and/or boiling down birch tree twigs, which released the sap. Again, sugar and yeast, were added to cause fermentation.

His mother most likely used orange peels for their orange oil, and citric acid, plus sugar and yeast, in creating orange soda. She may have used some fresh orange juice, but the oil extracted from the peels made the best tasting orange soda. The finished sodas were bottled, in glass quart bottles. A cork-lined metal bottle top was applied, sealing the fermenting beverage. Three times throughout the summer, his mother would get out the copper kettles, and brew another fifty to sixty cases of the popular home-brewed beverages. Franklin and his older brother, Charles, were the taste testers, enjoying the freshly made brews over ice. If they could produce a good belch, then his mother knew she was successful.

When the weather turned cold, the tables and chairs were brought into the store, where loafers and slot machine players, could relax out of the cold. Franklin wasn't school age, as he recalls, a customer remarking about 'the onion snow'. He asked his mother, "where the onions were", because he wasn't seeing any onions with the snow. She explained about the old saying, that it was a dusting of snow, in the early spring, after the onions had been planted and were starting to shoot through the ground. Thus, the name 'onion snow' became popular.

Even though, they had access to all the products in the store, his mother maintained a huge garden. She canned most everything, she raised. Franklin recalls his mother was also a great cook, and he especially loved her seasonal dandelion greens with a bacon and hard-boiled egg dressing.

***

Franklin's dad, Calvin Earl, was born in the Perdix log homestead, as was Franklin. His dad traveled by train to attend Harrisburg schools, at the urging of Harrisburg School Superintendent Graef, whose family members had a summer cottage in Perdix. There were six to eight other children from Perdix, who rode the train to and from Harrisburg each day, to attend school. Calvin graduated from Harrisburg Tech High School.

His dad was an accomplished musician. He played the piano, violin, clarinet and saxophone. He passed on his love for music and musical talent to Franklin, teaching him to play the clarinet and saxophone. Franklin, in his high school years, also received private lessons.

In fact, it was Calvin's violin that tugged at the heart strings of Franklin's mother. Anna Emma Ebersole (no relation to the Perry County Ebersoles), worked for the owners of the Herman Cigar Factory in Harrisburg, where they manufactured King Edward Cigars. The Herman family had a summer cottage in Aqueduct, northeast of Duncannon, along the Juniata River, across from Amity Hall. They entertained friends and employees with lavish picnics, during the summer months. Franklin's mother was the Herman family nanny. She cared for and tended to the needs of the children.

Anna, who attended Marysville Schools, was riding the train to Aqueduct, on a Sunday morning, when she decided to stop over in Perdix and attend church at the Perdix Chapel. Calvin was playing the violin, in church that Sunday. The rest is history.

Calvin and Anna had three chidren, Dotty, Charles and Franklin. Dotty had Downs Syndrome and did not go to school. She was very helpful around the house. Charles was always repairing or painting something, keeping the store clean, and doing odd jobs for people.

The customers called Franklin's parents by their first names. And because they were helping out in the store, most every day, it became natural for the children to call dad, Calvin, and mom, Anna. His parents took it in stride.

***

The school bus that transported Franklin in 1942, to first grade at Penn Township School, outside of Duncannon remains an icon at Rohrer Bus. The Perry County bus company on Route 11 & 15, a short distance from Perdix, has been transporting students and tourists, plus selling and repairing buses for over one hundred years.

Believe it or not, students in the Allen Cove area, outside of Duncannon, (The area where Kinkora Pythian Home is today) were first transported to school by Rohrer's horses and wagon in 1920. Howard Rohrer, Sr., then got the bright idea of building a wooden school bus frame, onto a metal car chassis --- another example of Perry County ingenuity. The transportation company, that buses students from central Pennsylvania to school, has thrived, for over one hundred years, at the edge of Perdix.

There just weren't many kids in Perdix, because it was a seasonal community. That being said, Franklin really enjoyed going to school.

A rite of passage for most youngsters, was getting that first haircut and especially getting spruced up before the first day of school. Franklin had long blonde hair, and his dad decided that he didn't want Franklin to look like a girl. They didn't motor down the road, in the first car his dad owned, a faded blue Plymouth, which Franklin called "my burple car". Instead, he put Franklin on the special wooden box he had made, so Franklin could see out of the Ford Pick-up. Off they went to Ben Fisher's Barber Shop, on the square of Marysville, to cut off his golden locks. A Ford Coup replaced the Plymouth.

***

World War ll and Rationing
Times were challenging, for everybody, in the 1940s. But Franklin's family took everything in stride and did their part to support the family. By then, his father's federal accounting job required him to spend the week, at Langley Field in Virginia. He carpooled, with other men from central Pennsylvania, leaving on Sunday night. When he returned on Friday evening, regardless of the hour, he would wake the kids and ask about their week. Franklin's mother continued to manage the store, and care for the children.

Running a store and feeding the family, with government rationing in place, took ingenuity. Adults and children were issued books of government stamps, which allowed purchases for specific items. Otherwise, no stamp meant no purchase of specific commodities, like coffee, certain cuts of meat, butter, sugar, and even new tires for your vehicle.

Franklin remembers his brother hating the 'fake butter', that appeared on the market. In reality, it was a block of lard, with what Franklin described as a yellow-orange pill, embedded. The pill was broken and worked into the lard, to make it appear yellow. However, there is no mistaking real butter!

Breakfast often meant, a fine meal of toasted bread and hot cocoa. Franklin recalls the oval tins of Hershey Cocoa. His mother would use cocoa, a small amount of sugar, if she had any, and milk, to make a hot breakfast drink. There was also coffee soup and milk soup, ladled over toasted bread. Orange juice was not available to the consumer, during the war effort.

According to Franklin, the rationing stamps were the same for adults and children, with one exception. The stamps, for coffee were already punched, and not usable. This made his parents unhappy.

Packaged cigarettes were not available, and smokers had to roll their own using loose Bull Durham tobacco. Most could not get the hang of using paper and rolling their own smokes, so they switched to puffing on a pipe.

Schools received government commodities. Franklin remembers being given a few dry prunes each day, at lunch time. The school received boxes full of prunes, to distribute. Apples were also handed out, on a regular basis.

"You took care of your shoes!" Franklin remarked. One of those stamps was needed to get new shoes, even if you had money to pay for a new pair. This lasted from first through fourth grades. So, when Franklin was out playing in the snow and his shoes got wet, he made sure to clean them off and dry them.

The family patronized Lee Snavely's Clothing Store, on Market Street, in Duncannon. That is where Franklin would go to get new shoes. He had a pair of lace-up boots, that he wore to elementary school. The boots had a small pocket on the side, which snapped. The pocket was perfect, for securing a small pocket-knife. Franklin and his classmates would keep their pocket-knives, in their boots everywhere they went. At recess, the boys would go to the janitor's office, in the school basement, instead of outside to play. Robert Fox taught the boys how to properly sharpen their knives, and really looked after all of the kids.

Interesting enough, in deer season, when Franklin walked from Perdix to attend high school in Marysville, he carried an army knapsack full of books, and a deer rifle. He and his fellow classmates hunted the mountainside to and from school. Bob and Jerry Johnson, his neighbors, did the same. Their classmates, who lived in Rye Valley, west of Marysville, also hunted on their hike to school. Upon arriving at school grounds, they would unload the rifle's ammunition chamber, and secure the rifles in the clothes closet.

Franklin actually shot a doe, in doe season, on his trek home from school. When he got home with the deer, it was taken to a butcher shop out behind Duncannon. The deer was processed. Franklin's family rented a freezer locker, in Sam Michener's Ice House, on Market Street, in Duncannon, to store the venison. When they needed more venison to eat, Franklin's parents would travel to Duncannon and bring some back, to supplement their diet.

The Susquehanna River supplied many a home with a meal, during the lean post war years. Many men were unemployed, as there weren't jobs available. During that time, the game wardens did not fine men for not having a fishing license, because they knew it meant food for the families. Poaching deer was another story!

Franklin would fish for bass and perch, which his mother would cook for their Friday fish fries. If he caught a carp, it would be thrown back into the river. Oddly enough, Franklin wasn't fond of fish, but enjoys a plateful today!

During the lean years, he recalls shopping at Mader's Supermarket, in Marysville, where Dave's Pit BBQ is today. Zimmerman's Apple Orchard was a source for fresh fruit. Since local farmers, who butchered, were not regulated, they freely sold their meats and meat products. Hucksters like, "Pippy" Hench, traveled throughout the area, peddling vegetables, fruits, and meats, like smoked slab bacon, which did not need refrigerated.

***

Hand-me-downs, from his older brother, kept Franklin in clothing. In those days, snow suits and galoshes were unheard of, when you went out to play in the snow. Franklin remembers his feet getting so cold.

He loved sledding with his Lightning Guilder Sled, made in Duncannon, at the Standard Novelty Works, by local workers. Jack Rudy had a Flexible Flyer sled.

From Friday night through Saturday, the kids would be outside sledding, almost non-stop. Sometimes, they trekked up the mountain and used the retaining wall at Benny Kauffman's summer cottage, as a ramp. Other times, they started at the top of the hill, by the firehouse. The end results were the same. They were able to sled down the steep hill, right over the railroad crossing, and continue on down to the river. That was a heart pumping ride! It's no wonder, Franklin ignored his freezing feet!

When it snowed, Franklin recalled getting up in the morning, and seeing two tracks in the snow, on Route 11&15. The milkman was more reliable than the postal service. He would see the Duncan & Herr Dairy trucks, from Duncannon, delivering milk to customers. West Shore Dairy, in Enola, also delivered dairy products into Perry County. Back in the early days, milk was more widely consumed and used in cooking, facilitating daily deliveries of dairy products.

***

Treated like prisoners in their own home, Franklin's neighbors, across the street, were inspected weekly by the Federal Bureau of Investigation, during the war years. Richard and Elizabeth Frank were Jews, who migrated from Germany, settling in Perdix. Upon their arrival, they were basically quarantined, in the confines of their home. They were not supposed to own a radio, which in those days was the best source for news, and/or to communicate with the outside world. Newspapers and magazines were also forbidden.

Franklin's father had a key to the cottage, the Franks lived in, so the FBI would come to him, in the dark of the night, to gain access to the property. They also asked his dad about the Franks' activities, as they searched for banned items. It is unclear, if the Franks were suspected of being spies, or Nazis, who escaped Germany to avoid prosecution.

When the FBI left the area for the night, Franklin's dad kept and stored the radio for them. He was sympathetic to their plight and helped them when he could. The Franks eventually bought a farm, in Wheatfield Township, north of Duncannon. On the farm, they raised Schnauzers, a breed of dog, similar to Scottish Terriers. They also raised chickens. The chickens were loaded onto a pick-up truck, transported, and sold to the Kresge 5 & 10 store, in Harrisburg.

During the war years, most of the summer cottages were sold. The owners had become older; the business climate had changed, and there was a need for cheap housing. New owners upgraded the cottages, with heating, electric and plumbing, and began living there year-round. It was the beginning of Perdix's rebirth. There were a lot more kids to play with, at the Perdix Community Park, where the firehouse sits today.

1926, sitting in the living room of Franklin's home, above the store, his grandfather, Horace, and his dad, decided it was time to organize a fire company, for the safety and wellbeing of the Perdix community. This was right after the Reidlinger's Store and Dance Hall had burnt to the ground.

If a fire occurred, they had to rely on fire companies from Duncannon or Marysville, to put out the fires. Sometimes, they couldn't come to the rescue. Reidlingers, who were always very civic minded, decided to take the matter into their own hands, and do something to resolve the issue of fire safety.

Franklin's great-grandmother, Serena, donated the land for the firehouse and community park. She wanted the firehouse to also host community activities and be used by the public. The firehouse was first built at the top of the hill, from the current location, with the park directly behind.

The firehouse became a community center for activities, a helping hand for those in need, and a nurturing center for the children. At Halloween, the fire company would host a party, for the community, especially the children. Kids would dress up to win prizes, for the funniest, weirdest, etc.

Dressed in costumes, the children would freely walk the roadway, from home to home, in Perdix, trick or treating. There was little traffic to contend with, back in the early days. Did the kids play pranks? According to Franklin, there was the occasional tipping over of a local outhouse!

Even as late as the 1980s, the fire company would drive a fire truck to each end of Perdix. Proceeding up the road, to the opposite end of Perdix, with lights shining, they lit the way for safe trick or treating. The trucks also traveled at a slow speed, which slowed down the speeding vehicles, that ignored the thirty-five mile per hour speed zone.

The fire company sponsored bazaars, ice cream socials, bingo, and dinners. As the town center, the fire house hosted meetings, banquets, and special family events.

Christmas meant going to the party, sponsored by the fire company. There were gifts for each child, boxes of candy, plus fresh apples and oranges. If a child could not attend the party, the fire company would send Santa out to deliver their gifts and treats. Franklin remembers playing Mr. Claus, when the Santa suit had to be stuffed with so many pillows, to make him appear as the real deal. In the 1950s – 1960s, it was not unusual for one hundred and twenty-five children to participate in the annual event.

To Franklin, Christmas was the time of year, "that got your heart pumping", with all the special Christmas music, played at church and the school pageant. There was always a big Christmas dinner. His mother cooked a turkey, with all the trimmings, for a memorable holiday feast. She would also make dozens of sand tart cookies topped with a piece of walnut. They were a favorite, that Franklin and his friend Nick DiPaolo have made over the years.

Franklin really liked the roast beef dinners every Sunday. His mother used a cast iron Dutch oven, to braise and then cook the tender beef. According to Franklin, that was when well marbled beef tasted like beef!

***

Real Mountain Men lived up on the mountain side, opposite Perdix. It was there, on the flat areas, they had charcoal pits. Since the mountain was covered in trees, they had an unlimited source of wood, to burn and smolder, producing chunks of premium charcoal. Several times a year, the bachelors would load up wooden sleds, with the charcoal, and physically pull them down the mountain side. The charcoal was then put onto two buckboard wagons, and pulled by mules, to their destination. Franklin wasn't sure who purchased the charcoal. It must have been shipped on the railroad.

According to Franklin, a mountain man would wrestle a bear on Sundays at Archie and Jim Johnson's Dance Hall, which operated down over the hill, to the north of Perdix. To attract business, Johnsons had a menagerie of animals and birds.

***

Reidlinger's Dance Hall was an addition built onto the side of the store. It was there that Franklin's dad, the accomplished musician, and his musically talented friends, would perform nightly, for round and square dancing.

Franklin's father also played clarinet and saxophone, with big bands that came into Harrisburg and Hershey. When Guy Lombardo and the Canadians were scheduled for Hershey, they would reach out to Franklin's dad, to come join them, as they performed to packed audiences. There were no practice sessions before the band's performance, at Hershey's Starlight Ballroom. All the add-on musicians, were talented enough to read the music, knew the songs, and played right along.

It was an exciting time! Franklin's dad and the other musicians, from central Pennsylvania, would converge on Perdix and carpool together. When they returned to Perdix for the night, his dad, rented out some of the cottages to them. He, being an enterprising businessman, would split the proceeds with the cottage owners.

One musician that stood out in Franklin's mind, was Salvatore Colangelo. He joined his father, playing for the big-name bands. Franklin remembers Salvatore taught music at the J. H. Troupe Music Store, on the square in Harrisburg. Franklin took private music lessons on the clarinet and saxophone, from Colangelo.

His dad played with other bands locally, in Marysville and Enola.

So, it is no wonder that Franklin followed in his dad's footsteps, after playing the clarinet and saxophone, for Marysville and Susquenita High Schools. Franklin performed, with the Harrisburg Symphony Orchestra, for two years. Being civic minded and loving music, he also played with the Harrisburg Moose, and Harrisburg VFW bands.

But what he enjoyed best, was sitting in the kitchen and listening to Kate Smith belt out tunes, on the radio. Red Skeleton was another radio show favorite.

***

Franklin would rather play baseball, than eat ice cream, as a kid. He started to play little league baseball, with Duncannon, in 1947. The team did not have enough uniforms for all the players. Franklin was small, and the uniforms didn't fit him anyway. He wore a pair of gray nickers, to compliment the team shirts. However, team shirts were shared among the players, who swapped them out, each time a field position was changed.

To play ball, after attending his Penn Township school all day and riding the school bus home, Franklin had to pay ten cents to ride the West Shore based, Valley Transportation bus back into Duncannon. He often missed supper and a young Perdix lad was hit on the roadway while riding his bike, which caused his mother to put her foot down. No more little league baseball in Duncannon.

He also practiced with the Marysville Little League for a few weeks. He and Jack Rudy and Paul Dymond rode their bikes two miles over the hill to and from Marysville. This became more work than fun. So all three gave it up as a bad idea. While in high school, he played 'teener ball', with Marysville, where the Marysville Lions Club is located today. Franklin was older now and had grown, so he played better and enjoyed the game more.

When Franklin was active with the Marysville Methodist Church, his dad and Paul Ellenberger, were the Sunday School teachers. They were pro-active in traveling to Philadelphia, with the sixteen to twenty boys in the group, to see ball games in the old Connie Mac Stadium, plus football games.

Ellenberger decided to travel to Williamsport, with five of the boys, in 1947, to see the National Little League game, when Nevin Magee, Walter Mutzabaugh, Donny Dieter, Corky Kulp, and Tommy Bornman of Duncannon; Earl Shope, Leslie Lutz, Gene Hammaker, and Donald "Russian" Snyder of Marysville; and George Plantz, Earl Stotlzsus, Dick Herzog, Bill Seitz, and Charley Sheaffer, Enola ball players, made up the West Shore Little League. It was an exciting time, for Perry County Little League players. Unfortunately, by the time Ellenberger arrived, after the long journey, the ball game was over.

The over-the-hill ball players still meet regularly at the Marysville Diner, to talk over old times, replaying ball games from their youth.

When kids want to play ball, despite the logistics, you form your own teams and make-believe league. Jack Rudy and Paul Dymond recruited ball players, like Franklin, Bob King, and Randy Supko, and Donny Boyer from the Cove to form a team. This is just to name a few, from Perdix and the Cove, that formed a team.

Bob Asper started a Duncannon team, with Ronny Barrick, Walter Wright, Kresge, and many others. They played every two weeks, rotating between the two towns. Perdix hosted the Duncannon team on the makeshift ball field, in the woods, near the firehouse... which dates back to the early days of Perdix where they played softball. They played without arguing or fist fights. When several of the local men weren't working on the railroad, or at the Navy Depot, or fighting fires, they would umpire the games. They used Valley Transportation to get to and fro. They had fun! That's all that mattered!

***

Like father, like son! Franklin's dad not only remained active with the fire company, he was a Justice of the Peace in Perdix for eighteen years. His involvement in the community ignited a keen interest in politics and civic duty, in Franklin.

Franklin was a Boy Scout and in later years, he was a scoutmaster for Marysville Troop 56. He was a Justice of the Peace in Perdix for eighteen months; president of the Perdix Fire Company, and the Perry County Fireman's Association; chairman of the Republican Committee of Perry County; appointed tax collector for Penn Township; and director of Civil Defense for Penn Township. Franklin was the first to serve two terms, as President of the Marysville Lions Club, (1986 -1987 and 1988 -1989).

When he married, he was a clerk for the Commonwealth of Pennsylvania. In 1956, he became a telegraph and teletype operator for the Pennsylvania Railroad. He moved onto the 'switching tower', and then to the 'movement office'. He ended his career with the railroad, serving as wire chief, of the Harrisburg Wire and Communications Division.

Franklin married Linda Cook of Duncannon. They made their home in Perdix with daughters Charlene and Carla. Both daughters graduated from Susquenita High School. Charlene enlisted in the United State Air Force, serving in the military police. Her unit was deployed to take part in the mother's and children's lifts from Vietnam. Two years after, she was discharged, she was diagnosed with cancer and died after a long hard battle, in 2012. Carla lives in central Pennsylvania.

Franklin and Linda remained in Perdix, celebrating fifty-two years of marriage, until Linda passed away suddenly in 2007.

***

In 1958, during the cold war, the local Civil Defense team, continued with bomb shelter drills. Wearing their yellow, red, and blue CD armbands and hard hats, they conducted air raid drills at the local schools, as in the war years. The local fire chief or police chief would assist. Students were escorted to the school lavatories, in the basements, told to hunker down and place their hands over their heads. Of course, it varied from school to school, as to where the students went.

One drill during WW ll, they did not perform anymore, was to call for a 'black-out' in the community. Perdix residents would be notified through the Marysville Telephone Exchange, when the 'black-out' was to occur. Also, the firemen would get out the fire truck and blow the siren, through Perdix, to announce when it was time to close their window curtains. The 'black-out' lasted for one and a half hours. It was a tactic used to prevent enemy aircraft from detecting a city or populated community, with which to bomb.

Franklin and the volunteers worked with radar detection equipment. He took college courses and graduated, having learned more on emergency management for communities.

His training and college courses came in handy, during Three Mile Island, when the entire area was constantly tested for radiation, after the leak at the nuclear power plant.

He experienced the devastation of the 1962 ice jam, which started at Duncannon, traveling down river, and caused widespread flooding along the river bank and the railroad tracks. People, who had homes in the stretch of land between the river and the tracks, were forced to move out. The fire company came to the rescue, using their panel and utility trucks to remove the stoves, refrigerators, freezers, and other items of value. Everything rescued was stored in the firehouse.

The same scenario occurred again in 1972. Only this time, Perdix was cut off from the rest of Perry County. The water was eight foot high over the roadway, in the Cove, where Forrer's Garage is today. Nobody could get through, from Duncannon, which was also extremely flooded and in dire need. Marysville was in the same boat, literally. People were trapped around the area of the archway of the Rockville Bridge, only to be rescued by boat.

Food and supplies couldn't be delivered. The National Guard was called in to assist. Luckily, they brought generators because the area around the fire house did not have electric. The Perdix Fire Company opened its doors, and prepared meals to feed the homeless. Fortunately, the fire company had planned for an Easter ham raffle, a turkey raffle, and grocery bingo. The fire house freezers and shelves were stocked with foods. The fire company fund raising prizes were shared by everybody as they enjoyed hot meals.

***

Per Franklin ….

I had strong-willed parents. I never saw my mother cry. Not even, when word came that my brother, Charles, was missing during the Korean War. However, I did hear her pray for his safe return. Those prayers were answered. Charles was awarded the Bronze Star, for his performance in action, and earned recognition in the history book, "The Forgotten War."

Charles was killed in an auto accident below Marysville in 1991.

Our parents seemed to have a saying to fit every occasion. My dad, Calvin, told us, "Your relatives are wished on you, but your friends you choose, so choose wisely." This meant don't get in with the wrong crowd. He reminded us every time we left the house!

My mother, Anna, told us, "That into everyone's life a little rain will fall." I now know about that rain!

It started, when we lost our dad, Calvin, who was also a good friend. My sister, who seemed to be much better off, in passing. My brother, Charles, my confidant and buddy, in so many ways, left us. My mother, Anna, who had alzheimers and who was no longer the dynamo, she always was. Lastly, my daughter, Charlene, who went from a beautiful young lady to a very sick lady. Even though, it was clear and cold that day at Fort Indiantown Gap Cemetery, I felt the rain.

***

"Growing up in the 1930s and 1940s, in a small community and rural county, there was a lot more interaction between boys of your own age. Lots more friendships and comradery, than today. It prepared me to grow up a little smarter and wiser. I was able to except bumps in the road and, yet look out for some things, that I normally would not have been able to do, had I not lived in a small community. We relied on what our parents said and taught us. Life's little lessons came about through interactions with our parents, as they rolled education and experience, all into one!" Franklin Reidlinger

The Reidlinger name is synonymous with Perdix! His grandparents and parents created a legacy, of community service and civic duty, which is still proudly carried on by Franklin, today.

Perry County Jargon

Storyteller Steve Hower

We Perry Countians seemed to have had our own unique jargon when I was young. Of course, at the time I didn't know it since these words and phrases just seemed normal. This was made clear to me when I entered the military in the 1970s and interacted with other men from all over the United States who had never heard "Perry County talk" before. Sadly, I've noticed that very few local folks still use these words although occasionally a few of the older residents still do. A few examples are listed here.

I don't pretend to know the origin or even the correct spelling of some of the words since I've never seen them in print, but hey, that's probably because outside of Perry County they aren't real words anyway. But they were real to us and we used them in our everyday conversations.

Examples:

If you were told that a friend recently bought a car but no details about the car were provided, to learn more you would ask your friend, **"What *fer* car did you get?"** and then maybe, **"What fer size engine does it have?"**

If your friends were going somewhere and you wanted to know where, you would ask them **"Where are *you'ens* going?"** or **"What are you'ens up to?"**

Many of the older people at that time would follow up a statement with "So it is."

"They're sayin' it's goin' to be a scortcher today. So it is."

If you were riding in your friend's car and you wanted to have him or her drop you off at the post office you would say, **"*Leave* (not let) me off at the post office."**

I can recall hearing some of the older ladies in our area using the words "Lands sake" (or was it Lans sake?) when expressing surprise after hearing a comment made by another.

Person 1: **"I hear Paula's man lost his job."**

Person 2: **"Well, lans sake!"**

Parents at that time would always be telling their children to: **"Get in there and red (read?) up your room!"**

And finally, in addition to our history of speaking differently, our uniqueness was (and still is) always demonstrated when we are visiting another area and someone asks, "Where do you live?" and instead of naming the closest town we simply answer, "Perry County". And for some reason that answer always suffices.

Little Germany Childhood Memories

Storyteller Donna Rudy Neely

The small community called Little Germany is nestled in a very remote farming area west of New Bloomfield, the county seat, and east of the village of Elliottsburg. This small community in the 1950's increased to five families with my family's arrival.

The road through Little Germany was unpaved and potholes appeared year-round. The township workers, after a summer rain, would hitch a wooden disk behind a tractor and drag it up and down the road to fill in the holes. In the spring mud; in the dry summer; clouds of dust would billow from the rare slow-moving vehicle. In the winter months the untreated icy road could be dangerous for travel. The cars and trucks would use tire chains. These were chains that were wrapped usually around the back tires of the vehicle for added traction.

Dum's dairy farm was immediately in your vision as you turned onto Little Germany Road. There was always activity at the farm. The dairy cows, several with bells about their necks, crossed the road from the barn to the meadow the same time each day, twice a day. These majestic animals, 85 total, would stop traffic as they ambled across the dirt road.

In the spring the farm fields were planted with corn and wheat. The dairy cows grazed along the stream in the meadow until late afternoon. Then just like clockwork, cow bells could be heard ringing, as they made their daily sojourn back from the meadow across the dirt road to the barn for milking. We decided these bells must be to alert Mr. Ben Dum of the cows comings and goings and that he needed to be ready for their scheduled arrival and departure at the barn.

The mailman was a daily traveler of Little Germany Road. His name was Mr. Bill Wilson. He drove a station wagon filled to the gunwales with packages and boxes on the back seat for easy access. A very large leather satchel with letters, magazines and catalogs shared the front seat with him. He sat in the middle of the front seat and from this position he could steer the station wagon from one mailbox stop to the next and reach everything around him with ease. This post office on wheels, like the cows, arrived the same time each day. So, we would watch for him. If we needed postage stamps, money orders, or certified mail we met him at the mailbox. Mr. Wilson would talk while filling the requests, sharing community news of people, neighbors and events. His body appeared smaller than it was as he sat amidst all the packages and his satchel. He was kind, always smiled and as he spoke, he would raise his eyebrows and look over his glasses rather than through them.

Aunt Mary lived about 3 miles west of us, on the other side of the hill, which was called Clouser Hollow. She visited twice each month. She played the piano at Little Germany Church and sold Blair Products throughout the community. She was tall, with tiny wire framed glasses sitting upon her rosy cheeks. She wore her long silver hair pulled back in a neat bun, held in place with a decorative toothed comb. She walked miles in good weather, carrying a wicker basket with samples of all she sold. It contained items like vanilla for baking a birthday cake to liniment for aches and pains. As she sat visiting, bringing news and stories, she would take out her pretty cloth hanky and wipe her brow. She was a real storyteller. We would have tea, biscuits and jam, as all activities stopped and we took in her every word. We couldn't wait for her return in two weeks with our order, news and stories.

Everyone had large gardens for fresh vegetables but also for canning and preserving for the winter months. The morning activities always included time in the garden weeding, working the soil and watering plants. We were always excited when Mom announced we were going berry picking. Our berry picking adventures lasted the biggest part of a day; providing fresh berries and berries for jams and jelly for the winter months. We would pack a lunch, water for drinking, berry containers and hike to areas where the wild berries were plentiful. Mom would make us a supper of fresh baked berry roly poly and sweet milk.

During the long hot days of summer there was canning of vegetables, fruit from the local orchard, jams and jellies. In the afternoon and early evening, it was fun to go stream fishing, river fishing, play hide and seek, or catch lightning bugs.

It was our third Thanksgiving in Little Germany and Mom shared her idea for Thanksgiving with us. This fall we would collect the black walnuts as we did every year, dry them, pick them, but this year we would fill quart jars with black walnuts and sell them in the community for $1.00 each. With the money from these sales Mom would buy our Thanksgiving turkey. It was well received by the community. The walnuts were delivered to everyone in advance of their holiday baking and candy making; and our Thanksgiving table was adorned with a big, beautiful turkey and all the trimmings.

During the winter months, the cold and icy road, left untreated, would become slick, providing the perfect surface for fast sledding. We did not hesitate! It was dark by the time we finished getting in all the wood and our other chores, so we used a lantern most of the time. On rare occasions, the full moon did light our way. The older kids were matched up with younger ones and a sentinel would watch for the rare sighting of headlights, indicating a vehicle. The goal was to go as fast and as far as the road would take us. Winter evenings were filled with homework of course, but we also read, played cards or board games. Dad would often tell us stories or play guitar. We had a very nice selection of paper dolls with many outfits; so, we would have a fashion show of sorts.

In the winter for a birthday or other special celebration we would get fresh milk from the farmer; ice from the frozen creek behind the garden; vanilla purchased from Aunt Mary; and eggs from the chicken farmer in the valley over to make homemade hand-churned vanilla ice cream. We would take turns turning the handle until it was difficult to turn, the ice cream was ready. Deciding whose turn it was to get the ice cream paddles was left to Mom.

The Little Germany Church of God was our place of worship and community events. The pianist was Aunt Mary. The church was within walking distance for most while others drove cars. The pastor was shared among other churches so Sunday School was scheduled first, then church which provided the pastor the necessary travel time.

You have heard the stories of walking 2 miles each way uphill through 3-foot snow drifts to get the school bus. Well, it's not all fiction. The kids in Little Germany walked 1 mile each way, each day in all kinds of weather, to meet the school bus at the end of the unpaved road, just beyond the dairy farm. Eventually, as more families moved into Little Germany the school bus traveled the unpaved road to pick us up and dropped us off at our homes. Mr. Lester Kell was the school bus driver. He also operated Kell's Store, a small country store with a pot-bellied stove surrounded by benches; where you could sit, chat, have a soda in the summer and stay warm in the winter. The kids from Little Germany attended the grade school in the village of Loysville where Ms. Hench (2nd Grade) and Mrs. Duncan (1st Grade) were the teachers. The Landisburg Elementary where Mr. Owen was the principal was for 3rd, 4th, 5th and 6th graders. Miss Helen Briner was the 3rd Grade teacher, and she encouraged her students in penmanship. Mr. William Nicholl, who himself was an educator, was the janitor. He spent much of his time in the boiler room across from the cafeteria in the basement area. If you helped in the cafeteria, you got your lunch free, so I helped. I could see the boiler room from my workstation as I stacked lunch trays and noticed Mr. Nicholl had a desk there with pens, paperwork neatly stacked, and lots of brooms and mops. He ate his lunch in the boiler room. He was tall and spoke softly. He took care of the heating system, building and playground issues, cleaning the school and he even replaced the heel of my shoe when he saw I was having a problem.

Innovation was upon us. In the 1960s, came the installation of the telephone. The telephone line was shared with as few as two other families. Our telephone was a black rotary phone. It was important to learn the sound of your telephone ring. If it wasn't your phone ringing and you picked up you could find yourself being scolded or accused of listening in.

The road was paved shortly after the telephone installation. The black and white television was now part of our lives. The antenna was mounted on the roof of our house. When the signal was weak and the TV became snowy then one of us would climb on the roof and walk the antenna back and forth until someone hollered "that's good". Sunday night television was "Bonanza" with Hoss, Little Joe and Adam Cartwright, plus the car commercials with Dinah Shore singing the Chevrolet jingle.

In life things change, and there are those things that will remain the same. The cows don't cross the road twice a day, but we still have milk. We can access the United States Postal Service through technology and it remains the USPS on wheels as it stops at my mailbox each day. We have fewer and fewer telephone landlines, rarer still are the sightings of a telephone booth, now cellular phones have opened up a new world in ways for us to stay connected any time from most anywhere.

Someone said "Life is a journey not a destination"; embrace the journey, embrace life, befriend people from all walks of life, hold onto memories but make new memories, be kind, be humble, stay connected to friends and family, give of your time and your talents to others and your community, say please and thank you, and remember school is never out, it's these things that connect us and matter greatly, to each of us, where ever we might be in life's journey.

Growing Up In Perry County

Storyteller Carl E. Tressler

We lived in a very unique spot in Perry County. We were about half a mile west of Wila, a small village about 5 miles north and west of Newport, on 8 acres that had no road frontage. From the story I remember, a farmer gave his daughter a couple of acres on an inside corner of his farm when she got married. Mom and Dad bought that a year or two before I was born. We said our lane was one-third of a mile, through the original farm fields. What a great place to grow up; we couldn't see our closest neighbor's house. Nothing but fields and woods.

Dad used our 8 acres for a huge garden, sometimes divided into two or three sections, and then grow some grain that would become feed for the bull he always raised. So, we grew what we would eat. And there were always chickens running around, what would be called free-range today. About any day in the summer, we kids, running around bare-footed, would find some place the chickens had been. All we did was wipe our foot on the grass and keep going.

As we got older, we kept exploring more and more of the woods and fields around us. Mom encouraged us by taking us on walks on Sunday afternoons. As we would walk through Wila, we often picked up more kids who came along. The neighbors and some cousins all started to look forward to the Sunday afternoon walks. There were times we had 15 to 20 people on the walk. I think a lot of the kids gravitated to Mom because she taught Sunday School and was the 4-H leader.

And we didn't stay just on the roads. Mom would take us through the woods – sometimes on old logging roads but often not – and fields, making sure we did not damage any crops. We probably looked funny, 20 people walking single file along the edge of unharvested corn and oat fields; especially when there was only one adult – Mom. And she had control of all of us.

We got to play in the woods beside our house, too. Mom got a bell and put it on the house right outside the door. We were told, "when you hear the bell, get your butt home". And we did. No matter where we were, when we heard that bell, we started home at a trot.

Dad's parents lived about a mile west of us. Granddad and Dad each had tractors; both were Farmalls; grandad had a Super H and Dad had an A. Depending what was going on, sometimes both tractors would be at either place. I remember riding with Dad from an early age. He would sit down and then I would sit on the front of the seat, between his legs. He would let me put my hands on the steering wheel and put his hands over mine. This started about age 6.

A couple of years later, he had me put my hands on the wheel, he put his hands on too and we started from granddad's to home. We hadn't traveled very far on the road when he took his hands off and let me drive. I was scared but so proud I would have busted my buttons if I had any. But Dad had a hidden agenda. It didn't take too long until he was driving behind me in the car while I drove the tractor.

Then it started. I would get a note to take the A to Granddads and walk home. A few days later, I was told they were done with the A and tomorrow, I was to walk there and drive it home. Or I walked there to drive the H back home. I did that a lot of times for a lot of years. There were times Uncle Max or Roy would call and ask me to bring the tractor. And I never complained. This all started before I was a teenager and would continue until Dad had both tractors.

And winter was always a special time. With our lane running through the fields and being lower than the fields, anytime it snowed and the wind blew, all the snow would fill the lane with drifts. Of course, if there was a chance of drifting, Dad always took the car to the end of the lane and left it there. Many times, we walked the fields to get to the car to go to church or town.

Often the drifts in the lane would be so bad that Mom or Dad would call a local excavating business to bring dozers and clean out the lane. Now, the lane started at the state road and would immediately start up hill. This hill was usually the place with the biggest drifts. Many times, the dozer would clean out the very end of the lane, and then climb into the field to get to the top of the hill and push the snow downhill; it just couldn't do it uphill.

Of course, as we all grew up and got cars of our own, we would put them at the end of the lane as well. So, it was nothing to have 3 cars there, which reminds me of a big snow.

It was the early to mid-1970's. I had just started working and my sister also lived at home. There was supposed to be a big blizzard, so we all drove our cars to the road and walked home. And it snowed and snowed and blew and blew and snowed some more.

The next morning broke crisp and sunny. Dad and I donned our hip boots – the snow was over knee high – grabbed shovels and started down the lane with Dad in the lead and me walking in his tracks. We were not quite halfway down the lane when he stopped and looked at me. He said, "you lead awhile". So, I went past him and broke the path. It was hard going. About 30 yards from the end, we swapped again.

When we got to the end of the lane, it was drifted straight across. There were 3 cars there, and we could see about 3 inches of one of the antennas. We made a silly bet whether it was from the middle car facing up the lane or the last car facing down. And then we took off our coats and started shoveling.

We cleared out Dad's car first and opened the hood so the sun could melt the snow from the engine compartment. Then we did my sister's car. Mine was the last one cleared. It was my antenna we saw. Then we helped the neighbor from across the road get his car to the top of his road.

I learned priorities from that snowstorm. Dad was the breadwinner so his car needed to be out first. And it continued until the lane was cleared. See, I worked 11:30 at night to 7:30 in the morning. Dad started work at 7 in the morning and my sister at 8. So, I would leave the house by 10:15, walk down the lane, and the cars would be in this order: my sister's car would be first, Dad's car would be in the middle, and mine would be last. I would start my car, start Dad's car, start my sister's car, pull it out onto the road and park it with the 4 ways on, pull my Dad's car out and park it with the 4 ways on, then I could pull my car out and park it, again with the 4 ways on. Then I would move my sister's car into the lane and park it, get Dad's car into the lane and park it. Finally, I could get in my car and start to work.

Helping people and priorities were learned at other times as well. As I said, Dad always raised a bull. My brother and I were to feed it in the mornings before our own breakfast. Dad always said, "the bull eats before you do". And any time you started to complain about feeding the bull, Dad would tell you that you wouldn't have to eat any of it when it was butchered. He only ever told me that once.

We always butchered the bull in the middle of February. Uncle Max always came to help. It was an all-day family event with taking the stomach out, skinning, quartering, carrying, cleaning up. One time, I was about 13, Dad put a piece of twine around the stomach and told me to drag it to the hollow. About 20 minutes later, I was only halfway there. He came with the tractor, and we drug it the rest of the way.

We always weighed the quarters from the bull to see how much meat we had. I was always interested in how much weight the bull put on in just about a year. One time, I named the bull George. I don't know why, but I did. After two years I wanted to change the name, but Dad would have nothing to do with it. Seems once I named him George, he started getting bigger. Dad said we wouldn't change a good thing. That one was the first one to top 600 pounds; and they kept getting bigger. I guess I learned the importance of tradition.

Of course, just being half a mile from Wila, we were involved in everything that went on there from church to Sunday afternoon softball or football games, to ice skating at the dam to sledding or 4-H and swimming in the summer. We got there however we could; bicycle, walking, in the winter, we often skated from 3 Square to Wila. 3 Square was a small area along the creek that was made into a picnic area. The owner let just about everybody use it. We also used inner tubes to float to Wila.

And we learned that someone is always watching you and that you can't get away with anything. One day my brother and I had ridden our bikes to Wila and were playing with the kids there. I don't remember what we did but obviously, someone thought we shouldn't have done it because when we got home, Mom asked us about it.

It was a great time and place to grow up. We learned responsibility. This was really driven home to me one day when Dad told me that we would go fishing that evening if I pulled weeds in the garden. Dad always had a huge garden. I didn't pull the weeds while he was at work; I didn't get to go fishing as we pulled weeds instead. The worst part of that was you could see how disappointed he was. He really wanted to go fishing.

There were other times that taught responsibility. One New Year's Day, Dad fell in the barn when we were catching chickens and broke his elbow and several vertebrae. My brother had graduated so at 16, I became the man of the house for about 12 weeks. I had to feed the bull before school and in the evening after I got home from basketball practice. My brother still lived at home, so we got to share any snow shoveling. I think some of the issues we are having at this time across the country would not be happening if people would have been taught responsibility at a young age.

Other lessons learned were: if you wanted something, you needed to earn it as it wouldn't be given to you for no reason; faith and work in the church are important; learn something every day; if you are going to do something, do it the best you possibly can and do it so you don't have to do it again tomorrow; respect for others, all others.

I could go on about the softball and football games at Wila beside the church every Sunday afternoon. Sometimes the teams were those who came from Newport versus Wila Tech, as we were sometimes called; sometimes the kids from Markelsville would make the 4-mile trip and challenge us. I'm not sure where the name came from, but for as long I can remember, we were called The Wila Wildcats. I think that name was around 20 years before I was born. Often, when the games were over, Mrs. Lyons would open her store so we could buy something to drink. She showed us love and we respected her for it.

I've only scratched the surface of what growing up in Perry County means to me. When I went to computer school, I was offered a teaching job there right before I graduated. Even though I probably could have gotten twice what my first job paid me, I wasn't going to stay in Fairfax, VA, just 15 miles from Washington, D.C. I came home. And I've never lived more than 3 miles from that 8-acre farm just outside Wila.

With all the walks Mom took us on, Dad taking us fishing, and hunting, and just walking on Tuscarora Mountain at Uncle Harry's, we learned a love of wild things and wild places. And that love will always draw me home, home to Perry County.

Cloverleaf Connections

Storyteller Lynn McMillen

I believe it was early summer, 1961, because I think it was when I was nine years old. Mr. Bill Downs, who was Associate County Agent for Perry County, knocked on our front door. I answered the door, and Mr. Downs asked to speak to my Dad, Mr. L. Dean McMillen. Dad was preparing to go out to the barn to do the evening milking, but he came to the door to speak to Mr. Downs.

Mr. Downs explained that some folks in Perry County were interested in forming a new 4-H Club… for horses and ponies!

In the 1930s and 1940s, my dad had been a beef feeder like most farmers, but in 1957 he began milking a small herd of Holstein cows and shipping eighty-pound cans of milk. Throughout the 1930s, dad's father had been, among other things, a dealer in Percheron draft horses. My dad, though only a small boy, had demonstrated a knack for breaking and training those untrained and poorly trained Percherons. Apparently, his reputation for horsemanship had survived the sixteen plus years, because that is why it had been suggested to Mr. Downs to contact my dad to be an adult leader for the Perry County 4-H Horse and Pony Club. It took a couple of days, but dad agreed to help, with the club, and I was able to join as a brand-new spanking member!

In about two weeks, the time arrived to conduct the very first meeting of the Horse and Pony Club. I had no idea what to expect! I believe my dad was excited also!

The meeting was to be held at the "Courthouse Annex", in New Bloomfield. That's a heck of a name to throw at a nine-year-old boy. Dad and I opened the squeaking front door to see no more than a long stairway leading up to a dimly lit second floor. We tramped up each of the steps and entered a brightly lit room containing a mixture of people, all of which were much older than me.

Somehow, everyone in the room managed to get introduced. In addition to my dad agreeing to be a leader, there were several other adults. I remember Mrs. Louise Mohler, from Newport, Mr. John Sledzinski, from Shermans Dale, and several other adults that agreed to help as volunteers. Next came the election of officers. As I remember Johnny Sledzinski, Jr. was elected president. Some other "big kids", that were elected officers were Carol Stone and Kathy Mohler.

(Please try to understand, that I'm trying to remember 4-H events from sixty years ago, without doing any research. My multiple years as a 4-Her tend to run together.)

Some other early club members, that I remember, were Linda Pottiger, Barry Luckenbaugh, John Reed, Dennis Gilbert, and Johnny Sunday. In those early days, nearly three-fourth of the club members were from the Duncannon and Shermans Dale area.

On our way home, from our first 4-H meeting together dad stopped at Emlet's Grocery in Loysville and bought two cans of Pepsi from the machine. That was the beginning of a tradition that lasted throughout my 4-H career.

While at our first meeting, the calendar for the year, was announced. In addition to a big event at Colonel Denning State Park, across the mountain at Doubling Gap, and some other special happenings, Mr. Downs mentioned we would have a club "Roundup", at the end of the 4-H year, probably in August. Oh, my goodness! A Roundup meant we'd have some sort of competitive horse show! Dad and I were going to have to find something for me to ride in the Roundup.

Dad was still in contact with a number of the area horsemen and horse dealers so he began making phone calls and we soon had some prospective mounts to be considered. Dad finally ended up purchasing a grade Welsh pony, from a man outside of New Bloomfield, by the name of Joe Yohe. We named our new pony "Ginger". Ginger was a very red bay, meaning she was the color red, with black ears, mane, tail and stockings. (Ginger was somewhat larger than a Shetland pony, because Welsh ponies had been bred to pull the coal cars, in the coal mines in Wales.)

August arrived and it was time, for our first Horse and Pony Roundup. It was to be held on the farm of Tom Baskins. I think that was in the Duncannon area. It was a normally hot, dry, dusty August day for the Roundup. My dad was the Ringmaster. I don't recall who the judge was. I was the youngest in the competition, and Mr. Sledzinski told me I was in the upcoming class. I was to ride into the ring, turn to the right, and just follow everybody else. All the while, I was trying to remember to do everything I had been told and taught.

Near the end of the day, at the conclusion of a class competition, my number was called for me to ride up to the ringmaster and receive my blue ribbon for having won first place in Junior Western Equitation! Shortly thereafter, Dad and I loaded Ginger onto my Great-Uncle's 1949 Ford pickup truck. We headed to Emlet's to celebrate with two more Pepsi's.

I was very active in Perry County 4-H. That first-year lead to eight or nine more. As far as the Horse and Pony Club was concerned, we moved up to larger venues for our roundups. Most of my years, I remember showing at John Sledzinski's new show ring, on the south side of Shermansdale. Then there was a year, that the Horse and Pony Club was asked to join the Perry County 4-H Fair, at the farm outside Ickesburg, that was later Knouse's Nursery, and now Greenwood Nursery. This was all in the years preceding the present-day Perry County Fair.

Ginger and I traveled the roads around Kistler, selling 4-H cookies, Butter Mints for the school band, and magazines for the Blain School.

I was active in the 4-H Horse and Pony Club, every year I was a 4-Her. Some of those years, I qualified to compete at the District 4-H Horse and Pony competition and show, which was held in Reedsville, Pennsylvania.

In addition to the Horse and Pony Club, I participated in the Dairy Club for two or three years. I qualified for the Dairy Judging Team, but I chose to go to Penn State, where the competitions were held, with the Horse Judging Team, because they needed me to complete a county team. I also participated in a community 4-H club, called Kistler Clovers. I did projects such as photography, woodworking, and electricity.

"Learning by Doing" with the 4-H projects, was enjoyable and beneficial to me, but 4-H is much more than projects. Learning parliamentary procedure by participating in, and leading meetings was very helpful, in later years. Working with qualified adults and peers on committees and projects was a great experience! Serving as elected officers, leading a club, was a tremendous experience! Learning social skills, while meeting new peers, and making new friends, some friends to this day, was tremendously important and beneficial, to me.

This article was not written to be about me. It is simply an effort to show that there is a great deal more to the 4-H Cloverleaf, than just green and white ink! 4-H activities occur at a child's very formative years, which is why so many 4-H activities are remembered! My story only scratches the surface of what 4-H has to offer. Every child, or grandchild, or stepchild, or neighbor kid deserves a chance to learn what they can do, and more importantly, what they can be! 4-H will show them!

Perry Countians Serving in the Spanish American War

Storyteller James Michael McAteer

I have always had an interest in the Spanish American War, as my ancestor, was a Medal of Honor recipient during that conflict. I began to research Lebanon County veterans of the Spanish American War after noticing a Hiker statue while I attended a Veterans Day service in Lebanon city. The Hiker, a statue dedicated to veterans of the Spanish American War, listed 11 Lebanon County veterans on the base of the statue. My subsequent investigation uncovered more than 200 Lebanon County veterans who served during the Spanish American War (1898), the China Relief Expedition (1900) and/or the Philippine Insurrection (1899 -1902). My interest then led me to join the national organization of Spanish American War veterans and I later became national president of the organization, in 2012, I organized the Alexander M. Quinn Camp of Lebanon County to honor my ancestors.

Since I lived in New Bloomfield for 28 years prior to moving to Lebanon County, my veteran investigation soon expanded to veterans of Perry County. There were over 200 veterans who lived in Perry County when they enlisted for service between 1898 and 1902. Even though I was a past president of the Historical Society of Perry County, I had not previously found information on Perry County veterans of the Spanish American War. After researching Perry County, I expanded my research to include all Pennsylvania veterans, expanding to all 67 counties. The Spanish American War was the only war where the United States fought a European military power, one on one. The result transformed the US into the international military power that it is today. The Pennsylvania veterans who volunteered need to be recognized for their achievements.

Currently I have a history on over 30,000 Pennsylvania veterans who served between 1898 and 1902. To honor our ancestors, I now give presentations on the Spanish American War Era that includes personal histories of veterans from the area who served in the military. Below are the results of my research:

Edwin A. Adams of Marysville: 1874-1903 Buried in Marysville
Pvt Jesse Dennis Baker of Markelsville: 1874-1950 Buried in Altoona
Pvt William Harvey Barrick of Newport: 1873-1954 Buried in Oliver Twp

Mus Foy Snyder Baskin of New Buffalo: 1876-1946 Buried in Williamsport
Cpl Ira Irving Beichler of New Germantown: 1877-unknown
Cpl W. Albert Bergstresser of unknown: 1880-1905 Buried in Duncannon
Pvt Anapolas Severa Bitting of Ickesburg: 1879-1955 Buried in Arlington
Pvt Charles Smiley Black of Marysville: 1872-1942 Buried in California
Pvt John Black of Tuscarora Twp: 1875-1998 Buried in Millerstown
Pvt William Ashley Blain of Greenwood Twp: 1879-1958 Buried in Millerstown
Pvt William Harvey Blakely of Millerstown: 1875-1936 unknown
Pvt Frank Bothwell of Duncannon: 1874-1928 Buried Huntingdon County
Pvt Grant C. Burd of Newport: 1878-1929 Buried in Newport
Wag John W. Burd of Buffalo Twp: 1875-1932 Buried in Camp Hill
Pvt James Henry Caldwell, Jr of Millerstown: 1877-1941 Buried in Titusville
Mus Duke William Carbaugh of Perry Co: 1905-1930 Buried in Harrisburg
Pvt Charles Edward Carl of Newport: 1878-1947 Buried in Ohio
Robert Orr Crist, MD of unknown: 1878-1907 Buried in Markelsville
Cpl Enoch H. Curry of West Fairview Twp: 1873-1934 Buried in Duncannon
Pvt John H. Daugherty of Marysville: unknown
Pvt John Blanchard Delancey of Newport: 1873-1957 Buried in Maryland
Pvt Patrick Thomas Doran of Elliottsburg: 1878-1939 Buried in Pittsburgh
Cpl Wesley H. Elliott of unknown: 1874-1900 Buried in Duncannon
Pvt Eugene Raymond Esler of Millerstown: 1875-1938 Buried in Indiana
Pvt Charles Franklin Etchberger of Newport: 1877-1956 Buried in Chambersburg
Pvt James William Fenicle of Duncannon: 1878-1962 Buried in California
Pvt William H. Fissell of Duncannon: unknown
Pvt David Henry Ford of Newport: 1880-1950 Buried in Newport
Pvt John J. Fosselman of Tuscarora Twp: 1872-unknown
Pvt John Raisner Frank of Newport: 1869-1958 Buried in Arlington
Pvt James Henry Galbraith, Jr of Landisburg: 1873-1958 unknown
Pvt Harry Kuhn Gamber of Marysville: 1874-1939 Buried in Marysville
Pvt Edwin Roy Gault of Marysville: 1881-1944 Buried in Paxtang
Cpl Harry Albert Gettys of Marysville: 1872-1932 Buried in Marysville
Sgt John Bennett Gossert of Marysville: 1873-1923 Buried in Mechanicsburg
Pvt Reuben E. Gotshall of Sunbury: 1876-1940 Buried in Liverpool
Pvt James P. Graham of Landisburg: unknown
Sgt William M. Graybill of Duncannon: 1877-1944 Buried in Duncannon
Pvt John Edward Greene of Millerstown: 1876-1954 Buried in Washington, PA
Pvt Edward Clinton Gunderman of Newport: 1876-1948 Buried in Newport
William J. Hain of unknown: 1875-1924 Buried in Tyrone
Pvt Charles Zinn Hartzell of Newport: 1877-1944 Buried in Harrisburg
Pvt Herbert Melvin Hartzell of Wheatfield Twp: 1877-1950 Buried in New Bloomfield
Jesse W. Hartzell of Dellville: 1880-1915 Buried in New Bloomfield
Pvt Benjamin Calvin Heck of Marysville: 1877-1951 Buried in Marysville
Pvt Clarence Perl Hench of Saville Twp: 1876-1939 Buried in Dover
Pvt John C. Hess of Middlesex: 1875-1901 Buried in Shermans Dale
Pvt Charles Hight of Newport: 1869-1933 Buried in Union County

Pvt Joseph Harry Hillard of Newport: 1872-1957 Buried in Dallas, Pa
Pvt David Vernon Himes of Duncannon: 1871-1939 Buried in Paxtang
George F. Houser of Duncannon: 1872-1921 Buried in Duncannon
Mus Charles Albert Hunter of Duncannon: 1874-1960 Buried in Duncannon
Pvt William Henry Idle of Rye Twp: 1866-1933 Buried in Rye Twp
Pvt William J. Jackson of Marysville: 1875-1934 Buried in Marysville
Pvt Frank M. Jones of Newport: 1874-1955 Buried in Michigan
Pvt Harry Elmer Jones of Marysville: 1873-1924 Buried in Harrisburg
Pvt Frank Legree Kline of Duncannon: 1882-1961 Buried in Duncannon
Sgt Orrie Dobbs Koontz of Blain: 1872-1954 Buried in Arlington
Pvt Arthur Clair Landis of Newport: 1875-1942 Buried in Newport
Pvt Charles W. Laney of Millerstown: 1878-1943 Buried in Fort Worth, TX
Pvt Harvey Fisher Liddick of Duncannon: 1873-1936 Buried in York County
Pvt John E. Lukens of Duncannon: 1865-1928 Buried in Indiana
1Sgt Robert Jesse Marsh of Fishing Creek Valley: 1869-1948 Buried in Oregon
Pvt John Penrose Martin of Duncannon: 1874-1948 unknown
Pvt John M. McNeely of Marysville: 1874-1950 Buried in Chambersburg
Pvt Franklin Silas Miller of Landisburg: 1874-1953 Buried in Landisburg
Pvt Harry I. Milliken of Duncannon: 1876-1930 Buried in Duncannon
Pvt Charles W. Moyer of Liverpool: 1876-1951 Buried in Liverpool
Pvt Thomas Clayton Mutzabaugh of Duncannon: 1868-1936 Buried in Duncannon
Pvt Charles Levi Ney of Marysville: 1877-unknown
Pvt David R. Osborne of Duncannon: 1869-1899 Buried in Duncannon
Pvt Harry Allen Patterson of Marysville: 1880-1936 Buried in Berwick
Pvt William Henry Patterson of Rye Twp: 1878-1951 Buried in California
Cpl Adolph Rudolph Pfafflin of Maryville: 1871-1941 Buried in Florida
Pvt Edward Henry Powell of Newport: 1878-1965 Buried in Oregon
Pvt Hayes Benton Raffensperger of Mannsville: 1877-1938 unknown
Pvt James N. Ragar of Newport: 1853-1915 Buried in Newport
Pvt Harry Reese of Duncannon: 1881-1962 Buried in Duncannon
Harry B. Rhinesmith of New Bloomfield: 1867-1938 Buried in New Bloomfield
Pvt Francis Brady Rice of Saville Twp: 1879-1943 Buried in Hanover
Pvt Harry Rice of Duncannon: 1866-1924 Buried in Duncannon
Pvt Lawrence Rice of Perry County: 1876-unknown
Pvt Orlando Chester Rice of Saville Twp: 1877-1951 Buried in New York
Pvt Samuel W. Ryan of Shermans Dale: 1870-1898 Buried in Rye Twp
Joseph William Saul of New Bloomfield: 1866-1954 Buried in New Bloomfield
Pvt Harvey Sellers of Marysville: 1877-1959 Buried in Minnesota
Pvt Elmer Erwin Shaffer of Wila: 1868-1940 Buried in Millerstown
Pvt Austin C. Sharon of Liverpool: 1876-1898 Buried in Liverpool
Pvt Elmer C. Sheriff of New Germantown: 1873-1950 Buried in Erie
Pvt Charles E. Soule of New Buffalo: 1865-1935 Buried in Watts Twp
John K. Stansfield (Blacksmith) of Wheatfield Twp: 1880-1937 Buried in New Bloomfield
Pvt George Stroup of New Buffalo: 1880-1956 Buried in Florida
Sgt William Henry Stump of Bayleysburg: 1879-1955 Buried in Arlington

Sgt Charles Wilbert Taylor of Marysville: 1877-unknown
Pvt Thomas E. Toland of Duncannon: 1878-1953 Buried in Gettysburg
Cpl Simon Roscoe Wert of Millerstown: 1876-1952 Buried in Altoona
Pvt Harvey Franklin Wertz of Newport: 1880-1960 Buried in Ft Bliss, TX
Pvt William I. Winters of Harrisburg: 1872-1901 Buried in Liverpool
Pvt Harry Orville Wise of Newport: 1879-1942 Buried in Harrisburg
Pvt Walter Edward Wise of Marysville: 1879-1898 Buried in Marysville
Pvt Harvey Fager Wolfe of Marysville: 1875-1943 Buried in Marysville
1Sgt William Lyle Woods of unknown: 1869-1899 Buried in S.W. Madison Twp
Cpl Jesse William Wright of Newport: 1874-1943 Buried in Newport
Pvt Charles Mauris Zimmerman of Marysville: 1875-unknown

(Jim has in addition to the names above, researched the Company assigned, date of Muster and Discharge or Desertion. He included the names of parents, spouses, and children.)

In Perry County Everybody Knows Your Name

Storyteller Jane Cameron Simonton

As I think about growing up and living my whole life in Perry County, I realize just how lucky I am to live in this area. Three clichés immediately come to mind.

First – It Takes a Village. When I was growing up in Millerstown, I had to not only worry about my parents knowing everything I did, but also relatives, neighbors, family friends, and even teachers. Anything good or bad was always soon known by everyone.

Second - the lyrics from the Cheers theme song describes our area so well! Sometimes you want to go where everybody knows your name and they're always glad you came. People in Perry County are so friendly, and it was nice to live in an area where everyone knew who you were and you felt safe. When I was young, I don't remember my parents ever locking the doors of our house or car.

Third – Perry County towns are like a Hallmark movie town. With all the small businesses, sport activities and fundraising events, the people come together to show their support.

Each year the Millerstown Carnival was a special happening for me. I would meet up with friends to ride the rides, eat the food, and play the games. I can remember that for a dollar I could buy French fries, ice cream and soda. Rides were only one ticket, and a book of tickets was only one dollar. Another memory is on Halloween, I would go trick or treating with friends. You didn't just go by the house and get candy, you had to go in and sit down until they guessed who you were.

At Christmas time we would go out to my dad's farm and cut down our tree. It was placed in front of the large picture window and decorated with lights, ornaments, and tinsel. Since there were four children in our family, we would get one large present and a few smaller things in our stockings. The afternoon would be spent at my grandma's house with my aunts, uncles and cousins.

I am so glad I grew up in Perry County and that I was able to raise my children here.

"Baby Boomer"

GROWING UP IN THE 1950s

Storyteller Fred C. Noye

I'm considered a "Baby Boomer". Born in 1946, just after the end of World War ll. My dad, Charles Noye, was discharged from the Army after seeing action in North Africa and France. He was wounded on three separate occasions and was awarded the Bronze Star and the Purple Heart. He actually died on the operating table in England but a determined doctor saved him. He was a true hero, but you better never say that in front of him. In fact, don't even bring up the subject of the war. I tried numerous times as a youngster to learn about his time in the army and all I ever got was bits and pieces. I was reminded about his military service every time I saw him without a shirt and the numerous large holes in his back.

Dad came home in 1944 and married my mother, Marie Heckert, in 1945, and exactly twelve months later I joined them. They lived in a small apartment, and then rented a small home on Ann St. until 1949. My mother's grandparents lived a few doors up the street and my great-grandmother died unexpectedly. My parents then moved in with my great-grandfather to help him.

I was fortunate to grow up at the greatest time to be alive, the 1950s. It was a time of peace, change and adventure. General Ike was in the White House and the public had tremendous trust in his leadership. After all he guided the armies through World War ll. A newfangled type of entertainment captured our minds and our hearts. It was called television. It showed us people, places, and events we only had been able to read about or hear on the radio.

Living in the small town of Duncannon, everyone knew most everybody and would spend time talking and helping their neighbors. With the war in the past, people were finally starting to feel carefree and outgoing again. Business was rebounding from the sacrifices they had to make during the war. With rationing over, people felt rich and blessed as store shelves were full and many new products came on the market. More and more homes bought a new TV (although we only had a couple channels) and new refrigerators, stoves and washers which made chores easier.

At first, I hated school. I liked my teachers, but all that learning interrupted my carefree schedule. Life was good, even when we lived through some dangerous times. We had our drills to prepare for a possible nuclear attack and we were faced with the scourge of polio. I had a bigger fear of a needle compared to everything else. We didn't need psychiatrists or psychologists to get us through. We looked after each other. We played games to win and not everyone was given a trophy for participating. We didn't have a safe place to run to if we were offended by something someone said or disagreed with us. We respected our elders, our teachers, and people in positions of authority. We could make fun of each other and ourselves and laugh about it. And, we had a sense of humor about our own shortcomings.

When there was no school, we kids got out of the house early and spent our days playing baseball, cowboys & Indians or just games we made up. We only came in to eat and then we would be back outside. Parents didn't worry where we were. If we weren't in the usual places we played, they knew we were at a friend's house.

To me, summer only meant one thing-----**BASEBALL**. That was my life. I studied every team and player (there were only sixteen teams then). Many years later when I started writing a sports column for the Duncannon Record, the Editor Dick Swank, wrote a very flattering column introducing me as the new sportswriter for the paper. He mentioned that when I was just a young kid, I knew more about baseball players and teams than most adults. I didn't quite remember it that way but was pleased to accept his accolades anyway.

My dad "Bumps" was a bartender for a while at the Duncannon American Legion. In 1952, late one night, baseball's greatest third baseman, Billy Cox from Newport, a member of the Brooklyn Dodgers stopped in at the Legion. I was home in bed and my dad rushed home to get me and took me to meet Billy. He gave me a World Series program and signed it. Sixty-nine years later, I still have that program and I still "bleed Dodger Blue"!

Every waking minute I would play ball. If my friends (Bob Barton and his brother Roger, John Vogel, Bill Cooper, and a little later Lee Bolan) weren't available, I made up ball games for myself. I was always throwing a ball against something. It's a wonder whoever was in the house didn't go mad from the thump, thump, thump. Someone introduced me to the game of "dice baseball" where you rolled the dice, and each number combination was either a hit or out. We would spend untold hours playing, using the line-ups of major league teams and players, and keeping statistics on each.

In the evenings or weekends, when the Duncannon town team played a home game up on the old High School football field (now known as Cooper Field), I would trudge up to see my heroes play the likes of Blain, New Bloomfield, Newport, and other teams from the Perry-Juniata League. And then Duncannon decided to switch to the West Shore Twilight League. Now the opponents were Enola, New Cumberland, Mt. Holly, Lisburn, Mechanicsburg, and others.

Some of the players took time with me before games, and then I was taught how to keep the score book. Soon I was the team's scorekeeper and was traveling with the team to all the games. It was an experience that I wouldn't have traded for anything. It is one of my fondest memories of growing up. Names that meant so much to me in my youth: Max Cooper, Roger & Neil Hickoff, Myron Rohrer, Bernie Britcher, Sid Klinepeter, Ken & Frank Bornman, Nevin Magee, Warren Barton, George Peterman, John & Jim Nearhood, Earl Renshaw, Vance Bolan, and Abe Leiter.

Then came little league. We started playing on a very crude field at the Penn Twp. school. The next year a new field was developed downtown next to the old town dump and along the railroad tracks. (It is now next to the town sewer plant.) It was named after the revered former high school principal, L. W. Bell. My dad coached our team for two years. I either played first base or caught. It truly was the "joy of victory and the agony of defeat". We were undefeated the first year, and winless the second.

And then, there was wiffle ball. It became a compulsion with me, Lee Bolan, John Vogel, and Jim Ford. We spent all our free time playing wiffle ball. We built mythical ballparks and mapped out where you had to hit the wiffle ball to get on base. It was sort of like monopoly. The games went on and on and on.

Life changed in 1954 when my parents bought a house outside of town along the Juniata River. At first it was difficult being away from my friends. Arrangements had to be made to go anywhere and schedules didn't always allow for transportation. We lived in Aqueduct along the old canal. The road was very narrow, allowing for only one car at a time. If you saw a car coming, someone had to get off the road to allow the other to continue. (Twice I put the car over the edge and had to get it pulled out). There were ten homes along the road. Of the ten, only five were full time residents. The other five were summer cottages.

The first house was owned by an attorney from Harrisburg, who also happened to be a State Representative (H. Joseph Hepford). He is one I believe helped to plant the seed into my head about politics. As a teenager I would go down when he was home and visit. He had a neat shuffleboard. It is quite humbling to be fifteen and constantly lose at shuffleboard to his seven- and eight-year-old daughters.

The second home was the Bowman family cottage. They were the owners of Bowmans Department Store in Harrisburg. Next was a doctor/surgeon from Harrisburg, John & Marie Sherger. They had traveled all over the world and would enthrall us for hours, with slide shows of their trips. They also had a swimming pool. Need I say more.

The doctor was a little eccentric. He dug a cement pit for his garbage. He imported two of the largest snapping turtles I have ever seen to take care of the garbage. They could snap off a broom handle in an instant. John was probably one of the best story tellers I ever met. His delivery and timing were as good as any stand-up comic I ever saw. In later years, he tended to repeat stories and they were just as funny as the first time you heard them. Of course, he was even funnier after a few adult beverages.

The next cottage was a Steelton family that seldom visited. We lived next door. The family of Karl and Ruby Zerfing, the owners of the local hardware store on the square in Duncannon, lived beside us. Beyond the Zerfings were Paul and Gwen Wueller. They kept pretty much to themselves and didn't socialize much. We didn't know much about Paul. It was only later that I learned that he was the Budget Secretary for several Pennsylvania Governors.

The last of the permanent homes belonged to Ken and Kate Snyder. They were the owners of the very famous and popular Barbeque Cottage on Front St. in Harrisburg. If you were a teenager and had a car you took your date to the Barbeque Cottage. (Even when you were older!) If you didn't have a date, that's where you went to look for one. Cars would constantly cruise around scouting the scene. It was almost like going to Al's on Happy Days. It was the happening place! It was at the Snyder home I saw my first color TV. They invited friends in to see the Rose Bowl Parade in "living color".

The last two properties were cottages. One we never knew who owned it, and the last one was a dentist from Harrisburg, Paul Martin.

Life along the river was fun. There weren't many kids along the Towpath. Next door was Ginny and Jane Zerfing. Ginny was two years older and Jane was a year younger. The others were Sue and Ken Snyder. Sue was the same age as Ginny and Ken was the same age as Jane. I was in the middle.

We spent a lot of time on or in the river in the summer. I wasn't much of a swimmer. Dad constructed a wooden raft and fitted it with barrels allowing it to float. He would anchor it for people to use while swimming. We had a small boat for fishing, which we used to get up and down the river.

If we wanted to go fishing, we had to sneak away from our little beagle, Nutmeg. She loved the water. If she saw us leaving in the boat, she would jump in the water and follow us. More than once, we had to turn around and bring her home. She once followed us down river to below Amity Hall, about a half mile from home.

Occasionally I could coerce the girls to play baseball or softball, especially when their cousin Sandy Balsbaugh would visit. I always thought I was the best player until Sandy showed up. No one could hit a ball farther than Sandy and she did it hitting cross handed. She was unbelievable. Kenny wasn't into baseball. He was more into football, and we spent a lot of time in the fall playing, especially in his yard where they had lights. Night football in those days was still quite a novelty in our area. I even had a white football for just that occasion. Consequently, Kenny had a very successful college football career at Cornell University.

In the winter, a lot of our spare time was spent playing board games or cards. The Zerfing girls and their grandparents introduced me to a card game called Hoffenpeffer. To this day I still don't remember how it was played, but we played it for hours. The Zerfings also had the best spot for sledding. You started on the Towpath, went down a hill across their driveway and on a good snow could go all the way to the river. It was during this time that they introduced the aluminum metal round discs. Boy were they a blast going down that hill!

Since there were few families living along the Towpath, occasionally parties were held bringing everyone together. Also attending was Sam and Marge Snyder, who was Ken's brother and lived along the river, but on the other side. Sam was part owner of the Barbeque Cottage, until he opened the legendary Red Rabbit near the Clark's Ferry Bridge. (Still open to this day with the 3rd generation.)

Winters were sometimes challenging. To get to Aqueduct, you traveled down a steep and narrow winding road and crossed the railroad tracks. We were like at the bottom of a bowl. There were three roads out of the area but the road I described was the only paved one. When it snowed, our area was not at the top of the priority list for plowing. We had to wait until someone could come to plow the very narrow Towpath. Getting up your driveway to the Towpath was always an event.

In the mid-1960s, the river froze and the snow piled up. We were stranded for about a week. No way in and no way out. The question arose about some food shortages. Sam Snyder to the rescue! On the other side of the river the roads were open and you could move around. Sam could get to a store so he and his family, with sleds full of supplies, trekked across the ice to provide home delivery. What better time to have a neighborhood party! Sometimes when life gives you lemons, you just have to make lemonade!

I was a board game nut and enjoyed playing cards. My parents didn't have a lot of time or desire for board games, but my grandmother, Alta, bless her soul, would spend hours playing anything I wanted to play EXCEPT------------Monopoly. That's where "Nannaw" drew the line. Many of the card games I learned or played were with her. She lived in Annville and had a circle of ladies that she played cards with regularly. When I visited her, I was always invited to play. We would play Canasta and Samba with the ladies, and at home we would play Rummy, Cribbage or War!

My mother "Nuncy" was a waitress for years, first at the American Legion and then at The Kings Inn, in the Cove. She was quite good and her tips reflected it. I remember how we would go through her tips the next morning, looking through the old coins. In those days, she would get coins that collectors today would pay large sums to own. It was nothing to get Peace or Morgan dollars, very early dimes and quarters (Morgan and Barber) and of course, it was all silver. And we were always looking for that elusive 1909 VDB Lincoln penny.

A lot of people ask me, "weren't you lonely being an only child?" If I was, I didn't know it. There were so many things I liked to do and I did them. I had a great imagination and I could make a game out of most any situation. I was so into sports of all kinds that I would make up a game and play against myself. I put up a small basketball hoop in the garage. In the dead of winter, with freezing temperatures, I would spend hours playing basketball. I played for both teams and kept score. I never wanted for something to do. Many a Friday and Saturday night were spent at the house by myself while my mother and father were working. I had the place to myself. I watched Your Hit Parade, Paladin, Gunsmoke, and Have Gun Will Travel on the TV, while enjoying Chef Boyardee pizza or Jolly Time popcorn. Plus, I had the games I made up. I was in heaven!

It's true that I spent a lot of my time growing up around adults. Looking back, I believe I was given the greatest gift I could have ever been given, and that was the gift of common sense by members of the "greatest generation".

The 1960s was the age of rock & roll. I loved the music and bought lots of 45 records (29c each at Ken Delanceys Jewelry store on the square in Duncannon) to play on my hi-fi record player. Along came stereo and that changed everything. I learned all the songs and singers, but I never got into dancing. That is one of the biggest regrets of my life. It seems my mother and dad were known as one of the best dance couples around. In those days, the Duncannon American Legion was one of the hottest dance locations. They had a large ballroom and brought in some of the biggest names during the great band era. When I became a teenager, they wanted to teach me all the dance moves, but for some reason I was either too shy or too embarrassed (some would say dumb) to let them show me. Did I mention that I wasn't born with much musical rhythm? While my friends were dancing to all the different new music, I was an observer. It took me years before I got enough confidence to dance, and then it was only slow dances.

I heard many a story about the dance contests at the great dance venues up in Lykens and Tower City in the late 1940s. That area was crazy for music. After all, three of the greatest names in band music came from there. Tommy & Jimmy Dorsey and Les Brown were from what everyone called the coal regions. They constantly held dance contests and my dad and Spike Hennessey from Duncannon were considered two of the best. I would always cringe when they told me stories of how they would get together and dance with each other to learn the latest dance steps and to practice. I was told it paid off because they each won their share of competitions.

We were referred to as the innocent generation. Maybe we were but we enjoyed a lifestyle that few have experienced. We weren't rich, but we sure thought we were. We had parents whose only goal in life was to give us a better life than they had. They were generous to a fault. We were happy and life was good and carefree. The future looked exciting for everyone who either was planning a career or looking forward to marriage and a family.

And then came the 1960s and Viet Nam, protests, riots and assassinations.... and the whole world changed…....

My Thoughts, Observations, and Story!

Storyteller Debra "Debby" Kay Noye

As I was reading everybody's stories, and the significant historical submissions, I discovered a common thread and tone.

"A strong love for, and a great pride in having grown up in Perry County.... which is cherished!"

We are a proud bunch. Not ashamed to have been dirt poor, because in the 1930s – 1960s, that was the way of life! You had the clothes on your back; shoes on your feet during the winter; food on the table; dirt under your nails from harvesting those vegetables and grains; grease on your clothes from rendering lard while butchering; cow manure on your toes from milking Bessie; chopped wood or dusty coal for the cook stove; water from the outside hand pump; outhouses with pages from catalogs used as toilet paper; hay in the fields to feed the animals; a roof over our heads; support of family and community; and the Bible presented upon joining the church.

As I read the stories, and did the interviews, there were several foods that everybody is wishing they could taste one last time, from back in their childhoods. Not the faux representations available today, was a resounding reply!

Ponhaus or **scrapple** from the family butchering topped the list. **Puddin' meat**, again from butchering hogs seemed to be another favorite, with that livery taste profile. Not a big puddin' fan, as I never liked hog liver!! Yuck!! Most often the fried scrapple was slathered with homemade **apple butter** or **King Syrup Molasses**. Molasses was a household staple, overlooked today!

I know first-hand about butchering hogs. My favorite treat was the head meat, having been boiled with the other odd cuts of meat and organs. Adding some salt to the tender cooked hog jowl or cheek… that was down to earth real food!! I also absolutely loved a boiled tongue sandwich, with salt and sometimes regular ole' yellow mustard. You do realize that the cooked tongue had to have the outer skin scraped off before thinly slicing and eating! My mouth is watering remembering those all-day butcherings.

My family never enjoyed the cracklin's. We would put the thick cakes of fatty, crunchy, rendered hog fat into paper grocery bags. My dad would give a shout out to Sam Martin of Elliottsburg. He'd come a running, because he loved the freshly made snacking treat. Double Yuke!!

Cornmeal was another staple that is under used in today's cooking. **Mush,** made from freshly ground cornmeal, eaten right out of the kettle or fried crispy on each side, was belly filling. Molasses and possibly a bit of butter made it seem a sweet treat, rather than an inexpensive way to feed a large family. Again, today's products do not come close, to the home-raised, dried and milled cornmeal of yesteryear, per you story tellers!

Springtime **dandelion greens** cooked in a sweet and sour bacon dressing was another favorite, that just doesn't seem to taste the same today. The reason being the bacon is quickly processed from hogs that are fed diets different from years back.

Fortunately, there was indoor plumbing and modern appliances in the farmhouse, outside of Elliottsburg, midway on that steep Limestone Ridge Road, when I was growing up. However, my grandmother, Esther Freeman, who never learned to drive, preferred to use her **outhouse** in the summer months. When I would visit my grandparents, who owned the Bernheisel Mill property on Montour Creek, by the shortcut road to Green Park, I loved to go into the outhouse to see all the colorful calendars on the wall! She had pretty much wallpapered the interior with the prettiest glossy calendars.

Gram's decorating expertise was the inspiration for the stories in "City Cousins Spend the Summer", my sequel to "The Treasures in Great-Granny's Scrapbook". She also had a washhouse, which provided the setting for some of the city-slicker cousin's adventures.

I liked to go exploring in the abandoned mill, which had a large water wheel, and the grindstones still intact. It was a magnificent structure that my grandparents tried to preserve. Attached to the mill was a small garage, which protected the Plymouth Business Coupe, from the elements. There was not a true back seat, and I sat on a wooden stool or box, when I was taken along to pick strawberries. I was a fast and clean picker...not destroying the plants. I loved freshly picked strawberries, or any berry for that matter. We went to Cumberland County, as I recall, to acres of strawberry plants, bursting with bright red berries. Just because I picked the berries didn't mean my participation was over. Taking the caps off with my fingernails was the only way allowed...no knives or gadgets. My fingers would get sore, because there were probably twenty-four quarts at least, which would be frozen and made into jam. Lots of strawberry shortcake made from Bisquick filled the bellies of the six of us. That was our meal!

My grandparents would also have me tag along to see the horse races at the Carlisle Fairgrounds, where Carlisle Productions holds the Carlisle Car Shows today. I can remember two magnificent horses collapsing on the dirt track on a hot summer day. You could see the sweat rolling off them as they passed the grandstands. It was unusual for that to happen, especially in two separate races on the same day!

I was introduced to Golden Books by my Gram. She was a small woman, but would sit me on her lap, scratch my back, and read them over and over to me. She mimicked the characters, which is what I did while reading to my two sons, and their children. When I would visit and stay over....she lived a quarter of a mile from our dairy farm.... I would sometimes walk barefoot to my cousin's house at the other end of the short-cut road, past the Green Park one room schoolhouse. This was usually in the summer months, when the tar on the road would bubble. I liked to take my big toe and burst the bubbles. Hot, heck yes!! My soles were like heavy workman's boot leather! I could step on tacks and thorns and not be bothered! Gram would send me to get things from my Aunt Fay Wilson, and I would spend time with cousin Fran.

This triggers the memory of Fran spending the day at the farm. My mother, Fern Freeman, had baked a chocolate cake complete with peanut butter icing. It like all her baked goods looked pristine and irresistible. She should have hidden it better, because Fran was sneaky and swiped a hefty portion of the icing! Guess who got the blame for that maneuver? Yepper!! It was me!

Oh my gosh!! In the summer, the Tressler Lutheran Church in Loysville hosted a church festival, complete with chicken corn soup. Some years my dad, Wayne Freeman, would plant extra sweet corn for the festival. Church goers would come to help husk and cut the corn from the cobs for the chicken corn soup. They would bring the entire family to help. Our yard would be swarming with people, corn husks and cobs plus pesky yellow jackets.

One time in particular Jody Morrow and her sister Jennifer showed up. There were other children too. For some reason, not recalled, Jody discovered my mother's lipsticks, in the master bedroom, as we were pretending to be Indians. Yes, we did! Those bright red lipsticks soon adorned our faces and torsos! Once seen, we were scrubbed, in the cellar, by our mothers, till our skin was bright pink. That thick stuff just wouldn't come off easily. Sure, you already know who got the blame once again!! The chicken corn soup was delicious, but our faces were still a bit pink at the festival.

Speaking of church and grange summer festivals, my grandfather, Harry Smith, who had the turkey pens that lined the north side of Loysville from the center of town to opposite Johnson's Garage, would take me along to many events. I loved the food, meeting new people, the attention, and the company of Pappy. I would often walk to his large, red brick house off the town square, from Walter Smiley's home, beside Johnson's Garage. Mr. Smiley taught me how to play the piano. I remember being allowed to play pool on his massive pool table, prior to my lessons.

I was never a truly accomplished pianist but did manage to play a hymn or two during adult Sunday School at Tressler Memorial Lutheran Church. Baird Collins, school band director, always led the singing. Well, his directing and my playing were not simpatico. I stopped playing, and declared we were going to start over! It was perfect!

The church had a large unused library, full of ancient books. I loved to read and probably read them all. I would go home most Sundays with armloads of books up to my chin. Folks thought it was great that I was utilizing the library. However, they had no clue as to the book's contents! Yep, they were dusty and musty!

The church was kind enough to allow the local 4-H club, spearheaded by my mother, to meet. Since the church had a full kitchen in the basement, we were able to do cooking projects. The club would sometimes meet in our home, especially if it required a lot of extra pots and pans. I was totally immersed in 4-H. It gave me the outlet to learn; to shine as I gave demonstrations to our club members as well as on the county level; and to **Dare** to be myself, which was actually a 4-H award.

I, too, had an Angus baby beef, and since I was an older club member, I had the opportunity to show Caesar at the Pennsylvania Farm Show. That twelve- hundred-pound beast **pinned** me against the truck when I was bathing him; **dragged** me through the aisles at Silver Spring Market during a county show; and was so contrary my dad would tether him to the back of the tractor to get him to learn how to lead. I was not unhappy to see him on the auction block after the Farm Show. These experiences are front and center in my sequel, as the cousins team up to bathe Caesar and Titus.

I liked helping out around the barn, and being with the animals, but it was pure hard labor! We had high school boys, like Gary Mohler and his siblings from Erly Road, help out in the summer, during hay season. That's when my mouth started to be washed out with Lava Soap by my mother, because I learned a new language and ways of expressing myself! Oh did I mention, they also smoked! You get the picture! The chicken house is still standing!

Now, you would've thought that my mother would've been too busy sewing, cooking, canning, washing clothes, ironing and cleaning, to stop long enough to grind soap into my teeth! She, being an excellent seamstress, made all of my clothes. I never wore feedbag creations though!

I was responsible for the gardening, picking bushels of peas and beans, and tons of weeds. Afterwards, I had to lend a hand in shelling, snapping, and bagging the blanched veggies for freezing. We also canned hundreds of jars of tomatoes, pickles, red beets, fruits, and jams. When I wasn't in the huge garden, I was expected to clean all the rooms in the house, including hand scrubbing the kitchen floor every weekend. Taking the clothes from the clothesline and neatly folding everything was an unwelcome task. Washing occurred more than once a week, with that old wringer washing machine cranking out lots of dirty farm clothes. "Pap", James Freeman got the sleeve of his arm caught in the wringers when he was trying to lend a hand with the cantankerous machine. My dad helped to dislodge his arm and hand, but it required medical attention.

The barn and my books were my escape. Pappy Smith would also rescue me, if the chores were all done, and off we'd go to that festival or to his house to watch television. We'd sit and eat cans of sardines preserved in mustard, with crackers. Simple pleasures in hard times!

My dad took us fishing on the Montour Creek, and we'd catch trout, sunfish, suckers, rock fish and snapping turtles. The Montour also was a source of cooling off in the summertime, when I'd visit with my cousins. We'd go wading in the meadow beyond my grandparents' house. We could see Chester Noll's farm, as we kept an eye out for snakes, frogs and crayfish hiding under the rocks. By that time, Sunnydale Farms, in Elliottsburg, was dumping their wastewater from processing milk into the creek. We could see a pink cloud of bubbles floating high above the water, coming down stream towards us. It was like taking a bubble bath. Just not so clean!

We'd take the crayfish to Fran's house and boil them till they turned a bright red. It was like a science experiment, but not too tasty! I was encouraged to hunt wild game, by my dad. My favorite was squirrel hunting. I enjoyed the challenge of blasting squirrels midair between trees. One fall day, I was very successful with a hunting vest full of squirrels. Proudly showing them to my dad, he promptly proclaimed, "Why'd ya shoot these pine hackies?" We didn't eat them, being as they were so small. The second question was, "Is your safety on?" He didn't ban me from hunting that day! Lessons learned!

The worst hunting experience I had was during deer season, at Stony Point, on my Uncle Wendell Smith's property. All the extended family was placed strategically at the base of the Conocochcague Mountain and in the tree lines around his farm. It was a clear crisp day, which generally meant the deer would take refuge high up on the mountain. Well, not this day! All of a sudden, a herd of deer raced across the open fields. The gunshots rang out from both sides of those fields. Two other large families from the area were putting on a drive.

I was watching from a position that gave me clear line of sight. One can only imagine the Civil War in times like these! I watched as a small deer bounded in my direction. It tried to jump over a partially downed fence and was not successful. I dubbed it my mercy killing! The button buck couldn't have survived its wounds, and most of the meat was not salvageable. I rarely hunted after that incident. I left that up to my three younger brothers.

Having three brothers, left me fending for myself! They always threatened to throw me into the cow's watering trough, which was in the barnyard. They were chuckleheads, and never followed through with their threats. Probably because they knew, I was very strong from all the farm work, and I could defend myself very well, with martial art stances unknown to man.

They didn't complain though, when they needed an extra to play baseball. I was usually the pitcher and could whack a ball way out into the fields. Of course, I could kick a football barefoot, into the garden. And the basketball hoop on the side of the wagon shed, had us kicking up dust, from the dirt driveway beaten down by the weight of all the heavy farm equipment.

Since we were a hunting family, it seemed only natural that my parents, one Christmas, gifted my young brothers with air rifles. Those little buggers shot some of the decorative balls off the Christmas tree. The antique balls shattered everywhere! It was as if the tree was covered in glitter!

We rarely left the farm. There was so much work to do on a daily basis, and cattle needed a watchful eye round the clock. It was our livelihood. We went to church and church activities. Attended school and school activities if the workload was covered. Once in a while, we were loaded into the car, transported to Ickesburg's Hi-Way Theatre and watched John Wayne star in a western movie. John Wayne is still my hero!

Sometimes, the Sunbonnet Restaurant, in Loysville, was the destination for a cone of soft serve ice cream. Sunday drives, just to see the county, and visit family, were common. However, I was prone to car sickness, and would often lose my ice cream without warning, if we didn't head straight home.

My story sound familiar? You and I grew up mostly under the same circumstances, and in some cases lived not too far apart. Yet our lives were different. We had **our** own family traditions and made new ones as the years progressed. With new technology, came changes that chipped away at the very soul of the family and community. Technology brought some relief, though very expensive, in the daily struggle to survive, particularly on a family farm.

That is our heritage, our legacy, and we own it! Thank You for sharing your stories, so our children's children and their children can hold in their hands something tangible and cradle it in their arms after reading the passages and traveling back through time.

***Cherish* your Memories!!!**

www.ingramcontent.com/pod-product-compliance
Lightning Source LLC
Chambersburg PA
CBHW082105280426
43661CB00089B/876